JOANNA BLYTHMAN is Britain's leading investigative food journalist and an influential commentator on the British food chain. She has won five Glenfiddich awards for her writing, including a Glenfiddich Special Award for her first book *The Food We Eat*, a Caroline Walker Media Award for *Improving the Nation's Health by Means of Good Food*, and a Guild of Food Writers Award for *The Food We Eat*. In 2004, she won the prestigious Derek Cooper Award, one of BBC Radio 4's Food and Farming Awards. In 2007, *Good Housekeeping* Magazine gave her its award for Outstanding Contribution to Food Award 2007. She writes and broadcasts frequently on food issues.

....

BY THE SAME AUTHOR:

The Food Our Children Eat
Shopped
Bad Food Britain

Food that's good for your health, pocket and plate

What
to
Eat

Joanna Blythman

FOURTH ESTATE · *London*

First published in Great Britain by
Fourth Estate
an imprint of HarperCollins*Publishers*
77–85 Fulham Palace Road
London W6 8JB
www.4thestate.co.uk

'Bangers and Mash' Words and music
by Herbert Kretzmer and David Lee
© 1960, reproduced by permission of
Francis Day and Hunter Ltd/EMI Music
Publishing Ltd, London W8 5SW

'Run, Rabbit, Run' Music by Noel Gay.
Words by Noel Gay & Ralph Butler.
© Copyright 1939 Noel Gay Music
Company Limited, worldwide rights
except the United Kingdom, Ireland,
Australia, Canada, South Africa and all
so-called reversionary rights territories
where the copyright © 1994 is held
jointly by Noel Gay Music Company
Limited and Campbell Connelly & Co.
Limited. Used by permission of Music
Sales Limited. All Rights Reserved.
International Copyright Secured.

9 8 7 6 5 4 3 2 1

A catalogue record for this book is
available from the British Library

ISBN 978-0-00-734142-9

Designed by Sonya Dyakova
Typeset by Birdy Book Design

Printed in Hong Kong
by Printing Express

Introduction

One night I was talking to a friend who was complaining about how hard she found it to shop for food. She was tight for cash, she explained, which made it difficult to afford the more ethical, progressive food she aspired to. She tended to shop on the way home from work, when only one smaller-format chain supermarket with a limited, overpriced selection, heavily skewed to convenience food, was still open. And that was only half the problem. Tired and uninspired by the dullness of the food on offer, she still had to dream up ideas for something to cook when she got home, then prepare it, and fit all that in with other activities, like going to the gym and doing the washing. Net result? 'I'm not eating as well, or as healthily, as I'd like to,' she said. 'Food is just so *complicated*.'

This got me thinking. Is food really that complicated, or does it just seem that way? Surely there must be a clear, practical way to help people recognize and locate food that's good in the broadest sense of that word: food that's healthy, affordable, doesn't trash the environment, exploit producers or cause unnecessary animal suffering, and, last but not least, tastes great?

So I wrote this book, a distillation of many disparate types of information about common foods that are not yet, as far as I know, brought together in any other place. Being impatient and, like many people, often short of time, I am a great believer in executive summaries, so any reader can cut to the chase, so to speak, by reading my 20 guiding principles for eating good food.

But broad generalities can't answer many of the pressing food dilemmas of the day, so all the foods we eat commonly are then discussed in detail, either individually, or in their family groups. Each section is free-standing. *What to Eat* is a reference book after all, so you can dip into the section on breakfast cereals, say, without having first read the one on grains. This inevitably means that there is some repetition, but of course you can skip over that.

To steer readers in the direction of the best food – what to eat – I have dished up some unsavoury facts about the worst stuff – what *not* to eat. This isn't meant to put you off eating, just remind you of why it's worthwhile seeking out something better.

Food is a contentious subject, so as well as picking up lots of useful information and the odd flash of inspiration, anyone who reads this book will get a mini crash course in the live debates in this field. *What to Eat* looks at food from a 360-degree angle (or at least takes a few purposeful steps in that direction). I hope it will help anyone, anywhere, make the best possible all-round choice, irrespective of personal circumstances.

The 20 principles of eating, made simple

Base your diet on real, unprocessed food

This is the bedrock principle of this book, and you can't go too far wrong if you follow it. Nature is a very clever, intricate system and natural foods in their whole, unprocessed form have an intrinsic nutritional integrity. We know this because humans have been eating them for centuries. We don't yet, and may never, fully understand all the complex inter-relationships between the major and minor nutritional components that go to make up familiar foods such as eggs, meat, fruits, vegetables and grains, but we do know that they act in synergy, supporting and enhancing one another, adding up to one wholesome entity. If you choose mainly unprocessed, or only minimally processed food, and regularly eat a variety of different foods from all the major food groups, then you really don't need to worry too much about being healthy.

See the value of cooking

Even if you can't cook meals from scratch all the time, it is important to recognize that cooking from raw materials gives you infinitely more control over the quality of what you eat than if you rely on convenience foods. The more food you eat that isn't home-made, the poorer your diet is likely to be, both in terms of nutrition, and the quality and provenance of the ingredients used. If you surrender sovereignty of what you eat by becoming dependent on convenience foods, the fatter you, and any other members of your household, are likely to become and the more readily your nagging concerns about not eating well can be exploited by food manufacturers selling you technofoods that make dubious health claims. Every meal that you take back under your control by cooking yourself, the better your health and your spirits will be, and the more pleasure you will get from the act of eating.

If you have got out of, or have never acquired, the habit of cooking, revisit this default setting. Cooking needn't be arduous. If you are one of those people who only think about food at the last minute, you may find yourself in shops where your choice is likely to be very restricted, and therefore forced to buy a lot of expensive rubbish. To alter your habits, you will need to decide in advance roughly what you are going to eat, then make sure that you have the ingredients. Other more creative cooks get ideas from shopping in stimulating places with inspiring ingredients, such as markets and small food shops, and then just come home and throw it all together. Either way, you can make life easier for yourself by cooking more than you need so that you can have the same thing later in the week, perhaps in a slightly different form or with different accompaniments. And here, your freezer will prove to be a trusty friend. Cook once, eat twice, or even thrice.

Don't be a sucker for processed foods

Here's one thing you need to know: the more processed a food is, the worse it is for you. Food processing is the food industry's way of making profit by taking apart natural foods and reinventing them in more lucrative form. Not usually to your nutritional benefit either, irrespective of what the label might claim. Commodity crops like wheat and corn, stripped of most of their beneficial nutrients, then loaded with sugar, salt and a sprinkling of synthetic vitamins, are presented as a nutritious breakfast. Industrially refined oils are chemically hardened, mixed with additives and water then reborn as 'heart-healthy' spreads. Who needs them?

Reconstructed, over-processed foods don't have the trustworthy track record of whole foods in their natural form. They contain novel ingredients and obscure additives produced by hi-tech methods and have only been on our plates for a relatively short period of time. This is already long enough to suggest that they are significant contributors to the major modern problems of obesity, food allergies and diet-related disease.

OK, there are exceptions. Cheese, butter, yogurt and bread are all processed foods, and, let's face it, few of us are going to get round to making these ourselves. But you can buy those that were made in the traditional way, using time-honoured techniques to alter primary ingredients.

Don't buy food with ingredients you won't find in a domestic larder

It's a safe bet that you don't have mono- and diglycerides of fatty acids in your storecupboard, nor high-fructose corn syrup, guar gum, partially hydrogenated vegetable fat, soya protein isolate, liquid pasteurized egg nor maltodextrin. The only people who have these, and other weird but not wonderful synthetic chemical food ingredients lining their shelves, are lab-coated food technologists whose job is to find new and ever more inventive ways to make even more money from the over-processing of food. And guess what? Your health is not their priority. So if you don't know what an ingredient is, or it has a long, unpronounceable name that reads like an algebraic formula, then don't buy any food product containing it. Every item you see listed on an ingredient label should be readily understandable and familiar. If it isn't, avoid it like the plague.

Be sceptical about nutrition advice from 'experts'

The dietetic establishment has led us to believe that food is merely fuel and healthy eating is just a straightforward matter of calculating the number of calories we need for our body weight and activity level. Grub in, energy out. That's all there is to it. This mechanical approach plays right into the hands of the food industry. Following this nutritional script, it doesn't matter whether we eat technofood or natural food because everything comes down to a simple arithmetical calculation. Common sense alone dictates that there is more to food and eating than that.

Don't hold your breath for learned, silvery-haired nutritionists to spell out the universal magic formula for healthy eating. Research into what constitutes optimum nutrition is best thought of as a work in progress, and anyone who tries to tell you otherwise is being simplistic and misleading. So instead, use your common sense. Base your diet on tried and tested unprocessed foods, studiously ignoring fads and showing healthy scepticism towards everything from top-down government health orthodoxy to the latest trendy diet.

These days, many foods come with an abundance of nutrition labels and supposedly helpful logos to help you assess the healthiness or otherwise of their contents. Mostly this is a confusing waste of time. Sometimes it is a deliberate red herring used by the manufacturers to bamboozle you and make you think a low-grade processed food is better than it might otherwise seem. Ignore nutrition labels and logos, and cut to the chase by looking at the ingredients label. Basically, the more ingredients listed, the more suspect the product is.

Don't dismiss traditional food knowledge

Certain foods – beetroot, celery, raw milk, ginger, suet, garlic, yogurt, cabbage and carrots, for instance – figure in traditional medicine systems around the world as having beneficial medicinal and nutritional properties. It is currently fashionable to dismiss any such collective wisdom on the grounds that it isn't 'evidence-based' – in the narrow, western, medical sense – and so little better than superstition. This is blinkered thinking. There is much to be said for the quasi-medical, nutritional knowledge that has been built up by different cultures and tested out and observed informally in human populations over time. When your grandmother told you that a hot honey and lemon drink would do you more good than any cough medicine, she wasn't making it up. She was simply passing on the accumulated wisdom and experience of the generations that came before her. That knowledge is like gold dust.

Practise vegetable-centric eating

Of course, it doesn't make sense to shut your ears entirely to ongoing discussions of nutrition, and there is some overlapping middle ground where otherwise diverse researchers and would-be authorities can agree. There is, for instance, no argument that vegetables are brilliant for you. It's not just all the vitamins, minerals and soluble fibre that are beneficial; research is gradually identifying a number of phytochemicals, or natural compounds in vegetables, that are both health-enhancing and protective against disease. The early twentieth-century view, that vegetables were relatively unimportant in the diet because they consist mainly of water, has been radically revised. Currently, putting vegetables more at the core of your diet seems to be a key strategy for being healthy. Think in terms of vegetable-centric eating, where protein, fat and carbohydrate-based ingredients play second fiddle to vegetables, not the other way round.

Eat some protein

Realistically, you aren't going to live solely on vegetables. A bit of protein still has its place, whether it's from fish, meat, eggs, dairy foods or from vegan sources, such as pulses. Protein is emerging in research as the macronutrient most capable of satisfying hunger. As your grandmother might have put it: 'It keeps you going.' If you do eat protein in the form of meat, poultry, milk and eggs, try to make sure that it comes from free-range animals that have been fed on grass and other natural pasture foods. It will be better for you.

Rethink what you have been told about fat and cholesterol

That big bad dietary bogeyman – saturated fat – is being rehabilitated. Contrary to what we have been led to believe, there is an absence of evidence to support the nutritional mantra that fat is bad for health, or even to back the assumption that the naturally occurring fat that you find in whole foods is intrinsically fattening. Increasingly, the health benefits of natural saturated fat are being acknowledged. Saturated fats are key components of cell membranes and essential for the production of certain hormones. They act as carriers for important vitamins, and are needed for mineral absorption and lots of other biological processes. The 'saturated fat is bad for you' gospel is likely to melt away in coming years. This is one to watch.

Likewise, while we were once told authoritatively that foods that naturally contain cholesterol, such as eggs and whole, full-fat milk, were bad for the heart, this nutritional script is being hastily rewritten to concede that the cholesterol we eat in food does not lead to heart disease, and acknowledge that some dietary cholesterol is actually essential for maintaining health. Cholesterol is a vital element in our cell membranes. It's no accident that human breast milk is very rich in the substance. Is it likely that nature would design a baby's first food that was a killer?

Saturated fat and cholesterol found in natural foods such as butter and meat have a place in an aware diet. Man-made fats manufactured from artificially hardened, hydrogenated polyunsaturated oils, on the other hand, which were once recommended as the healthy alternative, have now been shown to be pretty lethal. This just goes to show how the nutrition establishment cannot be relied on for sound eating advice.

Cut back on sugar, sweeteners and refined carbohydrates

All nutritionists whose salaries aren't paid by the sugar industry agree that sugar is a nutritional disaster. The main problem with sugar is that in its refined form we can consume huge quantities of it, in products such as drinks and sweetened fromage frais, almost without noticing. Unlike honey or treacle, refined sugar has no redeeming nutritional features. It's difficult, because many foods that contain sugar are enticing, but there's a strong case for keeping your consumption to a minimum.

A body of research suggests that high-fructose corn syrup, also known as corn sugar and glucose fructose syrup, a very modern ingredient now found in many soft drinks and a growing number of both savoury and sweet processed foods, is even more damaging to health than refined cane or beet sugar. Deeply implicated in the rise in obesity in the US, it is best avoided absolutely.

Don't imagine that artificial sweeteners are better because they contain fewer calories. There is already research that suggests that these novel chemical concoctions actively *encourage*, not *discourage* weight gain. It looks likely that they will turn out to be very bad for us indeed, even worse than standard table sugar. Why give them the benefit of the doubt?

Fresh fruits contain a lot of natural sugar, but they also contain a number of phytochemicals, similar to those found in vegetables, that are thought to be extremely beneficial. So the sugar in fruit is not something to get worried about, unless you eat vast quantities, or are trying to control your weight.

All carbohydrate foods have the capacity to disrupt blood sugar levels. In their whole, unprocessed forms they at least contain some useful amounts of vitamins. But over-consumption of refined carbohydrates, such as white pasta, flour, rice, couscous and sugary drinks, is increasingly coming into the frame as being more fattening than fat, another probable cause of the obesity epidemic that is sweeping through affluent countries.

Make time to sit down at a table and eat meals

Satisfying your appetite is not just about what you eat, but also about how you eat. Sometimes the pace and pressures of modern life make us overlook this. If you bolt down food on the hoof, on your lap, upright in the kitchen, in bed or at your desk, your stomach may feel satisfied, but your brain and your emotions most certainly will not. If you make time – even just fifteen minutes – to sit down and eat a meal at a table, taking long enough to appreciate what's on your plate, then your brain has the time to register that your stomach is full. Rushing food inevitably leaves you feeling psychologically unsatisfied by what you have consumed. In this state, you will be much more tempted to eat the next thing that comes into view and graze your way to obesity.

In all food cultures and over thousands of years, a certain ceremony and ritual has grown up around the whole business of eating. This is no accident. The act of eating is about more than simply filling the stomach. Meals have the capacity to make us feel nurtured, to nourish us emotionally and promote a sense of contentment that goes beyond any purely physical measure of wellbeing. If you can share meals with family and friends, then the pleasure of eating is further enhanced. But if you can't, treat yourself like a worthwhile member of the human race anyway, and sit down to eat a meal at a table.

Boycott factory-farmed meat, poultry, eggs and dairy

Factory-farmed meat comes from livestock kept indoors in cramped, insanitary circumstances that create huge animal suffering. Factory farms are also incubators for diseases that affect animals and which can, in certain circumstances, spread to humans.

Factory-farmed animals are fed on vast quantities of cereals. These feedstuffs could be used more efficiently and less wastefully to feed humans directly. The planet simply cannot continue to produce meat, milk and eggs by rearing livestock in this way.

The availability of cheap, factory-farmed meat has encouraged many people to eat much more meat, poultry and dairy products than is good for health and to see large daily amounts as some sort of democratic entitlement. An overabundance of animal-derived foods in the diet isn't healthy and, unless you are prepared to pay a small fortune, insisting on such quantities will necessarily mean that you end up eating cheap, inhumanely and unsustainably produced foods from miserable factory-farmed animals.

If you want to eat meat, poultry, eggs and dairy foods, buy less of them but maintain your spend by trading up to buy higher welfare, more extensively farmed, free-range, grass-fed products.

Adopt a 'closest to home' buying policy

It makes sense to favour food produced close to home. Of course, just because a food is locally produced doesn't mean it's good. A local chicken can be factory-farmed. The local baker can make lousy bread. But all other things being equal – the product tastes good and it has been humanely and ethically produced – then your food will automatically be fresher and more seasonal, and considerably less trauma will be inflicted on the environment in its transportation. The shorter the distance that food travels, the less energy is used. Transport relies heavily on oil, which is a rapidly depleting, non-renewable resource. A reduction in transport also helps bring down carbon emissions. By eating more local food, you can substantially reduce your carbon 'foodprint'.

The money you spend on local food will support and encourage our native food producers, which strengthens communities and the economy and helps build our self-sufficiency in food. At the moment, we produce only 58 per cent of the food we eat, not a great situation to be in when we face a future where there will be more competition for globally sourced food resources and the energy costs of bringing imported foods to our shores will become greater and greater.

The supermarkets' policy of treating the planet like one big global shopping basket has created a bizarre situation where many of us eat little or no local or regional food, and surprisingly small quantities of nationally produced food, even though we live in a rich and productive land and ought to be more or less self-sufficient. With the world's population set to grow by 50 per cent by 2050, and global warming and a shortage of oil putting pressure on the world's ability to feed itself, this dependency on imported food looks increasingly reckless. There is something fundamentally unsound about relying on faceless producers in faraway places to keep us fed, people who owe us nothing. Instead we need to make the country more resilient by buying more food that's grown here, not flown or shipped here. What on earth are we doing eating Brazilian chicken, Dutch carrots, Danish pork or New Zealand onions? Are we crazy?

Another bonus of buying local food is that the production process – everything from the welfare of animals to the treatment of workers – will be much more transparent than that of foods that have travelled thousands of miles through the multiple links in an opaque supply chain. Let's face it, shining a light into the dark highways and byways of industrial farming and food production is hard enough even within these shores. Suffice it to say that factory farms and food-manufacturing plants here don't go out of their way to welcome us in for 'Doors Open' days. So what chance do we have of knowing what's really going on in similar operations thousands of miles away?

Of course, we have been eating imported foods for centuries, and only the most pleasure-denying, hair-shirt-wearing eco-fanatic would seriously suggest that imported foods have no place on the plate. No chocolate? Or lemons? Unthinkable. Obviously, there is a list of foreign ingredients that few of us would like to live without, such as spices, olive oil, avocados, citrus fruits, cocoa, bananas and rice. We can't produce them, and they enliven our diet immensely. These foods are not usually air-freighted, but generally shipped or trucked. There is no need to forgo them. Even those that are transported by air – Indian mangoes or lychees from Mauritius for instance – can have a small place in the diet as an occasional, exotic indulgence.

But then there are foods that we are perfectly able to grow or farm here, at least for some part of the year, but which are routinely brought in from all over the globe via a convoluted cold chain: fruits and vegetables such as green beans, blueberries, asparagus; and meat and dairy products such as lamb, pork, chicken and yogurt. There's no need to have such foods supplied from abroad and their air-freighting, shipping and trucking, with its energy-intensive cold chain, is undeniably environmentally destructive. They almost invariably taste inferior to the native equivalent too.

Companies involved in the importation of fresh produce argue that the air-freighted trade in premium fruit and vegetables gives producers a much needed source of income, but any jobs created are precarious ones, based on a trade that is utterly fickle. Foreign workers can, and do, lose their jobs in a split second, at the whim of a supermarket buyer who decides to cancel a contract, or because transport costs make it cheaper to source food elsewhere. And in many places, crops are being grown for export at the expense of local people. In Peru, for instance, the production of asparagus is depleting the water resources on which local people depend. From Bolivia, there are reports that local people can't afford to eat quinoa, their staple grain, because foreign demand has sent the price shooting up. What's more, the dividends from such trade are more likely to end up in the pockets of wealthy elites than to stay with the people who do the work.

So rather than buying into the supermarkets' 'the food world's your oyster' proposition, apply a 'closest to home' buying policy. Make locally and regionally produced food your first choice, English, Scottish, Welsh and Irish your second, European and Middle Eastern your third and world your last.

When you do buy foreign foods, favour those with a Fairtrade label. It guarantees that producers get a more equitable, reliable price for what they grow and also means that their working conditions are better than most. Fairtrade allows us to build better relationships with foreign food producers, relationships that aren't mired in exploitation and neo-colonialism. Fairtrade products aren't prohibitively priced. You're talking pence, not pounds, to support this more progressive type of world trade.

If you can, buy organic products too. The use of pesticides is less regulated outside the European Union and many workers have to apply them in risky conditions that would not be allowed here. They have to work and live in an environment contaminated with toxins to provide us with food. When you choose the organic alternative, you will know that the workers in distant places didn't have to damage their health to produce it.

Get your food variety over the year, not in a week

Supermarkets have encouraged us to think that true variety is being able to buy every agricultural product on the planet 365 days of the year. This expectation is not environmentally sustainable. To add insult to injury, it is also extremely monotonous because the selection of food on offer doesn't ever seem to change.

A more refreshing approach is to get your food variety over the course of the year, and let it be dictated by the seasons. This is how people used to eat. You feast on a glut of one thing when it is in season and eat it until it is coming out of your ears. Just when you are beginning to think enough is enough, it will disappear again to be replaced by some other food that feels refreshingly 'new' and this will often invigorate your cooking ideas. And so the cycle continues. This way, your diet is constantly changing and you will be eating food that suits the time of year and the weather: clementines at Christmas, asparagus in spring, berries in summer and sweet root vegetables in autumn and winter.

Don't eat crops that trash the planet

Precious natural habitats all over the world are being cut down at an alarming rate to make way for large, intensively farmed plantations of soya and palm oil. Soya is used to provide the protein element in the feed of factory-farmed livestock. Both soya and palm oil are ubiquitous ingredients in thousands of common processed foods that we eat every day.

From the rainforest of Amazonia, through the Cerrado grassland savanna of central Brazil to the swampy tropical forests of Indonesia and Malaysia, these crops are powering massive habitat destruction. The impact on wildlife has been devastating. Magnificent species, such as the Borneo orang-utan and the Sumatran tiger, are now endangered because the habitat that sustains them is rapidly disappearing. These habitats are rich in biodiversity, not only in the form of animal and bird species, but also in plants. Such biodiversity is already alarmingly rare. We cannot afford to lose any more of it.

These vital habitats also act as massive carbon sinks, absorbing and storing potentially damaging carbon dioxide from the atmosphere. When these habitats are dug up to plant soya and oil palm, this carbon is released into the atmosphere, accelerating the pace of global warming.

Many people feel appalled by the destruction of our natural world, but feel powerless to do anything about it. One contribution is to stop buying products that contain soya and palm oil. Environmental groups have tried to set up systems to identify more sustainably grown soya and palm oil, but these have been hijacked by powerful companies active in these industries. For the time being, there's good reason to strike both soya and palm oil off your shopping list.

Understand the benefits of organic food

Don't fall for the line that organic food is just a trendy lifestyle choice for the neurotic rich. There's nothing new or modish about organics. Until

1950, all the food we ate was organically produced. It is organic food that should be considered as 'normal' not the Johnny-come-lately, factory-farmed, industrial equivalent.

These days, there are many compelling reasons for buying organic food. It will almost never contain the residues of pesticides that are commonly found in food grown with the aid of agrichemicals. Just six pesticides are approved for organic farming and these can only be used in extremely limited circumstances. Conventional farmers have over 300 at their disposal and use them routinely. The powers-that-be parrot the food industry line that we should not be the slightest bit alarmed that our food regularly contains residues of toxic pesticides because they are all below 'safe limits'. But pesticides are poisons. They are designed to kill things. Surely the only truly safe limit would be zero? Why eat toxins if you don't have to?

The list of additives that can be used in organic food is small – just 32 of the 290 additives permitted in Europe. Only additives derived from natural sources such as lecithin and citric acid are allowed and no artificial preservatives, colourings or flavourings are acceptable. Among the additives banned are those that have been linked to health problems. So if you are buying processed foods, the organic sort won't contain any dodgy ones.

GM (genetic modification) is not allowed in organic food production and organically reared livestock cannot be fed on GM feed. Evidence is emerging to suggest that GM crops increase the use of pesticides, produce super-weeds and super-pests and compromise animal and, possibly, human health. When you choose organic food, you have a cast-iron guarantee that your food is GM-free.

As well as missing out on the bad stuff, you may be getting more of the good stuff when you buy organic food. Some research suggests that organic foods, such as milk and strawberries, have higher levels of vitamins, minerals and other healthy micronutrients.

Organic standards for raising livestock are the most humane, animal-friendly sort around. Organic farming methods encourage and protect wildlife. Chemical-dependent agriculture, on the other hand, has been shown to harm and deplete it. For all these reasons, there is a lot to be said for eating organic food when you can.

You don't have to get hung up on eating 100 per cent organic though. There are many high-quality, wholesome foods around that do not come with organic certification – such as grass-reared meat, game, wild fish and hand-made cheeses.

Organic food is cheapest when bought direct from a farmer or producer, either via a box scheme, or at markets and farm shops. This sort of organic food will often cost less than the non-organic equivalent. But because most organic food costs more to produce and doesn't come direct from the producer, it will tend to be more expensive than the basic non-organic equivalent. That said, it may sometimes cost less than premium non-organic products, so don't always assume that organic will automatically be more expensive. Every now and then, compare like with like. You may get a pleasant surprise.

If you have to watch what you spend, and would like to buy more organic food but can't see how to afford it, then you can prioritize your purchases. There are stronger arguments for some organic foods than others. It is more important to spend money on organic pork or chicken, for instance, than it is to buy organic lamb or beef.

The extra you will have to pay for some organic products is more manageable than for others. Items such as organic flour, milk, bread and butter can be quite affordable, as can fresh seasonal products, such as salad leaves and herbs. If you do compare prices, you may actually find that many organic brands are cheaper than their conventional equivalents and are often on special offer. Throughout this book, the foods that you might want to prioritize for organic purchases are flagged up.

Support small-scale producers and independent shops and food outlets

Supermarket chains' commitment to small-scale foods and producers is skin-deep. At a structural level, these dinosaurs of food retailing are locked into bulk buying, globalized sourcing and centralized distribution, which favour the large supplier every time. Supermarkets just aren't equipped to respond to fleeting availability or to handle foods that are produced in small numbers, even if they truly wanted to. What this means is that if everyone keeps shopping only in supermarkets, many of our smaller-scale foods will disappear because supermarkets do not deem them reliable, consistent or significant enough in turnover terms to merit stocking them.

If you love interesting foods, and want to ensure that you will always have real diversity in your shopping basket – items such as rare-breed meat, traditional fruits, distinctive local specialities with a sense of place, more unusual varieties of fruits and vegetables that keep precious biodiversity alive, artisan farmhouse cheese and naturally grown produce that haven't been groomed to fit the big chains' body fascist cosmetic grading requirements – then make a conscious effort to do some of your shopping in alternative outlets like markets, farm shops and independent shops. By shopping this way, you lend your valuable support to producers who are maintaining our food traditions and heritage and people who are offering something refreshingly different to the cloned supermarket offer. You also help keep your locality alive and more vibrant with shopping outlets that offer an alternative to the homogeneity and sameness of the over-dominant retail chains.

Recalibrate your attitude towards the cost of food

There's lots of 'cheap' food on offer. Well, cheap that is, as long as you ignore its less obvious costs, such as its impact on your health, the misery of farm animals, the poor pay and conditions endured by workers in the global food industry, and environmental damage. Like clocking up debits on an out-of-control credit card, cheap food is stacking up a debt that we will have to pay at some future point.

Many people would like to buy something better, but feel that cheap, mass-produced food is the only type they can afford. More wholesomely and ethically produced food has a reputation for being expensive food, even though it usually represents much better value for money.

But there are a number of strategies that you can employ to keep down your overall spend, yet still eat higher-quality, more ethical food, simply by readjusting and rethinking certain strands in your diet. If, for instance, you cut out expensive, ready-made food, such as lunchtime sandwiches, pricey ready meals and pre-washed vegetables, you can free up a surprising amount of money to spend on something else: a free-range or organic chicken, say, instead of a factory-farmed one. By reducing the amount of meat you eat, choosing the less expensive, but arguably more delicious cuts, and bumping up the proportion of vegetables in your diet, you can afford to eat better meat and still be quids in. If you plan your meals in advance, you will almost certainly waste less and the money saved can go towards buying better ingredients. And of course, if you cut out sweet drinks, squashes, sodas and bottled water, and make tap water your default thirst-quencher, then you will instantly be awash with money that allows you to trade up on something else you regularly eat: a nicer hand-made cheese, some Fairtrade bananas, a special olive oil for salads. Throughout this book, ways to improve the quality of what you eat without spending more money overall are flagged up.

Save money outside the supermarket

Never assume that supermarkets are the cheapest place to shop. They most certainly are if what you want is processed food, say a bumper pack of crisps or a two-for-one offer on fizzy drinks. No corner shop or indie outlet can beat them on that stuff. They also offer bargain-basement prices on the handful of 'known value items' – such as bananas, milk and white bread. They price these products at an unrealistically low level to surround everything else they sell with a halo of value and convince us that they are cheaper than their competitors. But there's one very important thing to understand about supermarkets: they aren't cheaper places to shop for fresh, unprocessed foods. You will routinely pay more for fish, meat, fruit and vegetables in supermarkets than you will at the fishmonger's, the butcher's or the greengrocer's. On some products, the mark-ups charged by supermarkets are astronomical. Try comparing supermarket spice prices with those in your average Asian grocery store. Or check out the cost of supermarket lemongrass, spring onions or fish sauce against the Chinese supermarket. Supermarkets routinely charge eye-popping premiums on any food that isn't mass-market or industrialized. If you are looking for real fresh food, then take your business elsewhere.

Don't become an ideological eater

A number of different considerations now influence us when we are deciding what we eat. This is a positive trend. What's clever about swallowing mystery food without giving any thought to what it may be doing to you, food producers and the planet? But while some understanding of these concerns can undoubtedly inform and influence your choice of food, it is important not to become over-cerebral and to remember that, first and foremost, food should be a life-enhancing pleasure.

There's no need, for instance, to cut out meat from your diet entirely just because you are worried about the depletion of the rainforest or the conditions of farm animals. Many species of fish are below safe biological limits, but don't draw the conclusion that there is no fish left in the sea that you can eat. Nor is there any necessity to commit to eating only politically correct, right-on food. People who seriously suggest this are driven by ideological goals and you can't assume that they have any inherent love for, or great understanding of, food. Similarly, it's spirit-crushing and life-denying to sign up for an extremely limiting diet of 100 per cent healthy food. It's only human, every now and then, to eat things you know aren't that great, just because you like them.

It's good to be a thoughtful eater, but if you are excessively ideological in choosing what you eat, it's too easy to become neurotic and end up with a rapidly diminishing list of food you are prepared to eat. Instead, just try to head in the right general direction, but don't make a fetish of it. Be led by the stomach as well as the head. Eating well can seem complicated, but, actually, it's simple.

10 ways to save money on food without compromising your principles

As your till receipts will testify, the cost of food has climbed alarmingly of late. And it looks as if higher food bills are here to stay, not just for years, but for decades. A series of global factors – climate change, a growing world population, shortage of oil, market speculation and a weak pound – are combining to drive up the price of food. The underlying trend is that food prices will continue to rise in real terms for the next 30 years. So we have moved into a period when food will become a much more significant item in the household budget.

It's wearing having to worry constantly about the bottom line, but when money is tight there's no need to abandon your ethical and progressive instincts and buy the cheapest (and potentially nastiest) food on offer, or fill up on stodge. Instead, look on rising prices as an opportunity to hone your 'domestic economy' skills – yet still eat well – by employing these strategies:

Waste nothing - use up every last bit of food you buy

Cut out waste by shopping as frequently as possible, and try to buy only what you need for the next couple of days. Never bin food that could have a further use. For instance, sour milk makes great pancakes and scones, old bread gets a new lease of life when made into breadcrumbs, salads and puddings. Eggs that are past their 'use by' date can be safely eaten in recipes where they will be well cooked, such as a cake or fritatta. Don't throw away fat from meat or poultry roasts – use it for frying. Make old fruit into crumbles and compotes and tired vegetables into soups and purées. Save the leathery ends of Parmesan wedges to flavour soups and sauces.

Be super-suspicious of supermarket promotional offers

Three-for-two deals, buy-one-get-one-free, multisavers and more of that ilk need to be treated with deep scepticism. Their whole purpose is to get you to buy more food than you might otherwise do. With non-perishable foods, they might possibly represent a chance to stock up on products that you'll get through in the fullness of time, although, if you're controlling your weekly budget carefully, it might be better to buy only what you need, as and when you need it, rather than stockpiling potentially useful foods. But apparently good deals on fresh food rarely save you money. They not only coax more money than you had intended out of your pocket, they also encourage you to overbuy. Chances are that some of what you pick up will be wasted because it was more than you really needed. A promotional deal isn't a bargain if it ends up in the bin.

Check out cheaper sources for foods you buy regularly

If you tend to shop for food on auto-pilot in the same place, compare prices in other outlets once in a while. For example, fruit and vegetables generally cost much less in greengrocers and markets than in supermarkets; certain products, like Parmesan, are often significantly cheaper in foreign discount chains; spices are much better value in Asian shops; nuts often cost less when bought in larger quantities in Chinese supermarkets; organic vegetables and eggs from a farmers' market or box scheme may well be cheaper than the equivalent in supermarkets.

Stick with meat from free-range animals rather than switching to factory-farmed, but consider reducing the quantity you eat

In a typical stew or curry recipe, for instance, cut the quantity of meat specified by a half to a third, and make up the difference with vegetables or pulses. Bone up on how to cook cheaper, but delicious, cuts of meat such as beef shin, pork cheeks, neck of lamb and duck legs and make a little go a long way. Choose cuts of meat with some bone and fat. They may not look as neat and tidy, but they often have more flavour and richness than so-called 'prime' cuts, and cost much less.

Go for cheaper, less well-known types of fish

Forget the pricy premier league species like cod, tuna and halibut and concentrate on second division species like megrim, rockfish, coley, herring and mackerel. They taste good but sell for less largely because people are less familiar with them.

Cook more food from scratch and keep processed convenience foods to the bare minimum

Unless you're prepared to live on bargain-basement, poor value, low grade processed food, then buying convenience foods, like ready meals, is an extremely expensive, not to mention unsatisfactory, way to eat. By doing most of your own cooking you will not only improve the flavour and freshness of what you eat, but also save a mint. Ready-prepared foods constitute rotten value for money. Most of what you're paying for is packaging and marketing.

Take lunch to work

Buying your lunch from takeaways eats into your finances in an insidious way. A drink, a sandwich and a sweet bite easily clocks up £5 a day, usually for something that's deeply inferior to what you'd make at home. For the price of a floppy sarnie filled with rubbery cheese, you could make an infinitely superior home-made one, using decent bread and your pick of the country's finest artisan cheese. If it's the planning that defeats you, just scale up what you cook the night before to make sure that there's enough left for lunch the next day. Last night's leftovers, however random and variable, often taste even better at lunchtime.

Drink tap water

Bottled water costs anything from 500–900 per cent more than tap. Quench your thirst with this and it's as much of a drain on your financial resources as paying up a car loan, or signing up for a private club. Give up that pricy habit and you'll feel flush in no time. If you don't like the taste of tap water, drink it with ice and lemon, leave it to sit in the fridge so that the chlorine evaporates, use a jug filter, or make a one-off investment in a plumbed-in water filter.

Grow any food you can and make the most of cheap, seasonal, UK-grown produce

Even if it's just a snipping of herbs from a pot on the window sill, or some cut-and-come-again salads grown in a container on the balcony, a bit of home-grown food can not only transform your meals, it can also save you a surprising amount of money. Buy fresh, UK-grown fruits and vegetables at the height of their season when they are cheapest, and at their nutritional peak.

Forage enthusiastically whenever you get the chance

Both in rural and urban settings, there is a free larder of interesting foods at your disposal. Sniff out wild garlic leaves in city parks in spring, pick blackberries from roadside thickets in late summer, and scour the woods for wild mushrooms in autumn. Get your revenge on the ground elder in your garden by eating it.

Vegetables

Asparagus

If ever there was a vegetable made for indulgence, it's asparagus. It has the thrill of luxury – no other vegetable has that Cadillac alley, platinum status. There's no need to get too fancy with asparagus or dream up inventive ways to cook it when the old favourites have such perennial charm.

Some European countries, such as France and Germany, favour blanched white asparagus with its characteristic violet shading and yellow tips, which is grown by mounding up earth around the emerging spears to protect them from light. This type of asparagus has a taste not unlike that of salsify. The British, in company with the Spanish, prefer their asparagus green and grown in full light that gives it a flavour rather like peas. Purple and red asparagus are also popular with keen gardeners. They tend to turn green when cooked, so are better used ultra-tender and fresh, thinly sliced in salads. All shades of asparagus taste special in their own way.

Asparagus ranges in size from the young, slender 'sprue' to the thicker 'kitchen' and jumbo grades that have a more developed flavour.

Asparagus is one of those vegetables, like corn on the cob, that deteriorates rapidly after cutting. The older asparagus is, the more it dries out and develops a bitter, tinny taste. Wizened, greying lower stalks of asparagus are a dead give-away. Tender fresh asparagus should have tight, firm tips and the stalk, when pressed lightly with your nail, should still feel moist and sappy within. If you put pressure on a spear it should 'snap' and look moist inside. It should never be pliable and woody. Fresh-cut British asparagus easily upstages the imported stuff that has come to us over long distances by road and sea or air. This is partly because it is fresher: from a taste point of view, jet-lagged imports from thousands of miles away just can't compare. But there is also a school of thought that because it grows more slowly in our cooler climate, it develops a fuller flavour.

Things to do with asparagus

- You can't put a foot wrong if you roast or griddle asparagus – rubbed in olive oil and cooked for just a matter of minutes, until tender – then anoint with good extra virgin olive oil and liberal shavings of Parmesan.

- One of the best and simplest dishes to celebrate asparagus is to dunk the lightly cooked spears into soft-boiled, freshly laid eggs, then dip the eggy spears into breadcrumbs fried in butter.

- If you have been feasting on a glut and have exhausted the familiar treatments, it might be time to go for a more gutsy approach and serve your asparagus with a salsa verde (see Things to do with herbs), punchy with anchovies and mint.

- Use thin sprue asparagus, lightly cooked, in a salad, with crispy lardons of bacon, soft-boiled egg and fried croutons.

- Thick and medium spears, simply steamed, deserve the effort of an hollandaise or beurre blanc sauce.

- A quick, weekday asparagus risotto feels like a weekend treat and is a good way to use cheaper, less regularly shaped spears and stems.

- Delicate pale green asparagus soup, made with stems and topped with a drizzle of cream and a couple of tender tips, is one of the classiest soups. You'll want to sieve it if your stems are a bit woody.

Is asparagus good for me?

Asparagus is packed with beneficial micronutrients. It is rich in beta-carotene, which is needed for healthy skin and good vision; folate, which protects against birth defects; soluble fibre, which slows down the rate at which sugar is released into the bloodstream; and potassium, which helps moderate blood pressure. It is also one of the best sources of rutin, which, along with vitamin C, helps protect the body from infections. A mild diuretic (it makes you pee), it has been recommended traditionally for ailments associated with sluggish digestion and fluid retention. Don't be alarmed if your urine has an unusually strong smell after eating asparagus; this is quite normal and harmless. Asparagus contains certain sulphur-based compounds and their breakdown products in digestion are thought to be responsible.

How is asparagus grown?

The plants or 'crowns' that produce asparagus spears take about three years to become established and longer still to become fully productive. They do best in a well-drained rich loam – the most prized type of agricultural land. Some growers cover the asparagus mounds with polythene to warm up the soil and encourage the spears to grow earlier. The delicate spears have to be harvested by hand; mechanization is out. White asparagus is particularly time-consuming to harvest because only the very tip of the spear peeps out from the soil, so it takes an experienced eye to spot it.

Although we eat some Spanish asparagus that precedes our native crop by a couple of weeks, most of the out-of-season asparagus we eat in Britain comes from Peru. Peru has cornered the world market for this vegetable because the US decided to subsidize its fledgling asparagus industry in order to encourage alternatives to the cultivation of coca, the raw material for cocaine. So Peru's asparagus exports have grown rapidly over the past decade, but by several accounts the benefits have not filtered down to the asparagus workers or improved their lives. A number of charities have reported that asparagus workers operate in sub-standard conditions and poverty and that child malnutrition is increasing. In the arid Ica region where Peruvian asparagus production is concentrated, this thirsty export vegetable is also depleting the water resources on which local people depend.

Is asparagus a green choice?

The carbon 'foodprint' of air-freighted asparagus is very heavy indeed. It is not necessary to have such foods supplied from abroad and their air- freighting, shipping and trucking, with its energy-intensive, fuel-guzzling cold chain, is undeniably environmentally destructive. Binge on asparagus when the British crop is in season, then forget about it for the rest of the year.

Where and when should I buy asparagus?

Throughout mainland Europe, no vegetable stirs the same excitement as asparagus. Its appearance in mid-April on market stalls and on special restaurant tasting menus heralds the arrival of early summer. In the UK, our asparagus season is short and sweet, six to eight fresh, green, sappy weeks from the third week of April onwards, depending on the weather. Harvested after the 'hungry gap' of March and early April when British and Irish vegetable production is at its lowest ebb, asparagus provides a welcome splurge of fleeting, green vegetable after the sturdy roots and brassicas of winter months and before the tender salads of summer. British asparagus has become very sought after in recent years and there is more of it around as growers now increasingly see it as a worthwhile crop to cultivate.

THE MOST EAGERLY AWAITED SPRING FOOD

Before imported foreign spears became a fixture on supermarket shelves, asparagus, which had traditionally been an eagerly awaited spring food, most strongly associated with the Vale of Evesham, but also East Anglia and Cambridgeshire, was regarded as a gourmet food, rubbing shoulders with caviar, truffles and oysters. In 1931 an Asparagus Society was set up at Cambridge University's Trinity Hall to savour the new season's crop. The customary start date of the British asparagus season was 1 May.

Until the 1980s, most people's experience of asparagus – unless they had the good fortune to live in one of our traditional asparagus-growing areas such as the Vale of Evesham – was tinned. Tinned or bottled asparagus is a far cry from fresh, but it is one of the more successful tinned vegetables. Then imported asparagus spears began to appear in swanky, fine-dining establishments. In recent years, however, asparagus has become a fixture in our restaurants, shops and supermarkets. No longer a precious, seasonal crop, a steady flow of air-freighted imported spears has made asparagus available all year round. Is this progress? Most definitely not. Familiarity breeds contempt. It's hard to get worked up about the 365-day supply of jaded, imported asparagus, but the arrival of our fantastic native crop never fails to thrill.

Will asparagus break the bank?

You always pay quite a lot for good asparagus. Weight for weight, it can cost as much as meat or fish. But the compensation is that even a few spears can elevate a dish based on otherwise unremarkable ingredients and make it seem rather luxurious.

Never waste the bottom part of an asparagus spear. Once peeled, the tender inside can be chopped and added to soups, quiches, pastas and risottos. Thicker, less tender stems are good liquidized in soup along with cheaper green vegetables, such as leeks and peas.

Aubergine

There is something miraculous about the way that raw aubergine can be transformed from a bland, spongy vegetable, with a taste and texture about as interesting as blotting paper, into luscious, yielding flesh, impregnated with sultry flavours. To get the best from this languorous vegetable, observe two principles. First, aubergine eats lots of oil. Yes, it does go against the grain to keep on adding it, but if you are not prepared to give aubergine the oil it needs, then eat something else instead. Or at least don't stint on the oil but then drain off any surplus after cooking. Second, water — and other liquid ingredients such as tomato pulp and wine — is a potential enemy of aubergine. If you add liquid before the aubergine has absorbed enough oil and softened thoroughly, then the skin will stay squeaky-tight and tough and the skin and flesh will remain firm in the mouth and won't absorb as well the flavours of other ingredients.

Aubergine has a slightly bitter taste, which is part of its charm. This characteristic is most evident in recipes where you keep the skin on and slightly char it. It is often recommended that you slice or chop aubergine before cooking and leave it sprinkled with salt for half an hour or so to reduce this bitterness. Most of the aubergines we buy are not particularly bitter to start with, so this isn't really necessary. However, salting does have the advantage of drawing out water from the aubergine, which is helpful because, as a result of the way they are grown, most aubergines we cook with in Britain and Ireland are more watery than those grown outdoors in hot countries. Salting also enhances the flavour (even if you rinse the salt off thoroughly) and firms up the flesh, which means that it absorbs less oil.

The aubergines on sale in Britain and Ireland tend to be much of a muchness. The dark purple, pear-drop-shaped aubergine of uniform size and dimensions rules the roost. Middle Eastern and Asian shops often sell more varied types, with different shapes, sizes and skin tones from white through violet to purple-black. These can have subtly different flavours, being more and less bitter, and a smoother texture when cooked. Whatever sort of aubergine you go for, choose fresh ones. These should look smooth-skinned and firm and feel heavy for their size.

Things to do with aubergine

- Using a ridged, cast-iron grill pan or under a grill, char whole aubergines until the skin is stiff and papery and the interior is completely soft. Skin, then finely chop or liquidize the flesh with light tahini (sesame) paste, garlic and a little olive oil to make a dish in the style of the Lebanese *moutabal*, or pan-Middle Eastern *baba ganoush*.

- In Sicilian *caponata*, aubergines provide an almost meaty bulk in a sour-sweet partnership with celery, tomatoes, capers and vinegar.

- Aubergines love lamb, and flatter it immensely, in a Greek moussaka perhaps, or by adding melting texture that thickens a curry.

- Aubergines hit it off well with Thai flavours, basking happily in a hot, fragrant coconut broth.

- For lighter, more unusual lamb meatballs, use half-and-half cooked, chopped aubergine and meat.

- Tomatoes and garlic are best friends with aubergines. Cook them together in olive oil over a very low heat for hours in a shallow frying pan without a lid until they collapse into a delicious sludge. A stick of cinnamon will nudge the dish in a Middle Eastern direction. Season with salt and pepper and serve warm as a vegetable accompaniment or at room temperature as a starter, with bread or crudités, or sprinkled with parsley and salty white cheese.

Are aubergines good for me?

Even though they don't have the showy colours that we take as markers flagging up the healthiest vegetables, aubergines have much to commend them. They provide a lot of soluble fibre, which slows down the rate at which sugar is released into the bloodstream, are a good source of B vitamins, which aid brain and nervous system function, and folate, which helps prevent birth defects. Aubergines are particularly rich in useful minerals, especially potassium, manganese, copper and magnesium. Research into the aubergine suggests that it contains very beneficial phytochemicals, such as phenols and terpenes and sterols, which may help protect the body against cancer, microbial infections and viruses, and promote heart health.

How are aubergines grown?

Most of the aubergines we buy are grown either in the UK or Holland in glasshouses in the same way as peppers (see PEPPERS/How are peppers grown?).

Are aubergines a green choice?

Glasshouse production of aubergines raises the same issues as for tomatoes (see TOMATOES/Are tomatoes a green choice?).

Where and when should I buy aubergines?

Standard glasshouse aubergines are available all year round. Most come from Holland, some from Spain, and UK-grown ones are on sale from March until November. For more varied types of aubergine, check out Asian stores and supermarkets and Middle Eastern grocers. Italian food shops sometimes import outdoor-grown aubergines from Italy.

ALL BECAUSE OF ELIZABETH DAVID

Aubergines were more or less unheard of in Britain until they were introduced by way of the cookbooks of Elizabeth David. Now they have become a fixture in our vegetable repertoire. That said, many British cooks still lack the sure touch with this vegetable that comes as second nature to Asian and Middle Eastern cooks. UK public health advice to cut down on fat often makes people reduce the amount of oil used in cooking, but seemingly wanton quantities of oil are the key that unlocks the potential of this vegetable.

Will aubergines break the bank?

Aubergines aren't an expensive purchase and can provide cheap bulk in many dishes. Their meaty fleshiness makes them a good, inexpensive vegetarian substitute for meat in lots of recipes. The hidden cost with any aubergine dish is the oil required to cook it.

Aubergines keep well when refrigerated. Older aubergines may begin to sag in their skins and have golden-brown patches that indicate that they are rotting. When you cut into them, their internal pips will look darker and more obvious. If you end up with aubergines like this, there is no need to chuck them out. Just cut off the bad bits and then use as normal.

Broccoli, cabbage, cauliflower and other brassicas

(Brussels sprouts, kale, cavolo nero, bok choy and pak choy, romanesco, kohlrabi, radishes, Chinese leaves, spring greens)

For decades, brassicas were greeted with indifference, or worse, and seen as the least sexy, most unappealing of all our vegetables. Now, in a welcome reversal of status, they have been rediscovered as some of the most chic, interesting and useful vegetables we have to hand. The whiff of overcooked, school dinner cabbage and waterlogged hotel cauliflower no longer hangs over the land. Inspired by foreign cuisines and a new guard of progressive chefs more focused on home-grown vegetables, we have learned new ways with brassicas, be they eaten raw, al dente or cooked to melting softness.

Vegetables in this family don't show their age as much as lettuce, but with the exception of hard white and red cabbage, which store beautifully, they deteriorate surprisingly quickly, both in appearance and taste. So don't see brassicas as something to keep in the fridge for future use; eat them as soon as you buy them. UK- or Ireland-grown brassicas will naturally be fresher than the imported (usually Spanish) equivalent.

In cabbage and Brussels sprouts look for good, firm hearts and perky, tight outer leaves. For cauliflower and its pale green relative, romanesco, a compact, hard head is a must. Avoid any that are bendy or yielding. Brassicas such as radishes and kohlrabi should feel hard to the touch. When buying leafy brassicas such as bok or pak choy, or cavolo nero (black cabbage), look for leaves that stand up to attention and are vibrantly green. Don't buy any that are floppy or dull-looking. You can tell whether purple sprouting broccoli is fresh by testing it with your nail: it should sink into the stalk, which should not be woody or fibrous. You can also use the nail test for the more common chunky, dark green type of broccoli (calabrese). If your nail doesn't sink in, but the florets are tight and firm, don't discard it, simply pare off the hard exterior of the stalk with a knife until you come to a softer centre. Cut out the fibrous stalks from kale and use just the frilly green leaves.

When cooking brassicas, timing is critical. Cooking should be either short and sweet, or long and slow, as in cabbage soup, or braised red cabbage. Nothing in between will do. Over-boiled brassicas release sulphurous odours and turn to unappetizing mush. The best way to capture the fresh flavour of brassicas is to use as little water as possible. Either stir-fry, sauté or steam them, or use the half-boil/half-steam 'conservative' method. This involves putting the vegetables in a wide, shallow pot with only a little boiling water, so that they are not covered, and then cooking them briefly and furiously with the lid on.

Things to do with brassicas

- Peppery brassicas such as radishes and kohlrabi make excellent salads when shredded, or crudités when cut into batons. Along with hard types of cabbage, commonly eaten raw in coleslaw, they offer that attractive crunch.

- Nutty-tasting brassicas such as cauliflower and romanesco work in raw salads too, as long as they are broken down into tiny florets and generously anointed with a punchy dressing.

- Raw, shredded or torn, tender new inner leaves of cavolo nero and de-ribbed kale add vigour to a green salad.

- Cauliflower is good roasted. Blanch florets in boiling water for two minutes, slice thickly and roast with oil, ground or cracked coriander seed and sea salt.

- Kale and Chinese broccoli (kailan), in common with crisp, juicy pak and bok choy and other Chinese greens, are great steamed for a couple of minutes then finished off with soy sauce and a drop of sesame oil.

- Sauté stems of calabrese broccoli in a mixture of butter and oil, flavoured with chilli flakes and chopped anchovies in a lidded pan until soft, adding the florets two minutes before the end of cooking. You can do the same with purple-sprouting or tenderstem broccoli, but cook both stem and florets simultaneously.

....

- Cavolo nero lends dark green colour and adds its interesting iron-tinged flavour to hearty winter broths with root vegetables and pulses, such as Scotch broth and white bean soup.

....

- Thinly sliced Brussels sprouts make a less predictable winter gratin when baked in a white sauce with fried bacon lardons and chunks of blue cheese.

....

- Sauerkraut (sour, fermented cabbage), bought in a jar, can sharpen and jazz up otherwise plain meals involving cooked ham or sausage, along the lines of the celebrated Alsatian *choucroute garni*.

Are brassicas good for me?
....

Brassicas offer a truly impressive package of health benefits. The nutritional profile varies from one to the other. Red cabbage, for instance, has much higher vitamin C levels than white cabbage, but collectively these vegetables share many positive nutritional attributes.

They are loaded with vitamin C, which is protective against many diseases and supports the immune system; vitamin K, which is important for blood clotting and bone health; soluble fibre, which slows down the rate at which sugar is released into the bloodstream; and folate, which helps prevent birth defects. In addition to all this, brassicas contain a collection of useful minerals and phytochemicals, such as sulforaphane and indoles, which are thought to have a strong anti-cancer action, and have an anti-inflammatory effect, which is believed to help reduce the risk of heart disease and stroke.

If you want to lessen your exposure to pesticide residues, choose organic brassicas. If this isn't an option, discard more of the outer leaves than you usually would as they are more likely to trap residues from spraying.

How are brassicas grown?
....

Brassicas are grown all over the UK and particularly thrive in coastal areas. Most production is centred on Lincolnshire, Cornwall, Lancashire, Kent and the east of Scotland. The robust, hardy brassicas – cabbage, cauliflower, romanesco, kale, broccoli and Brussels sprouts – are usually grown in open fields, although they can be started off in an open, unheated polytunnel then transplanted for an early crop. More tender, leafy brassicas, such as pak choy, are commonly grown in greenhouses or polytunnels. Some brassica growers specializing in indoor production are now using hydroponic methods, where the vegetables are grown, not in earth, but in a soil substitute and nourished with water and nutrients.

Are brassicas a green choice?

Since brassicas grow well in the UK, there is never any need to eat the imported sort. These come from further afield, using up lots of oil in transport, so they leave a heavier carbon 'foodprint' than home-grown. Most imported brassicas come from dryer countries such as Spain where water usage in crop production has put further pressure on already depleted water resources.

Brassicas are very susceptible to insects, pests and diseases, so unless they are organically grown, they are likely to have been given repeated pesticide treatments. These can pollute soil and water and have a negative impact on wildlife. Non-organic British brassica growers are trying to reduce their dependency on pesticides, not least because several products they relied on are being phased out or restricted by the European Union. They are using various techniques to minimize spraying as well as regular crop rotations (not growing the same crop in the same place for too long) to prevent any pest build-up in the soil. That said, many conventional brassica growers still use several controversial pesticides that most consumers would probably prefer were not used to grow their food.

Polytunnel and glasshouse production of brassicas can raise a number of environmental issues too (see TOMATOES/Are tomatoes a green choice?).

Where and when should I buy brassicas?

British-grown brassicas are either in season or available from store as below. If you see these vegetables at other times, they are likely to be either imported or grown in heated glasshouses.

> *Cabbage*: all year
> *Cauliflower*: all year, best in summer
> *Spring greens*: March to June
> *Brussels sprouts*: October to March
> *Broccoli (calabrese), romanesco*: June to October
> *Purple sprouting broccoli*: January to April

Chinese greens: March to December
Kale: September to March
Kohlrabi: July to February
Radishes: March to August

THE SMELL OF SCHOOL DINNERS

Although cabbage and cauliflower have long featured in the British diet, unlike other cultures, we rarely celebrate them. Indeed, many people have an antipathy to them. Koreans go mad for pickled fermented cabbage, kimchee. Eastern and central Europeans celebrate sauerkraut. Say cabbage or cauliflower to British people, and you are more likely to hear remarks about the sulphurous school dinner smell of over-boiled vegetables.

In recent years broccoli, which was rarely eaten in the UK until the 1980s, has become the country's favourite brassica and a whole range of leafy vegetables once seen as oriental, and only available in Chinese supermarkets, is now being cultivated in the UK. As sales of these newer vegetables have boomed, production of the more traditional cabbages and cauliflower has declined. The area in the UK now planted with these crops has shrunk substantially, partly as a reflection of reduced demand, and also as a consequence of supermarkets paying growers unsustainably low prices for crops, which they then sell with a very healthy profit margin. This is a great pity, because, thoughtfully cooked, these are vegetables any nation should be proud of. Recently both cauliflower and cabbage (the latter often reinvented as 'seasonal greens') have earned the patronage of top chefs. Combined with the growing interest in local food, the fortunes of these two familiar vegetables may yet revive.

Will brassicas break the bank?

Since vegetables such as purple sprouting broccoli, spring greens and cavolo nero have become fashionable and calabrese has been hailed as a 'superfood', their price in supermarkets has increased noticeably. But in markets, farm shops and independent greengrocers, you can usually buy them for less, with a price tag that more accurately reflects the current wholesale price.

Probably because fewer people can think of something to do with them, radishes, kale and kohlrabi are notably cheap, so they are particularly good buys.

Hard white and red cabbages keep really well in the fridge, so ignore use-by dates that suggest otherwise. Although other brassicas are best eaten nice and fresh, there are ways to rescue those that haven't yet started to yellow, but are nevertheless past their prime. You can strip off and discard the floppier outer leaves of loose-headed cabbages and sprouts and use just the heart. Few people will notice that cauliflower isn't as fresh as it might be when it's cooked in a curry. Cut out any hard ribs and stems on brassicas that are green and leafy, such as spring greens and kale, wilt them in salted, boiling water, then drain them and dress with olive (or nut) oil and lemon juice or a splash of vinegar, in the style of that Greek staple, *horta vrasta*.

Carrots and other root vegetables

(parsnip, swede, white turnip, celeriac, sweet potato, Jerusalem artichokes)

Root vegetables have a reliable, comforting sweetness. They work well together, each one enhancing the other's flavour. People who find them boring have often had bad experiences with eating ones that were watery and fibrous because they were boiled or steamed. With the exception of soup, where their flavour and perfume suffuse the liquid, water is their enemy. You get the best from root vegetables when you fry, sauté, roast, bake or stew them, or, in the case of carrots, beetroot, Jerusalem artichokes and celeriac, eat them raw.

When it comes to carrots, mature, deep orange-coloured ones will be the sweetest and most flavoursome. Unwashed carrots are likely to taste better than washed ones. The soil may be a pain to wash off, but it really helps to protect the roots and keep them moist and firm in storage. It can be surprisingly hard to get decent-tasting carrots in supermarkets. Sweetness is often lacking and they can have a flat, almost soapy taste.

This is partly a reflection of their growing method but also a consequence of our large chains' body-fascist vegetable specifications that are driven by cosmetic appearance. They stipulate that carrots must always be of a similar length and girth, washed and looking appetizingly orange, fresh and wet. To achieve this look, they have to be washed and rotated in a vegetable-processing machine, a bit like a domestic washing machine. The considerable agitation involved in this treatment weakens the carrots and when they are then wrapped in plastic bags they deteriorate further. This is why many supermarket-bought carrots go soft and rot in parts. If you buy carrots washed, take them out of their plastic bag to allow the air to circulate around them and keep them in the fridge.

Tender, young baby carrots have their appeal, but they are never going to be heavy hitters in the flavour stakes unless you get them from the garden, when they can be a delicate treat. Slender, new carrots, usually sold in bunches with their green leaves still attached, look rustic, but they are a bit of a gimmick. Their taste is mute compared to properly mature carrots.

Pre-prepared carrot sticks sold in puffy 'pillow packs' may look fresh because they have been stored in a modified atmosphere made up of nitrogen and carbon dioxide, but they taste about as carroty and juicy as blotting paper.

It is an interesting exercise to compare the flavours of organic and conventionally grown root vegetables. The difference is most noticeable with carrots. The organic ones often taste better, which is perhaps why carrots are the most commonly bought organic vegetable.

Beetroot has a sweet, earthy flavour and a sumptuous colour. Unless you get a chance to buy small, tender summer varieties, go for larger beetroots because they keep better, and choose roots that are hard and not wrinkled. Don't discard the leaves on beetroot if they are still fresh and green: use them as winter spinach or salad leaves.

Celeriac is a big continental favourite which has become more popular in Britain in recent years. It has a mild celery flavour and tastes slightly nutty.

Parsnips have a unique, unmistakable flavour. They taste sweetest and best in the depths of winter when frost has converted their carbohydrates into sugar.

The fantastic, complex flavour of Jerusalem artichokes makes a spectacularly velvety, rather aristocratic soup.

Sweet potatoes have luscious, melting flesh and a taste that is reminiscent of chestnuts.

Swede is good in traditional winter broths but can be very fibrous, so chop it finely or grate it and cook long and slow. The smaller white-violet turnips that are in season in the spring, on the other hand, are tender and need only very light cooking.

Things to do with root vegetables

- Coarsely grated carrot and beetroot (along with kohlrabi, if you like) dressed with toasted nigella (*kalonji*) seeds, lemon or Seville orange juice and olive oil, make a striking-looking and unusual winter salad. Stunning with grated fresh turmeric root added, if you can find it.

- Roast beetroots in their skins, then peel, slice and serve in a salad with watercress, creamy goat's cheese and walnuts.

- Juice carrots and beetroot with tart apples and celery for a winter breakfast drink.

- Grated celeriac, dressed with equal amounts of natural yogurt and mayonnaise and a little horseradish or Dijon mustard, goes brilliantly with thin slices of cured or roast ham and sizzling hot bacon or pancetta.

- Par-boil quartered parsnips, roll in flour, egg, then a mixture of breadcrumbs and grated Parmesan. Shallow-fry them, dust with smoked paprika and dip in soured cream.

- Deep-fry ultra-thin slices of any root vegetable (cut on a mandolin, if you have one) for home-made vegetable crisps.

- Par-boil sweet potato, celeriac or parsnip, slice thinly, brush with oil and chargrill on both sides on a ridged, cast-iron grill pan. When nicely marked with lines, remove and serve warm, drizzled with more oil, chopped fresh herbs and chilli flakes.

- Par-boil and mash sweet potatoes, then fry with ground cumin, coriander and onions. Add canned tomatoes and chickpeas and simmer for five minutes, then stir in chopped or baby spinach at the last minute. Good with sausages or any grilled meat.

- Finely sliced or chopped raw Jerusalem artichoke gives sweet crunch to winter salads.

Are root vegetables good for me?

Carrots and sweet potatoes are an exceptionally rich source of antioxidant vitamins C and E, which help neutralize the damage done by harmful free radicals that can predispose the body to disease, and a very good source of beta carotene, which converts to vitamin A. The deeper and more orange-coloured the carrot or sweet potato, the more beta carotene it has. Among other things, carrots may be protective against heart disease and certain cancers, and help safeguard vision against degenerative conditions such as cataracts. Much of the nutrients in carrots lie just below the skin, so they are most nutritious when eaten unpeeled. Some research suggests that organic carrots have higher levels of nutrients than their conventionally grown equivalents and higher nutrients generally means bigger flavour. Organic growers do not rely on nitrogen-based fertilizers to boost crop yield, so their carrots and other root vegetables grow more slowly and contain more dry matter, which may account for the higher nutrient levels.

The purple pigment in beetroot, betacyanin, has been identified as having powerful anti-cancer properties. This vegetable is also a really rich source of folate, which helps protect against birth defects. Some research suggests that beetroot is anti-inflammatory and strengthens the immune system. It is used in traditional medicine in many countries as a treatment for anaemia and as a general tonic.

Celeriac, parsnip, swede and other types of turnip are all good sources of soluble fibre and minerals. Parsnip and swede rapidly release sugar into the blood, which means that they are not foods to be eaten in large quantities by anyone who is trying to lose weight or make their blood sugar levels more stable.

A light was shone on the environmental and human health impacts of pesticides on root crops in the 1990s when government tests found that carrots contained high levels of organophosphate residues. Since this problem was highlighted the situation has improved. Consumer concern about the toxicity of the chemicals used encouraged growers to find less malign alternatives, such as using protective fleece to act as a physical barrier to pest attack at a critical point in the growing year. Pesticide residue levels in carrots have diminished, but unless they are organic, they are still a crop routinely sprayed with insecticides, herbicides and fungicides. Government tests have shown that about half of all conventionally grown carrots contain residues. The government insists that any residues are so minute that they pose no risk. However, if you want to minimize your exposure, choose organic carrots.

How are root vegetables grown?

Root vegetables are mainly grown in open fields throughout Britain and Ireland. When the roots mature in autumn, the fields are often covered in straw, which makes it easier to harvest them when the ground is very cold in the depths of winter. Sometimes they are sowed in among crops like barley and mustard to give them cover and to stop the topsoil blowing away. Carrots, beetroots and white-violet turnips can also be grown for the early summer market in large, unheated polytunnels. Carrot production is most associated with the sandy soils of eastern England, Norfolk, the Fens, Cambridgeshire and Suffolk and the peaty land around Lancaster. Nowadays considerable quantities are also grown in Nottinghamshire and Scotland. All our sweet potatoes are imported, usually from Israel, because they only grow in hot countries.

Are root vegetables a green choice?

Root vegetables that are harvested in the autumn can be stored for months in a cool place as they are well nigh indestructible, giving us a constant supply of affordable and versatile vegetables. As such, they contribute greatly to our self-sufficiency, or food security. Why buy imported root vegetables, such as Dutch carrots or Australian parsnips, which will have been shipped and trucked to these shores and clock up unnecessary food miles? These imported root vegetables are marketed in spring as newer, fresher roots, at a time when the previous autumn's UK crop is beginning to look a bit old. However, these stored UK-grown roots will still be fine to eat, and other home-grown new vegetables such as asparagus, broad beans and purple sprouting broccoli will be coming on stream.

As supermarkets' cosmetic specifications stipulate that root vegetables must have uniform dimensions, they routinely reject roots that do not fit that bill. It is thought that a typical supermarket 'pack-out' rate (rejection) might account for anywhere between 35 and 50 per cent of the crop, which is a profligate waste of perfectly sound food. Supermarkets also add to waste by refusing to sell carrots unless they have been washed and put through a 'polishing' machine. This leaves the carrots looking pretty but weakens them. They don't keep as well and often rot in the bag. Root vegetables sold in farm shops or market stalls won't have been graded as they are in supermarkets, so they will be different shapes and sizes, dirtier and perhaps not so visually perfect, but they should taste at least as good and make a more ecological choice. Supermarkets also generate unnecessary packaging with their insistence that roots like swede must be shrink-wrapped in plastic. Root vegetables are pretty robust so that packaging is redundant.

Supermarket cosmetic standards for root vegetables have also encouraged growers to use more chemicals to meet the retailers' expectations. Every now and then, supermarkets sell less perfect-looking roots at a cheaper price, but mainly they insist that growers supply only Grade One roots.

Where and when should I buy root vegetables?

Root vegetables are on offer year-round so it might not be obvious from looking at supermarket shelves but, in the natural run of things, they are more seasonal than you might think. There are winter and summer crops of both carrots and beetroot. Tender violet-white turnips are a spring pleasure. But other roots mature in autumn and although they do store well, they are best for winter eating. So if you are still eating parsnips in May – not a great idea – then you can be sure they won't be home-grown.

Will root vegetables break the bank?

As a general rule, root vegetables are wonderfully cheap, but watch out for those – usually carrots – that have been processed or prettified to lend them 'added value'. Expect to pay a premium for having your carrots washed or chopped, while baby carrots or slender new carrots are almost always an expensive disappointment. Supposedly superior carrots from named varieties cost many times more than the basic mature root and generally taste worse.

You will also pay over the odds for small beetroots that are sold in bunches with their leaves still attached. Harder, larger, more mature beetroot are cheaper and will keep much better.

As Jerusalem artichokes and celeriac have become trendy, supermarkets often sell them pre-packed or shrink-wrapped as boutique, speciality vegetables and charge accordingly. Look out for them sold loose, and for much less, in alternative outlets.

There's no rush to use up root vegetables: they keep well for ages, irrespective of the limited longevity suggested by their use-by date. If they have softened, pare off any yielding bits until you get to a firm core, then use it chopped in recipes such as soup, gratins, stews and purées, where the vegetable is well cooked, not served raw.

THE UK'S FAVOURITE VEGETABLE

Unlike celeriac, which is a relative newcomer to these shores from mainland Europe, swedes and parsnips are vegetables particularly associated with the UK. On the Continent, many people do not know what they are, as there is no tradition of eating them there. Those who do recognize them generally consider them to be more suitable for animal feed.

Carrots are the UK's favourite vegetable, one that we have been cultivating and eating since the sixteenth century. As a vegetable that was plentiful and home-grown, carrots became a key plank of the Ministry of Food's 'Dig For Victory' campaign during the Second World War, which encouraged people to grow their own vegetables to boost food security. They also featured prominently in government wartime nutrition advice, with a cartoon character called Dr Carrot who encouraged people to try recipes such as carrot jam and carrolade, a mixture of carrot and swede juice. Carrots were strongly promoted as a healthy food, particularly stressing their benefits for vision, and featured on posters that read: 'Carrots keep you healthy and help you to see in the blackout'. The British government spread the rumour that the accuracy of their fighter pilots was due to all the carrots they ate. Subsequent research on the antioxidant effect of carotenes in carrots, and their beneficial effects in helping vision and protecting against macular degeneration, suggests that these claims were well justified. An example of how science sometimes takes time to catch up with traditional medicinal wisdom.

VEGETABLES

Celery

Celery packs more punchy flavour than any other vegetable, although, served raw, it isn't to everyone's taste. Its ubiquity on our shelves is explained by the fact that it is cheap, keeps well in the fridge and can be relied on to lend a welcome juicy crunch to salads. What is often overlooked is that celery can be a wonderful vegetable once cooked, when its potential brashness gives way to more interesting flavours reminiscent of those we associate with highly desirable vegetables, such as asparagus or artichokes. It merits a bigger role in cooking than being used just a stalk at a time as a minor aromatic.

There are two ways to present celery successfully. Either serve it raw, preferably chopped very, very small, or so well cooked that you can cut it with a fork. Anything in the middle can put people off this vegetable for life.

Celery comes in two types: the more common, stronger-flavoured green one and the less available white one. Snap up the paler white celery when you see it. It has a superior, subtler taste than the green sort: sweeter, nuttier and with aniseed notes. Many people find the fibrous threads that run down the outside of celery stalks unpleasant and spoil their enjoyment of the vegetable, but these are easily and quickly removed using a potato peeler. The inner stalks and heart of celery are less fibrous.

Things to do with celery

- Make a classic Waldorf salad of finely chopped celery, sweet apple and walnuts, bound with equal amounts of mayonnaise and soured cream or natural yogurt. Add leftover chicken to make it into a substantial, portable lunch.

- Celery makes a subtle, elegant, eau-de-nil-coloured soup. Just let it sweat with onions for a long time, then add chicken stock or vegetable bouillon. Liquidize, sieve and finish off with cream and parsley.

- Along with carrots and onions, celery is an essential component in the classic French *mirepoix* and Italian *soffrito*, those gently sweated mixes of finely chopped vegetables and aromatics that are used as a flavour base for many dishes. Use this to start off a Bolognese-style ragù, stew or soup that will be liquidized, and taste the difference.

- Slice it razor-thin over a bed of watercress or rocket, dress with olive oil, lemon juice and lots of black pepper, then crumble over a salty, mature, cheese such as Parmesan.

- Braise it long and slow with chicken stock and cream. This goes brilliantly with roast chicken and provides a creamy gravy.

- For a cheaper – and much more interestingly textured and flavoured – tuna or egg mayonnaise, add very finely chopped celery.

- Cut into batons, you can eat it with Middle Eastern-style dips as a healthier alternative to pitta bread.

Is celery good for me?

Celery is an excellent source of vitamin C, which boosts the immune system and may be protective against heart disease and cancer. Celery also has useful amounts of soluble fibre, which slows down the rate at which sugar is released into the blood; vitamin B6, which is necessary for metabolizing the amino acids in protein and the formation of red blood cells; potassium, which helps regulate blood pressure; and folate, which helps prevent birth defects. Green celery contains more vitamin C and folate than white.

In many types of traditional medicine, celery is recognized as lowering blood pressure. This may be due to its richness in minerals such as potassium, but also to the presence of plant compounds called phthalides, which may help relax the muscles around arteries and allow them to open up. Celery has a history of usage as a treatment for nervous conditions as it is thought to have a calming effect.

Celery is generally accepted to have a diuretic effect; that is, increase the production of urine. Some research suggests that this property may encourage the elimination of excess fluid in the body and possibly help reduce the severity of inflammatory joint problems, such as gout and rheumatoid arthritis. In many countries, celery is regarded as a cleansing vegetable with tonic properties.

Some research has identified certain natural plant compounds in celery – acetylenics, phenolic acids and coumarins – which may help prevent cell damage and inhibit the development of cancer.

UK government tests conducted in recent years identified a problem with residues of an insecticide in celery that is known to be toxic to wildlife and can have adverse health effects for people heavily exposed to it. The maximum residue limit for the insecticide in question has been tightened. The latest results of testing, however, still show that almost half of all celery samples contained residues. So it is a good idea to buy organic celery whenever possible. Pesticides are not used in organic celery production.

A BRITISH TRADITION RIPE FOR REVIVAL

White blanched celery, grown as an autumn and winter vegetable, is a great British speciality. Its production is mainly centred in the Lincolnshire Fens, Lancashire and Bedfordshire. Less is grown now than in the past, as the earthing-up of soil is quite labour-intensive, which adds to the grower's costs. It is also a crop that is susceptible to frost. Many consumers find the appearance of green celery more attractive and assume that it is fresher and healthier, which isn't necessarily true. For all these reasons, this once distinctive British-grown vegetable has been pushed off the shelf by a steady, year-round supply of green celery grown in warmer countries, mainly Spain. But seasonal white celery, with its less one-dimensional flavour, is ripe for a revival.

How is celery grown?

The traditional way to grow celery is to cultivate plants from seed in a greenhouse, then transplant them into deep trenches where they are earthed up to blanch them. Keeping the heads out of the light reduces the amount of chlorophyll in the stalks and leaves, and produces white celery that is pale and tender with a more nuanced flavour than green. More commonly these days, however, celery is grown above the ground like other crops and sold green. White or green, it is cut by hand.

Where and when should I buy celery?

Green celery, usually imported, is always on sale. White and green British-grown celery is a seasonal treat to snap up from the end of September until the end of December.

Will celery break the bank?

Celery is extremely affordable. Organic celery is consistently one of the lowest-priced organic vegetables you can buy. Celery is a very forgiving vegetable so it makes a great fridge stand-by and there is never any need to waste any. However old it may be, once trimmed, it will still have a use, even if only to add flavour to a stock made from a well-picked chicken carcase.

Courgettes, marrow, squash and pumpkin

The eye-catching contours and colours of courgettes, marrow, squash and pumpkin flag up a useful and easy-going family of vegetables. They keep well, for months in the case of the harder winter squashes, and their obliging ability to soften down to a pulp and combine unobtrusively with other ingredients, almost as a thickener, makes them very handy indeed.

With courgettes, colour is a distraction – green or yellow, they all taste the same – but small is beautiful. If you can get the finger-slim, new-season crop, they have a sweeter, slightly nutty flavour and a firm texture. The larger they grow, the more watery and insipid they become. They contain lots of water, so there's no need to add any. Other thin-skinned summer squashes, such as the dinky little gem and the flying saucer-shaped patty pan, have similar-tasting flesh to courgettes, but their high ratio of skin to flesh doesn't appeal to everyone and makes them more of an occasional novelty crop than a trusty staple. The main thing marrow has going for it is size and shape – perfect for stuffing – although if you are going to go to that bother, cabbage, tomatoes or peppers will produce tastier results.

Among the orange-coloured squashes, it's easy to be impressed by the quirky ensemble of turban-shaped Turk's head squash, stripy green kabocha, and heart-shaped, ribbed acorn, but they take a while to prepare and the flavour doesn't always merit that investment of time. Butternut squash gets the popular vote. It isn't so time-consuming to prepare because you can use a potato peeler, and the velvety, sweet orange flesh is wonderfully rich, sometimes so rich and sugary that it is almost too much and on its way to being a pudding. Pumpkins look fantastic, but their flesh is meek and insipid by comparison. If you feel inspired to do something with them other than carve a Hallowe'en lantern, go for the heaviest and firmest you can find to be sure of getting the maximum amount of usable flesh.

Things to do with courgettes, marrow, squash and pumpkin

- Grill long thin slices of oiled courgette on a ridged, cast-iron grill pan. Serve at room temperature drizzled with extra virgin olive oil, lemon juice, chopped fresh mint and crumbly white cheese such as Lancashire or feta.

- Use larger, more watery courgettes to thicken up and add bulk to any liquidized vegetable soup, instead of stodgier potato or lentils.

- Butternut squash rarely disappoints in a soup but, to stop it resembling baby food, sweat the flesh with onions and lots of fresh ginger then finish it off with coconut milk and a very generous dusting of grated nutmeg. Add red lentils if you want to make it heartier.

- You can make something of larger courgettes by sautéing slices in a heavy pot with unsalted butter, a soft, over-ripe fresh chopped tomato, a garlic clove, sea salt and a generous grind of black pepper, then cooking very slowly with a lid on until they soften. Chuck in a handful of torn fresh basil at the end.

- Marrow finds a purpose in chutney, where its bland flesh comes alive with the assertive flavours of vinegar, sugar and spices.

- The best recipes for pumpkin are American, such as custardy pumpkin pie and pumpkin cheesecake. Pumpkin works really well in desserts with treacle and sweet spices such as cinnamon, nutmeg, cloves and cardamom.

Are courgettes, marrow, squash and pumpkin good for me?

Courgettes, marrows and other types of thin-skinned squash such as patty pan are mainly made up of water, but they do provide some vitamin C, which supports the immune system, and soluble fibre, which slows down the rate at which sugar is released into the bloodstream, along with useful minerals like manganese, magnesium and potassium. The harder, heavier, orange-fleshed types of squash, such as butternut, kabocha and pumpkin, have more going for them nutritionally because they contain less water and are a more concentrated source of these vitamins. They are also a rich source of carotenoids, such as cryptoxanthin. Some research suggests that people who eat more carotenoid-rich food have a lower risk of cataracts, heart disease and certain cancers. The darker-fleshed the squash or pumpkin, the more carotenoids it contains.

Pesticide residues have been a concern with courgettes in recent years, so much so that the European Commission has issued EU-wide alerts. Since pesticide residues are toxins, it is best to minimize exposure, and therefore to buy organic courgettes. Marrows, pumpkins and squash seem to be more or less free from residues.

How are courgettes, marrow, squash and pumpkin grown?

Courgettes, marrow, squash and pumpkin are field-grown crops. Sometimes in cold weather they are grown under polytunnels or covered with plastic or fleece to protect them from cold and encourage them to mature earlier. Courgettes, marrows and pumpkins all grow in the UK and Ireland, although many of the courgettes we eat also come from Spain and France. Hard-skinned winter squashes are imported from Europe, usually Italy and Greece, and also from South America, South Africa and Egypt.

Are courgettes, marrow, squash and pumpkin green choices?

To cut down on needless environmentally destructive food miles, eat courgettes, marrow and other thin-skinned squashes in summer, pumpkins in autumn, and thick-skinned British winter squashes in winter. Try to avoid imports at other times of year by focusing on seasonal vegetables grown closer to home. If you find yourself choosing among imported winter squashes such as butternut, go for those grown in Italy and Greece over those from further afield. If you buy these Europe-grown winter squashes when they are on offer, and store them for future use in a cool place, like a garden hut, cellar or unheated room, they will keep for months.

INEDIBLE GIANTS

The enduring popularity of courgettes and marrows in our gardens speaks volumes about how easily they grow. Even the least dedicated gardener with the shortest attention span can produce courgettes. In no time you get yellow flowers which, given a couple of warm, sunny days and a bit of rain, can turn into edible courgettes in the blink of an eye. Left ignored, a modest courgette will reinvent itself as a marrow.

For its part, the super-sized marrow drops into the scene like an alien invader from outer space. One minute there is only a flower. The next, it is taking over the garden. The English have something of an obsession with this watery vegetable, which has nothing to do with taste, and everything to do with scale. Rural competitions for prize marrows are hotly contested, and debates over judging can become as acrimonious as those over the lightest Victoria sponge. As evidence of the English dedication to the marrow, in 2008 a Norfolk grower, Ken Dade, went into the *Guinness Book of Records* for producing the world's biggest marrow on record. Weighing in at sixty-five kilos, and resembling a gigantic gherkin, it took two men to carry it. The prize-winning seeds were retained to produce more massive marrows in future years, and the flesh dutifully composted. Needless to say, no one seriously considered eating it.

Where and when should I buy courgettes, marrow, squash and pumpkin?

UK- and Ireland-grown courgettes, marrows and other thin-skinned summer squashes such as little gem and patty pan, are in season from June to September. The more unusual types generally only turn up in organic vegetable box schemes and at farmers' markets. UK- and

Ireland-grown pumpkins and winter squashes are in season from late August until November. Imported, thick-skinned, winter squashes, such as butternut, are available year round.

Will courgettes, marrow, squash and pumpkin break the bank?

Courgettes and marrows are always cheap. You will pay more for novelty summer squashes like patty pan. Fresh pumpkins are great for making lanterns, but for pies and other recipes, tinned pumpkin pulp might end up being cheaper. Imported winter squashes cost more than courgettes or marrow, but they contain a lot less water and a little goes a long way. Half a butternut squash, for instance, will make a decent quantity of soup. You pay a premium in supermarkets for the more unusual-looking winter squashes, such as acorn, Turk's head and kabocha, largely because of their novelty value. Those in vegetable boxes and at farmers' markets will usually be cheaper.

Green beans and runner beans

There's no real substitute for the satisfying crunch and bite of juicy green beans. This is the vegetable that comes closest to asparagus in the sophisticated, sexy vegetable stakes. Also known as French or round beans, they are long, thin, smooth and stringless. They can be eaten simply topped – although fastidious people might prefer also to tail them – as they have no fibrous strings. The fine or extra-fine grades represent skinny supermodel standards for cosmetic desirability, but thicker 'bobby' or 'round' beans, and more unusual types, such as long (snake) beans and wax beans, which are used in Asian cuisines, have every bit as much flavour.

Green beans go rapidly downhill with age as their attractive sweet, bright flavour gives way to a dull, even bitter, taste. Most of the imported green beans on sale in the UK are a good few days old by the time we buy them. Telltale signs of beans that are older than they should be are that they have a dull, matt finish and look limp or puckered. A really fresh green bean should be juicy, stiff and snap cleanly when bent. Some people believe in boiling them briefly so that they are still crunchy and squeak when you bite into them, but while beans should never be overcooked or soggy, they are better when just soft and cooked through.

Flatter, longer, rougher-skinned runner beans with their less predictable shape don't have the same crunch as green beans, but bring a satiny texture to the table. They need their strings removed and are usually served not whole, but thinly sliced. Runner beans are more fibrous than green beans, but, on the plus side, they last much better than green beans, and there are those who prefer their more buttery taste. They are at their best when they are small and tender, so avoid those that look extra-long, coarse and knobbly as they may be a little woody within.

Things to do with green and runner beans

- Combine cooked pasta with cubes of boiled potatoes, halved cooked green beans and pesto in the Ligurian tradition.

- Raw and very thinly sliced green beans add crunch to Asian-style salads dressed with lively ingredients such as lime juice, fish sauce, fresh chilli and sesame oil.

- Green beans blanched in boiling water for three minutes, strained, refreshed in chilled water to keep the colour bright and cut into small batons, are a must in a proper salade Niçoise.

- Steam green beans and smoked haddock and top with poached egg.

- Add crunch to crunch by dressing blanched green beans with nut oil and adding crushed toasted hazelnuts or pecans.

- Runner beans turn soft and voluptuous if you stew them slowly in olive oil with tomatoes and garlic. Add oregano and/or a stick of cinnamon during cooking or throw in some chopped mint or dill at the end.

Are green and runner beans good for me?

Feel free to eat green and runner beans until they are coming out of your ears. They are an abundant source of the antioxidant vitamins C and beta-carotene, which help neutralize the damage done by harmful free radicals that can predispose the body to disease, and vitamin K, which is important for bone health. They also provide the body with soluble fibre, which slows down the rate at which sugar is released into the bloodstream, folate, which helps prevent birth defects, and beneficial minerals, most notably manganese and potassium. If you want to get the maximum nutrition from fresh green beans, avoid those that have been pre-prepared. Topped and tailed beans keep less well than the whole sort as the cutting weakens the structure of the beans and speeds up vitamin loss.

There is an ongoing problem with pesticides in green and runner beans. Government tests in recent years have detected relatively high levels of residues, almost always in imported beans. They have found samples of beans with multiple residues, residues of pesticides that are illegal in the UK, and residues that have been above the maximum permitted limit. The situation has been serious enough for the Food Standards Agency to issue rapid alerts to retailers and importers. If you want to reduce your exposure to pesticide residues, choose organic beans. Organic standards more or less outlaw the use of pesticides, and no residues have been found in recent years in organic beans.

How are green and runner beans grown?

Green and runner beans are grown in open fields. Most of those we eat come from Kenya, Zimbabwe or Morocco. Green and runner beans from Africa are transported using an elaborate chain that ensures that they are rapidly chilled after picking, then kept refrigerated at every stage in their journey to the store. Supermarkets and exporters insist that they can get African beans from field to plate within forty-eight hours, still really fresh, but the reality is that they do not emerge from this process radiating true vitality and freshness. UK-grown beans will almost certainly be fresher, especially if you get them from a farmers' market or farm shop.

A tiny proportion of imported beans are now Fairtrade, and these are preferable because workers are better paid, growers receive a higher price for their production and more money goes back into the community to support community projects.

Are green and runner beans a green choice?

The importation of vegetables such as green and runner beans from far-flung countries is extremely controversial. As they are fragile and fresh, they must be transported by air, and air-freighting is particularly damaging to the environment because it uses up much more fuel than other sorts of transport, leaving a very heavy carbon footprint that is likely to accelerate the pace of climate change. Many of the countries that grow produce for the UK will be in the front line for feeling the effects of climate change because they are short of water and drought-prone, a situation that has already been worsened by global warming. Thirsty vegetables need lots of irrigation to grow, so this trade puts further pressure on already stretched water resources.

Some development groups argue that the environmental damage done by air-freight is offset by the fact that the air-freighted vegetable trade provides much needed income for people in producer countries. They say that if UK consumers stopped buying air-freighted produce, these countries would suffer. In their opinion it is unfair to deprive poorer countries of a lucrative trade when their overall carbon footprint is much lower than that of affluent countries.

Other development groups think that this trade is inherently precarious and gives no true security to producer countries, as retailers in wealthy countries can abandon their suppliers at the drop of a hat. They argue that poorer countries would be better to build their own 'food security', or self-sufficiency in food, by concentrating on growing food to feed their own people. There are also question marks over whether the financial benefits of the air-freight vegetable trade filter down to agricultural workers, or whether they are mainly creamed off by local elites and retailers in the UK. Vegetable workers, although happy to have a job at all, typically work long, hard hours for low pay.

On environmental grounds, it is hard to justify the air-freighting of vegetables, not least because it undermines local production. The never-ending supply of vegetables from other continents continues right through the summer months, even when the UK- and Europe-grown crop comes on stream, so it clearly competes with beans grown closer to home. While there may be a very small place for air-freighted imports for produce that can't ever be grown in the UK, such as passion fruit or baby corn, the same cannot be said for those that can, such as green and runner beans.

Where and when should I buy green and runner beans?

UK-grown green and runner beans are in season from June until September, as are European imports. Imported beans from further afield are sold year round.

UNIFORMLY-PROPORTIONED CLONES

Green beans have a definite cachet, thanks perhaps to their time-honoured association with French cooking. Unlike sliced runner beans, which were more commonly used in domestic cooking, many British people first encountered the stringless green bean in the pages of post-war cookbooks, nestling in the classic salade Niçoise or as an accompaniment to the Gallic steak-frites.

In a few decades, green beans have gone from being a seasonal summer vegetable with irregular dimensions and curves to being ever available, uniformly proportioned clones that stack up as neatly as matchsticks. The standard supermarket specification for fine beans is that they must be straight and measure between ten and thirteen centimetres long and six to nine millimetres in diameter. What this means is that growers have to grade out 20 per cent or more of their crop, as retailers and wholesalers will otherwise reject it.

British chefs have been besotted by green beans and their aura of luxury and chic. In the 1980s and 1990s, bundles of imported green beans, blanched and tied with chives, became a common sight at functions and in aspiring restaurants. These days, imported green beans have become so over-used and so over-represented that they are increasingly being eclipsed on progressive restaurant menus by home-grown vegetables like celeriac and spring greens. UK-grown green and runner beans, on the other hand, are now seen as a special, seasonal treat worth seeking out.

Will green and runner beans break the bank?

At any time of year, there will always be a much cheaper, fresher and more interesting seasonal vegetable alternative to imported beans. Imported green and runner beans are always considerably more expensive than the seasonal UK- and Europe-grown equivalent. Fairtrade beans sell for a further premium, but they do represent a more ethical choice.

If you have any space at all to grow things, even a patio, or a large pot on a balcony, consider growing beans. They grow very easily, crop abundantly and look really pretty.

Herbs

Without herbs, you'll be cooking with one hand tied behind your back. They offer an easy, quick and varied toolkit for adding flavour and interest to even the most basic dishes. No dish looks or tastes mundane when fresh herbs have been used. On the contrary, they are the cook's instant 'fixer', a transformative ingredient whose green presence makes the humdrum look and taste special. There is scarcely a dish that is not improved with a final scattering of fresh herbs.

The flavours of individual herbs are unique, and even different varieties of the same herb can be markedly distinctive. The peppery basil you will see in markets in Italy, for instance, smells and tastes quite different from the more aniseed-flavoured sort that we commonly buy in our shops, or the small-leaved Greek bush basil. Flat parsley always tastes greener and more pungent than the curly type. Apple mint is quite unlike spearmint. On smell alone you can easily tell lemon thyme from the more common sort. And never make the mistake of buying a Russian tarragon plant instead of a French one, as the former tastes of zilch; the latter is the one you want.

If you can't grow a few of your own herbs, then it is best to buy those cut herbs that come simply wrapped in a thin, slightly stiff plastic pouch. Some herbs are still sold in rigid plastic packs, which often look good superficially, but tend to hide herbs that are rotten in the middle because they have been squashed and have had no air circulating around them.

Herb plants sold for harvesting in the kitchen are fine if you only want a very small amount and no better loose-cut herbs are available, but they tend to produce rather spindly, leggy growth and have a pretty faint flavour and less aroma than you might expect from a herb plant bought in a garden centre and planted in soil. This is because they are really just clumps of overgrown, overcrowded seedlings – the sort that a gardener would normally thin out – that are competing with one another, rather than one healthy vigorous plant. These supermarket herb plants typically last for a shorter time than you might suppose.

Dried herbs are worth considering in place of fresh but are not usually a substitute for fresh herbs as the drying process intensifies their flavour and perfume and produces a stronger, more intense effect, so they are better thought of as seasonings, like salt or spices. Some herbs do dry better than others. Dried parsley or coriander, for instance, is a waste of space, but dried tarragon, oregano and mint, on the other hand, can be more effective and more delicious in some dishes than the jet-lagged, flaccid, fresh equivalent, particularly outside the summer months.

Things to do with herbs

- Chop finely or blend fistfuls of basil, flat parsley and mint with smaller amounts of garlic, anchovy, Dijon mustard, capers, olive oil and vinegar or lemon juice to make a vibrant salsa verde that can be served with asparagus or any roasted meat or fish.

- Make an omelette with thin discs of soft goat's cheese and masses of chopped mint added at the last minute.

- Tomatoes taste great sprinkled with fresh breadcrumbs that have been mixed with fresh thyme, sea salt and black pepper, drizzled with oil, then roasted.

- Bay leaves have an affinity with lamb. Use them to perfume a lamb stock-based soup made with barley or spelt and chopped root vegetables.

- Roast chicken legs in olive oil with chopped rosemary and quartered lemons. Make a gravy by deglazing the rosemary-lemon roasting juices in the roasting tin with white wine, scraping the tin to get all the bits.

- Sage leaves are excellent when you sizzle them for seconds in hot oil until they become crisp. Handy for finishing off a herby risotto or for tarting up a soup.

- Sorrel sauce is brilliant with fish cakes or baked fish. Just sweat chopped shallot in butter, deglaze the pan with white wine or vermouth, add cream and bubble up. Add shredded ribbons of sorrel, cooking only for a minute or two until the sorrel wilts and turns olive green.

- Snippings of chive and chervil enliven simple scrambled eggs.

- Thyme is a non-negotiable ingredient in the marinade for Caribbean jerk chicken.

- Potato salad is vastly improved by heaps of chopped dill or fennel herb and chives.

- Fresh pesto, made by blending basil, pine kernels, grated Parmesan and olive oil, puts the bought stuff in the shade.

....

- Pour boiling water on fresh mint, fennel herb, lemon balm, bay leaves or verbena to make a fragrant tisane.

Are herbs good for me?

Each herb has its own precise chemical make-up but, collectively, herbs are mini treasure troves of the beneficial compounds that we associate with green plant foods, which is why they have been used medicinally for centuries. Fennel and mint have been used to soothe indigestion and colic, for instance, while thyme is used in many traditional medicine systems for coughs and as an antiseptic. Even if you only eat herbs in small quantities, they give you the opportunity to pick up small, but nevertheless useful amounts of natural plant compounds that are often lacking in diets top-heavy with processed food. Rather than thinking of herbs as just a flavouring or garnish to be used in small amounts, incorporate as many fresh herbs into your food as possible. Think handfuls of herbs, not decorative sprinkles.

How are herbs grown?

For simplicity's sake, you can divide 'fresh' (undried) herbs into three groups. First, there are the hardier more shrubby herbs, such as rosemary, thyme, lavender and bay. These thrive outdoors in the UK and can often continue to grow throughout the winter months. The second group is the more tender-leafed herbs such as basil, coriander, tarragon, chervil, dill, oregano, marjoram and sorrel, which flourish in Britain only in summer months. Somewhere between these two groups – depending on the local climate where they are grown – come chives, parsley, mint, lovage, fennel and sage. They will appear earlier and have a longer growing season outdoors than the most tender herbs, but a really cold snap will usually see them off.

For most of the year, the tender cut green herbs on sale in our super-markets and greengrocers are imported by air from warmer countries, most commonly Israel, often Cyprus (especially flat parsley, mint and dill) and sometimes from Spain. From spring until autumn, most chains buy British herbs from milder areas of the UK and from the Channel Islands. Usually the more delicate herbs grown on any scale are cultivated under polytunnels, either to protect them from the heat of the sun or to shelter them from inclement weather, but herbs sold through outlets like farmers markets, farm shops or specialist herb suppliers may have been grown outdoors. Large-scale growers in both Britain and in Holland also cultivate herb plants for harvesting in the kitchen.

If you are trying to keep an eye on where your herbs are coming from, it can be quite confusing. Some UK herb packers have adopted geographical-sounding names which suggest that the herbs come from Britain all year round when in fact they are only growing their own herbs in summer and simply packing imported herbs the rest of the time. So use your common sense. Would a tender leaf like basil come from northern Britain in January? It's highly unlikely, whatever the label might suggest.

Supermarket herbs state their country of origin on the label, but even this can be less than straightforward. Herbs grown on Israeli settlements in the Israeli-occupied Left Bank, or Palestine, are sometimes labelled as coming from the West Bank rather than Israel. West Bank herbs should not be considered as Palestinian or as an alternative source for people who prefer not to buy Israeli produce as a protest against Israel's occupation of Palestine.

FOOD AS MEDICINE?

Although herbs have always featured among the culinary plants grown in Britain and Ireland, they were more commonly grown for medicinal purposes, everywhere from abbey cloisters to physic gardens. Other than parsley, fresh herbs rarely featured in any abundance in our cooking until the 1980s. Once seen as rarefied or specialist ingredients generally imported from sunnier climes, they now seem like a kitchen essential. This has opened up the market for herb growers in the UK and they are helping us to appreciate the range and diversity of herbs that can be grown here.

Are herbs a green choice?

Flying herbs thousands of miles just so we can make fresh pesto in December, or decorate dishes with chervil and mint in February, is environmental lunacy and contributes to unnecessary, avoidable carbon emissions. It is better to let your cooking be informed by the seasons.

Hardier herbs like thyme and rosemary go well with heartier autumn and winter food and feel right for that time of year, while the fleshier, tender green herbs like dill, chives and chervil work best with lighter spring and summer ingredients.

Where and when should I buy herbs?

Tougher, hardier herbs like rosemary, thyme and bay can be grown outdoors in the UK year round so they can be considered as kitchen staples that are always at your disposal. British-grown tender green herbs like basil or chervil are available from June until September. The more prolific, vigorous home-grown green herbs like mint and chives have a slightly longer growing season from April through to October.

Will herbs break the bank?

Even though the pick-up price of fresh herbs may seem relatively small, herbs have some of the steepest mark-ups (several hundred per cent) of any food we buy. The retailer's explanation for this is that they are highly perishable so wastage is high, but this is also true of salad leaves, which have much lower mark-ups. Another defence is that they are imported by air, which is expensive. However, as the price of herbs doesn't vary much, if at all, throughout the year even when home-grown herbs are in prolific supply, this argument needs to be taken with a pinch of salt.

Whenever possible, buy herbs in Asian shops and supermarkets, from grocers specializing in Middle Eastern foods, or from farmers' markets and farm shops. You will get a fistful of herbs for the cost of a few stems in the supermarket.

One way to get better value out of supermarket herb plants like basil and chives is to break each one up into much smaller clumps of roots and repot in new pots, giving them more space to grow. This will produce a more usable herb and more vigorous, healthy growth. Treated like this, a purchase of one herb plant can give you a summer's worth of supply.

Despite their often high price, herbs can help you cook quite economically because they have the capacity to transform otherwise humdrum, cheap ingredients into something special. By using herbs to lend colour and flavour to your food, you can cut down on more expensive ingredients such as meat and cheese and make much more of vegetables, grains and pulses.

Lettuce and other salad leaves

The umbrella terms 'lettuce' and 'salad leaves' do not do justice to the exciting portfolio of salad greens that can be grown in the UK. British salad need never be boring at any time of the year.

There are six broad categories of salad leaf:

Dark green and peppery
Mustard cress
Watercress
Landcress
Rocket
Tatsoi
Mizuna
Mibuna
Nasturtium

Soft and sweet
Lamb's lettuce/corn salad
Butterhead (curly)
Oak leaf
Lolla rossa (red)
Lolla bionda (green)
Salad bowl

Juicy and sweet
Pea shoots
Purslane

Juicy and sharp
Sorrel
Claytonia
Red chard
Spinach
Red orach

Bitter
Belgian chicory
Red (Treviso chicory)
Frisée endive
Radicchio
Dandelion
Escarole
Batavia

Crunchy
Cos/Romaine
Buttercrunch
Little Gem
Webb's wonderful
Lakeland

To make a great 'green' salad, the art is to combine leaves with different colours, textures and flavours so that the salad is packed with interesting contrasts. For extra freshness, you can add any seasonal herbs that you have to hand.

While vegetables like carrots can be stored for months and still taste good, salad leaves need to be ultra-fresh to deliver on the taste front.

Hearts of Little Gem lettuce, for example, may stay looking green in the fridge for a week or more but their fresh sweetness will give way to an unpleasant, flat bitterness.

Puffy 'pillow' packs of salad leaves are filled with 'modified atmosphere' (nitrogen and carbon dioxide gas) to prolong their life. They may look fine when you buy them, but often flop dramatically when exposed to air. This is because their life has been extended unnaturally and so they just don't have the natural vitality, or the flavour, of freshly picked leaves. It makes more sense to buy fresh whole lettuces and leaves that have not been packed this way so you can more easily assess their freshness.

Modern supermarket distribution systems can mean that it takes several days for salads to reach our shelves. They must be ready picked by growers in anticipation of a supermarket order, sent to a factory for trimming, or full cleaning and bagging, then on to a distribution centre, which may not be close by, before being trucked from stores where they will be sold with a 'best-before' date a few days on. Traditional greengrocers, market stalls and box schemes cannot rely on refrigeration to store salads so when you buy salad leaves from these outlets, it is much more obvious whether they are really fresh or not.

Things to do with salad leaves

- Combining the more ordinary salad leaves with fresh herbs such as whole mint leaves, flat parsley, fronds of chervil, dill and oregano – including any that are flowering – will make the mix much more inspiring.

- Dress the more bitter leaves, such as radicchio and curly endive, with nut oils (walnut or hazelnut) and cider or sherry vinegar.

- Use whole, crunchy leaves (such as Little Gem or Cos) as a 'plate' for hot minced pork or duck that has been stir-fried, mixed with a little ground toasted rice, fresh coriander and mint leaves, then dressed with lime juice, palm sugar and fish sauce in the style of an Asian 'larb' (meat salad).

- Salad leaves become the basis for a meal if you put them together with crisp-fried bacon, soft-boiled egg and croutons of fried bread.

- For a fail-safe, classic vinaigrette, use three parts extra virgin olive oil to one part red or white wine vinegar. To obtain a good emulsion, combine the vinegar with a little smooth mustard, sea salt and pepper before whisking in the oil. If you like a sweeter taste, add a drop of honey to the mustard and vinegar mix.

- Sweat watercress in butter with some onion and potato and/or peas, add stock and liquidize to make a verdant, punchy, easy soup.

- Braise halved Little Gem or baby Cos lettuce in butter and chicken stock until soft and juicy, adding a little cream to finish off.

- Heads of chicory or crunchy lettuce hearts, either blanched or steamed, make an unusual winter gratin when wrapped in thin slices of ham and baked in a béchamel sauce.

Are lettuce and salad leaves good for me?

Leafy salads are sometimes dismissed as being mainly water, which is true up to a point, but also misleading since they also provide valuable levels of antioxidant vitamins, minerals and trace elements that we particularly benefit from because we eat them raw. Lettuce has also figured in traditional medicine for centuries as a sleep-promoting food.

Levels of micronutrients vary from one type of salad leaf to another. Cos lettuce, for instance, is packed with vitamin C. Watercress stands out as a nutritional treasure trove. It is loaded with vitamins C and E, and beta-carotene which help neutralize the damage done by harmful free radicals that can predispose the body to disease; folate, which helps prevent birth defects; and zinc, which supports the immune system. All salad leaves contain these, but at lower levels. Watercress has a time-honoured place in traditional medicine as a tonic, purifying food and as a remedy for skin problems.

The nutritional value of salad leaves starts to diminish as soon as they are picked so it is important to eat them as fresh as possible. Research suggests that bagged salads sold in puffy 'pillow' packs filled with modified atmosphere have fewer vitamins and folate than the freshly cut equivalent. This could be because although the modified atmosphere keeps the leaves looking fresh and green beyond their natural shelf-life, some nutrients are depleted by the storage process. This deterioration is likely to be even more rapid in bags that contain leaves that have been torn and cut.

Bags of salad leaves that are sold as ready-to-eat will have been washed in water. Unless they are organic, this water usually contains chlorine, an oxidizing disinfectant, which may also reduce their micronutrients. Some retailers now have their salad leaves washed in spring or ozonated water instead to improve the taste and reduce the chance of chlorine by-products lingering on the leaves. But unless your salad bag label says otherwise, assume that chlorinated water has been used. It is always a good idea to wash bagged salad leaves even if they are ready-to-eat as an extra precaution, both against food poisoning bugs that might have colonized the packs during processing, and to rinse off any lingering chlorinated water.

Due to their open leafy shape, lettuces and salad leaves are particularly likely to trap pesticides. Since the early 1990s government testing of UK-grown salad leaves has revealed an ongoing problem with pesticide residues, so much so that the government now checks them on a regular basis. This residue problem has been most evident in lettuces, both UK-grown and imported, that have been cultivated in glasshouses and in polytunnels, rather than the open field, because they get particularly heavy fungicide treatments. The protected environment creates the perfect climate for the development of rot and the carry-over of disease from one crop to the next.

Follow-up action taken by the authorities against growers producing lettuces with unacceptable levels of pesticides has reduced the incidence of residues somewhat, but lettuces are still routinely found that have multiple residues of various pesticides. Illegal use of pesticides not approved for use in the UK is often also detected. If you want to reduce your exposure to pesticide residues, there is a strong case to be made for buying organic salad leaves. Hardly any pesticides are approved for use in organic growing and no pesticide residues have been found in recent years in organic salad leaves.

How are lettuces and salad leaves grown?

Lettuces and salad leaves were traditionally grown outdoors in open fields, but nowadays many of the lettuces and leaves we eat, whether home-grown or imported, are cultivated in polytunnels or glasshouses. Growing salad leaves under some sort of cover allows growers to extend the growing season because it keeps the crops warmer and protects them from weather damage. In recent years there has been a technological revolution in growing some salads under cover in a temperature-controlled environment using soil substitutes (see PEPPERS/How are peppers grown?).

British watercress is grown in a different way to other salad leaves. Traditionally foraged from streams, these days it is cultivated in shallow, gravel-lined concrete beds in a gentle flow of water from natural springs and underground bore-holes. In the UK, the key watercress-growing areas are Hampshire, Dorset and Wiltshire. As the cress grows in water, it doesn't freeze in winter as tender, soil-grown green leaves would do. This means that although watercress used to be considered a late spring and summer crop, we now have year-round watercress production.

Are lettuces and salad leaves green choices?

From an environmental perspective, it makes no sense to eat lettuces and salad leaves that have been imported from abroad. These have to be trucked long distances in refrigerated vehicles, which uses up a depleting resource – oil – and contributes to climate change in the form of vehicle emissions. As a wide variety of lettuces and salad leaves can be grown in the UK for the best part of the year, there is no need for environmentally destructive imports. Watercress is a 'green' choice in more than one respect: watercress beds provide a particularly attractive natural environment for kingfishers, warblers and other rare birds and encourage otters to set up home in nearby rivers. In wintertime, when the availability of UK-grown leaves and lettuces is more limited, a more environmentally aware approach is to ring the changes with native seasonal vegetables.

Where and when should I buy lettuces and salad leaves?

Salad leaves used to be thought of as a summertime food. Now we tend to think of them as something we can eat year round. If you want to eat UK-grown salad leaves and lettuces, then the selection will change throughout the year and be smaller, but still worthwhile, in the winter. When buying salad leaves, use your common sense and think seasonally. As a rule of thumb, the more bitter-tasting leaves such as chicory will continue to grow in Britain in winter and many other types, such as landcress, watercress and lamb's lettuce, make excellent winter salads. More tender leaves and lettuces don't naturally thrive outdoors in the UK except from early summer until autumn. Supermarkets offer a year-round availability of salad leaves and lettuces. In the winter months they will be imported, usually grown in glasshouses and polytunnels in North Africa and southern Europe.

If you feel daunted or bored at the thought of getting through a whole head of lettuce, check out the fresh mixed leaves selections on farmers' markets stalls, from box schemes, farm shops and natural food stores which usually offer a more interesting array than the supermarket equivalent. Another way to transform your supply is to grow your own 'cut-and-come-again' salad mix, sometimes called 'misticanza' or 'saladini' in a container (on a patio, balcony or windowsill) or in the garden. Even the smallest space will give you a varied summertime crop that you can snip away at, enlivening other more humdrum lettuces and leaves.

Will lettuces and salad leaves break the bank?

Weight for weight, it is much cheaper to buy a whole lettuce and wash it yourself rather than just stumping up for a bag of salad leaves. At a glance, the contents of these bags might look quite adventurous, but on closer inspection, you will probably find that they are padded out with cheaper substitutes – red cabbage instead of radicchio, for instance – which makes them unexciting and poor value for money. There is no point in paying more for ready-washed salad leaves because it is best to wash them yourself at home as a health precaution.

If you think you can't get through a whole lettuce at a time, simply strip off a few leaves and return the heart to the salad compartment of the fridge. If you want to use a mix of leaves, but can't see how you can use them all at once, you can wash them all together, take what you want for that meal, then keep the rest inside a plastic salad spinner with a lid on in the fridge where, if truly fresh to start with, they should keep for a couple of days. If you live on your own, or in a smaller household, eat small quantities of one salad at a time, say lamb's lettuce or mustard cress, and then choose a different leaf next time. This way you avoid waste and get your salad variety, not in one bowl, but over a period of time. The same 'mix' of salad leaves inevitably becomes tedious if you never vary it.

Tender, young pea shoots and tendrils are all the rage for salads and sell for a premium price. Rather than shelling out for them – excuse the pun – if you don't have a garden, then you can grow your own either indoors, or on a patio or balcony. Just fill a container with compost in spring or summer, plant some shop-bought dried peas, put them in a light place and then water them regularly. The shoots will pop up in around two weeks and you can harvest the shoots and tendrils for weeks, just like a cut-and-come-again lettuce.

THE EVERLASTING ICEBERG

Salad leaves have always featured in our diet. In 1699 the English gardener and diarist John Evelyn's book, *Acetaria*, catalogued an astonishing diversity of plants that could be used for 'sallet'. He also recommended 'a particular Composition of certain Crude and fresh herbs, such as usually are, or may safely be eaten with some Acetous Juice, Oyl, Salt, &c. to give them a grateful Gust and Vehicle': what we now know as a French dressing or vinaigrette.

The dark ages for British salad leaves were in the post-Second World War years when a salad typically consisted of a couple of flaccid leaves of curly lettuce, topped with boiled egg and tomato, temptingly garnished with that peculiarly British condiment known as 'salad cream'. When the American iceberg lettuce arrived in the 1970s, it felt revolutionary. We devoured them with enthusiasm despite their almost total lack of flavour because they delivered that welcome juicy crunch. The cabbage-like iceberg could be kept in the fridge, apparently fresh, for weeks on end. For a nation that ate green salad infrequently, more out of a sense of duty than anything else, the everlasting iceberg was just the job.

Throughout the 1980s and 1990s, restaurants began to showcase more exciting salad leaves such as curly endive and oak leaf lettuce, stimulating consumer demand for what we took to be foreign varieties. The dreaded iceberg has now been relegated to crummy sandwich bars and we have embarked on a love affair with rocket. British salad leaves have perked up no end in recent years as neglected native varieties have been complemented by fascinating newcomers from as far afield as Japan. This diverse selection is now in small-scale commercial production around the UK.

Mushrooms, cultivated and wild

(large white, button, chestnut, portobello, oyster, enoki, shiitake, porcini (ceps, boletus) chanterelles, morels)

Mushrooms, or edible fungi, come in lots of different forms, each with its own colour, scent, texture and flavour. Wild chanterelles, for instance, have an almost apricot-like perfume, while shitake can have a smoky presence. Large black portabello and field mushrooms are distinctly meaty. Chestnut mushrooms have more of that woodland taste than the white button sort. But, taken as a family, they share certain characteristics. They taste earthy and savoury, and are one of a few plant foods capable of producing the rich flavours found in meats and cheeses. Japanese people refer to this quality as 'umami', and consider it to be the fifth component of taste along with sour, sweet, salty and bitter. Mushrooms have this rich savoury flavour because they contain glutamic acid, a naturally occurring flavour enhancer – not to be confused with the synthetically made food additive, monosodium glutamate (MSG) – along with other natural flavour enhancers. When mushrooms are dried, these natural flavour enhancers are intensified, which is why dried mushrooms pack more punch than their fresh equivalents.

Whatever type of mushrooms you are buying, the same rule applies: look for firm, dry heads and avoid any that look wet or shiny as this is a sign that they are starting to decompose.

Things to do with mushrooms

- A basic liquidized soup made with fresh mushrooms, onion and stock is transformed by the inclusion of a couple of soaked, dried porcini before blending.

- Fill large flat mushroom heads with herby butter (try thyme or tarragon), top with breadcrumbs and bake or grill until they are soft below and crunchy on top.

- Sauté mushrooms with strips of bacon or pancetta, some fresh sage (if you have it), season with black pepper and sea salt, and add thick cream and chopped parsley: an instant sauce for spelt, pearl barley or pasta.

- Brush toasted sourdough bread with olive oil and a thin layer of Dijon mustard, then top with a pile of pan-fried wild or cultivated mushrooms, tossed with chopped tarragon, and a fried egg for a quick, filling supper.

.....

- You can turn the remains of a beef stew into a cheat's stroganoff by stirring in sautéed, sliced mushrooms and soured cream. A dusting of chopped dill adds sparkle.

Are mushrooms good for me?

.....

Mushrooms may not look that promising, but they have many nutritional strengths. They are a good source of soluble fibre, which slows down the speed at which sugar is released into the bloodstream, and B vitamins, which provide energy and support brain function. While it used to be thought that vitamin D was not found in plant foods, a plant sterol – ergosterol – has been identified in mushrooms, which converts to vitamin D when exposed to light. Vitamin D is increasingly being recognized as protective against a wide range of diseases and it is thought that many British and Irish people do not get enough of this for optimum health. For vegetarians especially, mushrooms are a welcome source of vitamin D.

Mushrooms are also a good source of key minerals such as copper, which helps blood cell production, and selenium, which is thought to be protective against certain cancers. Some research suggests that the fatty acids in mushrooms, particularly conjugated linoleic acid, may inhibit breast cancer cell growth. Other research has suggested that certain mushrooms, such as shitake, have immune-modulating effects; that is, they help regulate and strengthen the immune system.

Cultivated mushrooms are usually treated with fungicides while they are growing. Use of insecticides and chemical disinfectants, such as chlorine, is also routine for sterilizing mushroom sheds between growing cycles. If you would rather that your mushrooms weren't grown this way, choose organic. Organic growers are not allowed to use these chemicals and their mushroom sheds must be steam-cleaned.

Eating mushrooms collected from the wild is a risky business as it is quite easy to confuse edible and poisonous types. However enthusiastic you are about foraging, it is vital that any you intend to eat have been correctly identified by a reliable, experienced person – a poisonous one can kill you.

How are mushrooms grown?

The cultivated mushrooms we eat are nearly all grown in Britain and Ireland. They are cultivated in indoor environments that mimic the natural stages of mushroom growth. Many types of mushroom can be grown this way, not only the familiar white- and brown-capped types such as button and chestnut, but types that are often thought of as wild, such as oyster mushrooms and shitake. First a growing medium, or compost, is prepared, typically a mixture of straw, gypsum (a mineral used to make plaster) and poultry litter. Poultry litter is a euphemism for bedding cleaned up from the floor of indoor poultry production units. It consists of straw, poultry droppings (manure), feathers and possibly uneaten feed. Compost for growing organic mushrooms is mainly made from organic straw, but sometimes sawdust or woodchips are used. It can also contain manure from organic, but not intensively farmed, livestock.

Once mixed, the compost is allowed to decompose naturally for a time, then it is pasteurized to kill off any potentially dangerous bacteria or moulds. This method produces the crumbly dark compost that you see clinging to the base of mushroom stems.

The compost is then inoculated with mushroom spores (mycelia) and put in bags, or spread out on trays, blocks and shelves, in hot, humid, dark sheds. This encourages the spores to multiply throughout the compost. When the spores have thoroughly colonized the compost, it is covered with a layer of 'casing', usually peat mixed with sugar beet lime, and the temperature is reduced to encourage the mushrooms to fruit. The mushrooms come through in flushes, and are harvested by hand in low light. Some types of mushroom can also be grown on inoculated logs.

Wild mushroom spores spread underground in woods, then, given the right weather conditions, they 'fruit' or produce edible mushrooms in among vegetation and decaying leaf mould. Wild mushrooms are harvested by foragers, usually for cooking at home, although some semi-professional foragers supply them to shops and restaurants.

Are mushrooms a green choice?

Commercial mushroom growing, both conventional and organic, is a major user of peat and this is helping to drive the depletion of peat bogs in Britain and Ireland. Peat bogs, which take centuries to form, provide a very special and rare habitat for plants and animals. They also act as very effective 'carbon sinks', storing carbon dioxide below ground. When peat is drained and dug up, this escapes into the atmosphere and speeds up global warming. Some mushroom growers are trying to reduce their dependency on peat and looking at greener alternatives, such as fine waste from coal mines and quarries.

Mushroom-growing sheds and buildings are very energy-intensive because they need to be heated to high temperatures for much of the year. This makes them high users of non-renewable fossil fuels. This is to some extent offset by the fact that most of the mushrooms we eat are cultivated in the UK and Ireland, so no energy is involved in transporting them from abroad. Some producers are trying out alternative types of fuel that may be more environmentally friendly, such as old mushroom compost.

COMPETITION IN THE WOODS

With all our dark, mossy woods, Britain and Ireland make ideal territory for mushroom foragers, so it is perhaps surprising that wild mushrooms have not featured greatly in our traditional food repertoire. Instead, we have been largely indifferent to the natural bounty of fungi on our doorsteps, unlike people in continental Europe where wild fungi are widely valued as a free food source and figure prominently in many popular recipes.

Until recently, most of our wild mushrooms went unpicked, so any keen foragers and mushroom enthusiasts scouring the woods for species such as chanterelles and boletus (ceps, porcini) had expanses of woodland more or less to themselves. Much of what they harvested was exported to Europe, or sold to upmarket restaurants, and there was little home consumption. All that has changed with the arrival of migrants from eastern Europe, notably Poland, whose love for fungi in all forms does not allow them to leave nature's bounty rotting untouched. Nowadays, by all accounts, our woods are on the picker's map. Set out into the woods now with your mushroom knife and basket and chances are you'll have company.

VEGETABLES

Where and when should I buy mushrooms?

Fresh mushrooms cultivated in the UK and Ireland are available year round. The best season for picking the most popular wild mushrooms species is late summer and autumn. Dried porcini – the most aromatic type of dried mushroom – are widely available in delicatessens and supermarkets. Asian supermarkets stock the best selection of dried oriental mushroom varieties.

Will mushrooms break the bank?

Cultivated mushrooms are blissfully cheap. Mushroom soup and mushroom risotto are some of the most inexpensive dishes you can make. Mushrooms on toast, fried with a little garlic and tossed with parsley, can make a surprisingly substantial main course. Mushrooms can also be used in quantity to spin out more expensive ingredients. For instance, you can considerably reduce the amount of meat in a recipe for beef stroganoff, and up the amount of mushrooms, without spoiling the dish.

Dried mushrooms, especially porcini, have a particularly intense flavour and aroma that can be used to perfume a dish. You get an astonishing amount of flavour from a very small pack. Water left over from soaking wild mushrooms should never be thrown away, but added to the dish to intensify its taste.

Fresh wild mushrooms are either free or extremely expensive, depending on whether you have picked them yourself.

Onions, garlic, shallots, leeks and spring onions

Onions are one of the simplest and most effective ingredients for getting flavour into any savoury dish. They lend a warm, sweet depth and their ability to caramelize beautifully creates the potential for further flavour notes. Onions that are marketed as specially sweet and mild are often watery and don't have such a good flavour when cooked. Red onions are usually sweeter and less pungent than white ones but do not brown as well. It is common to see them used raw in salads, but check how hot your red onions are before you do this, as some are much too strong to be used this way. For real sweetness, imported Breton onions, sold in 'Onion Johnny' strings, are unbeatable.

Garlic adds pungency and strength to everything it touches. From the way it is sold, you might get the impression that it keeps for ever, but it doesn't. It is best to think of it as a fresh vegetable, not a storecupboard item. If you don't get through garlic very quickly, keep it in the fridge to slow down the rate at which it deteriorates.

Garlic is often old and tired, even though it looks superficially fine, but the sweet pungency it initially had has given way to a stale, ever-so-slightly rotten over-dominance. This can be disguised up to a point in cooked dishes, but it is only too apparent when used raw. Old garlic, and pre-prepared garlic paste, often used by the catering trade and processed food manufacturers, are the causes of 'garlic breath'. Truly fresh garlic never has this effect.

If you want to use garlic raw, say for an aioli, or a chilled Spanish *sopa de ajo* (garlic soup), then only the freshest, sweetest, new summer crop is really up to the job. Garlic is at its very sweetest in May and June when it is 'wet'; that is, the skin around each clove is moist and pliable. When it dries out, a head of still-fresh garlic will feel hard, and the cloves will be juicy, crisp and white when cut, without any 'give' or yellowness. Fresh green leaves of garlic, gathered in the wild, have a striking green colour and mild flavour, a bit like garlic-scented chives.

If you want to cook recipes that major on cooked garlic, such as whole roasted heads, or the classic French chicken with forty cloves of garlic, do so in summer and autumn when the home-grown and European crop is still fresh and firm. Heartbreaking though it is, any old, stale garlic is best abandoned. You can't make a silk purse out of a sow's ear.

The charm of shallots lies in their silky sweetness and their champion ability to caramelize, although they need long patient cooking to achieve this. Their mildness means that they are often better for using raw in a salad than either red or spring onions. Eat them raw or cooked to obliging collapse – anything in between is unpleasant.

Leeks are the most laid-back, mellow members of the allium family. They work especially well with cheese, ham and potato. It's important to cook them thoroughly until they are truly tender: undercooked leeks that squeak when you try to cut them are a bit of a challenge.

Some spring onions are just immature onions, picked while still green. In this case, the white bulb end will be quite large and prominent. These spring onions are full of flavour, but sometimes they can be too powerful for salads. On the other hand, they can be delicious when lightly cooked, chargrilled for instance, when they exhibit some of the gentle savoury-sweet character of leeks. Other spring onions are from milder varieties specifically bred for use in salads. The white end is usually more of a slim tip than a bulb and they don't keep as well as the more bulbous sort. Like red onions, it's a good idea to nibble spring onions before using them to see how strong they taste.

Things to do with onions, garlic, shallots, leeks and spring onions

- Thinly sliced onions, fried in oil or ghee until golden and caramelized along with fresh chilli, sliced garlic and cumin or ajwain seeds, make a seasoned oil or 'tarka' to round off and enrich a simple lentil dal.

- Slowly sweat lots of chopped leeks in unsalted butter until very soft (allowing for shrinkage) and use them as the principal ingredient in a quiche along with cheeses such as Cheddar, Gruyère, Parmesan and ricotta.

- Whole heads of new summer garlic can be drizzled with olive oil and sprinkled with thyme and roasted in a hot oven until soft. The sweet, hot garlic pulp can be spread on toast or eaten with grilled or roasted meat.

- Roast small new potatoes in baking parchment parcels with half their quantity of unpeeled garlic cloves, some sea salt, pink peppercorns and olive oil.

- Thinly sliced, dark-fried, crisp shallots and garlic make a venerable garnish for many Asian noodle and soup dishes.

- Spring onions, softened in unsalted butter and puréed, make a mellow, easy-going accompaniment to white fish.

- To make an Irish champ, simmer floury potatoes in milk until soft, then mash them with thinly sliced spring onions and unsalted butter. This recipe also works well in early spring with leaves of wild green garlic instead of, or as well as, spring onions.

- If you stumble on a prolific source of wild garlic leaves, use them to make a garlic pesto, substituting the garlic leaves for basil.

- Vary a standard potato gratin by including a layer of sweated spring onions or leeks and grating Cheddar on top to form a crust.

- The sweetness of shallots works especially well when it is cut with the acid taste of vinegar, as in shallot red wine vinegar to splash on oysters.

- Whole shallots are an essential ingredient in a proper coq au vin.

Are onions, garlic, shallots, leeks and spring onions good for me?

Onions, garlic, shallots, leeks and spring onions all belong to the allium family of plants, which is thought to have many health virtues. It is no coincidence that in many cooking traditions a bowl of onion or garlic soup is often recommended for anyone who is feeling poorly. Each family member has its own make-up but, taken as a group, these vegetables are good sources of vitamin C, which supports the immune system and is protective against many diseases, several B vitamins, which help give you energy and support brain function, and beneficial minerals such as potassium, manganese, chromium and copper.

In addition, onions, garlic, shallots, leeks and spring onions contain a number of phytochemicals, natural plant compounds, which research suggests bestow many health advantages. The quercitin in onions, for instance, may slow down cell damage. Alliums contain natural sulphur compounds, which some research suggests may protect against infections, assist blood flow, help lower blood pressure and ease conditions such as bronchitis and asthma. These phytochemicals are present in all members of the allium family, but onions and garlic have the most. Some research suggests that the more freshly pungent the bulb, the more active these compounds are. So boutique varieties of onions and garlic bred to be mild may be missing the point.

How are onions, garlic, shallots, leeks and spring onions grown?

Allium crops are field-grown. Most of the garlic we consume is imported, usually from France and Spain or from the southern hemisphere, although some very fine garlic is commercially cultivated on the Isle of Wight and in Aberdeenshire. Onions, leeks and shallots all grow well in these shores. French growers, particularly the Bretons, seem to have cornered the market in elongated types of shallots, grown in the traditional way from sets of bulbs, rather than seed. Shallots grown from seed tend to be rounder and frequently come from Holland. Spring onions are often imported from abroad, from countries such as Spain, Mexico, Egypt and Thailand.

Are onions, garlic, shallots, leeks and spring onions green choices?

A surprising number of onions are imported from countries as various as Italy, Holland, New Zealand and Chile, which seems a little bit crazy, given that both the UK and Ireland can grow onions very successfully. Imports reach their peak in spring and early summer when the native crop is thinnest on the ground but they are often on our shelves at other times of the year when stored home-produced onions are still perfectly firm.

Supermarkets have encouraged the idea that rather than eating up the stored crop, customers want new season onions, even if this means transporting them from the other side of the world and charging considerably more for them. This is another example of supermarkets' global sourcing, carried out in the name of the consumer, who, one suspects, isn't really that bothered. In practical terms, there is never any need to buy imported onions. Visually, stored onions may not look as attractive and they won't be quite as firm as fresh imports: you may need to peel off an extra layer. But unlike garlic, the flavour will still be good, and it is a lot more environmentally aware to eat onions grown closer to home. Think twice before you eat imported spring onions in winter or, for that matter, baby leeks. They will very likely have been chilled and air-freighted, which leaves a heavy carbon 'foodprint'. Choose spring onions that have been grown here, not flown here.

A DEGREE OF CULINARY SOPHISTICATION

Garlic is the one member of the allium family that barely featured in the native cookery of these isles. Then, in the 1960s, we embraced it enthusiastically as one of those exciting foreign ingredients whose availability signalled a break from the plain tastes and austerity of the war years. To eat garlic displayed a degree of culinary sophistication. Undaunted by lack of experience or knowledge about how best to use garlic, we set about making this vegetable our own, armed with the latest kitchen kit, a garlic crusher, an implement forever destined to become rank and rusty with stale, adhering garlic.

Garlic bread – a baguette spread with butter mixed with salt and crushed garlic cloves – became a modern British classic without any clear European precedent, something to be served, perhaps, as an accompaniment to an Italian lasagne. It bore a resemblance to the French parsley butter that is served with snails, but the meatiness of snails is more of a match for garlic butter than bread. There were echoes of several European recipes such as the Catalan *pa am tomaquet* or the Italian *bruschetta al pomodoro*, which sometimes, not always, call for the bread to be rubbed lightly with a cut clove of fresh garlic. But in such treatments, the garlic presence is infinitely more restrained than in the now traditional British garlic bread. Garlic bread epitomized the British ability to take ingredients and techniques from other culinary repertoires and reassemble them in a mongrel, hybrid form.

Nowadays, garlic baguettes are a staple of the supermarket chiller cabinet, a symbol of how the food industry has traduced and debased many ingredients and culinary traditions to invent popular lines of highly profitable, 'value-added' convenience food. What you have in the typical pre-prepared, pappy garlic baguette is a pile of refined white flour with dubious 'flour improvers' and additives that has been spread with extremely salty butter laced with anonymous dried green herbs and dollops of factory-prepared garlic pulp with a taste and odour that will pollute your breath until it eventually works its way through every pore in your skin. Do we really understand garlic? Looking at the supermarket baguette, perhaps not.

Where and when should I buy onions, garlic, shallots, leeks and spring onions?

UK- and Ireland-grown onions and shallots are available year round, sometimes from stored supplies. They are at their freshest and newest in summer. Leeks are harvested from August until March. Spring onions are at their best, not surprisingly, in spring and early summer. The European and home-grown garlic crop comes on to the market from late May and stored bulbs are available until early spring. After Christmas, the new crop of southern-hemisphere garlic comes on to the market.

Will onions, garlic, shallots, leeks and spring onions break the bank?

Onions, garlic, shallots, leeks and sping onions are all extremely affordable. Wild green garlic leaves grow abundantly in woods in early spring and announce their presence with a distinctive aroma. Follow your nose and pick them for free.

Tresses of onions imported from specialist onion growers in France cost more than the standard equivalent, but they do tend to have a superior eating quality. They are characteristically pink, or slightly mauve-tinged, exceptionally juicy and soften down to a delicious mush. If you are making a dish where the onions need to be really melting, such as an onion jam or a French onion tart, then these onions are worth the expense.

Peas, broad beans, mangetouts and sugarsnaps

By way of native vegetable delights, it's hard to trump summery garden peas, fresh from the pod, or rival their crunchy green sweetness. New broad beans, which crop in the UK in late spring and summer, are a great pleasure too, offering that green pea flavour all wrapped up in a velvety, floury texture.

To get the best from fresh seasonal peas and broad beans, you have to taste them before their sugar starts turning to starch. Look out for pea pods that are smooth, vibrantly green and plump. Avoid those that are puckered and fading towards khaki, or that look matt or webbed. These will be rather elderly specimens, which means that the peas within will be mealy. Broad bean pods should look well filled and stiff, not undulating and floppy. Broad beans are at their best when they are small and new, and you can just about get away without slipping them out of their inner skins. But if you are using more mature broad beans, these skins will have toughened up and will interfere with the taste of the bean. Peeling – best done by plunging them in boiling water for a few minutes – is essential.

For most people, garden peas are a stalwart, workaday freezer staple that comes in a packet, not in a pod. But there's no need to be sniffy about frozen peas – or indeed broad beans for that matter. In fact, there is a lot to be said for them. They do, however, have a more slippery texture than the fresh sort – a consequence, perhaps, of the fact that they are blanched (plunged briefly in boiling water) before freezing. They tend to have firmer skins and a more one-dimensional sweetness than the fresh equivalent. These characteristics make them a very different animal from peas or broad beans fresh from the pod. When buying frozen peas, choose the small sort (petits pois) for preference as they are generally sweeter and have more delicate skins than the larger ones. Broad beans freeze even better than peas: their flavour and texture is closer to the fresh ones. Once again though, go for small ones as the larger ones you get frozen in bulk can be tough.

While fresh British peas and broad beans are only seasonally available and not always easy to find, mangetout and sugarsnap peas are ubiquitous. Opinions are divided about the merits of these flat, pea-free, wholly edible pods. Some enjoy them, but not everyone appreciates their icing sugar-like crunch. If you get them fresh, British-grown mangetouts and sugarsnaps can be delicious. If you shop in farm shops and farmers' markets, you may be lucky enough to find a brief supply of mangetouts and sugarsnaps, which are the vegetable equivalent of a packet of sweets in an edible wrapper.

But most mangetouts and sugarsnaps are imported from Africa, Asia or Latin America, and despite all those supermarket guarantees that read 'air-freighted for freshness', they often have a palpable bitterness to them that can make them actively unpleasant. Imported mangetouts may come to us via an elaborate cold chain, but keeping a vegetable cold and looking good during its long journey is one thing; retaining its sweet freshness is quite another.

Things to do with peas, broad beans, mangetouts and sugarsnaps

- Sizzle nigella seeds (*kalonji*) in coconut oil, or other oil, until they pop, add a small handful of fresh curry leaves, sea salt, fresh or frozen peas, mangetouts or sugarsnaps and stir-fry until they start to soften.

- For an easy, pleasing soup, soften onion in unsalted butter, add frozen peas, sea salt, pepper and stock, bring to the boil, then blitz the soup together with a large handful of fresh mint leaves. Frozen broad beans make a heartier, if less elegant, version.

- Broad beans make an interesting and authentic substitute for chickpeas in no-soak falafel recipes. If you haven't got a food processor, boil frozen broad beans for a couple of minutes until soft and bash up using a potato masher, then add the other falafel ingredients, form into falafel shapes and chill well before frying.

- Braise peas or broad beans in unsalted butter with chopped spring onions and crunchy lettuce hearts, then finish off with fresh chervil, mint or basil.

- Make a pea and bacon risotto along the lines of the Venetian *risi e bisi* (rice and peas).

- Raw peas, blanched broad beans and mangetouts or sugarsnaps – the latter two finely sliced horizontally – add colour and crunch to soft-textured salads based on grains such as quinoa, cracked wheat and brown rice.

Are peas, broad beans, mangetouts and sugarsnaps good for me?

Peas, broad beans, mangetouts and sugarsnaps vary in their nutritional make-up, but collectively are a very good source of vitamin C, which supports the immune system; vitamin K, which is needed for healthy bones; beta-carotene, zeaxanthin and lutein, which are important for the eyes; and certain B vitamins, which are vital for the nervous system. They also contain useful minerals, such as potassium, which helps regulate blood pressure, and soluble fibre, which slows down the rate at which sugar is absorbed into the bloodstream. Being legumes (pulses) as well as a vegetable, they contain more protein than many vegetables and make a great storage food if dried.

The frozen food industry is always keen to improve the marketing profile of its products and peas have become something of a standard-bearer for the argument that frozen vegetables can be healthier than fresh. This argument is based on the observation that peas deteriorate rapidly after picking and that frozen peas retain more of their nutrients than 'fresh' peas that may have been hanging around in the shops for a few days. There is some industry-funded research to support this point of view. Some processors boast that their peas are frozen just two and a half hours after harvesting, whereas fresh peas take much longer to appear in shops. Following this logic to its conclusion, there is no point bothering with fresh peas as they will be nutritionally inferior. Obviously, peas, like many other fresh vegetables, do go downhill after picking, but this is no reason to abandon the fresh article entirely, since fresh peas offer a very different eating experience to frozen. The trick is to look out for fresh peas in really tip-top condition and then eat them straight away.

How are peas, broad beans, mangetouts and sugarsnaps grown?

Britain is the largest producer of fresh garden peas in Europe. Most of the peas we eat come from growers on the east coast of England and Scotland, under contract to frozen food companies.

Peas and broad beans grow in open fields and are usually planted in drills. If they are to be frozen, they are taken to a factory where they are podded, blanched, then rapidly blast-frozen.

In spring and summer, mangetouts and sugarsnaps are widely grown by small-scale market gardens selling through farmers' markets and farm shops. The rest of the year, they are imported, so very little is known about growing methods or the conditions of the workers. For more equitably produced imported peas and mangetouts, look out for those with a Fairtrade label, usually from Kenya.

Are peas, broad beans, sugarsnaps and mangetouts green choices?

Peas, broad beans, sugarsnaps and mangetouts belong to the legume family of plants, which means that they are able to make use of nitrogen in the atmosphere to enrich their protein content and 'fix' nitrogen in the soil. When the roots are left to decay, the nitrogen in the root becomes available to the following crop, acting as a natural fertilizer and reducing the need for synthetic ones made from rapidly depleting fossil fuels. Many farmers use peas as a 'break' crop to introduce nitrogen back into the soil as part of a rotation after four or five years of cereal or root vegetable cultivation.

Unless they are organic, pea growers have at their disposal a number of pesticides, although many increasingly emphasize more natural biological control methods such as pheromone traps to catch insects. Pesticide residues are rarely found in peas.

A minority of the peas and the majority of the mangetouts and sugar-snaps we eat are imported from thousands of miles away. Mangetouts from Guatemala, for instance, travel some 5,000 miles. Air-freighting vegetables raises major environmental issues (see GREEN BEANS AND RUNNER BEANS/Are green and runner beans a green choice?).

Where and when should I buy peas, broad beans, mangetouts and sugarsnaps?

UK-grown peas, broad beans, mangetouts and sugarsnaps are in season from May until September. Air-freighted imports are on sale all year round.

Will peas, broad beans, mangetouts and sugarsnaps break the bank?

Fresh peas never feel like the best deal, simply because they look so inconsequential when shelled, and broad beans can be even more disheartening, but neither is especially expensive and the price will reduce considerably when the British season is at its peak. Rather than using them as a bulk equivalent of the frozen sort, use them in small amounts, either raw or just lightly blanched in salads where their colour and texture will make their presence felt, or make them go further by cooking them lightly with other summer vegetables, such as new potatoes, young carrots and slim courgettes.

Don't throw away empty pea pods. They can be used to make a vibrant soup, especially with a handful of summery green herbs; just make sure to sieve the soup to remove any fibrous bits. Broad bean pods are usually too coarse for this treatment, unless they are the extremely tender spring sort.

PEASE PLEASE

Peas have been an important crop in Britain for centuries, although they were mainly dried and used as a cheap, staple protein. Traditionally they were soaked then cooked with onion to make a versatile, filling, grey-green-coloured pudding, known as pease pudding, pease pottage or pease porridge, essentially a very thick soup that firms up in a mould. This cheap, filling food would be made using water, or ham stock and was commonly served with a bit of ham or bacon, and could be eaten in different ways, as the old nursery rhyme records:

> Pease porridge hot, pease porridge cold,
> Pease porridge in the pot, nine days old;
> Some like it hot, some like it cold,
> Some like it in the pot, nine days old.

In more recent times, mushy peas – dried, soaked marrowfat peas cooked until they collapse – have been considered as an iconic British food, the traditional accompaniment to the fish and chips first brought to the UK by Italian immigrants. With a much wider, fresher range of vegetables to choose from now than ever before, mushy peas have become a nostalgia food most appreciated by older generations, and since the tinned sort commonly contain added synthetic green colouring and sugar, increasingly peas have come to mean the fresh green garden sort, not their grey-green, rehydrated cousins.

In the 1980s, because peas were generally considered as a rather low-rent frozen vegetable, many chefs in Britain latched on to imported mangetouts as a more sophisticated choice and also because there was a supply 365 days a year, but they became something of a cliché. Now, the tables have been turned because mangetouts are widely regarded as both a dated and unimaginative choice, and fresh home-grown peas are seen as one of the most desirable vegetables that you can eat.

Peppers

Peppers are sweet, sunny, quintessentially Mediterranean vegetables. There are those who can find a use for peppers eaten raw, to give crunch to a salad or for dunking in a dip perhaps, but they make a much more compelling vegetable cooked, when their excess water has been driven off, their flesh has become meltingly soft and yielding, and their sweetness has concentrated and caramelized.

Multicoloured packs of peppers are a distraction. All peppers start off green when unripe, then they ripen and become yellow, orange or red, depending on variety and ripeness. Although green peppers have an honourable place in Middle Eastern cuisine where their slight bitterness is used to good effect, red peppers are otherwise preferable for most cooking purposes because at this stage they are at their ripest, sweetest and most flavourful. That familiar red/yellow/green pepper sprinkle we see on pizza toppings is all about supplying colour, not taste. Choose either green or red peppers, depending on the recipe, and don't mix them.

Ubiquitous 'bell' peppers dominate our shelves. Retailers like these because they have an exceptionally long shelf life and consumers have appreciated them because they can languish in the domestic fridge for weeks without going bad, but they may well be the least exciting variety in pepperdom. The thinner-skinned, more elongated Romano or Ramiro peppers that have been introduced to add a bit of interest to the homogenous pepper category are closer to the genuine Mediterranean article and have a little bit more of the complexity you get in chilli peppers, minus the heat, and small green Padrone peppers have a likeably bitter taste.

As a consequence of how they are grown, the bell peppers that hog our shelves have a high water content that interferes with taste, so you have to work harder to get them to show any of that elusive Mediterranean promise. Rather than refrigerating them, leave them sitting on a windowsill or in a bright place at room temperature until they begin to wrinkle and dry out and darken in colour. Check them every day or two to make sure that they aren't going bad. They may not look so ornamental, but the longer you mature them in this way, the better their flavour will be when cooked. Red peppers that have been roasted, skinned and then covered in oil deserve a place in any kitchen box of tricks.

Things to do with peppers

- Pulverize roasted red peppers and tomatoes in a blender along with toasted almonds and a little sherry or red wine vinegar and olive oil to make a Spanish romesco sauce to serve as a dip, or with fish or grilled meat.

- Finger-sized green Padrone peppers are great eaten whole when they are stir-fried in olive oil until they char and begin to wilt, then sprinkled with sea salt. A no-fuss but unusual nibble to serve with drinks.

- Brown chicken or rabbit legs in a shallow sauté or frying pan with onions and garlic, then add canned tomatoes, thin slices of roasted red peppers and a pinch of paprika and simmer, without a lid, until the meat is tender, in the style of French *poulet Basquaise*.

- Fleshy, syrupy roasted peppers and soft goat's cheese make a succulent lunchtime sandwich.

- Anoint roasted red peppers with olive oil and chopped preserved lemons, green herbs and toasted pine kernels.

- A trickle of Middle Eastern pomegranate molasses gives roasted peppers a sour-sweet edge that enlivens grilled or fried fish.

Are peppers good for me?

Peppers are a brilliant source of the antioxidant vitamins C and beta-carotene which may help neutralize the damage done by harmful free radicals that can predispose the body to disease. Red peppers contain higher levels than green or yellow peppers. Red peppers also contain lycopene, a plant pigment that some research suggests may inhibit certain cancers, and two pigments, lutein and zeaxanthin, that some research suggests are active against macular degeneration, the main cause of blindness in the elderly.

Peppers have a bad track record when it comes to pesticide residues. Government tests regularly find peppers with multiple residues. Occasionally, traces of pesticides not approved in Europe have been found. Pesticide residues in peppers regularly trigger Europe-wide Rapid Alerts to warn regulatory authorities, retailers and wholesalers. This is one vegetable where it is well worth considering buying organic. Pesticides are all but outlawed in organic production and in recent years residues have not been found in organic peppers.

How are peppers grown?

In hot, sunny countries, peppers grow happily outdoors. In Britain, they can also flourish outside, if cultivated in a sunny, sheltered spot in areas with a mild climate. But unless you have a garden, allotment, or market garden source – and even then these are likely to have been brought on in a greenhouse before being planted out – any peppers you buy will have been cultivated using hydroponic techniques in a state-of-the-art glasshouse. Cucumbers, aubergines and some salad leaves are also cultivated using the same techniques.

Glasshouse production is about as far away from any notion of 'natural' growing as it is possible to get. Production is not pegged to the seasons but can start at any point in the year as the glasshouse creates an artificial climate-controlled environment that can be heated in winter or cooled in summer. Computerized sensors monitor temperature, humidity, carbon dioxide and light, automatically adjusting levels in response to variations in both external and internal climate.

The essence of hydroponic systems is that plants grow not in earth, but in an alternative growing medium – gravel, coconut fibre, clay pebbles, granular rockwool (like fibreglass), perlite (volcanic glass granules), vermiculite (a mineral), even air – and are fed nutrients in a liquid solution. There are various hydroponic techniques. The nutrient solution can be sucked up into the growing medium using a wick, dripped on to the base of each plant, pumped to the roots, or misted directly on to the roots. The same nutrient solution can be used throughout the plant's growing cycle, but by varying the formula to support different stages of growth – root, leaf, flower – the plants can be encouraged to provide a heavier crop. For more information on the pros and cons of this type of production see TOMATOES/How are tomatoes grown?

Are peppers a green choice?

It's hard to think of any vegetable that is quite so monotonously standardized and so devoid of interesting variations and biodiversity as the bell pepper. This dull, techno-pepper plant can be made to grow resolutely and produce heaps of watery fruits in its glasshouse world, come wind come shine, so it rules the roost. Supermarket cosmetic specifications compound the insult. Thanks to them, our larger-than-life peppers might as well be cloned as they share identikit proportions and gleam like fake plastic vegetables.

The whole pepper category is ripe for innovation. The pity is that there are many more interesting sweet pepper varieties that could be cultivated and which are still widely grown in southern and eastern Europe and the Middle East. Seeds for a more biodiverse, and genuinely varied, range of peppers are available for home-growing. If you have access to peppers from a domestic greenhouse, allotment or garden, then you may get a flavour of them.

Glasshouse cultivation raises a number of environmental issues (see TOMATOES/Are tomatoes a green choice?).

Where and when should I buy peppers?

Imported peppers, usually Dutch or Spanish, are available all year round. English peppers come on to the market from March until October.

AN APOLOGY FOR A PEPPER?

Peppers were an alien vegetable (or more correctly, fruit) until the 1960s and 1970s when they earned the patronage of distinguished cookery writers such as Elizabeth David and Jane Grigson, who testified to how delightful they could be when consumed on their home turf. By the 1980s, our sweet pepper market had been more or less sewn up by the Dutch horticultural industry, which kept us supplied with a never-ending supply of the glasshouse-grown sort. Neither Spanish nor English-grown pepper growers have ever really challenged its supremacy. Britain's meek acceptance of what southern countries might see as an apology for a pepper may have something to do with the fact that our experience of eating the sun-grown, hot-country sort was limited to foreign holidays, so we were less aware of how different, and how much more rewarding such peppers might be.

The sheer dogged reliability of unseasonal hothouse peppers has won them a near invincible place in our vegetable repertoire. At any point in time, while wholesale markets and suppliers will have fluctuating stocks of other vegetables, they will always be able to supply peppers. 'Mediterranean vegetables', showcasing the pepper, have become a menu cliché. Ratatouille, roasted peppers and red pepper soup have become thoroughly embedded in Britain's vegetable lexicon.

Peppers are a commodity glasshouse crop, but this doesn't stop supermarkets charging unjustifiably high prices for them. As a general rule, peppers are cheaper in greengrocers and from market stalls. Don't be put off by peppers that look a little soft and wrinkled, instead snap them up at bargain prices. They will taste better than their smooth, still waterlogged, more expensive equivalent. Don't turn up your nose at discounted peppers that are soft or rotten in parts. Peppers are one vegetable where you can happily cut out the bad bit without any off flavours tainting the rest.

Potatoes

Potatoes are a bit like a dependable old friend. They are always there for you. Whether it's a plate of home-made chips, an oozing gratin or a buttery potato purée, potatoes offer solace and comfort. You can snuggle up with them like a warm quilt. Too often used in a routine way as a ubiquitous, stodgy sidekick to the main act, potatoes have patrician potential and can rise to the special occasion when cooked thoughtfully and creatively.

For cooks, the crucial distinction in potato type is between waxy (firm flesh, good for salads) and floury (more granular, good for roasting and mash), although some varieties (Desiree, Wilja, Romano) fall between these two categories. The mainstream potato industry grades potatoes on a scale from one (waxy) to nine (floury), but most commercial effort goes into developing and marketing a few 'all-purpose' varieties.

The flavour and texture of potatoes come down to a combination of the variety grown and the growing method, but even the best grower can't make duff varieties taste of much. Our shelves are loaded with potatoes that look the part, but disappoint on the flavour and texture front. Under the influence of supermarkets, plant breeders have developed potatoes for yield, processing quality and appearance. They must be free from deep-set 'eyes', all similarly shaped, and have no knobbly bits, which instantly knocks out many of our distinguished traditional varieties. Eating quality has barely entered the brief. Old varieties (see Potatoes with a sense of place), prized for their flavour, their flesh of various colours and their distinctive textures, have lost out to anonymous-tasting, white-fleshed modern varieties, such as Maris Piper, Santé, Estima, Cara, Rocket and Nadine, that produce high yields when given lots of water and chemical fertilizers.

If you want real spuds, not duds, then seek out varieties with character and personality. Among the most readily available, the best-tasting waxy varieties include Charlotte, Nicola, Jersey Royal, Pink Fir Apple, Yukon Gold and La Ratte; the best-tasting floury varieties include Golden Wonder, Marfona, King Edward, Duke of York, Valor, Cosmos and Kerr's Pinks.

Things to do with potatoes

- Roast unpeeled potato wedges in olive oil and generously dust just before serving with smoked paprika and sea salt.

- Vary the classic gratin Dauphinois (thin slices of floury potatoes baked with cream, nutmeg and garlic) by substituting turnip, Jerusalem artichoke, celeriac or parsnip for half the potatoes.

- Greek *skordalia* – smooth potato, garlic and olive oil purée – served warm makes an unusual dip to serve with crudités.

- A couple of finely chopped anchovies turns a basic, creamy gratin into that full-bodied Scandinavian dish, Janssen's temptation.

- For a cheap, but interesting starter, purée potatoes with olive oil and a little poached salt cod to make a French *brandade*. Serve with rustic toast brushed with olive oil.

- Thinly sliced potatoes and onions baked with stock – *pommes* Anna – make a lighter gratin.

- Home-made potato gnocchi beat the ready-made vacuum-packed sort hands down.

- Instead of the usual mayonnaise approach, make a more Germanic potato salad by dressing still-warm waxy potatoes with oil, wine or cider vinegar and lots of smooth mustard, then add fresh dill and chopped gherkins. Serve with crisp lardons of bacon on top, or with ham or smoked meats.

- Grate par-boiled waxy potatoes, season well with sea salt and pepper and shallow fry in thin, flat piles to make crunchy Swiss rosti.

Are potatoes good for me?

Potatoes are best thought of as a starchy carbohydrate food, an alternative to rice or pasta, rather than as a vegetable. Potatoes do contain some vitamin C, which supports the immune system, and this makes them nutritionally preferable to other popular starchy foods like couscous, pasta and white rice. Vitamin C levels are higher in new potatoes (the thin-skinned sort) than in older potatoes (the thicker-skinned sort). They also contain useful amounts of vitamin B6, which is necessary for metabolizing the amino acids in protein and the formation of red blood cells; vitamin B1, which is needed for healing and the smooth running of the nervous system; iron, which helps prevent anaemia; and folate, which helps prevent birth defects.

Like other starchy foods, potatoes do release sugar rather rapidly into the blood and this can encourage a surge in the fat storage hormone, insulin, which encourages the body to lay down fat. Different types of potatoes affect insulin in different ways. New potatoes raise your blood sugar level less than older, maincrop potatoes. Older maincrop potatoes are not great for people who want to lose weight, despite all those diet sheets that seek to persuade us that a baked potato is the slimmer's friend. That said, if you eat potatoes along with foods that contain protein and fat, like meat, fish and eggs, this significantly slows down the release of sugar into the bloodstream.

In the past there have been concerns about residues of pesticides in potatoes, mainly in new potatoes. In recent years, the situation seems to have improved with around two-thirds of potatoes sampled in government tests coming up residue-free. More progressive conventional growers use ethylene gas to protect the potatoes in cold storage, rather than spraying them with post-harvest chemicals. You can reduce your exposure to chemical residues by choosing organic potatoes. One pesticide can be used in organic potato growing, but only in extremely restricted circumstances.

How are potatoes grown?

Potatoes are planted outdoors in rows, and the soil is mounded up around the emerging leaves to encourage the tubers to grow. Organic growers approach the challenge of growing potatoes without pesticides by choosing varieties that are less susceptible to disease, such as Valor, Nicola, Cosmos, Desiree, Charlotte, Raja and Saxon, and, increasingly, by growing the new, blight-resistant organic varieties that are being developed. Instead of using chemical fertilizers, they grow potatoes in long rotations, interspersing them with other crops. Organic potatoes are often planted after a crop such as red clover, that naturally fertilizes the soil, and the soil is then dressed with manure. Jersey Royals, though not organic, are treated with a natural seaweed fertilizer called 'vraic'.

Most older potato varieties are very prone to blight (see Are potatoes a green choice?), so although they can be grown organically on a back-garden scale, they are susceptible to crop failure when cultivated on a more commercial scale.

Are potatoes a green choice?

An underlying problem with potatoes is their narrow genetic base. There are some 150 different species of potatoes in the Andes where the potato family originates, but all the potatoes grown outside that region come from one sub-species. This lack of biodiversity, or genetic similarity, leaves the world's crop more susceptible to disease, in particular, blight, the same devastating fungus that caused the Irish potato famine of the 1840s and which destroys 20 per cent of the world's annual potato harvest.

One solution advanced for blight is genetic modification, but this is extremely controversial. The leading International Potato Centre in Lima, Peru, has imposed a moratorium on planting GM potatoes in South America because of fears that genes introduced into GM potatoes might escape into wild potatoes. Meanwhile, plant breeders in Hungary and Scotland have already come up with a non-GM solution, successfully breeding blight-resistant new varieties, such as the organic Sarpo Mira and Axona, using conventional breeding techniques. These new organic varieties have shown unprecedented blight resistance and also virus resistance, while other supposedly blight-resistant varieties, such as the ubiquitous Sante and Cara, have been wiped out within weeks. Biotech evangelists love to make out that only their industry has the solutions to intractable farming problems like blight, but here's a glowing example of how it is possible to breed a crop with a desirable trait without using highly unpredictable GM techniques, such as the introduction of antibiotic resistance marker genes, that open the door to major environmental and health risks.

POTATOES WITH A SENSE OF PLACE

For as long as anyone can remember, the potato has been a stalwart ingredient in the British and Irish diet. Back in the Second World War, it was considered such an essential, healthy food that potato growing became a key plank in the British strategy for survival. It figured prominently in the Ministry of Food's 'Dig For Victory' campaign, which enlisted a cartoon superhero, Potato Pete, to encourage the nation to grow and eat more potatoes, successfully doubling the acreage planted. Nowadays, only the Portuguese and the Irish eat more than we do.

Potatoes grow quite well in our climate and Britain has always been a leading centre of expertise in potato cultivation and breeding. Some rare, traditional potato varieties are still in small-scale commercial production, popular with allotment holders and gardeners and very much in vogue with chefs. Taste them blind, and the taste contrast with the standard spuds we eat is striking. They look discernibly different too. Some have deep-set eyes, others thick, netted skin – like the scruffy East End cousins of cosmetic modern varieties. Their skin tones employ a palette of colour from mercury black through rosy pink to midnight blue. Their flesh can be alabaster white, butter yellow, imperial purple, indigo or claret. Their shapes go from elongated and knobbly via oval to round and smooth. Their names have all the interest of a Grand National line-up: Highland Burgundy, Kepplestone Kidney, British Queen, Edzell Blue, Red Duke of York, Purple-Eyed Seeding, Epicure, Shetland Black, La Ratte, Peachbloom, Pink Fir Apple, Red King Edward, Witchill and Mr Little's Yetholm Gypsy, to mention a few. These are potatoes steeped in history and traditions, potatoes with a sense of place.

Where and when should I buy potatoes?

The potato year begins with the arrival of 'new' or 'early' potatoes. They are lifted young when they still have thin skins that can be rubbed off with the fingers and their consistency is slightly waxy. In February, imports from Egypt, Israel and Cyprus start arriving in shops, followed by Jersey Royals in March then Cornish and Ayrshire varieties in May and June. If you want to reduce unnecessary food miles, then stick with

UK new potatoes: they are worth waiting for. Next come the 'second earlies' grown in colder, more frost-prone areas of the UK, followed by early 'maincrop' potatoes in August, then the true maincrop potatoes that come on stream in September and October. These maincrop potatoes have a higher dry matter content than earlies and thicker skins. They can be sold directly from the field or kept in cold storage throughout the winter to preserve them until the next year's home-grown new potatoes become available.

Supermarkets are now stocking a few more interesting 'heritage' varieties, but for a better range check out specialist potato suppliers and look out for more unusual, characterful varieties at farmers' markets.

Will potatoes break the bank?

In early spring, before the new season's Irish- or UK-grown potatoes are available, imported new potatoes go on sale. These can make the maincrop potatoes from the season before look rather old, but they will still be fine for most purposes – they just need to be peeled – and will cost a fraction of the price commanded by the new, more attractive-looking imports.

You pay an awful lot for the privilege of having your potatoes pre-prepared. Products such as ready-made gratin, baked potatoes and fried wedges come with a huge mark-up. Save a small fortune by making your own at home. And, of course, they will taste better.

Don't throw away older potatoes when they start sprouting. This happens naturally when maincrop potatoes are stored over winter. Just knock off the sprout and use the rest of the potato. Don't use potatoes with large green areas, as these have been exposed to light and could be slightly poisonous. It's fine, however, to eat potatoes with only a little patch of green on them. Simply cut it off.

Spinach and Swiss chard

For a concentrated blast of greenness in your diet, spinach is hard to beat, a supremely versatile leaf that earns its keep both cooked and raw. There are two sorts of spinach. The most common type in shops is true spinach, sometimes called summer spinach, which is fine, silky, tender and smooth when cooked. It has an affinity with cream, eggs and both mild and pungent cheese. A coarser type of spinach, known as perpetual or winter spinach, is more often grown by gardeners, or supplied by small-scale growers in vegetable boxes or at markets. It is slightly less green, with a less pronounced spinach flavour and is more fibrous. If you want elegant spinach, then perpetual spinach isn't it. For cooking purposes, it is better treated like spring greens, lightly blanched and then dressed with oil or butter, or stir-fried.

Swiss chard is excellent when cooked and hugely under-appreciated. You can think of it as two vegetables packed into one. Its pearly central stalks offer a unique taste that bears some comparison with artichoke, palm heart and salsify. The green leaves, which initially seem quite coarse, will soften down beautifully when sautéed gently. Rainbow chard has red and yellow central stalks, but it tastes the same as the white-stalked sort.

Things to do with spinach and Swiss chard

- Pearly central stalks of Swiss chard make a fantastic creamy, cheesy bake.

- The classic eggs Florentine tops a half muffin with buttery cooked spinach, a poached egg and hollandaise sauce.

- Chopped or blitzed cooked spinach adds thickness, texture and colour to curries and Middle Eastern stews.

- Make a salad by throwing garlic-rubbed fried bread croutons on baby spinach leaves dressed with olive oil, lemon juice, sea salt, and lots of black pepper and Parmesan.

- Spinach goes brilliantly with ricotta cheese. Use as a filling for cannelloni topped with béchamel sauce, or to make Italian green gnocchi, or as a filling for a vegetable tart.

- Chopped Swiss chard, both stems and leaves, is great stir-fried with chilli and sliced onions, then served on a potato rosti with a soft-fried egg.

- Green Swiss chard leaves make an interesting green ingredient for a meat stuffing.

- Add shredded leaves of Swiss chard to an autumnal minestrone.

Are spinach and Swiss chard good for me?

Spinach and Swiss chard are rich in the antioxidant vitamins C and E, which help protect against free radicals that can predispose the body to disease; vitamin K, which promotes bone health; folate, which helps prevent birth defects; and iron, which prevents anaemia. They are also a good source of soluble fibre, which slows down the rate at which sugar is released into the bloodstream. The green colour of the leaves hides the fact that chard and spinach are also a good source of carotenes, such as lutein and zeaxathin, which may perform many beneficial functions, including protecting the eyes against age-related degeneration and lowering the risk of heart disease, certain cancers and stroke.

Spinach is a vegetable that in the past has been shown to contain pesticide residues above safe limits. The most recent tests suggest that the residues in spinach do not pose a threat to health, but small amounts of residues have been detected in over half the samples tested. As pesticide residues are a toxin, it makes sense to minimize exposure to them, and buying organic spinach would be a good way to do that. As Swiss chard is considered to be something of a minority vegetable, it has not been monitored for pesticides in any systematic way. However, it is popular with organic growers because it is less susceptible to disease than spinach, and therefore more easily cultivated without pesticides. Even conventionally grown Swiss chard is likely to have lower residues than spinach.

How are spinach and Swiss chard grown?

Spinach and Swiss chard are grown in open fields or in polytunnels. Spinach is grown in the UK and Ireland throughout the year but considerable amounts of spinach are imported, usually from Spain, Portugal and Italy. Swiss chard, too, is cultivated in the UK and Ireland all year. Imported Swiss chard, generally organic, comes from Italy.

Where and when should I buy spinach and Swiss chard?

In the coldest months, hardier perpetual spinach and Swiss chard may be easier to find than the more tender true spinach, which is susceptible to frost. Swiss chard is less widely available, but it is a staple of the organic vegetable box and prominent on farmers' market stalls.

Will spinach and Swiss chard break the bank?

By washing your own spinach, rather than buying it pre-washed, you can save a considerable amount of money. Your spinach will also be more robust because it hasn't been put through a pack house bath of water – often chlorinated.

Swiss chard is one of those vegetables that are rarely found in super-markets and where stocked is much more expensive than at a farmers' market stall. Gardeners insist that it is easy to grow, so if you do have any green space, try growing it from seed. It should keep going for months and save you lots of money.

Tomatoes

The defining quality of a really good tomato is a balance of sweetness and acidity. To achieve this, a number of different factors come into play. The variety grown is critical. The justly famous tomatoes of southern Europe, such as the Sicilian Pachino, San Marzano and Cuor di Bue tomatoes or the French Marmande have taste built into their DNA, whereas more recently developed varieties, such as the revealingly named Moneymaker, were bred to meet different goals entirely: regular appearance and size, split-resistant skins, long shelf life. Sun and heat are also essential to grow tomatoes with really memorable flavours.

Some tomato buffs argue convincingly that home-grown tomatoes, which have reached maturity slowly, growing outdoors (or only lightly protected from the elements) in a sunny, sheltered spot on fertile soil, can give imports from sunnier countries a run for their money. Very few tomatoes are now grown that way in Britain so nearly all the home-grown tomatoes you buy will have been grown in glasshouses which are notorious for producing high-tech tomatoes that look the part but don't taste it. The Germans have a word for them, '*wasserbomben*' – literally water bombs – an ironic description of those pinkish, mushy fruits that we have all tasted. That said, the eating quality of glasshouse-grown tomatoes has improved immeasurably as growers have selected more intrinsically flavoursome varieties, allowed them to ripen longer and picked them when they are more mature.

When choosing fresh tomatoes, as a general rule, and whether home-grown or imported, small is beautiful. Large plum and beefsteak tomatoes often disappoint – although they can be quite good for cooking as opposed to eating raw – but small plum and cherry tomatoes usually have the best flavour. Two of the most consistent cherry varieties from a taste perspective are Gardener's Delight and Sungold. Try to make a note of the name of the variety to build up your own mental checklist of which varieties pack a flavour and which are duffers.

Don't get sidetracked by tricksy appearance. Tomatoes come in all shapes, sizes and hues: beefsteak, cherry, yellow, black, gold, plum, mini-plums, cocktail, pumpkin and heart-shaped. The only way you can tell if they taste any good is by trying them. Don't automatically assume that pricier tomatoes with a 'vine-ripened' label will taste better. They might, but equally they might be from an inherently tasteless variety, or ripened in an artificially heated glasshouse, so cheaper, less upmarket tomatoes might outperform them on flavour and texture.

Whatever variety or size of tomatoes you have, and however unpromising they may look – wishy-washy pink or even slightly green – you can usually improve their taste, if not texture, by ripening them up at home. Don't keep them in the fridge because this hampers their natural ripening. Instead, put them in a basket, or on an old brown paper bag, laid out in a single layer, then leave them in a warm, bright place to soften and redden. If you want to use them for a salad, leave them until they colour up nicely. But if you intend to cook with them, leave them until they are blushing red and slightly wrinkled, as this will only improve their flavour and give your recipe a deeper, richer tomato taste.

For many recipes, such as tomato sauce, tinned tomatoes, creamed tomato or passata from a pack or bottle, will often give superior results to fresh. This is because riper tomatoes will have been used to start with, and the tomato flavour has been concentrated by the heat of processing.

Things to do with tomatoes

- A Niçoise *pan bagnat* makes a brilliant summertime packed lunch. Several hours before you intend to eat it, open up and hollow out the centre of a crusty, but pliant white roll or section of baguette, fill well with sliced tomatoes, a little finely chopped sweet red onion, some tinned tuna and/or anchovies, basil leaves and/or chopped olives. Season it well with sea salt, pepper and olive oil. Wrap in foil and squash under a heavy weight, so that the centre will be moistly pulpy and full-flavoured when you bite into it.

- Halve tomatoes horizontally, sprinkle with a mixture of breadcrumbs, chopped herbs (rosemary, thyme, oregano), sea salt, black pepper and olive oil, and bake until they are soft below and crunchy on top.

- Over-ripe tomatoes make a good salsa to serve with grilled meats. Just combine chopped tomatoes, a little finely chopped sweet red onion, a tiny amount of chopped garlic, sea salt, black pepper and olive oil. Vary your salsa by playing around with additions such as chopped capers, black olives, preserved lemon and any fresh herbs you have to hand.

- A liquidized Spanish gazpacho, made with squidgy-ripe red tomatoes, sweet onions, cucumber, red pepper, olive oil, sherry or red wine vinegar and water is ideal for a refreshing and healthy cold summertime soup, served with croutons fried in olive oil.

- Fry tomatoes, halved horizontally, in unsalted butter until browned on the cut side, stab the uncut side with a knife tip in a couple of places, then fry on this side. When the tomatoes are browned and soft, season with sea salt and black pepper, then pour in enough double cream or crème fraîche to deglaze the pan. Let the cream bubble up and turn golden, then serve.

- Put horizontally cut tomato halves in a bowl with enough olive oil to coat and shake around. Meanly sprinkle the cut sides with golden caster sugar and bake at your lowest oven setting for several hours until they have shrunk in size and darkened. Use these oven-dried tomatoes to make roasted tomato soup and sauce, or cover in extra virgin olive oil and keep in the fridge to use on top of bruschetta, or as a salad with crumbled ricotta or mozzarella.

Are tomatoes good for me?

Tomatoes are a good source of vitamins A, C and E and lycopene, which help combat cell damage that causes disease. Lycopene in particular, the red pigment in tomatoes, is thought to be protective against heart disease and several cancers. The riper your tomato, the more lycopene it will contain. Some vitamins are depleted when you cook tomatoes, especially vitamin C. But don't be sniffy about using tinned tomatoes, tomato paste or passata as there is also some research that suggests that certain other nutrients, such as lycopene, may become more concentrated in these products and better absorbed when they have been cooked with oil, as in a typical home-made tomato sauce.

How are tomatoes grown?

You will still find tomatoes grown in soil outdoors in gardens and allotments in the UK, but commercial-scale tomato production in soil here is a thing of the past. Nowadays the tomatoes we eat are produced under polytunnels in warmer countries, or, more often in the UK, in glasshouses. These range in size from scaled-up versions of the traditional gardener's greenhouse to massive glass and steel constructions that are the size of a large village.

The type of cultivation within these glasshouses varies. Some growers still plant the tomato vines in soil, but, increasingly, more growers use hydroponic systems where the tomato plants are planted in soil substitutes such as coconut fibre, rockwool (a bit like fibreglass), clay pebbles and perlite (volcanic glass granules), and fed a nutrient solution. This can produce many more tomatoes than growing in soil because water, nutrient and air is directed to the rootball, freeing the plant to use its energy for upper leaf, fruit, or flower development.

Growing tomatoes (and other crops such as peppers, cucumbers, aubergines and lettuce) has been revolutionized by these state-of-the-art technological growing methods, making it possible to produce warm-weather crops even in the depths of winter in sunless northern climes.

Are tomatoes a green choice?

Modern tomato production methods are mired in controversy. Back in 1996, Sainsbury's introduced a tomato paste made from the US-grown genetically modified Flavr Savr tomato. It went down like a lead balloon with consumers and was withdrawn from sale in 1999. Currently, no GM tomatoes are grown or sold in the UK.

More recently, large commercial polytunnels, widely used in warmer countries, have been criticized for generating large amounts of unrecyclable polythene waste and discharging nitrates from fertilizers into local water courses.

Soil substitutes are a debate in themselves. In colder northern countries like ours, spent soil substitutes can create another pollution source. On the other hand, when tomatoes were cultivated on a large scale in soil, the soil had to be sterilized regularly with chemicals to prevent disease and pest build-up and treated regularly with herbicides against weeds. Soil substitutes make this unnecessary.

Advocates of glasshouses also argue that the covered, controlled environment of the glasshouse makes for greener growing methods. In many UK, Irish and Dutch glasshouses, bumble bees are used as pollinators and beneficial predator insects are used to keep pests at bay. Commercial UK tomato growers say that these techniques are making pesticides more or less redundant and cutting discharges of nitrate and phosphate fertilizers into the environment.

The biggest environmental debate around the indoor growing of tomatoes and other crops such as peppers and cucumbers concerns the heating of glasshouses. Without such heating, British glasshouses would produce tomatoes only from May until October. Heating extends that season from February until November. This helps the UK and Ireland compete with imports, which account for about three-quarters of all the tomatoes we eat.

But conventional heated glasshouses guzzle up fossil fuels, contributing to carbon emissions and the global 'greenhouse effect', so UK tomato growers are looking at combined heat and power projects, such as capturing heat from power stations, to cut that heavy carbon footprint.

TOMATOES

Is it better to cut down on food miles and buy UK-grown or northern European tomatoes grown under glass with heat, or choose imported tomatoes that have travelled further but have been grown only with the heat and light of the sun? Brainy people spend hours attempting to calculate which option is best for the environment and no uncontroversial conclusion has yet emerged. In the absence of a definitive answer, there is an alternative common-sense solution. Gorge yourself on British tomatoes during the traditional British season when they taste best, then focus mainly on tinned tomatoes, passata or paste at other times.

GREEN TOMATO CHUTNEY

It is no coincidence that recipes for green tomato chutney feature in traditional British cookbooks. Tomatoes are not the easiest crop to grow in the UK or Ireland, the main problem being not enough sun to sweeten and ripen them, which is why we don't have the wealth of tomato recipes you find in Spain, Italy and France or throughout the Middle East.

Britain and Ireland had no tradition of eating tomatoes until the nineteenth century when the availability of sheet glass made commercial indoor growing feasible and the first glasshouses opened in Kent and Essex. Although tomatoes have been grown in Britain since the sixteenth century they were originally cultivated for their ornamental leaves and considered poisonous. Not without reason since, as members of the nightshade family of plants (along with aubergines, potatoes and peppers), their leaves are indeed poisonous. Some advocates of a macrobiotic diet (which originated in Japan and is based on eating whole grains, fruit and vegetables) still recommend avoiding foods from this family, as they believe that the alkaloid toxins in them are bad for health.

Where and when should I buy tomatoes?

If we are aware of the seasons at all, we tend to think of tomatoes as a summer food, but home-grown tomatoes, if grown using the most natural methods, either outdoors or in an unheated glasshouse, are at their best in the early autumn. The peak is September, but you can still get slowly ripened tomatoes as late as October.

Another approach is to stock up on flavoursome autumnal tomatoes in September and preserve them. Bigger tomatoes can be halved, slowly dried in a very low oven, then packed in small bags and kept in the fridge for a month or longer, depending on how thoroughly dried they are, and they will be much more delicious than those you buy. Overripe tomatoes can be turned into concentrated tomato sauce and stored in the freezer. In late September and early October, lay out mature, end-of-season UK- and Ireland-grown tomatoes in a cold room and they will still eat well at Christmas.

Will tomatoes break the bank?

Unless you want to buy the most standard type of hydroponic, glasshouse-grown tomato, supermarket tomatoes can be scarily expensive. Rest assured that you will have to pay through the nose for any better-than-average tomato. Small tresses of 'premium' tomatoes on the vine, or 'flavour-grown' ones command eye-wateringly high prices but because they are sold in small amounts, and customers rarely check the kilo price, we don't always notice. Almost invariably these boutique ranges of tomato are swathed in packaging, usually not recyclable, and this helps to obscure the fact that you are getting very little for your money. If you manage to find some delicious gems in among the upmarket tomato offerings, then look on them as an expensive treat, but don't assume that they are worth the price tag and keep monitoring what you are getting to check that they are worth it. Canny shopping at market stalls and in greengrocers is a good idea. They often sell perfectly good but ordinary tomatoes by the punnet or bag, for much less than supermarkets.

Meat

2

Chicken and other poultry

(turkey, ducks, geese, poussin, quails, pheasant)

There's something magnificent about a whole roast bird. It makes a natural centrepiece for a meal and brings to the table a mood of celebration and ceremony. From a weighty Christmas turkey to a relatively slight weekend roast chicken, there aren't many meat-eaters who are oblivious to the charms of that winnable combination of crisp, golden skin anointing succulent, tender white meat. As for the darker-fleshed duck and goose, they most definitely have VIP status. A day when you eat duck or goose isn't any old day – it's special.

Mostly though, we eat poultry in bits and bobs, breasts mainly, or already jointed. Here the emphasis tends to be on ease of use and speed of cooking, so we ask fewer questions about its provenance. But whether your poultry comes as a whole bird or jointed, if it is to taste really good, the method of rearing is all-important. Unsurprisingly, a chicken that has been outside, running around pecking away at grassy pasture for months won't taste the same as one that has been kept in a barn for weeks and fed on feed pellets full of soya. No prizes for guessing which one tastes best.

The standard factory-farmed turkey is a flavour-challenged bird with meat that resembles wet felt. It is a world apart from free-range and organic birds from tasty breeds such as the bronze and black-legged turkeys that are raised for the Christmas market. The minority of turkeys that have been hung for a couple of days after slaughter have a more pronounced, developed flavour than those that haven't. Dry-plucking, rather than wet-plucking in a machine that uses warm water, helps the skin go crispy and improves the overall eating quality. Only some small, free-range and organic producers go to the bother of hanging or dry-plucking their birds.

Quails and poussins (immature chickens) have benefited from a somewhat superior image to standard chicken because they are often presented on restaurant menus as a gourmet option. But as these small birds are too young to have developed much flavour and are almost always intensively reared, the anticipation is better than the reality.

Ducks and geese both have considerably more fat than white poultry, and their fat is famously tasty. Their flesh is a halfway house between white and red meat. Like chicken and turkey, ducks are commonly factory-farmed these days, which means that they often have spindly bones and a rather neutral flavour, but a free-range or organic duck from a good breed – Aylesbury, Gressingham or Muscovy – can be flavour-packed. Goose has rich, dark meat and produces lots of glorious white fat that can be used to make the ultimate roast potatoes.

Semi-wild pheasants have a slightly gamier flavour than chicken. Recipes involving whole pheasant are usually an unhappy compromise because legs and breasts need different cooking times and treatments. Pheasant breast is potentially very dry, so short, swift cooking is the order of the day. Leg, on the other hand, is potentially tough and needs long, slow cooking.

Things to do with poultry

- Make leftover cooked turkey or chicken exciting with a fiery, dark Mexican *mole* (sauce) made from sesame seeds or nuts, dried chillies and other warm spices, tomatoes and dark chocolate, cooked together for a long time, then blended. Serve with re-fried beans, tortillas and guacamole.

- Frizzle sage leaves in olive oil until crisp, set aside, then sear chicken or duck livers for a couple of minutes in the hot oil until they are only just browned and still pink. Season well with sea salt and pepper, deglaze the pan with wine or sherry vinegar, and add the sage leaves. Serve with potatoes roasted in duck or goose fat and a salad of punchy green leaves such as watercress or rocket, dressed with a robust vinaigrette.

- Sauté chicken thighs and/or legs in a skillet with olive oil and chopped rosemary. When almost cooked, add Dijon mustard and lemon juice. Finish off with a spoonful of crème fraîche and chopped chives.

- Roast a whole chicken with tarragon butter massaged under its skin, then deglaze the roasting pan with a little water or stock, add double cream and bubble up with a little chopped fresh tarragon to make a sauce.

- Chefs' recipes for stock usually call for uncooked poultry bones or joints, which are likely to prove expensive and impractical for most people. But you can make a perfectly good household stock with the stripped carcass of a cooked chicken, turkey, duck, goose or pheasant. Just cover the carcass with water, add chopped vegetables (gently aromatic carrot, onion, celery and leek are good), some black peppercorns and any fresh herbs you have to hand. Simmer gently, without a lid, for an hour or two until the liquid is reduced by half and smells savoury. This broth makes a good base for soups and risottos. Add salt to the final dish, not the stock.

- Spread duck legs with a generous layer of marmalade, season with sea salt and pepper, and roast until they are cooked through and look sticky and barbecued.

- Gently stew duck legs with finely chopped onion, celery, carrot, white wine and bay leaves until the meat is falling off the bone. Fish out the legs, pick the meat off the bones and discard them. Return the tender strands of meat to the gravy (reduced if necessary) and use to sauce pasta; pappardelle and tagliatelle work particularly well.

Is poultry good for me?

Poultry is a very good source of protein. Protein is essential for the regeneration of the body, and since it is filling and takes a long time to digest, it keeps you going for hours at a time, so you are less likely to snack on unhealthy things.

Poultry contains monounsaturated fat, which may be protective against heart disease and stroke. It also contains saturated fat, mainly in the skin – lots of it, in the case of duck and goose. However, there is an absence of evidence to support the nutritional mantra that fat is bad for health or causes heart disease, or even to back the assumption that the fat you find in natural foods is intrinsically fattening. Increasingly, the health benefits of eating saturated fat are being acknowledged.

Poultry also contains cholesterol, but this is not a worry. Cholesterol is a vital component of every cell membrane. Without cholesterol, the body cannot make certain hormones – cortisol, oestrogen and testosterone. If cholesterol is too low, the body may not be able to use the sun to make sufficient amounts of vitamin D.

Poultry is a good source of vitamin B3, which is needed for the effective functioning of the digestive and nervous systems, and vitamin B6, which is necessary for metabolizing amino acids and the formation of red blood cells. Duck and goose also have useful amounts of vitamin B12, which helps maintain a healthy nervous system and is essential for brain health. Eating poultry is a good way to get selenium. This mineral may be protective against cancer and many people may not get enough of it because there is very little in British and Irish soils.

Poultry meat presents a high food-poisoning risk. Tests have shown that around three-quarters of British-reared chickens harbour the campylobacter bug, which can cause diarrhoea, stomach cramps, even death and is the source of thousands of cases of food poisoning a year. Poultry meat is also frequently contaminated with other disease-causing bugs such as E.coli and salmonella which can, in some circumstances, prove fatal. This high burden of disease-causing bacteria is a reflection of the overcrowded and insanitary conditions on factory farms, which incubate diseases, and the high-throughput abbatoirs that spread them. It is important to cook poultry thoroughly to kill off food poisoning bacteria that may be present and to make sure that blood or fluids from raw poultry never come into contact with other foods during storage or contaminate work surfaces, cloths and so on.

On a global scale, large, intensive poultry operations have been pinpointed as epicentres for the emergence of H5N1, a new and more virulent form of bird flu. Factory farms keep large numbers of animals close together, which encourages the mixing and adaptation of viruses and enables their rapid transmission. Worldwide, intensive poultry production has expanded and this growth has been mirrored by an increase in outbreaks of H5N1. To date, this bird flu has only posed a risk to people who work with poultry and their families. Eating poultry meat appears to present no risk of bird flu. But the growth in poultry-related disease is a reminder of how intensive poultry operations are vectors of disease. Today's globalized intensive poultry trade is a vertically integrated industry, where the same companies produce breeding stock, operate feed mills, own transport and slaughter facilities and are represented or send their products, breeding stock, wastes and even diseases, across national boundaries. This is another good reason for choosing poultry that has been produced in a smaller-scale, healthier, more wholesome way, and getting it as directly as possible from its source.

Over the last decade, cheap chicken breasts imported from Europe have been injected with a mixture of water and protein, from either cows or pigs, to bulk up their weight and make them more profitable. This is legal, as long as it is declared on the label. Many processed chicken and turkey products that are made in the UK and Ireland contain added water, although this is apparent only if you read the small print on the ingredients listing. But repeated government spot checks have found that water- and protein-injected chicken is often sold to the catering trade unlabelled, destined to end up in everything from snack bar sandwiches to pub meals. This adulteration of chicken does not appear to pose a risk to health, although it does offend faith groups for whom either pig or cattle products are prohibited, along with those who feel, not unreasonably, that chicken should be 100 per cent chicken. This scam is a further reason to avoid bargain-basement chicken.

How is poultry farmed?

Most of the chickens, turkeys, ducks, poussins and quails we eat are reared in Britain and Ireland. The vast majority are kept on large-scale factory 'farms' in utterly squalid conditions. Some chicken is also imported from Thailand and Brazil, where the birds are reared in the same sort of system. In essence, the birds are put inside a shed and fed compound feed until they reach their desired end weight. In the case of chickens, as many as 40,000 birds can be kept in one shed. These sheds are generally bare, except for water and feeding points, and have no natural air or light. A low, artificial light is left on to encourage the birds to keep eating so they fatten up faster. There is litter on the floor to absorb their droppings but this isn't changed until the birds are taken out for slaughter, so it can become caked with droppings, ammonia from urine and uneaten feed.

When the birds are young, they have space to move around, but as they grow bigger they become closely packed and have less and less space. In the case of chickens, tens of thousands of birds can be housed in each shed so that by the time they are ready for slaughter, the birds look like one continuous moving carpet because there are hardly any gaps between them. Turkeys and ducks are given more space, but are still extremely tightly packed.

In these overcrowded conditions, the birds cannot exercise or express their natural behaviours, so they are put under great stress. Flocks are so big that the birds can't establish a pecking order and express their natural instincts. It can get very hot inside the sheds, and the air can become highly polluted with ammonia and dust. This is why intensively reared poultry often suffer from respiratory illnesses and eye problems. Standing all day in soiled, ammoniacal litter frequently causes them to develop painful hock burns on their legs and feet. These are often visible on the carcasses of chickens at point of sale.

As the birds grow much faster than they would naturally, this puts pressure on their legs and feet, so painful, often crippling bone disorders are fairly common. This is exacerbated because modern poultry strains have been bred to have heavy breasts and their legs struggle to support the weight. Fast growth rates also put a strain on their hearts and lungs. Millions of chickens die each year from heart failure.

Turkeys suffer from foot sores and painful joint problems, and because the male turkeys are too heavy to mate naturally, the females have to be artificially inseminated. Low lighting in enclosed sheds is used to make turkeys less active and prevent them from becoming aggressive. It is common for turkeys to have had part of their beaks cut off, without anaesthetic.

There are certain higher welfare brands of supermarket chicken and turkey where the birds are still kept entirely indoors but have more space, some natural light and are provided with straw bales to encourage natural behaviour like foraging and perching. Smaller producers often keep turkeys in more spacious, partially open barns with natural lighting and air. These brands are a marginal improvement on the most intensive systems.

When it comes to slaughter, animal welfare groups have accumulated a body of evidence that suggests that birds often suffer rough handling and injury on their way to and at the abbatoir, many of which are typically processing thousands of birds at a time. Often, the slaughter process is inhumanely done. Problems include dislocated and fractured bones while the birds are being held in shackles and ineffectual stunning, which means that the birds may still be alive when their throats are cut, or when they are plunged into the hot-water bath that removes their feathers.

Unless you feel happy about the idea of confining birds indoors for the entirety of their life, buy free-range, or better still organic, poultry. In free-range systems, the birds must be given continuous access to a grassy outdoor area during the daytime. In theory, this allows them to do all the things birds like to do such as pecking, scratching, foraging and exercising. Because they grow more slowly and have opportunities for exercise, free-range birds have better leg and heart health and a generally higher quality of life. They take longer to reach their end weight than intensively reared indoor birds. A standard free-range chicken will take about eight weeks, two weeks longer than the typical indoor bird. In the most basic free-range systems, however, there may be so many birds in the flock that, in practice, not all of them can get access to outdoors through the available popholes, so they live mainly indoors, with the chance of spending some time outdoors.

Organic birds are always free-range and are kept in flocks with fewer birds than the standard free-range system so that they can go outdoors easily. The smaller flock size means that the birds are happier and not stressed. Organic farmers also tend to use more traditional, slower-growing breeds so they take longer to reach their end weight, and the birds must also be given organically grown feed. In the best free-range and organic systems, birds live mainly outdoors in small flocks and have houses to retreat to at night. Other than eating grass, they are fed on home-grown cereals, not imported soya.

Organic birds take longer to reach their slaughter weight. Organic chickens will take around twelve weeks – about twice that of a factory-farmed bird. An organic turkey will live around five months, while its factory-farmed counterpart will live around nine weeks.

Geese seem to have resisted intensive farming and are always free-range. Pheasants are often thought of as wild birds, but most commonly they are reared intensively indoors when they are young birds and fed on pelleted rations, then released into the wild. Some are shot quite soon after release, while others may live for months or years in the wild.

A METEORIC RISE

Chicken has gone from being a food that we hardly ever ate to one that we eat all the time. Back in 1950, most British people ate less than a kilo a year. Now, we eat twenty-five times that amount. Chicken reigns supreme – excuse the pun – as the most popular meat.

The meteoric rise in chicken began in the 1950s when a new kind of bird, designed exclusively for meat production, was developed in the US. Known as a 'broiler', it was so named because its meat was tender enough to be grilled (broiled). Before then, all the chicken meat we ate came from breeds of birds that were dual-purpose; that is, they were kept for both eggs and meat. This meant that they were much older at slaughter and their meat was much tougher, especially the leg meat, because the birds, which were free-range, had been running around for long periods of time. As a result, they took much longer to cook and were more likely to end up in the soup pan than the roasting pan.

Before the arrival of the American broiler, the UK and Ireland had very little in the way of commercial chicken production. The broiler transformed all that. It arrived just as the rationing of poultry feed was coming to an end, and at a time when many farm outbuildings had electricity for the first time. It became possible to rear large numbers of birds, solely for their meat, entirely indoors. The animal breeders got to work, re-shaping the chicken, genetically 'improving' it to have big plump breasts. No matter that the bird's legs couldn't keep up with the increased weight, a profitable industry has grown up churning out unprecedented volumes of lean, white chicken breast meat.

The intensive broiler chicken industry, which is as fast-growing as its wretched birds, got another boost in the 1970s and 1980s as the nutritional orthodoxy became fat avoidance – a gospel that is now being widely challenged. In this misguided context, chicken became seen as a healthier meat than beef, lamb or pork, simply because it was lower in fat. In the 1990s chicken benefited again from the crisis in public confidence in red meat that emerged in the wake of the discovery of BSE (mad cow disease). Not only seen as leaner than other meats, it now became cleaner too, a warped perception, considering how the vast majority of chickens are produced for our tables.

These days, despite repeated media exposés of the cruelty and squalor on which the mass production of chicken is predicated, factory-farmed chicken breast is a ubiquitous product, on menus, in homes, at the sandwich bar and in the canteen. We only got into the habit of eating this miserable meat in the last half century. We need to get out of it in the next.

Is poultry a green choice?

The fast growth of intensively reared poultry is predicated on feeding
birds on large amounts of protein, mainly in the form of soya, which is a
disaster for the environment. Soya cultivation, along with cattle ranching,
is now one of the two main causes of deforestation in South America,
where vast expanses of rainforest and grassland are being cut down to
make way for huge soya plantations. These plantations are managed in a
very intensive way using high levels of synthetic fertilisers and pesticides.
The destruction of these precious habitats has a catastrophic effect on
wildlife and biodiversity and is a major contributor to climate change
because the carbon that was fixed in the soil is released into the
atmosphere, contributing to global warming.

Most of the world's soya crop is from beans that have been genetically
modified so that farmers can use it along with generous amounts of
weedkillers. Genetic modification raises major issues (see SOYA FOODS/
Is soya good for me?/Is soya a green choice?).

Where should I buy poultry?

The best place to buy free-range or organic poultry is from the producer
at a farmers' market because you can speak directly to someone who can
answer your questions about how the birds have been raised. Progressive
butchers usually stock free-range birds from local producers.
Supermarkets stock a small number of organic birds and more that are
free-range. However, these birds are more likely to have been slaughtered
in the same high-throughput slaughterhouses used for factory-farmed
birds than those bought from independent outlets. Factory-farmed
chicken is the norm, so go for poultry products that are very clearly
labelled as free-range or organic.

Will poultry break the bank?

Even if you are hard up, don't buy chicken and other poultry that has
been factory-farmed. The bird will have led an appalling, short life and
been raised in fundamentally insanitary conditions. Its meat will taste
poor and it may also be adulterated and carry food-poisoning bugs. Avoid
bargain-basement poultry, and unless poultry products are very clearly
labelled as free-range, assume the worst.

Judged against the bargain-basement cost of factory-farmed poultry, free-range, and particularly organic, birds can seem prohibitively expensive. Organic birds cost more because they are slow-growing and fed on natural, organic feed, not plumped up on imported soya. And the pick-up price of intensively reared poultry doesn't reflect the true cost of its production, either in animal suffering or environmental degradation. But even if you take on board these points, you may still wonder how you can ever afford a more ethical bird. The best way to approach this is to eat less, but better poultry. Think of it as a food you eat occasionally, not routinely. Buy the most humanely reared sort you can afford, free-range or better still organic, and use every last little bit of it.

If you can't manage a whole bird, then resist the knee-jerk urge to go for the most costly (and some would say rather dull) breasts and choose instead the legs, thighs and wings which offer that winning combination of more flavoursome darker meat and potentially crisp skin. Make a couple of chicken wings the centre point of a salad-based lunch, and you can save the money that you would have spent on a pricey chicken sandwich made with potentially dodgy, factory-farmed breasts.

If you get a whole chicken, make it do several meals. You could roast it and eat it hot, then take all the remaining meat off the bone and use it in another dish or in your lunchtime sandwich. Keep the giblets, and add the gizzard to the well-picked chicken carcase to make a stock.

Beef

With all their lush green pastures, Britain and Ireland are famously good at producing beef. All countries like to brag about having the 'world's best' foods, but when the 'best beef' trophy is up for grabs, we've got it in the bag.

A number of factors have a bearing on the eating quality of beef. Breed is of paramount importance. Our traditional breeds of beef cattle, such as the celebrated Aberdeen Angus or Hereford, seem to have flavour laid down in their DNA; no wonder their meat is highly rated. The main selling point of the more recently introduced continental beef breeds is that they reach maturity faster. This can make them attractive to farmers anxious to see a quicker return on their investment, but continental beef breeds don't taste as good as our native ones.

The way the cattle have been fed is also crucial. Beef from outdoor-reared, grass-fed cattle that graze for most of their lives on permanent pasture which has a rich diversity of green plants has infinitely more flavour and character than beef from cattle that have lived mainly indoors, chomping their way through a mountain of cereals and soya.

Taste doesn't just come down to farming. Expert handling at slaughter to minimize stress to the animal and experienced butchering thereafter is vital, otherwise all the good work of the farmer can be undone. The skill here is not only knowing how to cut up a side of beef, but also how to mature it. These days, most beef is sent straight from the cutting plant, packed in plastic to exclude oxygen, then supplied to the supermarket with little if any ageing, so it is ruby red, quite moist and floppy. This isn't always obvious until you open the pack, as most supermarket beef is routinely packed on an absorbent mat to soak up the moisture. Beef like this is soft, but not particularly tender.

Traditional butchers, on the other hand, still hang whole sides of beef in a cool, dry atmosphere for anything from fourteen to twenty-eight days so that they are dry-aged naturally by the oxygen in the air. During this period, the meat darkens in colour and loses excess moisture, which firms up the flesh. The intrinsic beef flavour becomes more developed, and the grain of the meat relaxes, making it really tender. So if you want the best-tasting beef, look for information about breed, feed and hanging. Choose beef that looks reasonably dry and dark red in colour.

Modern healthy eating orthodoxy has encouraged us to see fat in beef as the enemy but it is the fat that gives it much of its flavour and keeps it tender. Really good beef should have a marbling of fat through it and any covering of fat should not be white (a sign that the animal was grain- and soya-fed), but creamy white (a sign that the animal has grazed pasture). There are some good lean cuts, such as silverside and brisket, but these need slow cooking or they will dry out.

Things to do with beef

- Shin makes a particularly unctuous Indian curry.

- A French daube (beef and red wine stew) or beef carbonnade (Flemish beef and beer stew) made with cheaper stewing cuts is handy when you have to feed a lot of people and want no last-minute stress. They taste better reheated, so you can get ahead by cooking them the day before.

- Use big chunks of featherblade to make a melting beef rendang, the Malaysian dry beef and coconut milk curry.

- Tongue and heart of beef might sound scary, but with long, slow simmering in water with aromatic vegetables and herbs, these cuts taste like exceptionally tender beef. Fabulous served on sourdough or rye bread with chutney or mustard, or with a punchy Italian salsa verde made with parsley, mint, basil, anchovies, capers, mustard, lemon juice and olive oil. If you don't feel brave enough to cook tongue or heart, brisket suits the same treatment.

- Steak pie: just make a simple beef stew with onions, carrots, stewing beef – economy cuts like chuck, featherblade, skirt and shin are fine; there's no need to use pricier rump or round steak – and water, stock or a little wine. Top with all-butter puff pastry. To make a steak and kidney pudding, include a little chopped kidney in the stew and use a suet crust. (Suet is the fat found around beef kidneys.)

- For a celebratory starter, make carpaccio using raw beef fillet: 200 grams will feed four. Chill the fillet well, slice thinly, then beat out each round of beef with a rolling pin under greaseproof paper until it is paper-thin. Drizzle with good-quality extra virgin olive oil and lemon juice, season with sea salt and pepper, and serve with rocket and Parmesan shavings.

- Spin out small quantities of expensive prime cuts like fillet and sirloin by cutting them into strips and using them for stir-fries, or sautéing with mushrooms and cream for a simple stroganoff. Like this, one steak will serve two to four people.

Beef is a really good source of protein, which is essential if the body is to regenerate itself. Protein is the best macronutrient in food for satisfying the appetite: it keeps you going for longer than either carbohydrate or fat.

Beef contains monounsaturated fat – about half the fat in steak is of this type – which may be protective against heart disease and stroke. Beef also contains saturated fat. Contrary to the public health dogma that has prevailed over the last few decades, there is no good evidence to support the idea that saturated fat is harmful or causes heart disease.

Beef also contains cholesterol. It is increasingly accepted that eating cholesterol in food such as beef does not lead to clogged arteries and heart disease. Cholesterol is a vital component of cell membranes and allows the body to make vitamin D and certain hormones.

Beef is a good food for providing B vitamins, particularly B6 and B12, which, as well as helping brain function and providing energy, help lower levels of undesirable homocysteine that can build up in the blood. High levels of this substance are associated with an increased risk of heart attack and stroke. Vitamin B12 deficiency is quite common, especially among older people and vegetarians. Beef also contains useful iron, which helps prevent anaemia; zinc, which boosts the immune system and builds bone density; and selenium, which may protect against certain cancers. Most British and Irish soils are very low in selenium, so selenium deficiency may be quite common.

There is good reason to choose beef from grass-fed cattle. A growing body of evidence suggests that grass-fed beef is nutritionally superior to beef from more intensively reared grain- and soya-fed animals. Cattle fed on grass have been shown to have higher levels of omega-3 fatty acids in their flesh, probably because of all the green grass and wild plants they eat. Omega-3 fatty acids are important for healthy brain function and thought to be protective against heart disease. In particular, grass-fed beef is a good source of conjugated linoleic acid, which appears to reduce the risk of cancer, heart disease and obesity. All organic beef cattle are grass-fed, as are many traditionally reared beef herds.

Ever since BSE (mad cow disease) was discovered to be transmissible to humans, many people have worried that beef is not safe to eat. The cause of BSE was thought to be the unnatural practice of feeding beef and dairy animals with compound feeds that included the recycled remains of dead, possibly diseased cattle. Feeds like this are now banned and systems have been put in place to ensure the traceability of both beef and dairy animals. There is no reason to think that beef is unsafe.

The jury is out on any possible link between red meat consumption and cancer. Some research has shown an association, while other research has failed to find any link. If there is a risk, it seems to relate to the consumption of cured meats, such as salami, pastrami and bacon, which contain chemical preservatives, not fresh, unprocessed red meat.

How is beef farmed?

There are two different types of beef. You might think of it as 'beef beef' and 'dairy beef'. The most desirable sort is beef that comes from a herd reared exclusively for that purpose. This is called suckler beef because the calves are kept with their mothers and suckle from her, usually for at least six months. When they are weaned, they remain in family groups. The cattle graze outside for all, or most of the year – which is what cows are designed by nature to do – with their diet only being supplemented, if necessary, by hay (dried grass) or silage (preserved grass) in the winter. These free-ranging, outdoor-reared grass- and pasture-fed cattle take anything from twenty-four to thirty months to reach their target end weight. Beef from suckler herds of a traditional breed noted for its eating quality, such as Highland or Shorthorn, is generally agreed to be the best around and commands the highest price.

Some beef suckler herds use non-native, continental breeds such as the Simmental and Limousin, because they put on more lean growth faster. These are largely reared outdoors but they aren't hardy enough to spend the winter outdoors, so they will spend part of the year inside.

The other sort of beef is a byproduct of the dairy herd. Dairy cows are mated with a bull from a beef herd. Their offspring are what is known as dairy crosses. The meat from pure-bred dairy animals is generally regarded as inferior to that from suckler herds, which is why any meat from such animals tends to be sold for food processing. Meat from dairy cross cattle is better than that but it doesn't have the taste or eating quality associated with beef from suckler herds.

Dairy cross calves are taken away from their mothers soon after birth and fed on formula milk so their mothers can go back for milking. The growing animals can then either be kept entirely indoors in a system which is like a less extreme version of the notorious US feedlot, where large numbers of cattle are fattened up for beef, or they spend some time out grazing. But because they aren't pure-bred beef animals, they take for ever to fatten on grassy pasture and the end price of their meat won't repay the farmer's patience. So more commonly they are 'finished', or fattened for market indoors on cereals and soya so they can be slaughtered at between twelve and eighteen months.

In 2010 it came to light that a small amount of beef (and milk) from cloned dairy cattle has found its way into the British food chain. Cloning is a relatively new and highly controversial procedure that makes an identical copy of the most productive cattle and raises major animal welfare concerns. The idea is to breed herds of super-productive animals capable of giving large amounts of milk and meat.

The problem with this technology is that it is hit-and-miss and so entails extreme animal suffering. An embryo has to be implanted into a surrogate mother using a potentially painful surgical procedure. If they do not miscarry, these mothers often don't give birth naturally and must instead be delivered by caesarean. Very few cloned animals survive for more than a few months and those that do often suffer from defects and illness. Opponents of cloning are also concerned that because this technology narrows the genetic base of our herds, cloning could make cattle more susceptible to disease. This in turn could have negative effects on future food production.

Cloning also raises human health issues. The UK Food Standards Agency says that milk and meat from clones is 'hypothetically safe'. It bases this view on the assumption that since the primary DNA sequence is unchanged, cloned food is no different from the non-cloned equivalent. It admits, however, that there is 'no data on the composition of meat or milk obtained from the descendants of cloned cattle'.

In Europe it is illegal for breeders to create 'first-generation' clones for use in agriculture, and the European Parliament wants to have the cloning of animals for food banned. But farmers are nevertheless allowed to import embryos and semen from clones for breeding purposes. Usually these come from the US, the country driving this technology.

In the UK and Ireland there is widespread public opposition to meat (and milk) from clones and their progeny entering the food chain. One survey showed that 80 per cent of consumers were concerned about it, while 91 per cent wanted meat and milk from clones and their offspring to be labelled. But the UK government wants to allow food from clones and their offspring to be sold freely without any label that would distinguish it from normal sources.

There are no statistics showing how many offspring of cloned animals are now on British farms and to what extent their meat could be making its way into our food. It is thought that only a minority of farmers are currently using cloning technology and it isn't clear how common cattle cloning might become. If you want to be extra sure that you are not eating meat from cloned animals or their progeny, choose organic beef (and milk). Organic standards do not permit cloning.

Is beef a green choice?

The feeding of intensively reared beef cattle is a big environmental problem. Unlike organic or grass-fed cattle, they do not eat the natural diet of grass and other forage food, but rely mainly on feed rations or pellets. These rations are made up by feed compounders and consist mainly of cereals. Feeding cattle this diet means that they can be 'finished' or pushed to reach the required end weight at twelve to eighteen months old, when otherwise it could take up to thirty months or even longer. A diet of grass and forage food simply won't do the trick.

Feeding cereals to animals is a very inefficient use of the world's already stretched food resources because most of these crops' potential food value is lost during conversion from plant to meat. For every kilo of weight factory-farmed cattle gain, they have to eat at least five kilos of feed. These foodstuffs would generate much more in the way of human nutrition if they were fed directly to people. Using cereals as animal feed is also wasteful of the increasingly scarce resources of land, water and fossil fuel energy that are used to grow them.

Grass-fed beef, on the other hand, is a very sustainable food because the cattle convert something we cannot eat – grass and other green forage foods – into meat and milk. The great strength of outdoor-reared livestock is that they are able to use land that is generally not suitable for other forms of food production, so they do not compete with humans for food.

Where should I buy beef?

Most of the beef on sale in supermarkets, unless it specifically states otherwise, comes from dairy cross animals fed mainly on a cereal and soya diet. There are several labels and logos that indicate the geographical origins of beef, but these don't guarantee that the beef is from a free-range, grass-fed animal. If buying supermarket beef, choose organic, because organic cattle must be free-range and grass-fed, or go for premium-priced beef from a named breed that specifically states that it is free-range and grass-fed. It is unlikely that supermarket beef will have been hung so the flavour may be disappointing.

Traditional butchers often sell beef from native breeds that have spent most of their lives out on pasture. They should be able to tell you the breed of their beef, the name and location of the farm it came from and what age the animal was at slaughter. Traditional butchers are also expert at hanging meat and wrapping it in a way that preserves its good characteristics; unlike supermarket beef, which is usually smothered in plastic.

Many small-scale farmers rearing interesting breeds on grass sell their meat at farmers' markets or by mail order. The problem here is that health and safety regulations require that meat is vacuum-packed, which is not the ideal way to store it. If you buy beef like this, remove it from the pack a few hours before you cook it. Pat it dry with kitchen roll, put it on a plate and leave it at room temperature so that the meat can dry up a bit. This will help it cook better. The same technique will improve supermarket beef a little, but can't compensate for its other inadequacies.

Will beef break the bank?

Mince counts for over 50 per cent of the beef we buy because it's affordable and most people know what to do with it: that familiar roll call of lasagne, burgers, chilli con carne et al. It isn't a great idea to buy cheap, bargain mince, since it is likely to contain more fat than you will want for the dish. Equally, there is no need to buy extra-lean steak mince, unless the recipe calls for it, in dishes such as hamburgers, for instance.

If you are watching what you spend, there's more to beef than mince. In search of steak, forget those familiar cuts – fillet, sirloin and ribeye – and go for hangar steak (skirt). It is scrappier, so it does need to be well trimmed by the butcher, and chewier too, but it usually costs much less than other steaks and has a particularly rich taste.

For stews and casseroles, relatively cheap, flavourful cuts like oxtail, shin, silverside, brisket, chuck, skirt and featherblade are ideal. You have to wait longer for them to be ready, but preparing a nourishing, lip-smacking braise takes no longer than grilling a steak. Slow-cooked beef keeps well and can be prepared in advance and reheated.

Properly hung, dry-aged beef will always be more expensive than the bright red unhung sort because the carcase loses moisture in the hanging process and so the butcher has less wet weight at the end of the hanging period. But the beef will have a superior flavour, is likely to be healthier because it comes from a grass-fed animal that has lived a better life, so it represents value for money.

UNIQUE NATIVE BREEDS

Scotland, England, Wales and Ireland are home to some of the world's most highly rated beef breeds. The best known is the Aberdeen Angus, but there are other regional and local breeds that can also produce excellent meat, such as the Belted Galloway, Shorthorn, Longhorn, Devon Reds, Highland, Luing, Red Poll, Irish, Welsh Black, White Park and Dexter. Such breeds are an important part of our food heritage and our biodiversity. They were developed over time for their hardiness, their suitability for the local environment and weather and their ability to produce wonderful-tasting meat from nothing much more than pasture. Some of them are now only represented in such small numbers that they count as rare breeds.

After the Second World War, beef production moved away from traditional breeds to continental ones as a means of meeting the growing demand for larger quantities of meat at low prices. Now-adays, as their diet of cereal and soya no longer looks environ-mentally sustainable, or particularly desirable on health and taste grounds, our unique native breeds are coming back into their own as better suited to meeting the environmental and health challenges of the twenty-first century. Although it may sound counter-intuitive, eat beef from these breeds whenever you get the chance. It shows farmers that they are commercial and encourages producers to rear them.

Lamb and mutton

Lamb is the most reliable meat you can get. It's actually quite hard to buy poor lamb and the best lamb and mutton can be magnificent. While pork and chicken are much more of a lottery and can often taste rather like neutral protein, lamb is always lamb, with a distinctive smell and meaty taste that permeates other ingredients. It punches above its weight on the flavour front, which makes it a useful, economic meat. A very little lamb can go a long way but still impart its characteristic flavour. In recipes such as curries, casseroles, stews, shepherd's pie and Middle Eastern-style meat patties and rissoles, you can easily reduce the amount of lamb and increase the amount of other, cheaper vegetables, grains and beans, but still get a suitably meaty effect. Instead of lamb and vegetable stew, think vegetable stew, flavoured with a modest amount of lamb.

The character of lamb is laid down in the DNA of the sheep and in the unique flavour attributes of specific breeds. Our older sheep breeds tend to be more intrinsically flavourful than meat from more modern, commercial breeds designed for faster growth, but flavour in lamb is also a consequence of diet. Almost all the lamb we eat comes from free-ranging sheep that have spent their lives grazing on pasture made up of many different types of plants, grasses, flowers, herbs, brackens, heathers and clovers. The natural diversity of the sheep's diet makes for meat with a taste that reflects local geography. Lamb from hill sheep that have fed on heather, bracken and bilberries, for instance, will taste subtly different from lamb from sheep that have grazed on marshy, salty coastal land and fed on seaweed. Both will taste slightly different again from lamb from sheep that have fattened on lush, grassy pastures.

Lamb varies considerably in character depending on the age of the sheep at slaughter. The older the sheep, the fuller and more distinctive the flavour. The mildest-tasting lamb comes from sheep that are just a few months old. Sold as 'spring' or 'new season' lamb, the flesh is pale and the texture loose-knit, as the lambs have usually had little exercise. It is moist and succulent, with a mild, some might say feeble, flavour, often because the lamb has been raised on a diet of animal feed concentrates, rather than green pasture.

Most lamb on sale, however, is older than this, less than a year old, generally at four to six months. It has a deeper, redder colour, more of that distinctive lamb taste and a more obvious marbling of creamy-coloured fat. For many butchers and food lovers, this is young lamb at its sweetest and tastiest.

People who like a more mature, richer-flavoured lamb adore hogget (meat from sheep that are over a year old) and shearling (meat from sheep that are seventeen to twenty-two months old). Both these types of lamb have a more pronounced, richer taste because the sheep have spent longer outside, munching on green pasture.

The ultimate treat for those who like full-flavoured lamb with a deep, complex flavour is mutton (meat from sheep in their third, fourth or even fifth year). Don't be put off by that old 'mutton dressed as lamb' put-down. True mutton comes, not from tired old ewes, but from rams that are still in good shape. The strong, deep flavour that develops from time on pasture makes mutton hugely satisfying to eat. Good mutton should not be tough, but have a fine, firm grain, thanks to all the exercise the sheep has had. It need not be slow-cooked either: proper mutton can be roasted just like beef.

One of the reasons that lamb from a proper butcher's shop often tastes better than the supermarket equivalent is that professional butchers hang their lamb to improve the flavour and tenderize the meat. Young lamb is best hung for a week, hogget, shearling and mutton for two to three weeks. Most supermarket lamb is not hung.

Things to do with lamb

- In the traditional Moroccan *harira* recipe, a small amount of stewing lamb or mutton (neck fillet is perfect) turns a spicy tomato and chickpea soup flavoured with fresh coriander, onions and cumin into a satisfying meal.

- Fry very thin strips of lean lamb, hogget or mutton (leg, loin, or neck fillets) in hot olive oil with ground cumin, sea salt and black pepper until they are slightly charred. Allow the hot meat to cool until warm, then place a small amount on top of hummus flavoured strongly with tahini (sesame) paste, and dust with sour sumac (optional). Eat with hot bread and lemon wedges to squeeze.

- Make a plain stew of filleted neck or shoulder with onions, finely chopped carrots and turnip, and water, stock or wine. When the meat is cooked, add a generous pinch of saffron that has been lightly toasted and crumbled and a handful each of finely chopped parsley and mint. Good with boiled spelt or barley.

- Simmer shank, breast or flank in water with chopped carrot, onions, parsley stems and a little thyme until it is meltingly soft. Add chopped leeks and potatoes to make a chunky or liquidized soup. Pick off the tender strands of flesh from any fat or bone and use them to make sandwiches with tarragon mayonnaise and mustard cress.

- Use best end of neck or shoulder chops to make a traditional Lancashire hotpot with a crispy potato lid, or an Irish stew.

- A touch of cinnamon works well with lamb, whether it's in a Greek moussaka or a Moroccan tagine.

Is lamb good for me?

Eating lamb is a good way of getting high-quality protein in your diet, which is essential if the body is to regenerate itself. Protein is the best macronutrient in food for satisfying the appetite: it keeps you going for longer than either carbohydrate or fat.

Most of the fat in lamb is monounsaturated. This type of fat may be protective against heart disease and stroke. Lamb also contains some saturated fat. Contrary to the public health dogma that has prevailed over the last few decades, there is no good evidence to support the idea that saturated fat is harmful or causes heart disease. Since most sheep are free-ranging, grazing on pasture, the fat in lamb is likely to have the desirable balance of omega-3 and omega-6 fatty acids, and provide a rich natural source of conjugated linoleic acid, which is thought to protect against heart disease and cancer.

Lamb also contains cholesterol. It is increasingly accepted that eating cholesterol in food such as beef does not lead to clogged arteries and heart disease. Cholesterol is a vital component of cell membranes that allows the body to make vitamin D and certain hormones.

As well as supplying useful iron, which prevents anaemia, lamb is one of the best sources of zinc, a mineral that many people, especially young women, lack. Zinc is essential for helping to build bone density, healing, and supporting the immune system.

Lamb is also a good supply of B vitamins, most notably B12 and B3. Vitamin B12 helps lower levels of undesirable homocysteine that can build up in the blood. High levels of this substance are associated with an increased risk of heart attack and stroke. Vitamin B12 deficiency is quite common, especially among older people and vegetarians. Vitamin B3 aids brain function. Some research suggests that it may be protective against Alzheimer's disease and other age-related degenerative conditions.

The jury is out on any possible link between red meat consumption and cancer. Some research has shown an association, while other research has failed to find any link. If there is a risk, it seems to relate to the consumption of cured meats, such as salami, pastrami and bacon, which contain chemical preservatives, not fresh, unprocessed red meat.

How are lamb and mutton farmed?

Sheep are the most extensively reared and free-ranging of all our farm animals. With the exception of a minority of indoor-reared lambs destined for the early spring market, they do not suffer from the cruelties and deprivations associated with factory-farming, so lamb does not raise the common animal welfare concerns that relate to intensively reared, factory-farmed meats. Sheep don't quite look after themselves, however. They need a shepherd to check that they have enough to eat in cold weather, to help out with lambing, to move them from one type of pasture to another, to shear their fleeces and more, but they are left to their own devices most of the time.

Sheep farming varies slightly from one part of the country to the next, reflecting climate and topography. Hill and upland sheep, from Scotland, Wales, Cumbria and Yorkshire, graze on inhospitable, tussocky moorland and heath land in higher-lying areas. As this land is not fertile enough terrain to fatten up lambs before winter closes in, those not required to maintain the herd are moved as 'store' sheep to lusher, lower lying, greener pastures until they reach the desired weight. Hogget, shearling and mutton generally come from slower growing, hardy hill breeds in upland areas. Lowland lambs from southern areas and milder coastal strips just have to stay put and fatten up on grassy summer pasture. Slower-growing lowland lambs, like store lambs from hill and upland areas, are fattened up over the autumn on fodder crops such as kale, turnips and hay to supplement their grassy diet.

An exception to the rule that lamb comes from free-ranging animals is lamb sold as 'new season' or 'spring lamb' in early spring. Frisky baby lambs make their appearance in our fields at this time of year, but this is not what you will be eating if you go for this type of meat. Although there are certain breeds, such as the Dorset, that naturally give birth in the autumn when reared on fertile southern pastures, most new season spring lamb comes from flocks that have been specially manipulated so that the ewes give birth in November and December. These lambs are reared indoors, weaned early from their mothers and fattened up on high-protein feed, usually containing concentrated soya (which may be genetically modified) and cereal, so that they will be ready for the Easter market.

New season spring lamb is not to be confused with the new season lamb that appears in the autumn. This comes from upland sheep reared in the traditional manner.

AN ASTONISHING COLLECTION OF BIODIVERSITY

Sheep have been reared in Britain and Ireland from ancient times for milk, meat and wool. Britain has more than fifty native breeds of sheep, of varying type and appearance: Hebridean, Manx Loaghtan, Herdwick, Rough Fell, Speckle Face, Romney Marsh,

Manx, Portland, Welsh Mountain, Soay, Dalesbred, Swaledale, Derbyshire Gritstone, White Faced Woodland, White Faced Dartmoor, Hill Radnor and more. This is an astonishing collection of biodiversity.

Sheep are an enduring feature of our landscape. Many of them are 'hefted'; that is, they have adapted over time to a particular environment and geographical conditions. Hefted flocks have a sense of place with an inbuilt knowledge of a particular terrain that has been passed down from one generation to another. They know their patch – where to find the best food, where to drink water and so on – and never want to leave it, so they can roam freely without constant shepherding, or being penned in with walls. This is a very special farming system.

MEAT

Most hefted flocks are from hardy hill breeds that are relatively rare. Some of these breeds are at a healthy level, but others are endangered. Rare-breed, often hefted, sheep are harder to rear than those farmed on lush pastures as they are usually slower growing and grazing on more hostile land. The cull of sheep that followed the outbreak of foot and mouth disease in the UK in 2001 particularly affected rare-breed flocks, because they were fewer in number to start with than the more commercial sheep breeds.

As people have become more interested in smaller-scale local food, meat from rare-breed sheep has undergone a revival. It is good to eat meat from rare-breed sheep. You are not consuming the last vestiges of a dying species; instead, the demand for such meat shows farmers that there is a good market for their sheep and encourages them to keep such flocks in production.

In the past, most sheep meat was eaten not as young lamb, but as mature mutton. It was a staple of the British and Irish diet and considered to be superior in taste and texture. In the second half of the twentieth century, mutton all but disappeared from our shops as fattier meat became unfashionable and hearty red meat lost market share to poultry. In more recent years, mutton has been undergoing a renaissance. Chefs and food lovers adore its rich, complex flavour, and farmers are delighted because it restores some market value to their older animals.

Is lamb a green choice?

Lamb is one of the most environmentally friendly types of meat, since sheep spend most of their time grazing on land that is not fertile or productive enough for growing crops. Like lawnmowers on four legs, sheep convert land that cannot be used for cultivating crops into high-quality protein for humans. Although over-grazing by sheep can cause problems – they eat young trees and stop woodland regenerating – without sheep, much of our wilder, upland areas would revert to impenetrable scrub and bog. Most sheep will need supplementary food in the depths of winter, at lambing and towards the end of their lives to fatten them; nonetheless, sheep do not consume anything like the mountains of cereals and soya as pigs or poultry.

Since the UK and Ireland produce lots of lamb, there is no need to buy any imported from New Zealand. There is nothing wrong with New Zealand lamb but it makes sense to favour lamb that is local, regional or at least national, as it will have travelled substantially fewer miles than the southern hemisphere equivalent, and so leave a lighter carbon 'foodprint'.

As well as providing us with meat, the sheep's fleece gives us wool which is a renewable, biodegradable resource with many uses, everything from clothing and carpets to loft insulation and ecological nappies.

Sheep farming in upland areas has been an important way of maintaining small rural communities in remote areas by providing a source of income that keeps people on the land.

Toxic chemicals in sheep dips, used to control parasites, are a major environmental concern. These are a common cause of soil contamination and water pollution and known to be hazardous to the shepherds who are doing the dipping. Efforts have been made to regulate the use of sheep dips but it is hard to control parasites without them. Some of the most toxic chemicals used in sheep dips have been suspended or been withdrawn by their makers. Organic sheep farmers also use sheep dips, but the list of chemicals available to them is more restricted.

Where and when should I buy lamb and mutton?

There is never a problem finding English, Scotch, Welsh or Irish lamb, except in the early spring, when butcher's shops and supermarkets often sell imported New Zealand lamb. Although New Zealand lamb is available all year, in its chilled form, it is marketed most aggressively in this early spring period when our home supply of younger lambs has dried up.

Counter-intuitive though it may seem, what with all the talk of Easter lamb, spring is the worst time to eat lamb. Any home-produced lamb on sale at this time is likely to be from early lambing breeds or lambs raised indoors. So in spring, rather than going for this type of lamb or the imported type, you may prefer to eat other meats, or find a source for more mature hogget, shearling or mutton. After all, we are only talking about waiting a few months and although young spring lamb has some charms, lamb is better thought of as an autumn meat. Alternatively, fall back on home-produced lamb that you have frozen in autumn, since lamb freezes well.

By May, lambs that were born in the early spring, and which have been out feeding on grass on lusher lowland and coastal pastures, start to become available. As late summer moves into autumn, slow-growing lamb from less fertile, upland ground comes on to the market and continues until Christmas. Although hogget, shearling and mutton may be found year-round, they are most readily available from October until May, sold to fill the early gap between home-produced autumn and summer lamb.

If you want your lamb properly hung, use a traditional butcher. Most supermarket lamb comes straight from the cutting plant. For rare breeds, the best source is farmers' markets, farm shops and upmarket butchers.

Will lamb and mutton break the bank?

There is absolutely no need to shell out the premium prices charged for new season spring lamb as the taste is feeble. Nor is there any need to pay high prices for 'premium' cuts like loin or loin chops, leg or leg steaks, or rack. Although a roast leg of lamb is always a treat, for most slow-cooking purposes, cheaper cuts with a bit more fat and/or bone, like shoulder, shank and neck, will often give a more flavoursome result.

Rare-breed lamb and more mature hogget, shearling and mutton cost very little more, and often the same as standard lamb despite the fact that they usually taste significantly better.

Pork, bacon and ham and wild boar

A little persistence and dedication is needed when you're buying pork. Choose the right stuff and you'll be richly rewarded with impeccably crisp roast crackling and succulent, almost creamy meat with a mellow but distinctive porky personality. But there's an awful lot of pork around that doesn't fit that bill.

Like chicken, the quality of the pork we eat has been compromised by modern factory-farming methods, a pressure intensified by selective breeding. Our traditional breeds of British pigs were slow to mature, hardy animals that did well outdoors but were unsuited to the confinement of intensive indoor production. They had a good covering of fat as well as fat through their flesh, which made it succulent to eat. Happily, such pork, and occasionally wild boar – the meat from hardier, wilder breeds of pig – is still available from small pig producers keeping traditional breeds in free-range systems.

But for the mass market, animal geneticists have diligently produced modern breeds that can be reared entirely indoors. Consequently, most of the British national pig herd is now made up of animals from two foreign breeds, the Landrace and the Duroc, crossed with a British breed, usually the Large White. These genetically 'improved' breeds have been developed because they are regarded as more 'efficient'; that is, they put on lean weight faster. The Landrace in particular is adapted to indoor production – an asset for cost-conscious producers who want to turn out as many rashers as possible in the shortest time frame – but these modern pigs lack the intrinsic flavour of the older breeds. Eaten cured, either as bacon or ham, pork is so heavily salted that the taste deficit is somewhat masked. But eaten as a roast or a chop, the standard fresh pork can make for very unrewarding eating, offering chewy, dry, grey flesh with precious little character.

Fresh pork should look pale pink and have a slight sheen but some intensively reared pork can be of a particularly poor quality because the animals have been badly handled in the lead-up to slaughter. This can cause a fault described by the industry as PSE, short for pale, soft exudative flesh, in which case the meat is paler than usual, looks floppy and produces a lot of fluid. Or it can be DFD, which stands for dark, firm and dry. Even when factory-farmed pork doesn't have these textbook flaws, it is very often BA, or bloody awful, in anyone's language.

When it comes to bacon and ham, the taste and texture of the meat depend not only on how the pigs have been reared and bred, but also on how their meat has been cured (salted). There are two traditional methods. The pork can be dry-cured. It is covered with salt, saltpetre (the preservative potassium nitrate which keeps the bacon looking pink and stops food-poisoning bugs like botulism developing), seasonings such as juniper, bay, peppercorns, ginger and sometimes, if a 'sweet cure' is required, sweeteners such as honey or treacle. Then it is left to cure for up to a month and the ingredients massaged into the meat from time to time. Alternatively, the pork can be brined using the same ingredients for dry-curing, only mixed with water. Most producers of free-range and organic pork use one of these methods. Dry-curing generally produces the best results.

In modern times, the food industry has developed brine curing so that bacon and ham can now be made in a matter of hours. Wet-cured meat tends to absorb more water; indeed, for food technologists, a great triumph was to produce more rashers from less meat by incorporating polyphosphates (additives that help the meat retain water), sometimes along with the flavour enhancer, monosodium glutamate. This is done by injecting the bacon with brine solution, using very fine needles. This innovation has given us cheaper wet-cured bacon that tends to taste saltier and less porky than dry-cured, and which stews rather than crisps in the pan because the additives and water ooze out in a white scummy liquid. Most mass-market bacon and ham, both British and imported, is cured this way.

Once cured, bacon and ham can be left 'green' (unsmoked), or smoked over wood. Most is still wood-smoked, but for the very cheapest or 'economy' products, synthetic smoke flavouring may be used instead. Purely on taste grounds, streaky bacon or pancetta is likely to have more flavour and crisp up better because it contains more fat than leaner bacon cuts such as back, collar and middle.

If you are looking for pre-sliced cooked ham with a good flavour and texture, read the label to check what it says about water. By law, ham and bacon can contain up to 10 per cent added water without any declaration on the label. This means that if a label says that it contains, say, 15 per cent added water, it most likely contains 25 per cent. Unless you enjoy paying for water, go for ham and bacon with no added water. Be wary also of sliced cooked ham that comes in a very uniform shape. While the classic cooked ham is sliced from one intact cut of pork, such as the leg, many cheaper fresh and tinned sliced hams come from various different cuts of pork that have been re-formed into a ham shape by being massaged or tumbled into easy-to-slice blocks or rounds. These are bound together with other ingredients: water adds weight, polyphosphates help the meat retain the added water, yeast extract and hydrolysed vegetable protein flavouring give it a meaty taste, and gelatine helps hold it together. This kind of ham is easy to spot because it is typically very pink, shiny and wet-looking. A nice natural ham should be pale pink and have a slightly matt surface.

Things to do with pork, bacon and ham and wild boar

- Pork has an affinity with fennel. Use fennel seeds crushed with black peppercorns and sea salt to dust joints of pork or pork chops, or massage this mix into the slashed skin of pork belly.

- Combine minced pork, finely chopped bacon or pancetta, lemon zest, breadcrumbs, egg, chopped parsley and minced garlic, form the mixture into patties, and fry.

- Slices of pork shank – ask your butcher – make a cheap, but still tasty alternative to pricey veal for making an Italian osso bucco.

- Pig's cheek may sound off-putting but these little, flat discs of stunningly cheap and flavoursome meat can be used instead of more expensive cuts to make a tender, slow-cooked braise, stew or curry that even faint-hearted carnivores will love. Allow one to two cheeks per person. For an easy pork cheek stew, simply brown the cheeks whole with lots of onions, add root vegetables (carrot, turnip, celeriac, parsnip), a bay leaf and/or a few sage leaves and water, white wine or stock. Simmer slowly until tender. Serve with a gremolata (chopped parsley, garlic and lemon zest) on top.

- When you get bored eating up the ends of a cold cooked ham or gammon joint, serve it thinly sliced with a béchamel sauce, flavoured with a little onion and handfuls of very finely chopped parsley.

- Simmer a ham hock or ribs (smoked or unsmoked) with aromatic vegetables and herbs. Add lentils, chopped root vegetables, celery, leek and a few potatoes to make a chunky soup.

Are pork, bacon and ham and wild boar good for me?

Eating pork is a good way of getting high-quality protein in your diet, which is essential if the body is to regenerate itself. Protein is the best macronutrient in food for satisfying the appetite: it keeps you going for longer than either carbohydrate or fat.

Pork contains some monounsaturated fat, which may be protective against heart disease and stroke, and saturated fat. Contrary to the public health dogma that has prevailed over the last few decades, there is no good evidence to support the idea that saturated fat causes heart disease.

Pork also contains cholesterol. It is increasingly accepted that eating cholesterol in food such as pork does not lead to clogged arteries and heart disease. Cholesterol is a vital component of cell membranes that allows the body to make vitamin D and certain hormones.

Pork is a good source of B vitamins, particularly B1, which is essential for the nervous system and fertility, and B6 and B12, which as well as helping brain function and providing energy, help lower levels of undesirable homocysteine that can build up in the blood. High levels of this substance are associated with an increased risk of heart attack and stroke. Vitamin B12 deficiency is quite common, especially among older people and vegetarians. Pork also contains useful iron, which helps prevent anaemia, zinc, which boosts the immune system and builds bone density, and selenium, which protects against certain cancers. Most British and Irish soils are very low in selenium, so selenium deficiency may be quite common. It also has a high content of useful minerals such as iron, magnesium, zinc and potassium.

Some research has shown an association between high red meat consumption and colon cancer. Any risk seems to relate to the consumption of cured meats, such as bacon and ham, which contain chemical preservatives, not fresh, unprocessed meat. Four preservatives are permitted to prevent food-poisoning bacteria developing: potassium nitrate (saltpetre) E252, sodium nitrate E251, potassium nitrite E249 and sodium nitrite E250. It seems sensible to minimize exposure to these additives on health grounds. Choose bacon that contains no more than two of these preservatives, and preferably just one. Some cured meat also has added ascorbic acid (vitamin C) as this is thought to inhibit the formation of potentially cancer-causing substances when these preservatives are used.

There is good reason to choose pork from grass-fed, free-range pigs or wild boar. A growing body of evidence suggests that the meat of grass-fed livestock is nutritionally superior to that of more intensively reared grain- and soya-fed animals. It is likely to have higher levels of omega-3 fatty acids, probably because of the green grass and wild plants the pigs eat, in particular conjugated linoleic acid, which appears to reduce the risk of cancer, heart disease and obesity.

Left to their own devices, pigs would spend a lot of their time outdoors rooting around while foraging for food. Pigs convert rough pasture into edible meat (pork) more efficiently than any other farm animal. Given protection from the elements, pigs naturally organize themselves into family groups and, despite their mucky reputation, they keep their sties clean.

Most pigs, however, are factory-farmed in large herds with up to 1,000 pigs. The modern pig has been selectively bred to produce larger litters, now typically ten to twelve piglets, twice that of wild pigs. In intensive systems, a sow will have around five litters in two years – almost twice as many as normal. Factory-farmed pigs spend their whole lives indoors in sheds, often housed on concrete or slatted metal floors without any straw bedding to make it easier for producers to collect their slurry.

The piglets usually have their teeth clipped to prevent them from fighting with their siblings as they compete for teats. Around one month after birth, the piglets are 'early-weaned'; that is, taken from their mothers sooner than is natural, and put into a separate shed to be fattened up.

As large numbers of weaner or fattening pigs can be packed into a small barren space with nothing much to do apart from eat, they tend to get bored and start chewing each other's tails so 'tail docking', or cutting off part of the young pig's tail without anaesthetic, has been widely used to prevent this. EU law says that pigs must be given 'environmental enrichment' such as straw so that they can engage in their natural rooting and foraging activities and not become irritable and listless and has banned routine tail docking. But animal welfare groups say that many farmers are still docking tails and failing to provide straw, both on the Continent and in the UK. In many European countries, castration is also carried out routinely on male piglets. This severe mutilation is again performed without anaesthetic. In the Republic of Ireland and the UK, however, farmers generally no longer inflict this mutilation.

Indoor-reared pigs do not eat the fresh green foraged food that they would root up in nature. Instead they are mainly or exclusively fed on rations bought in from feed manufacturers. These are based on cereal, but also contain some added protein, usually soya (most likely GM in origin).

Although certain European countries, such as Sweden, operate extremely high standards of pig welfare, UK-produced pork is generally considered to be more humanely reared than is the case in most other European countries because the sow stall – a small enclosure where the sow does not have enough space to turn around – is banned in the UK. However, that does not mean that all is well with welfare on British pig farms. Like their European counterparts, British pork producers are still at liberty to use the farrowing crate. When near to giving birth, the heavily pregnant sow is usually moved from a group house into the farrowing crate. She will have her piglets and remain there for about a month until they are weaned. Like the now infamous sow stall, the farrowing crate prevents the sow from even turning round.

In recent years as concern about pig welfare has mounted, more British pig producers have turned to outdoor, or at least partially outdoor, production systems. Another incentive has been the fact that outdoor systems are cheaper to set up, although the producer's feed costs rise because the pigs are more active and eat more to keep warm. In such systems, the sows are allowed to roam on a free-range basis out in fields with shelter provided by huts or pig arcs. The sows live in groups while pregnant, and then are moved to individual huts with their own paddock when the piglets are due.

There is an important distinction to be drawn between 'outdoor-reared' or 'outdoor-bred' pork and true free-range pork. The first two terms only guarantee that the pigs are free-range for part of their lives. Once weaned, outdoor-bred or reared piglets can be put indoors for fattening and remain there until slaughter.

Under organic standards, pigs are always free-range, and when indoors they must be bedded with straw. Farrowing crates are not allowed and the piglets are taken away from their mothers later, usually at around eight weeks. The young pigs must be given straw and similar materials so that they can carry out their natural rooting and investigatory behaviours and to prevent them becoming aggressive. Tooth clipping, tail docking, castration and the farrowing crate are banned. The use of routine preventative medication in feed is not permitted and antibiotics are only used to treat ill pigs.

Until the 1960s, most of our pork, ham and bacon came from old, established breeds that thrived outdoors and were famed for their eating quality: Saddleback, Berkshire, Gloucester Old Spot, Large Black, Middle White, Welsh, British Lop and Tamworth. Now the number of such animals is so worryingly low in the UK that they are now referred to as 'rare breeds'. This means that it only takes a few farmers to give up rearing them, or an outbreak of disease in an area with such breeds, for these venerable breeds to disappear for ever. The Rare Breeds Survival Trust has already classified the British White and Middle Lop as 'endangered', the Berkshire, Large Black, Tamworth and Welsh as 'vulnerable' and the Saddleback as 'at risk'. Seeking out meat from farmers who still produce these breeds helps keep them in production and encourages a healthy genetic diversity in our pig herd.

Are pork, bacon and ham green choices?

Unlike their outdoor, free-range counterparts who will get at least part of their diet from foraging on pasture, indoor pigs are fattened up on large quantities of grain. As the world's population booms, there are more human mouths to feed and more competition for cereals, so it has been argued that it would be better for grains to be eaten directly by humans rather than fed to farm animals which are then sold as meat. For every kilo of weight a factory-farmed pig gains, it has to eat at least two and a half kilos of feed. The protein element in this feed is provided by soya, which is a disaster for the environment. Soya cultivation, along with cattle ranching, is now one of the two main causes of deforestation in South America, where vast expanses of rainforest and grassland are being cut down to make way for huge soya plantations. These plantations are managed in a very intensive way using high levels of synthetic fertilisers and pesticides. The destruction of these precious habitats has a catastrophic effect on wildlife and biodiversity and is a major contributor to climate change because the carbon that was fixed in the soil is released into the atmosphere, contributing to global warming.

Most of the world's soya crop is from beans that have been genetically modified so that farmers can use it along with generous amounts of

weedkillers. Genetic modification raises major issues (see SOYA FOODS/
Is soya good for me?/Is soya a green choice?).

Where should I buy pork, bacon and ham?

UK-reared pork, ham and bacon are always available but are under
continuous price pressure from cheaper, lower welfare imports. Some of
these imported products are packaged and labelled in a way that suggests
that they are British in origin such as bacon that is 'perfect for the British
breakfast' but comes from Denmark, or 'York' ham that has been cured
in the UK using imported pork. Similarly, York, Bradenham, Wiltshire,
Suffolk and Ayrshire are names for traditional British sweet cures for ham
and bacon that have no legal definition. Their presence on the label does
not necessarily mean that the pork is British or that it has any connection
with the geographical area mentioned.

The phrase 'Product of the UK', which ought to mean what it says, is very
misleading. As long as pork, ham or bacon has had something done to it
in the UK, such as packing and slicing or curing, it can be sold as British,
even if the pigs were not reared in the UK.

Some pork products are packaged with either the Union Jack, the flag of
St George, the Scottish Saltire or the Welsh dragon to indicate that they
are not imported. In the case of smaller, more artisanal producers, look
out for a more detailed, specific guarantee that the pigs have been both
reared and cured in the UK, such as 'Pigs reared and cured in Devon on
Sunnyside Farm'.

Farmers' markets are good places to look for pork products from
traditional breeds.

Will pork, bacon and ham break the bank?

Less humanely reared imported pork, ham and bacon consistently
undercut the UK-produced on price but if everyone buys them, then
British producers with more compassionate pig welfare standards will be
put out of business. The cheaper Irish, Danish and Dutch bacon and ham
that are widely on sale are likely to be reared to lower welfare standards,
and even gourmet Spanish, French and Italian hams and other cured pork
products, such as salami and pancetta, are likely to be factory-farmed
unless they state otherwise.

Rather than looking for cheap pork products, it is better to stick with British pork but to save money by concentrating on using cheaper cuts of fresh pork such as shoulder, hock, belly, cheek, neck and osso bucco.

Small amounts of bacon and ham can be used as a minor flavouring in a dish, rather than as a principal ingredient as they pack well above their weight on taste.

Venison

Venison, whether wild or farmed, is a full-flavoured, lean red meat with a slightly tighter texture than beef. Due to its leanness, it is important not to overcook it as it will become dry and firm. If you are using a prime cut, such as loin or saddle, it should be tender enough to be cooked pink. It is sometimes a good idea to add more fat (streaky bacon, extra oil) to recipes that involve slower cooking of cuts, like haunch, shin or shoulder, to compensate for this leanness. Lots of recipes recommend marinating venison in red wine, but unless you have meat from an older animal, this is not necessary and will give the venison a more powerful, robust taste that you may not always want.

In Britain and Ireland there are four main breeds of deer that we eat: red, fallow, roe and sika, which is very much like red. The breed of deer makes little difference to taste, although roe deer does tend to have a finer grain than red, sika or fallow deer.

The eating experience can vary widely, depending on how cleanly the deer has been shot and how the carcase has been handled thereafter. Much depends on whether it has been hung to tenderize the flesh and develop a more gamey flavour, and how it has been hung. Venison from a carcase that has been skinned will usually have a less obviously gamey taste than that which has been hung in its fur. The age and condition of the deer are also factors. Venison from younger deer will usually be more tender than that from older animals, and the eating quality of wild venison can dip from January to March when the animals are thinner and in poorer condition because they can't find enough to eat. Farmed venison doesn't vary in this way as the deer are given extra feed when there is not enough pasture to eat.

Since so many factors can influence the eating quality of wild venison, you have to put your faith in a good butcher or game dealer or specialist venison supplier to provide you with meat that will eat well. Wild venison can be splendid and most of it is very good, but every now and then you can get meat from an animal that was too old, too thin or not cleanly shot. Farmed venison may be less romantic, but it is a more consistent product than wild because it will have come from a deer that was in good condition and cleanly shot.

Things to do with venison

- Minced venison makes excellent, unusual chilli con carne. Add some smoked paprika, or smoked chilli, to make it feel less everyday and more special.

- Chopped haunch of venison is a prime candidate for a Thai red curry or a Massaman curry.

- Rich, lean, gamey venison works particularly well with dried fruits (prunes or apricots) and spices (cumin, ginger and saffron) in a Moroccan tagine. Choose shoulder or shin for this treatment.

- Minced venison can be used instead of beef to make burgers. Just include a little olive or nut oil with the usual additions of minced onions, egg, salt, pepper and chopped parsley. A slightly gamey venison burger stands up better than the beef equivalent to a potentially bossy blue cheese dressing.

- Casserole or stew cheaper, slow-cook cuts (shank, shin or shoulder) in sweet stout or dark fruity ale. If you have any raspberries, blackberries or blackcurrants to hand, you can reduce the gravy once cooked, and throw in a handful. Add a spoonful of redcurrant or similar jelly if you like the sauce sweeter. Add a square of dark chocolate for extra richness.

Is venison good for me?

Venison is an exceptionally healthy red meat with more protein than any other red meat we commonly eat, which means that it is excellent for satisfying the appetite and keeping hunger pangs at bay for a period of time. It contains very little fat. Venison has particularly high levels of iron – about twice as much as beef – which helps prevent anaemia. It also provides major amounts of B vitamins, such as vitamins B2 and B3, which help regulate metabolism, and vitamins B6 and B12, which can help lower undesirable homocysteine that can build up in the blood. High levels of this substance are associated with an increased risk of heart attack and stroke. Vitamin B12 deficiency is quite common, especially among older people and vegetarians. Venison is a good source of important minerals like zinc and copper and trace elements such as selenium. Thanks to the high percentage of wild food that deer eat (100 per cent in the case of wild deer), the small amount of fat in venison is likely to have the desirable balance of omega-3 and omega-6 fatty acids, and provide a rich natural source of conjugated linoleic acid, which is thought to protect against heart disease and cancer.

How is venison produced?

There are two different types of venison: wild and farmed. Wild venison, as the name implies, comes from deer that spend all their lives outdoors eating a wild diet. They are hunted and then shot in the wild.

Farmed venison comes from deer that live outdoors in enclosed paddocks and fields but which are otherwise free to roam. Farmed deer are never intensively reared. In winter, when it is very cold and the deer might suffer outdoors, deer farmers provide a large barn in which they can take shelter. The diet of farmed deer consists largely of grassy pasture, supplemented by hay, silage (preserved grass), grain and root vegetables in lean winter periods. Farmed deer live a semi-wild existence but are protected from the starvation and disease that affect wild deer.

Deer usually have a quick and stress-free death. Some do go to an abattoir, but most are shot in the wild or, in the case of most farmed deer, in the field.

Is venison a green choice?

There are good environmental reasons for eating venison, both wild and farmed. Wild deer can have an extremely destructive effect on the natural environment as they cause extensive damage to trees and crops, which is why forestry authorities and landowners carry out routine culls (kill a percentage of the deer population) to keep numbers within manageable limits. Buying and eating wild venison therefore helps keep the wild deer population under control. And an animal that would otherwise be considered a pest provides a prolific source of high-quality human food.

Farmed venison raises few, if any, of the issues raised by other farmed meats. Deer-farming enterprises are typically small-scale and local. The deer are born, reared, fattened and slaughtered, and often butchered, on the farm and sold quite locally, so little road transport is involved. Farmed deer are free-range and fed on a diet that is mainly grass, so they do not consume profligate amounts of cereals that could feed people. Deer-farming enterprises are generally found in colder, upland areas where it would be difficult, or even impossible, to grow crops that could feed humans. Farmed deer convert something that humans can't eat – grass – into high-quality human food.

A MEAT FROM THE MISTS OF TIME

Red deer and roe deer are native to the British Isles and Ireland and so the practice of hunting and eating wild venison extends back into the mists of time. The Normans brought fallow deer with them to England, and the Victorians introduced sika deer. Deer farming began in medieval times as landowners enclosed deer in their estates and parklands. Throughout our history, venison has featured in the diet of rural people.

From the 1980s, small venison-farming enterprises have been springing up, responding to consumer demand for meat that is healthy, sustainably produced and not factory-farmed. Increasingly, venison is finding a wider market, especially in restaurants.

Where and when should I buy venison?

Farmed venison is on offer all year round. The season for wild venison varies according to the breed, but some wild venison is usually available at any given point in the year. Wild venison supplies are likely to be most limited in March and at their best from June to December.

Most supermarkets do not stock venison, or offer only a limited range of products. For wild venison, the best source is a traditional butcher/game dealer, as he will keep an eye on the quality of the meat. Farmed venison is easy to find at farmers' markets or direct from farms, either online or by mail order. If availability is a problem, buy it when you see it and then freeze it.

Unless you are talking about sausages, burgers, or mince, venison is never especially cheap. Expect it to be priced on a par with good-quality, traditionally reared, grass-fed beef. Although wild deer are regarded as a pest and theoretically 'free' to shoot, the cost of processing venison to meet food hygiene regulations is high. Deer farmers have all the same costs as other livestock farmers. But don't feel you have to play safe with the more expensive prime cuts like saddle and loin. Check out cheaper options such as mince, shank, heart and sausages.

Thanks to its high protein content, venison is an exceptionally filling meat, and because of its leanness, it hardly shrinks in cooking. So it is possible to serve smaller portions of venison than you would of other meats. In most slow-cooked venison recipes, you can easily reduce the quantity of meat, and up the quantity of other ingredients, yet still produce a very satisfying, meaty dish.

Veal

Veal isn't exactly a heavyweight meat. Compared to robust red meat, or poultry, veal is meek and mild, cuddly rather than combative. It brings to the table a gentle, soft meatiness with a texture somewhere between pork and chicken, and a lightweight beefy flavour. Since it doesn't have the characteristic taste or appearance we associate with full-bodied red meats like lamb or venison, its light colour and delicate taste often appeal to red-meat avoiders. It also has that chameleon-like ability to take on other stronger flavours without vying with them.

Always go for pink-fleshed or 'rosé' veal as this will come from calves that have eaten a more varied, more natural diet which makes for more flavour. Avoid pale or 'white' veal as the calves will have been kept indoors and fed a milk-based diet, which produces meat that tastes like neutral protein and not a lot else.

Veal can come from animals aged anything from five to eight months, but in practice most veal calves are killed at around five to six months. The younger the animal, the more mild-flavoured and tender it is. The older it is, and the more time the calf has grazed outdoors, the more it comes to resemble beef.

Things to do with veal

- Half-and-half minced veal and pork is the mix you need to make an authentic Bolognese ragù to be served with tagliatelle.

- Chopped, boned shin or shoulder are in their element braised in a Hungarian goulash. Brown the meat and onions, add tomato passata, water, sea salt and pepper and lots of paprika. Simmer until the meat is tender, add chopped potatoes and cook until they are soft. Stir in a little soured cream and serve with a blob of soured cream on top and a generous dusting of chopped dill.

- Minced veal makes great meatballs. Cook them in a tomato sauce and serve with pasta and Parmesan. Or fry them first and serve with sautéed mushrooms, deglazed with Marsala or brandy, and finished off with cream.

- For *Wiener schnitzel*, place escalopes between two sheets of greaseproof paper and pound with a rolling pin until they are no thicker than a 50-pence coin. Dip in seasoned flour, then beaten egg and finally dried breadcrumbs. (Add lemon zest to the breadcrumbs if you fancy it.) Shallow-fry on both sides in hot oil, butter, ghee, pork fat or beef dripping until golden and crunchy. Serve with green salad and lemon wedges.

- Slice leftover cold, cooked veal as thinly as possible and cover with a smooth sauce made by liquidizing canned tuna, mayonnaise, olive oil and a little natural yogurt. Top with pink fillets of anchovies (optional) and capers, in the style of the Italian dish *vitello tonnato*.

- Gently braise slices of shin (osso bucco) with onions, water/stock, a little chopped carrot and celery until the meat is falling off the bone. Serve with a Milanese saffron risotto and gremolata (finely chopped parsley, lemon zest, garlic).

Is veal good for me?

Veal is a good source of protein, which is essential if the body is to regenerate itself. Protein is the best macronutrient in food for satisfying the appetite: it keeps you going for longer than either carbohydrate or fat. Veal is low in fat and leaner than beef. It is an excellent source of B vitamins, which, among other things, are crucial for the effective functioning of the brain and nervous system. In particular, it is a notable source of B12, which can help lower undesirable homocysteine that can build up in the blood. High levels of this substance are associated with an increased risk of heart attack and stroke. Vitamin B12 deficiency is quite common, especially among older people and vegetarians. Veal also provides a significant amount of zinc, which plays an important role in helping the body resist infection. Calves liver is a very good source of iron, which helps prevent anaemia.

Veal from free-ranging calves that have grazed outdoors on pasture will have a more desirable balance of omega-3 and omega-6 fatty acids than that from indoor-reared, milk-fed calves. It will also contain more conjugated linoleic acid, which is thought to protect against heart disease and cancer.

How is veal farmed?

The essence of veal production is that male calves from the dairy herd are fed mainly on milk, so their flesh has a pale colour and is nice and tender. But while much of the beef we eat in the UK comes from breeds raised exclusively for the quality of their meat, veal comes from breeds such as Holstein-Friesian, Jersey, Guernsey and Ayrshire, whose main purpose is to produce milk. In the dairy herd, female calves become the next generation of milkers, but there is no use for the male calves as they cannot lactate. However, if these calves are allowed to grow, for anything from five to eight months, they produce veal. Unlike calves specifically bred for beef, male dairy calves will never produce beef with the highest eating quality, although their meat can be delicious in a different way and offers an interesting, versatile addition to the range of meats we more commonly eat.

Veal had a bad reputation and was rightly reviled as a cruel meat thanks to the infamously cruel production system known as the veal crate, an animal-rearing system where calves were kept in individual cubicles, often tethered and without any straw bedding, and fed only on milky liquid, usually the by-products of cheese manufacture, such as whey and lactose, made up with water. This crate system caused considerable animal suffering and left the calves deficient in iron and other key micronutrients that would naturally nourish them if they were fed on pasture foods like grass and hay, but it produced the white, relatively tasteless flesh that was once considered desirable. Veal crates are no longer legal, and by law calves must be given some fibrous pasture food to prevent mineral and vitamin deficiencies, so disturbing images of miserable, weak calves stuck in metal crates that date back to this inhumane system are no longer relevant to the discussion of the veal we eat today.

These days, the most animal-friendly method of producing veal is to keep the calves with their mothers. If this isn't practical, because the cow is going back into milk production, the calves are put with another retired dairy cow that acts as a 'wet nurse'. In the best systems, notably on organic farms and those that specialize in rearing dairy cows outdoors whenever possible, the calves will be out with the cow when she is on grass so they will also munch away on green pasture. This grassy component in the calves' diet means that they grow healthy and strong and their meat takes on a distinctly rosy hue from the iron and other beneficial trace elements in their diet and develops more flavour than the purely milk-fed imported equivalent. This type of outdoor production produces meat known as pink or rosé veal.

A more common way of producing pink or rosé veal is to separate the calves from their mothers days after birth and house them indoors in groups where they are fed on milk formula and just the necessary amount of pasture food to prevent any dietary deficiencies until they are ready for slaughter. The more enlightened farmers keeping calves indoors house them in small groups on straw in airy barns. Some farmers operate a sort of halfway-house system where the calves are kept indoors, but are fed a diet that contains a larger element of pasture food.

Rules for raising veal are stricter in the UK than in the rest of Europe. For instance, younger calves in the UK receive double the amount of pasture food than their continental equivalents, the older ones must be given more space than is stipulated in EU law and must be provided with bedding for six months, rather than the two weeks that is required in the rest of the EU. So British veal is almost certainly a more animal-friendly option than imported.

Is veal a green choice?

There is a strong moral and environmental argument for eating veal. Unless you are a vegan and do not consume any dairy products, then it is both inconsistent and wasteful to boycott it. Female cows, inevitably, have male calves. One thing to be done with these 'bobby' calves is to raise them for veal. Thanks to the country's resistance to eating veal, most of these male calves – thousands every month – are currently shot at birth because they have no economic value and so the farmer cannot afford to feed them. This is not only sad, but a huge waste of healthy animals that could produce wholesome food. On organic farms, this practice is to be phased out by 2015. In the past, if the calves were not shot, they were exported live to Europe. These calf exports have stopped for the present time, and many more farmers are keeping the calves for longer than they would for veal – eight months is the maximum – and raising them for beef. This is a very positive trend.

A 'FOREIGN' MEAT

Although further back in our history farmers wasted nothing and almost certainly kept male dairy calves to rear for meat, in the more recent past veal has widely been seen as a 'foreign' meat and all the veal that was eaten, mainly for the restaurant trade, was imported from abroad, usually Holland, usually from crated systems. Perhaps due to heightened sensitivity to animal welfare issues in Britain, and probably also because the market for British veal was pretty well non-existent and so no commercial interests were threatened, the UK was the first country to ban the infamous veal crate in 1990. A Europe-wide ban did not come into force until 2007.

Despite the fact that the veal crate is banned, the prejudice against eating veal that has been so strong in the UK and Ireland lingers on. While more adventurous meats such as rabbit and venison that were once considered to be minority tastes have become increasingly popular, veal is rarely seen on restaurant menus, unless they are of the old-school Italian variety. Of late, as more people have taken heed of arguments that we must improve our 'food security' and increase our self-sufficiency in food, veal is coming back into the frame as a meat of which we should eat more, not less. A growing number of farmers are sickened by the waste and needlessness of helping cows give birth, only to shoot their calves soon after, and struck by the pointlessness of sending calves abroad where they will most likely be reared for meat in worse conditions than they would have been at home. So they are hanging on to calves and raising them for veal, but because of the persistent taboo, they can struggle to sell it. By buying and eating humanely reared veal, you are helping to put an end to one of the most unsavoury aspects of modern dairying and encouraging farmers who are doing something progressive with their calves.

Where and when should I buy veal?

British veal is available all year round but not always easy to find. Some upmarket branches of supermarket chains stock it. Independent butchers do stock veal but check that it is British. It's easier to find veal either at farmers' markets or mail order, direct from the farm.

Will veal break the bank?

There are few bargains when it comes to veal although cheaper, slow-cook cuts such as shoulder and breast can be quite manageably priced and minced veal isn't prohibitive. Prime and popular cuts of veal, such as escalopes or shin (for osso bucco), are always expensive but cheaper cuts can be stretched out with other cheaper ingredients – such as mushrooms in a stroganoff. Calves liver is considered to be the finest liver you can eat and it is invariably expensive, but because it is particularly filling and satisfying, a little can be made to go a long way.

Rabbit

Forget any old prejudices about eating bunny. If you want lean, white, flavoursome meat from a healthy, free-ranging animal that has had a natural diet and a great life, wild rabbit is just the ticket.

It tastes like slightly gamey chicken and the flesh is more springy and athletic than chicken. Being lean, rabbit dries out easily, so it's important not to overcook it. The best meat is on the back legs and saddle. It should have a nice rosy pink colour and a fresh, clean smell. Don't accept any rabbit that smells 'high' or pungently gamey, or one with darkened or bruised flesh: it may have been badly shot, will not taste so good and may still contain tooth-cracking lead pellets.

Things to do with rabbit

- The laziest approach to a rabbit is the classic Italian *coniglio arrosto*, where you marinate rabbit joints (saddle and legs) in olive oil, white wine, garlic and herbs overnight, then roast them at a high temperature. For such a treatment, you will need a plump rabbit with pale flesh, free from any gamey whiff.

- It doesn't take much effort to brown rabbit joints and slowly braise them in a casserole with wine and/or water and lots of onions. When the weather is hostile, root vegetables should go into the pot, while in the brighter months a gently cooked rabbit almost sits up and begs to be accompanied by young vegetables: thin carrots, new white turnips and bright green peas or broad beans. At any time of year, finish off the stew with fistfuls of fresh herbs: parsley in winter, chervil and chives in summer.

- For those who fret about choking on a rabbit bone, recipes for potted rabbit rillettes, terrine or pâté mean the cook has done all the picking off of the meat in advance. Since rabbit is so lean, add fat – usually pork or, better still, duck or goose – to the mix, or it will be too dry.

- To make the classic *lapin à la moutarde*, braise joints in the oven with white wine and/or water with onions. When the meat is tender, take it out and bubble up the gravy until it thickens and reduces. Then add a very generous amount of smooth or coarse mustard and a liberal amount of crème fraîche and reduce the sauce again, before returning the meat to heat through. A sprinkling of fresh tarragon just before serving won't go amiss.

Is rabbit good for me?

Wild rabbit meat offers cheap, lean protein. What fat it does have has the health benefits associated with pasture-fed meat (an ideal configuration of omega-3 and omega-6 fatty acids). It is an excellent source of selenium, which may protect against cancer, and vitamin B12, which can help lower undesirable homocysteine that can build up in the blood. High levels of this substance are associated with an increased risk of heart attack and stroke. Vitamin B12 deficiency is quite common, especially among older people and vegetarians. Wild rabbit is a good source of phosphorous, which is needed for strong bones and teeth, and also contains useful amounts of iron, which helps prevents anaemia, and zinc, which supports the immune and reproductive systems.

When UK rabbit consumption dropped after the end of the Second World War, the rabbit population soared. By 1952, the British government decided to follow the lead of other governments worldwide that had a rabbit management problem, and introduce the deadly myxomatosis virus to control the population. As a result, 99 per cent of the country's 60 million rabbit population died within two years. The sight of dead 'myxie' rabbits with swollen eyelids became common in the countryside. A couple of years later, the rabbit population had bounced back and developed immunity to the virus but rabbit meat had become synonymous with disease and our taste for it further declined, a persistent prejudice that still lingers. These days, the only potential hazard associated with eating rabbit is swallowing a bone or breaking a tooth on a piece of shot. For this reason, use only cleanly shot rabbits and either remove small bones from cooked dishes or warn people to look out for them.

Where is rabbit from?

Britain is simply teeming with wild rabbits, an estimated 38 million or thereabouts, and their population grows by around 2 per cent every year. That old maxim 'breeding like rabbits' is apt. The female rabbit, or doe, is fabulously fertile. At six months old, she typically produces six different litters, each with five baby rabbits, all within one season. Half of her offspring will be females who in turn will breed within the same season. No factory farm could ever hope to match the natural reproduction rate of the wild rabbit.

Wild British and Irish rabbits live in colonies in underground tunnels (burrows or warrens) and particularly appreciate light sandy soil. They have a good life and a quick, clean death. Wild rabbits are killed when they come out of their burrows. Usually ferrets are sent down holes to make the rabbits bolt out. Once they emerge they are either shot or caught in nets and killed by hand by pulling (breaking) their necks, which results in instant death. Their lives begin and end in the field.

Imported farmed rabbits, on the other hand, may never leave their hutch and may be reared entirely indoors on grain and feed pellets. They have as little flavour as factory-farmed broiler chicken.

Is rabbit a green choice?

Rabbits emerge from their burrows to feed enthusiastically on any green, growing thing in sight. Their staple food is grass and wild pasture, but they are also partial to lush plants, kindly provided for them by obliging farmers. Whether it's wheat, barley, oats, potatoes, carrots or turnips, an army of rabbits can munch their way through them with gusto. It is thought that six rabbits eat as much as one sheep, and collectively they cause millions of pounds of damage to crops every year. A newly planted orchard of fruit trees is irresistible to rabbits – all those new sappy trees just waiting to be scoffed. To be blunt, as far as farmers and many country-dwellers are concerned, rabbits are a pest that needs to be controlled. Eating them is one way to do that.

Where and when should I buy rabbit?

Rabbits are always in season and are at their best eaten between three and four months old. At this age they are plump, their eyes are bright and they have plenty of white fat around the kidneys. They are best eaten as fresh as possible. Young rabbits are suitable for roasting. Older ones need slow cooking.

Wild rabbit is best bought from a game stall at a farmers' market or from a traditional butcher/game dealer. The British Association for Shooting and Conservation has a website that helps you find an experienced game dealer in your area: www.basc.org.uk/content/find_a_game_dealer

Supermarkets don't generally stock rabbit because it has been regarded as too challenging a meat to sell to the British, despite its popularity in Europe. But this may well change as the economic downturn has made people open to trying cheaper types of meat.

Will rabbit break the bank?

For thoughtful consumers who are trying to balance eating more ethically with soaring food prices, wild rabbit is rapidly coming into the frame as a wholesome alternative to chicken. Rabbit is the cheapest white meat around, a really good economical alternative at a fraction of the price of a well-reared chicken. Don't neglect the liver, heart and kidneys, which can be used in a terrine or lightly fried in a warm salad.

A SUBSISTENCE DIET DOWN THE CENTURIES

The rabbit is not native to Britain or Ireland and there is a debate as to whether it was first introduced by the Romans or the Normans, but it is thought that it was the latter who brought the practice of farming rabbits for fur and meat by marking out suitable sandy land that was easy to dig to make walled earthen banks to create enclosures or 'warrens'. These were run by 'warreners' who were employed to look after rabbit colonies by feeding them and protecting them from predators such as foxes.

The area in Britain that was most associated with rabbit-rearing in Norman times was East Anglia. Lakenheath in the Breckland had specially constructed warrens that extended for miles. Place names like Thetford Warren in Norfolk and Trowlesworthy Warren on Dartmoor originate from the association with the rabbit. Once introduced, escapee warren rabbits began colonizing Britain, constructing their own natural burrows in the wild, and became a welcome free food source for people living on a subsistence diet down the centuries.

We relied heavily on rabbit during the Second World War when rabbit pie was never off the menu because it was the only cheap and plentiful meat on offer, a situation immortalized in the lyrics of the Bud Flanagan and Chesney Allen wartime hit, 'Run Rabbit Run':

> On the farm, ev'ry Friday
> On the farm, it's rabbit pie day.

After the war, consumers, previously starved of choice, ditched rabbit and moved to meats that had been less available during the rationing years and therefore had more cachet, such as chicken. Now that chicken is tainted by association with factory-farming, rabbit is being rediscovered. It is increasingly popular on the menu of fine-dining restaurants and trendy gastropubs.

Sausages

If you want to start a heated debate, ask people to describe their perfect sausage. Almost everyone has an opinion on what kind of sausages they like best, their taste, their texture and the best way to cook them. But British and Irish sausage-eating habits do tend to have one thing in common. Our palate seems to prefer a softer, less meaty, more open-textured sausage than the bouncier, meatier Italian or French type, but one that is still considerably firmer than the spongier German frankfurter or knackwurst.

It is possible to make almost any sausage taste quite appealing, at least initially, by loading it up with flavourings and heaps of salt. This type of sausage is easily spotted if you check the ingredient listing. Go for those with a short list and avoid ones with long lists of obscure ingredients and additives that you do not recognize from home cooking.

Sausages are as variable as all the different companies and butchers that make them. Recipes differ radically, as do the types of meat (pork, beef, lamb, chicken, venison) and other ingredients used. There are still plenty of cheap and nasty bangers around that consist of factory-farmed meat, padded out with excessive salt and additives, but there is also an ever-growing number of better quality, more natural sausages, made with higher-welfare meat. More upmarket sausages should have a subtler, but satisfying taste that comes mainly from the meat and simple seasonings.

Don't prick sausages before cooking as this makes them less succulent. They are best gently fried – anything from twenty minutes to half an hour – so that they have nicely caramelized extremities, or grilled. Good-quality sausages should exude no water or white liquid when cooking, a sign that they contain excess water and polyphosphates. They should leave very little fat in the frying pan or grill tray either.

Things to do with sausages

- Ring the changes by serving sausages with a mash of beans (butter beans, cannellini or flageolets) flavoured with softly sweated onion and herbs, rather than the ubiquitous potato mash.

- Hot, well-browned chipolatas go well with chilled oysters served on the shell.

....

- For an easy cassoulet, make a tomato and bean stew, add slices of fried sausages and lardons of fatty bacon. Top this mixture with breadcrumbs, drizzle them with olive oil and bake until the breadcrumbs are crunchy and the juices bubble up from below.

....

- Sausages, both smoked and unsmoked, go well with warm sauerkraut, steamed or boiled waxy potatoes and mustard.

....

- Cold cooked sausages, along with lentils dressed with olive oil, lemon juice and chopped green herbs or baby leaf spinach, make a satisfying packed lunch.

Are sausages good for me?

....

Sausages have an unhealthy image. Sometimes this is deserved, sometimes it isn't. It is argued that because sausages make use of fatty cuts, they are automatically bad for you, but there is no good evidence to support the idea that saturated fat is harmful. There is, on the other hand, a growing body of research to suggest that natural saturated fats have many benefits, such as enhancing the immune system, strengthening bones by helping us absorb calcium and stiffening cell membrane.

The healthiness or otherwise of a meal using sausages depends on how you use them. A main course consisting of a pile of cheap, low-meat-content sausages with heaps of stodgy mashed potatoes and liberal squirts of sugary ketchup, or the classic British toad in the hole where sausages are baked in a white flour batter, doesn't have a lot to commend it in nutritional terms. However, a main course where a couple of sausages with a high meat content are flanked by a generous quantity of salads, cooked vegetables or beans and lentils, has quite a lot going for it.

Cheaper sausages often have excessive levels of salt to compensate for their low meat content, the high amount of rusk they contain and the all-round lack of character of their factory-farmed meat. Excessive salt is easily spotted in sausages: they leave you gasping with thirst. Over-salting is rarely a problem with the better, meat-rich sausages.

In its simplest, purest form, a sausage is just finely minced meat and fat, combined with seasonings and something that will bind the mixture, piped into a casing. High-quality sausage-makers use the traditional sort of casing made from the intestines of animals that have been cleaned, bleached and preserved in salt. Most industrial manufacturers use collagen casings that have been made from animal skin or cellulose from plant fibre.

Sausages can be made on a small-scale basis – in a butcher's shop, say – or on a mass-production scale in a factory. Pork is the most commonly used meat for sausage-making followed by beef, but in recent years sausages made from meats such as lamb, venison and wild boar have become more available.

At the top end of the market, there are 'premium' sausages. Often, but not always, these superior sausages come from more expensive organic, free-range, or higher-welfare British or Irish meat. But you can't take this for granted. Most sausages are still made from intensively farmed meat where the pigs have been reared indoors. Many manufacturers use even cheaper, lower-welfare, factory-farmed meat, usually pork imported from Holland and Denmark. Confusingly, sausages can be sold as 'product of UK' even if the meat was imported. So, if you want to be sure that yours were made in the UK using British or Irish pork, only buy sausages that state that fact clearly on the label.

The term 'sausage' is best thought of as a fairly indiscriminate catch-all term that covers very different qualities of product. As a rule of thumb, the single most helpful indicator of how a sausage has been produced is its meat content.

The meat content of sausages varies considerably. A high-quality sausage should contain 85–90 per cent meat and a middle-market sausage around 65 per cent.

The minimum legal amount of pork in a product labelled as a pork sausage is 42 per cent. Anything labelled as a 'sausage', 'breakfast sausage' or 'chipolata' must have 32 per cent. For a product labelled as a beef, lamb or venison sausage, the minimum legal amount of meat is 30 per cent. The lowest meat sausage is anything labelled as a poultry sausage: 26 per cent.

When it is used in a sausage, by law, meat can include fat and connective tissue, what's known in the butcher's trade as 'broke' – bits of meat left over from normal butchery such as skin, jowl, ligaments, tendons and gristle. In a pork sausage, for instance, the meat element can be made up of 30 per cent fat and 25 per cent connective tissue, while in a beef or lamb sausage it can be up to 25 per cent fat and 25 per cent connective tissue.

It used to be perfectly legal to use mechanically recovered meat (MRM) – a low-grade meat sludge sprayed and sucked off already butchered carcasses – without declaring it on the label. Now MRM must be listed as a separate ingredient, 'recovered meat', and cannot be included in the meat content. The same goes for organs such as heart or tongue.

Sausages with a high meat content do not usually contain connective tissue; instead the meat is a mixture of lean and fat cuts of meat. In a pork sausage, for instance, a mixture of belly and shoulder is used.

Irrespective of the proportion of meat they contain, all sausages contain either breadcrumbs or more usually rusk (dried, crushed, yeast-free bread made from wheat flour, salt, bicarbonate of soda and water). This is added with anything from one to two times the amount of water to bind the sausage together and make it succulent. If a sausage was made just from meat, it would be too dry. In poorer-quality sausages, however, much larger amounts of rusk and water are used as bulking agents to pad out the product. Up to 10 per cent of a sausage can be water without listing water as an ingredient on the label. A really good-quality sausage should contain no more than 10 per cent rusk.

Almost all sausages, unless they are home-made, also contain a nitrate preservative, because without one they would have a shelf life of just two or three days. Some sausage-makers do sell preservative-free sausages that need to be cooked within a day or so, or frozen.

Sausages of all qualities are seasoned with salt. Good-quality sausages also contain herbs and sometimes spices, specially mixed for each recipe.

In addition, lower grade sausages also contain a long list of other ingredients and chemical additives, all well worth avoiding. These are extra fat (to fill out the sausage), sausage stabilizer (a mixture of lactose (milk sugar) and vegetable protein that gives a sweet and meaty flavour), sugars and caramel (to add flavour and give the mixture a brown colour), polyphosphates (to bind water and fat and increase weight), soya (to bulk out the sausage and retain fat), extra nitrate preservatives (to extend shelf life and give a pink colourant), antioxidants (to extend shelf life), colourings (to give a rosy hue to the grey meat), synthetic flavourings (including the controversial monosodium glutamate), natural flavourings (such as yeast extract, soy sauce, onion and garlic powder) and gum arabic or guar gum (to bind the mixture).

A MUCH RESPECTED NATIONAL DELICACY

Oh, how the British love their sausages or 'bangers' – the name they acquired during the Second World War because when they were fried they tended to explode with a bang.

Tales – apocryphal or otherwise – abound that in the past, British sausages have been seen by our butchers as a good way of getting rid of excess fat and parts of the animal that most view as less palatable. From the late 1980s, public anxiety that meat from cows infected with BSE (mad cow disease) was finding its way into processed meat products made many people deeply suspicious of what went into their sausages.

Now the public relations profile of the British sausage has bounced back with a vengeance. Bangers have been reinvented and are no longer seen as some potentially dodgy, cheap meat product, but a much respected national delicacy.

Are sausages a green choice?

In recent years, chefs and environmentalists have highlighted the amount of food that is wasted and been critical of the relatively modern tendency to seek out prime lean cuts of meat and discard other parts of the carcase, however edible. Sausages are one good way of using up wholesome, but neglected cuts.

Buying sausages from local farmers and butchers using local meat cuts down on the unnecessary food miles a sausage travels. The UK and Ireland have many high-quality, small-scale sausage-makers.

Where should I buy sausages?

The worst-quality sausages – those with little meat, lots of fat and additives – are commonly found in economy ranges in supermarkets and frozen food shops. Although there are exceptions, independent butchers do not tend to use the gamut of cheap ingredients, such as recovered meat and additives, that you find in the mass-produced, industrial sort. One of the best places to buy sausages is at farmers' markets, which generally have a better range of sausages made from different kinds of meat, such as venison, wild boar and rare-breed pork, and offer a wider selection of sausages made to interesting recipes than supermarkets.

Will sausages break the bank?

That old maxim, 'You get what you pay for' was never truer than when applied to a sausage. Buying cheap sausages means you will get low-grade specimens that represent rotten value for money. Top-quality sausages cost considerably more, but they still make for a relatively low-cost meal.

Dairy

3

Milk and cream

(cow's, sheep's, goat's and buffalo's)

If you are content with milk that tastes like white water, then there's a lot of that around. If, on the other hand, you're looking for milk with some intrinsic flavour, a pleasing viscosity and richness, then you may need to look a little further. Of all our staple foods, milk is the one that has changed dramatically. Until the 1960s, our milk was slightly golden in colour and creamy. Today, most of the milk we consume resembles watered-down whitewash and tastes as though it has had a flavour bypass. This is largely because most of the personality in milk lies in the creamy fat. Remove that, and it becomes a shadow of its former self. If you buy skimmed or semi-skimmed milk, your milk will instantly have less character. So go for full-fat, whole milk if taste matters to you.

The character of whole, that is, full-fat cow's milk differs slightly, depending on the animal and breed it comes from. Cow's milk is quite neutral and a little sweet. Most of the cow's milk we consume comes from Holstein or Holstein-Friesian herds. It is usually whiter, and less cream-coloured and creamy-tasting than milk from traditional dairy breeds such as Jersey, Ayrshire or Guernsey, which is often sold as 'breakfast milk'. Buffalo milk tastes like a creamier, richer version of cow's milk. Goat's milk and sheep's milk have a more pronounced flavour than cow's milk and can be more of an acquired taste. Whole milk from grass-fed animals can vary in richness depending on the time of year, and the lushness or otherwise of the land the animals are grazing.

Processing radically alters the flavour and consistency of milk. The most decisive intervention is pasteurization – heating the milk to a high temperature for a short time. Pasteurization kills off most of the beneficial bacteria and volatile aromas that give raw (unpasteurized) milk its flavour. If you have ever had the pleasure and privilege of tasting raw milk, then you will know that it has a much fuller, more complex taste.

Homogenization also makes a huge difference to the character of milk. In its natural, unhomogenized state, the cream in milk would gradually rise to the surface and accumulate, so you get that old-fashioned 'top of the milk' where there is a visibly thicker, creamier layer of milk at the neck of the bottle and a more liquid one below. But these days, because many consumers are unfamiliar with milk in its natural state and might mistake any visible cream as a sign that the milk is off, most milk is homogenized; that is, the fat globules have been processed so that they are redistributed evenly throughout the milk, making for a more even consistency. Unhomogenized milk is labelled as such and some brands use this as a selling point. It usually comes from traditional breeds of cows and is sold in bottles, not cartons, so that the cream on top of the milk is visible. Sheep's, goat's and buffalo's milks are naturally homogenized because the fat globules are smaller than those in cow's milk and evenly dispersed throughout the milk.

Most cow's milk is also 'standardized', a process that separates the fat from the more liquid milk then puts it back together to achieve a standard fat content. UHT (Ultra Heat Treated) and sterilized milk have been heated to high temperatures using an extreme form of pasteurization to kill off almost all bacteria. This means that they can be stored for long periods at room temperature without going off. These heat-treated milks have a distinct 'cooked' taste and smell which some people like, but which is totally different from other milk.

Cream varies markedly in taste terms. Cream from traditional breeds of cows with richer milk, and cows that have been grass-fed, generally looks more golden and less white than the snowy-white cream of Holstein-type cows that are fed mainly on cereals, and has a superior flavour. Crème fraîche and sour cream have a slightly sharp edge because lactic bacteria are added. Clotted cream has an appealing crust and a taste reminiscent of evaporated milk because the cream has been scalded.

Things to do with milk and cream

- Taking the trouble to warm your milk makes mashed potatoes extra unctuous. Cold milk can turn the mash gluey, rather than smooth and fluffy.

- The Tuscan *arista di maiale al latte* – a joint of pork slowly cooked in milk with herbs and garlic – gives melting, tender meat and demonstrates how a stove-top pot roast can rival the oven equivalent.

- A little milk or cream will fix many soups and soften and mellow meats, as in the classic Bolognese ragù.

- Crème brûlée made with slightly sharp crème fraîche is less cloying and rich than one made with double cream.

....

- Don't throw away slightly sour milk that's a day past its 'use-by' date. It's brilliant for making Irish soda bread and airy drop scones.

....

- Make quivering pannacotta (milk, cream and sugar set with leaf gelatine) fragrant by flavouring it with a little rose water. Marvellous with a rhubarb and rose water compote.

Are milk and cream good for me?
....

Milk is a straightforward, natural food that has been in our diet for centuries. It is one of the most nutritionally complete foods around and comes in a convenient form. It is a good source of protein, which helps the body regenerate; vitamin A, which strengthens immunity to infections and helps vision; vitamin B1, which is needed for healing and maintaining the nervous system; vitamin B2, which is needed for metabolizing food; and B12, which as well as helping brain function and providing energy, helps lower levels of undesirable homocysteine that can build up in the blood. High levels of this substance are associated with an increased risk of heart attack and stroke. Vitamin B12 deficiency is quite common, especially among older people and vegetarians. Milk is an important dietary source of vitamin D. This increasingly looks like a vitamin of which we need more. It is thought that many British and Irish people may have insufficient levels. Vitamin D deficiency may be linked to increased risk of heart disease, auto-immune diseases such as multiple sclerosis, and certain cancers. It also contains some vitamin E, which helps neutralize the effects of free radicals that could predispose the body to disease, and vitamin K, which is needed for healthy bones. Milk is also a good source of several minerals, notably calcium, which is needed for healthy teeth and bones. Sheep's and buffalo's milks contain more calcium than cow's or goat's.

Many people have been put off whole milk and cream because it contains saturated fat and cholesterol. Contrary to the public health dogma that has prevailed over the last few decades, there is no good evidence to support the idea that saturated fat is harmful. There is, on the other hand, a growing body of research to suggest that natural saturated fats, such as those found in milk and cream, have many benefits, such as enhancing the immune system and strengthening bones by helping us absorb calcium and stiffening cell membrane. It is increasingly accepted too that eating cholesterol in food such as milk does not lead to clogged arteries and heart disease. Cholesterol is a vital component of cell membranes, and among other things it helps the body heal and repair, supports brain function and allows the body to make vitamin D and certain hormones.

Even supposing you do want to eat less fat, whole, full-fat milk is not a high-fat food. Cow's milk usually contains between 3.7 and 5 per cent fat if it is made with richer cow's milk such as Jersey. Whole goat's, sheep's and buffalo's milks are a little richer containing around 7 per cent, 6 per cent and 8 per cent respectively. Semi-skimmed and skimmed cow's milk contains 1.0–1.5 per cent and 0.1 per cent fat respectively, so by switching to semi-skimmed or skimmed the reduction in your fat consumption is pretty negligible. Unless you drink gallons of milk, changing to lower-fat milks is unlikely to make any great impact on your fat intake.

Skimmed and semi-skimmed cow's milk is also less nutritious than whole milk because the fat-soluble vitamins A, D, E and K in milk are in the cream, and thus removed when this is skimmed off.

Several scientific studies have now supported the idea that organic milk is more nutritious than the non-organic equivalent. They have found that whole, organic cow's milk has more fat-soluble nutrients – omega-3 fatty acid, vitamin E and beta-carotene – than non-organic milk, as well as a healthier omega 3:6 ratio. This ratio is important because it is thought that many people today don't get enough omega-3 fats and consume far too many damaged omega-6 fats, mainly in processed foods. The ideal ratio is 1:1. One of these scientific studies found that organic cow's milk has on average 68 per cent higher levels of omega-3s than non-organic. Researchers are still exploring why this might be the case but one theory is that it is because organic cows graze on pastures sown with clovers, which act as natural nitrogen fixers, rather than those that are sown with one or two types of quick-growing grass and grown with the aid of synthetic nitrogen fertilizers and weedkillers.

There is also research that suggests that milk from free-range, grass-fed animals – organic or otherwise – has higher levels of vitamins and a superior fatty acid profile to that produced by animals kept indoors and fed on dried animal feedstuffs made from cereals and soya. In particular, grass-fed cows produce milk with higher amounts of the omega-3 CLA (conjugated linoleic acid), which is thought to reduce the risk of cancer. Grain-fed cows produce milk higher in less desirable omega-6 fatty acid and lower in more desirable omega-3 fatty acid. Sheep, goats and buffaloes kept for milk in the UK and Ireland are usually free-range and grass-fed, so it is likely that their milk has similar nutritional benefits to grass-fed cow's milk.

In recent times, cow's milk has emerged as a source of food intolerance. The theory is that some people find milk hard to digest and that this could be triggering conditions such as catarrh, asthma and eczema and some research does support this. In the past, cow's milk was not associated with these conditions in European countries although many Asian countries have higher levels of milk intolerance. Increased reporting of cow's milk intolerance in the UK and Ireland may simply be a result of heightened awareness, but it could also be connected with the fact that more of the milk we consume these days comes from grain-fed, rather than grass-fed animals. People who think they suffer from cow's milk intolerance may like to consider drinking only whole cow's milk from grass-fed and/or organic cows, or trying sheep's, goat's or buffalo's milk.

The healthiness, or otherwise, of raw, unpasteurized 'green top' milk is hotly contested. In England, Wales and Ireland it is still possible, although not easy, to buy raw milk for drinking, and it must be sold with a rather alarming cigarette packet-style health warning that reads: 'This product has not been heat-treated and may contain organisms harmful to health'. Raw milk for drinking is banned in Scotland, however.

Milk is pasteurized both to extend its shelf life and as a broad-brush safety measure. The health establishment's view is that because milk is often consumed uncooked, pasteurization is a necessary blanket safety measure against bad bacteria that could be lethal if the milk had been produced in dirty conditions. Advocates of unpasteurized milk argue that farms producing raw milk are more frequently and stringently checked by public health authorities, and must conform to higher hygiene standards than those producing pasteurized milk, as they cannot rely on pasteurization to kill off any harmful bacteria.

Advocates of raw milk also point out that pasteurization is a fairly brutal, blanket treatment that denatures milk, diminishing its nutritional qualities. Pasteurization reduces levels of some vitamins, destroys vitamins B6 and B12, denatures the proteins that carry nutrients in the bloodstream, and kills off bacteria that are beneficial to health. It has been suggested that raw, unpasteurized dairy products are much easier to digest and generally healthier. Some research has found that drinking raw milk can reduce certain allergic conditions and suggested that exposure to the healthy bacteria in raw milk strengthens the immune system. Another theory is that the switch away from the consumption of raw milk from grass-fed cows to pasteurized milk from grain-fed cows goes some way to explaining the modern rise in reports of milk intolerance. Public health bodies insist, however, that the nutritional benefits of drinking raw milk are outweighed by the food safety risks.

Some opponents of dairy production say that milk is full of pus and a hazard to health. What they are referring to is traces of pus-like white blood (somatic) cells in milk. Such cells are naturally present in cows' udders but at very low levels. When cows are suffering from an udder infection (mastitis), or when milk is produced in unhygienic conditions, then high levels of contamination with these cells can occur. All milk has to be tested regularly to check that the level of somatic cells never creeps above the level deemed acceptable by regulatory authorities. Farmers are paid less for milk with high somatic cell counts so there is a financial incentive to keep such contamination in check, but critics of dairy farming argue that the levels permitted are too high.

This tainted milk should never find its way into the milk supply because milk with higher levels should be discarded. There are, however, concerns that among intensively farmed dairy herds levels of sub-clinical mastitis are so high that milk from affected cows not showing obvious symptoms could pass into the general milk supply.

If you are concerned about this issue, choose organic milk. Raised cell counts are most likely to occur in intensively farmed herds where animals are more prone to mastitis because they are under constant pressure to produce high milk yields.

How are milk and cream produced?

The nursery-book image of Daisy, the dairy cow, chewing away contentedly in a grassy meadow, no longer gives the flavour of modern dairying. In the last few decades, pressure from supermarkets for cheap milk has encouraged the creeping industrialization of UK and Irish dairy production. Thousands of small dairy farms have gone to the wall as farmers have come under sustained economic pressure. For some years now, dairy farmers have had to sell their milk to processors acting on behalf of supermarkets for what it costs them to produce, or frequently less. One way for dairy farmers to try to increase profits and reduce production costs is to use more intensive methods. While a hundred or so cows were once considered to be a good-sized herd, there is strong economic pressure coming from some farmers to open US-style 'mega-dairies' that would house thousands of cows, either on a 'zero-grazing' (the cows never get out to grass) or limited grazing basis. Already, British and Irish milk comes from fewer cows on fewer farms than ever before, and this has transformed the nature of dairying.

In the past, dairying was based on traditional breeds of cow, such as the Jersey, Friesian, Guernsey and Ayrshire, breeds that were well suited to free-range production. They spent from Easter until autumn grazing out on pasture and then came into barns in winter where they were bedded on straw. Nowadays, such herds have been widely replaced by bigger, more productive cows by breeding the traditional Friesian cow with a modern 'extreme' dairy breed from the US – the Holstein. This 'super-cow' is genetically selected to produce a much higher milk yield, especially when fed on high-protein foods made from grains and soya.

On some of the most 'productive' farms, these cows are managed so that they lactate for ten months of the year. They are kept in individual cubicles, often on slatted metal or concrete floors (to make cleaning easier) and only go out briefly, even in summertime, their only exercise being walking to and from the milking parlour. A minority of dairy farms already operate zero-grazing systems where cows are housed permanently indoors.

The prodigious milk output of modern Holstein-type cows comes at a price. They are treated as high-yielding milk machines and pushed beyond their metabolic limits. In contrast to the neat udders of traditional dairy breeds, which were in proportion to their bodies, Holstein-type cows often have visibly heavy, bulging udders because they have been bred to produce so much milk. The excess weight of these distended udders makes it difficult for the cow to walk, so many suffer from painful lameness. This can be exacerbated when confined cows are standing indoors for hours at a time in their own slurry. At any one time, over 20 per cent of cows are lame. Mastitis, brought on by a range of factors, including over-production, is also a common ailment in intensive dairy herds and so cows often need repeat treatment with antibiotics. Longer term, the intense physiological pressure put on cows by such intensive milk production means that they are worn out after four years of milking and have to be slaughtered because their yield drops. In the natural order of things, cows would live for up to twelve years.

If animal welfare is an important concern for you, then buy milk direct from smaller scale dairy farmers who guarantee that their cows are out on pasture for a good part of the year, or choose organic. Organic cows are always put out to graze when the weather allows and kept in smaller herds. When bad weather keeps them inside, they are loose housed (able to walk about) and bedded on straw. Organic cows graze on organic land that has not been treated with synthetic fertilizers or pesticides and great emphasis is put on keeping them on rich pasture that contains diverse types of grass, clovers, flowers and herbs because this helps keep cows healthy and makes for better, more nutritious milk. Organic cows must get most of their food from grazing and any dry food must be either organic, or from a small number of permitted natural sources. GM feed is not permitted. The more natural diet of organic cows means that the cows have a lower milk yield, so are put under less physical strain.

This kind of milk and cream goes straight from the farm to the public or retailer, so farmers have a strong incentive to produce to the highest standard because their reputation is on the line. These days, many on-farm dairies have closed down and most farmers, conventional or otherwise, send their milk to a central milk processing facility where it is pooled with milk from many other farms. This sort of milk is picked up in milk tankers that drive around various farms and can be stored for some hours at the processing plant, so it may not be quite so fresh. Furthermore, individual farmers have less of a stake in it because it is a mixture from many sources.

In 2010 it came to light that a small quantity of milk (and beef) from cloned dairy cattle has found its way into the British food chain. Cloning is a relatively new, highly controversial technology that raises many issues and entails extreme animal suffering (see BEEF/How is beef farmed?). If you want to be extra sure that you are not consuming milk from cloned animals or their progeny, choose organic milk. Organic standards do not permit cloning.

Are milk and cream green choices?

The British Isles and Ireland have abundant green pastures and plentiful rain, making them ideal for dairy production. When dairying is conducted in an extensive way – that is, when the cows spend most of the year outdoors, feeding on pasture – then milk production fits in well with sustainable farming as the cows can convert something we humans can't eat – grass – into one that we can: milk. Hardy sheep, goats and buffaloes are particularly good at converting poor-quality foraged food on rough pasture into milk.

Grassy pastures that are used for grazing dairy animals, year in, year out, act as carbon sinks, cleaning up the atmosphere. If these permanent pastures were to be dug up and planted with other food crops, this stored carbon would be released into the environment, so contributing to global warming.

Most traditional farming systems work on the principle of a mixed farm, one that combines both livestock and crop production. On a mixed farm, dairy animals yield milk and eventually meat, all the time producing manure that can be used as a natural fertilizer for other food crops, so the farmer does not need to buy in chemical fertilizers from further afield. In an ideal model for a sustainable farm, cows or other dairy animals are part of a self-sufficient biological loop. They feed on pasture and leftover by-products of food crops, converting these into human food and producing manure to nourish other crops destined for humans.

In the UK, the industrialization of farming means that there are considerably fewer mixed farms than there were in the past. Many cows are farmed on dairy-only farms. On the most environmentally aware of these farms, the cows will feed outside on pasture, only coming in for milking, until the growth of the grass slows down and the weather becomes extremely cold. Then they will be brought indoors and fed on hay and home-grown, preserved grass (silage) until the grass starts growing again and the weather warms up.

On more intensive dairy farms, cows spend most of their lives indoors, and in the case of a minority of zero-grazed herds, never go out. Dairy cows kept this way are fed on large volumes of feed concentrates, usually derived from grains and soya. Most of the world's soya crop is GM. Even though your milk doesn't say GM on the label, unless it is organic, there is a high chance that it comes from cows fed on GM feed. Genetic modification is an imprecise and poorly tested technology that mixes genes across the species barrier. It has the capacity to trigger unwelcome changes that could have very negative impacts on the environment, animal and human health.

The bought-in feeds based on cereals that are used to nourish indoor cows are also of concern to environmentalists because, unlike pasture, these foods could be consumed by humans. In other words, there is competition between humans and animals for these food resources. They argue that it just doesn't make sense to feed grains and soya to livestock so that they can produce milk for people when it would be more efficient to use them to feed people directly. This argument seems ever more pertinent with a growing world population and mounting global anxieties that the world won't be able to produce enough food to feed everyone.

Intensive dairy farms can also be notoriously polluting. Large numbers of cows produce substantial amounts of manure and urine, and whereas on mixed farms this nitrogen-rich waste can be used as fertilizer, many large-scale dairy operations do not have sufficient land to use all the manure they generate so it has to be disposed of by some other route. This waste is usually held in slurry tanks before being spread on fields or diluted and sprayed over a larger area of land. Unless very carefully controlled, the over-abundance of nitrogenous nutrients in this slurry can contaminate both surface and underground water that feed the public water supply as a result of seepage, spills or even just heavy rain. Nitrogen-containing pollutants turn up quite commonly in drinking water. Excessive ammonia from dairy cows' urine can also make land too acid.

The near disappearance of the returnable glass pinta bottle for selling milk has had negative consequences for the environment. These bottles were environmentally friendly because they could be reused many times, and, once they were too well-used, recycled. The move away from these to other types of packaging has generated unprecedented volumes of waste milk cartons and plastic bottles, most of which end up on landfill sites. Some farm shops also sell milk in strong, but biodegradable bags that can be opened and decanted into a jug. This progressive form of milk packaging deserves to become much more widespread.

Where and when should I buy milk and cream?

Cow's and buffalo's milks are available all year, while sheep's and goat's milks are more seasonal, generally most obtainable in spring and summer. Raw, unpasteurized milk and cream can be bought in England, but only direct from the producer. Farmers' markets or farm shops are the best place to find them. For a list of raw milk producers see: http://www. natural foodfinder.co.uk/unpasteurised-raw-milk-uk and http://www. seedsofhealth.co.uk/resources/dairy/index.shtml

Cow's milk used to feature much more prominently in our diets than it does today. We woke up to the chink of the milkman's cart and the arrival of the doorstep pinta. The UK and Ireland had lots of small dairy farms, most of which did their own bottling and many also operated doorstep deliveries. Milk was a staple food in our diet and quite commonly drunk with meals. In primary schools, a third of a pint of milk, first in a glass bottle, then in a carton, was every child's break-time snack. Cow's milk was widely recommended as a good food for children because it aids growth, building strong bones and teeth. We were encouraged to 'Drinka Pinta Milka Day' to stay healthy. The crime writer Agatha Christie was a famous advocate of both the health properties and taste of cream. She liked to eat some cream every day and painted her house in Devon cream because it was her favourite colour.

Milk has become much less prominent in our diets with the dominance of the debatable government health orthodoxy that saturated fat is bad, and to be avoided. This put a question mark over whole milk in many people's minds and many switched from milk as a drink to supposedly healthier alternatives like fruit drinks, and for general use changed to skimmed or semi-skimmed.

In tandem with this, the arrival of centralized supermarket chains and their buying power in the market sounded the death knell for small farms with on-farm dairies producing milk with character. The daily, fresh doorstep pinta filled with milk that was only hours old from a named local farm became a thing of the past. Milk became an anonymous product of unknown pedigree that you buy in bulk from the supermarket and which will last you for days at a time, the only thing to watch out for on the label being whether it is full-fat or not. As a result, we now know much less about the origins of our milk, and drink milk that is less fresh and has travelled much further than it did before.

In some rural areas it is still possible to find cow's milk from small farms with dairies that deal direct with the public, either delivering milk to the doorstep or selling at a farmers' market or farm shop. This type of milk is a precious rarity and very well worth seeking out.

In the past, we had no tradition of drinking sheep's, goat's or buffalo's milk. The revival of artisan cheesemaking that has taken place in the UK and Ireland in the last few decades has seen cheesemakers look to the Continent and start to make cheese using these milks, and the wider potential of these animals as a source of liquid milk has been recognized. Sheep's, goat's and buffalo's milks remain a minority taste, but are becoming increasingly available and represent a viable alternative for those who suffer from intolerance to cow's milk.

Will milk and cream break the bank?

Grassy green pasture is the natural diet for cows, sheep, goats and buffaloes. Milk from pasture-reared animals is more expensive than that from grain-fed animals, mainly because the milk yield is lower. This is why milk from grass-fed and organic animals costs 20–25 per cent more than the basic milk from intensively farmed cows, but is still a relatively affordable purchase.

Butter, ghee and buttermilk

Butter is a versatile natural fat that graces everything it touches. It blends with other ingredients, both savoury and sweet, and enhances, even transforms them. Not for nothing is the adjective 'buttery' always taken as a compliment.

Butter tastes different depending on whether it is 'sweet' cream butter, 'lactic', also known as 'cultured' or 'ripened' butter, or whey butter. All types of butter are sold in unsalted or salted forms. Sweet cream butter has a neutral, fatty character, which is why many people prefer it salted. The majority of butter made and sold in the UK, and from New Zealand, is of this type. Lactic butter, which is more popular in Europe, has a milkier flavour and a slightly sharper edge that comes from the gentle fermentation that occurs when natural bacteria convert milk sugars into lactic acid. The process produces additional aroma compounds that produce a fuller flavoured result. Whey butter has a lower fat content and a cheesier, stronger taste. If you are unaccustomed to this, it can be confused with rancidity. Ghee is simply the Indian form of clarified butter – butter fat with almost all the milk solids skimmed off. It is very handy for frying. Buttermilk is the slightly sour tasting residual liquid or 'milk' left over once butter is churned.

Butter made from cream from cows kept in a shed and fed on concentrated animal feeds won't taste the same as 'free-range' or organic butters where cows are primarily pasture-fed, grazing on different grasses, clovers and green plants. The breed of cow also affects the taste of butter. Ayrshire and Jersey cows, for instance, produce a richer, yellower butter than those from the more common Holstein-Friesian herds.

Things to do with butter

- Peppery radishes, served with chilled unsalted butter and a small pile of sea salt crystals, make an effortless but elegant summer starter.

- Melted butter, allowed to sizzle to a nutty brown, then teamed with rinsed, chopped capers and a spritz of lemon juice, makes a simple grilled fish shine.

- A knob of butter stirred into a risotto at the end of cooking adds a glossy richness and improves the texture.

- A cheese sandwich can be rendered delicious by buttering it on the outside, then grilling it on a ridged, cast-iron grill for a couple of minutes on each side.

- Make a beurre blanc to accompany asparagus, sprouting broccoli or fish by bubbling up vinegar and black pepper with a little chopped shallot or onion until the liquid has almost evaporated, then swirling in cubes of chilled butter until you have an emulsion. Add herbs (chives, chervil, tarragon or basil are all good) to taste.

- Butter is the star ingredient that turns a load of stale bread and a little milk into velvety, light bread and butter pudding.

- For a lighter pannacotta, use half and half buttermilk and cream.

- For cooking, use unsalted butter. Salted butter – especially the sort with whole flakes of salt swirled throughout – is magnificent with good bread and briny oysters.

Are butter, ghee and buttermilk good for me?

In recent years, butter has become a dietary bogeyman because it contains saturated fat and cholesterol. While most people agree that it tastes better than margarines and spreads, many avoid it on health grounds. Indeed the UK Food Standards Agency advises us that: 'Margarine tends to contain unsaturated fats, which are generally better for us than the saturated fats found in butter.'

But the butter versus margarine debate is more complicated than that and butter's nutritional image is being rehabilitated. The simplistic theory that cholesterol eaten in food increases the incidence of heart disease is being revised. Cholesterol is a vital component of every cell membrane. Without cholesterol, the body cannot make certain hormones – cortisol, oestrogen and testosterone. If cholesterol is too low, the body may not be able to use the sun to make sufficient amounts of vitamin D.

The saturated-fat-is-bad mantra is melting away also. Several major scientific studies have failed to find evidence that reducing saturated fat intake significantly reduces your risk of heart disease, or cancer, or showed that saturated fat consumption causes weight gain. Increasingly, it is thought that natural saturated fats, like butter, can form a useful role in the diet because they satisfy the appetite and help stave off feelings of hunger. And as the case against butter softens, the case against the fats in spreads and margarines is firming up. Researchers are addressing the theory that a surfeit of polyunsaturated fats, of the type found in abundance in margarines and spreads, might be a risk factor for heart disease and type 2 diabetes.

Quite apart from being satisfying, butter has many nutritional strengths. It is one of the best sources of easily absorbed vitamin A, which is thought to be protective against heart disease, helps vision, aids the absorption of calcium and supports the thyroid and adrenal glands. Butter also contains vitamins E, K and D, which many Britons don't get enough of, and useful trace minerals. In particular, it is a very rich source of selenium, which may be protective against cancer.

Butter offers a good balance of omega-3 and omega-6 fatty acids deemed essential, among other things, for brain function and healthy skin. It is rich in short- and medium-chain fatty acids. These have strong anti-cancer properties as well as anti-fungal effects, which means that they may help prevent conditions such as candida and thrush. Butter also contains conjugated linoleic acid (CLA), which may protect against cancer, along with glycospingolipids, a type of fatty acids that protect against gastro-intestinal infection. In traditional Indian Ayurvedic medicine ghee is recommended for its digestibility. And some research suggests that butter protects against tooth decay.

Organic butter may be better for you. Several academic studies have found that organic milk has more vitamins, and a better balance of fatty acids, than the conventional sort (see MILK AND CREAM/Are milk and cream good for me?).

How are butter, ghee and buttermilk made?

Butter is a straightforward food. It is made by churning; that is, continuously agitating cream until it forms fat globules. The cream separates into butter and buttermilk. The latter is drained off and sold as a product in its own right, often to make Irish soda bread, scones or pancakes.

Sweet butter is made using fresh cream. Lactic butter comes in two types. The more artisan method is to allow the cream to sit for a few days until it naturally ripens and slightly ferments, developing natural lactic acids similar to those in yogurt. Larger-scale butter-makers usually add lactic acids to fresh cream to get that slightly sharp tang, but faster. Whey butters made from cream skimmed from whey, rather than milk, is usually a by-product of cheesemaking.

Anything from 1.5 to 3 per cent salt can be added to any type of butter, depending on whether you choose slightly salted or salted. Salt acts as a preservative in sweet butter, making it last much longer than it otherwise would. The acids in lactic butters do the same job. Without added salt, sweet butters would go rancid, so if sweet butter is to be sold unsalted, it is given a longer life by beating out all the whey – that's the milk solids left over after the cream is separated from the milk – and replacing these with fresh water.

True butter remains naturally solid in all but the hottest weather without any technological intervention. Easier spreading butter is a product devised to compete with the perceived convenience of spreads by remaining softer at colder temperatures so it spreads thinly straight from the refrigerator. Butter can be made spreadable in a number of different ways. Cows can be fed on a diet that is rich in oil seeds so that the fat in their cream has a softer consistency, vegetable oil or air can be incorporated into the butter, or softer 'fractions' of the fat can be separated out from the harder fats then recombined with a reduced proportion of the harder fats.

Ghee, or clarified butter, is useful in cooking and keeps longer. It is butter that has had almost all of its water and milk solids removed, leaving more or less pure butterfat. It has a very high burning point, which makes it handy, as it doesn't burn or smoke during cooking.

Are butter, ghee and buttermilk green choices?

See MILK AND CREAM/Are milk and cream green choices?

Will butter, ghee and buttermilk break the bank?

Apart from the gimmicky ones that trumpet special health benefits, spreads and margarines are cheaper than butter, but they are poor in taste, will give you less delicious results in baking and cannot always be used successfully as a substitute in recipes that call for butter.

Lactic butters, made in the traditional way by allowing cream to ripen naturally, are considered to be gourmet butters and can cost anything from 50 to 100 per cent more than standard, mass-market butters. More commercial lactic butters made by adding lactic acids to fresh cream, and organic sweet milk butters, are quite affordable.

You may use more butter than you need to if you are in the habit of storing it in the refrigerator. This makes it harder to spread thinly. In most parts of Britain and Ireland, in all but the hottest weather or overheated houses, there is no need to refrigerate butter. Covered, it will keep for weeks at room temperature and remain spreadable anyway. If you forget to leave butter out of the fridge, you can soften it up to a consistency suitable for baking. Just put the packet, still in its wrapper, on a flat surface, cover with a clean tea towel, and whack it hard several times with a rolling pin. Check it from time to time until you have beaten it into the required soft state. If you do keep butter in the fridge, make sure that it is well covered, preferably in a dish with a lid. Butter can pick up a taint from other strong flavours in the fridge, such as onions or garlic.

AN ARTISAN BUTTER RENAISSANCE

Butter is one of Britain's most traditional foods. We may not have olive groves, but we do have dairy cows. It has been the fat of our land that has helped sustain us for centuries.

Before the advent of large-scale creameries, butter was made on the farm and in small dairies. Cream was accumulated from several days' milking and when there was enough to make the effort worthwhile, it was churned into butter. Since much of the accumulated cream was several days old, ripened and slightly fermented by the time it was made, it had a more pronounced, fuller flavour. The character of the butter varied much more than it does today, depending on the breed of cow, the time of year and the lushness, or otherwise, of the pasture.

With the closure of many on-farm dairies and the opening of large, centralized creameries pooling milk from many producers, and the supermarkets' demand for a standardized product, British butter became rather uniform as there was a wholesale shift away from farm-made lactic butter made with ripened milk to mass-produced sweet butter. British butter seemed a rather lacklustre product, and chefs and food lovers tended to favour continental lactic butters that had more intrinsic taste and personality. Artisan British and Irish butter is enjoying something of a renaissance, however, as some small producers are finding a market for more flavoursome butters with an interesting pedigree.

Yogurt and yogurt drinks

Some people screw up their faces at the thought of eating plain yogurt, but if you get a good one it can be one of the most agreeable, yet simplest of foods, offering a pleasing, chalky creaminess cut by a clean, fresh acidity. No well-made natural yogurt should be unpalatably sour or tart, and should be pleasant to eat on its own without the addition of sugar. The acid test of any brand of yogurt is the intrinsic quality of the plain, natural version. There are too many distracting ingredients in flavoured versions to form any clear impression of the basic yogurt.

Yogurt is one of the most useful foods to keep in the fridge, with a vast array of savoury and sweet uses. Put it this way: with a pot of yogurt in the fridge and a few basic storecupboard ingredients, you'll never starve.

Although whole milk (full-fat) yogurts are outnumbered on our shelves by lower fat ones, yogurt made with whole milk will have a better essential taste because much of the flavour in milk comes from the fat, so flavour is impaired when the fat is skimmed off. Avoiding fat in yogurt is something of a red herring anyway, because yogurt is scarcely a high-fat food. Whole cow's milk yogurt usually contains 3.7 per cent fat, and around 5 per cent if it is made with richer cow's milk such as Jersey. Yogurt made from whole goat's, sheep's and buffalo's milks contains around 7 per cent, 6 per cent and 8 per cent respectively. And because skimmed milk has a thinner body, stabilizers – milk proteins, starches, gelatine, agar, pectin, guar gum, milk and whey powders – are commonly added to produce a thicker, some might say gluey, texture.

Middle Eastern, Asian and wholefood stores sell straightforward, refreshing, quite authentic yogurt drinks, such as ayran and kefir. Many of the more western-style yogurt drinks, on the other hand, are usually little more than flavoured, sweetened yogurt thinned down with water, or a combination of skimmed milk powder and water, with live bacteria added. They taste pretty fake.

If plain yogurt isn't your thing, and you generally buy flavoured or fruit types convinced that they are good for you, check the label to see how much sugar or artificial sweetener they contain and look out for colourings and flavourings that might give them a larger-than-life taste. The front label, for instance, might say 'With real Madagascan vanilla' and it is only when you look at the ingredients that you realize that it also contains synthetic vanilla flavouring. View with suspicion yogurt drinks aimed at children; most of them are loaded with excessive sweeteners and unnecessary additives.

The taste of whole cow's milk yogurt will vary according to the breed of cow (see MILK AND CREAM) and what they eat. Yogurt from cows kept mainly outdoors on organic pastures that contain a diverse mix of grasses and clovers will taste different to that made from cows kept indoors and fed on a diet of cereal and soya-based animal feed.

Yogurts made from sheep's, goat's and buffalo's milks come from free-range animals. Goat's milk produces a snowy-white yogurt. Sheep's and buffalo's milk yogurt look more like the cow's milk equivalent. Both goat's and sheep's milk yogurt have a pronounced flavour, more like those you find in cheese, so they can be something of an acquired taste. Buffalo's milk yogurt tastes like a creamier, richer version of cow's milk yogurt. It is popular with people who feel that most cow's milk has very little flavour.

Mass-produced yogurts taste the same all year round because manufacturers monitor milk to ensure that the milk and fat content doesn't vary in order to achieve a standardized product, but yogurt from small dairy farms will vary subtly, becoming slightly richer when the animals are eating lush summer pasture.

Most yogurt is made with milk that has been homogenized so that all the fat is evenly distributed through it. Some smaller-scale, more traditional dairies do not routinely homogenize their milk, so the fat will form a delicious natural creamy crust on top of the yogurt.

There are three different styles of yogurt on our shelves. The majority, though not all, of British and Irish brands tend to be homogenous with a gloopy texture. Greek-style and French 'set' yogurts have a more jelly-like consistency and the whey in the milk – the watery, slightly golden liquid – will separate in the pot. Greek-style 'strained' yogurt has had some of its whey removed and may also have some cream added.

Things to do with yogurt

- Blend natural yogurt, ice and canned Alfonso mango pulp to make an Indian mango lassi.

- Yogurt is a vital ingredient in many Middle Eastern foods. Strain overnight in the fridge through a sieve lined with muslin to make a *labneh* dip, which is also good as a vehicle for grated, salted cucumber and garlic.

- Minty yogurt soup, made with rice and egg yolk, is a great Turkish favourite; the Armenian equivalent uses barley instead of rice.

- Yogurt is a useful tenderizer and marinade for meat; it's one of the reasons why tandoori chicken is so moist and tender. Marinate chicken or lamb in yogurt overnight with spices, salt, lemon juice and fragrant herbs such as mint or coriander, then grill or barbecue, or bake in a clay brick or tandoor oven.

....

- If you find mayonnaise too rich, mixing it with yogurt will lighten it up. Equally, if you are serving a really intense, dark chocolate cake, a spoonful of sharp yogurt on the side will often provide a better counterpoint than cream.

....

- Mixed with just a pinch of lightly toasted, crushed saffron strands, runny honey, chopped toasted nuts and passion fruit seeds, yogurt makes an impressive, near-effortless pudding.

Is yogurt good for me?
....

There is plenty of research to suggest that in its simple, plain, natural form, yogurt is a truly healthy food. By way of an appetite-satisfying snack to keep you going between meals, natural yogurt is one of the best foods around. Benefits associated with eating it include immune system support, reduced constipation, stomach acidity and diarrhoea, lower body fat, less bowel cancer, anti-inflammatory effects, stronger bones and a fresher breath. People who are lactose-intolerant can sometimes digest yogurt when they can't tolerate milk because the lactose (milk sugar) is converted into lactic acid in the yogurt-making process. Some research also suggests that yogurt is better tolerated than milk because of the partial protein digestion that occurs when milk is fermented.

The health-promoting qualities of yogurt are due to its nutrients (see MILK AND CREAM/Are milk and cream good for me?), but also to its fermentation and the presence of beneficial 'live' (still active) bacteria. Some brands make a selling point out of containing live and 'friendly' or 'probiotic' bacteria (micro-organisms that confer a health benefit) as though this was a special selling point. They are developing and patenting strains of bacteria unique to their brand and marketing them as foods that have a special health-promoting property. Consumers can be forgiven for thinking that such brands have an advantage over other yogurt products that do not make such claims. In fact, any yogurt is live and has a probiotic effect as long as it has not been pasteurized after it is made. British yogurts are not pasteurized, so they can be considered live and probiotic, even if they don't say so on the label. The only exceptions here are the tiny number of long-life yogurts that have been pasteurized after fermentation to extend their shelf life.

If you like set yogurt, don't pour away the whey. This natural component of milk is rich in protein and contains beneficial vitamins and minerals.

It wouldn't be true to say that the only good yogurt is the plain, natural sort, but it is worthwhile checking the label to distinguish between wholesome yogurts with straightforward additions, such as slightly sweetened fruit purée, and the toothsome assortment of products that bear more resemblance to hi-tech desserts than they do to the time-honoured dairy food. Buyer beware: the word 'yogurt' is commonly used by food manufacturers to place an aura of health around products that don't merit that perception. Some yogurt products are so sweet that they would be better classified as desserts. Many fruit yogurts, including those that come in a dual container with a fruit compote to stir in, are either loaded with sugar – everything from straight sugar through all manner of sugary syrups (maple, cane sugar, high-fructose corn syrup, glucose) to condensed milk – or have artificial sweeteners added. Some research suggests that artificial sweeteners, though lower in calories than conventional sugars, may be even worse for your health (see SUGAR AND OTHER SWEETENERS/Is sugar good for me?). Lower-fat versions of flavoured yogurt often have higher levels of sugars, or contain artificial sweeteners, to compensate for the skimmed milk's reduced flavour. Toffee chocolate yogurt topped with caramel chunks anyone? Eat such yogurts-cum-puddings by all means, but don't mistake them for health foods. Consider adding your own sweet additions – berries, fruit purées, honey perhaps – to natural yogurt rather than buying already sweetened ones: they are likely to be less sweet than the bought equivalent.

Some research suggests that organic milk is better for you than the conventional equivalent, so organic yogurt may be better too (see MILK AND CREAM/Are milk and cream good for me?).

How is yogurt produced?

If you have ever left some milk unrefrigerated on a warm day and returned to find that it has thickened and set, then you have inadvertently made yogurt. Wild bacteria in the environment have colonized the milk and turned it into yogurt. On a domestic basis, the easiest way to make yogurt is to warm milk and stir in some yogurt that contains a live strain of the appropriate bacteria, although yogurt starters are also available in powdered forms. On a commercial scale, yogurt is made by adding lactic bacteria to milk, such as *Lactobacillus bulgaricus*, *Acidophilis casei* and *bifidus*, or *Streptococcus thermophilus*. Despite their potentially alarming names, these are benign bacteria that ferment and thicken the milk, so giving it its sharp, clean flavour.

A HEALTH-SUSTAINING FOOD

Fifty years ago, it was almost impossible to buy yogurt in Britain. This ancient food that sustained the populations of the Middle East and Mediterranean just didn't figure in our diet, but nowadays it is a fixture on our shelves. Since Britain came late in the day to the yogurt business, our dairies lacked experience in making it, so the first generation of natural yogurts in the UK was often challengingly astringent. This helped establish the notion that natural yogurt was more or less inedible unless you ate it with a thick crust of sugar. It also paved the way for the food industry to take a primordial, health-sustaining food and use it as the basis for products that are better thought of as a series of puddings. Nowadays, although big yogurt brands dominate our shelves, smaller-scale dairies in the UK have turned to making high-quality, interesting local yogurts, often using organic milk.

Is yogurt a green choice?

Some of the worst examples you can find of food over-packaging are yogurts that come in moulded plastic pots with packages or pots of sweet additions to stir in. If you care about what goes into landfill sites, these are to be avoided.

If you eat a lot of yogurt, you can easily generate a load of empty plastic cartons, few of which are likely to be recycled. So avoid brands that are made in thick, rigid plastic tubs and favour those that come in thinner, flimsier, more yielding cartons, those in glass jars that can be more easily recycled or, better still, those sold in biodegradable cardboard cartons from sustainably managed forests.

Yogurt is not an expensive purchase, but value-added yogurts – those with bits and bobs to add in, and those that look like desserts – represent much poorer value for money than those sold in the standard 450- or 500- gram carton. Yogurts sold in glass jars will always be more expensive, and not necessarily any better, than those sold in plastic cartons. If you are comparing yogurt of like quality, it is usually significantly cheaper to buy it in large cartons, rather than in one-serving pots.

Remember, there is no good reason to pay a premium for yogurt or yogurt drinks that appear to have unique strains of probiotic bacteria. All yogurt contains live and probiotic bacteria unless it is long-life.

Organic yogurt does not cost significantly more than many comparable yogurts and sometimes can even be cheaper as well as offering a number of extra health and animal welfare benefits.

Cheese

There's something miraculous about the way that one food – milk – can produce such a heterogeneous legion of cheese. The cheese world appeals to those with a collector's mindset, opening a door on to sets and subsets of related, yet distinct flavours and styles. What a pleasure it is to dig into a really well-composed cheeseboard, one that juxtaposes wedges, rounds, ovals and logs, offers different colours – everything from orange-rinded to stippled blue and charcoal – and which showcases flavour contrasts that span everything from the fresh and tangy to the aged and salty. Likewise, few food-shopping experiences stimulate the senses quite so keenly as does walking into a serious cheese shop, with wheels and rounds of hand-made cheeses and knowledgeable staff at the ready with morsels of cheese to sample. And of course, if your preoccupation is less with being a gourmet than feeding yourself and others, then cheese is a faithful friend.

Supermarket cheeses are commonly given a 'strength' rating from one (mild) to five (strong), which is about as unhelpful a way to describe the flavours, tastes and eating qualities of cheese as one could ever imagine. Several factors combine to give cheese its personality – or lack of personality, as the case may be. Sheep's milk cheeses tend to be creamy-coloured with a nutty, mellow, slightly caramel character, while goat's milk produces whiter, sharper cheeses with a distinctive goaty tang. Creamy-coloured cow's milk and buffalo's milk cheeses are initially more neutral, but they have the capacity to develop deep, rich, complex flavours when aged.

Perhaps even more than milk, cheese is a showcase for the nature of the animal's diet because the flavours of milk are intensified in cheese. So cheese made from the milk of grass- and pasture-fed animals will have more character than cheese made from animals that spend much or even all of their time indoors, being fed on a monotonous, unvaried diet of concentrates made from soya and cereal. Cheese is only ever as good as the milk from which it was made.

For all but the freshest cheeses, made relatively simply and quickly, good cheeses are the product of patience. They need to be carefully looked after and matured in the days, months and even years after they are 'made' and they need someone with experience to look after them when they are in the shop.

All other factors being equal – the skill of the cheesemaker, the quality of the milk – cheeses made from raw, unpasteurized milk will have a superior taste, simply because the milk had more essential character to start with, and all the bacteria that contribute to flavour and aroma have been left intact.

Individual cheeses vary and superficially similar-looking cheeses will have many different nuances and even the same cheese can look and taste quite different, depending on whether or not it has been aged. But for the sake of simplicity, they can be grouped into broad categories.

Soft white cheeses
Such as fromage frais, ricotta, cottage cheese, young (unaged) goat's cheese such as English Perroche, Ragstone and Golden Cross, Scottish crowdie and Italian mozzarella. These should taste fairly straightforwardly of fresh milk and have a clean lactic flavour. Some simple, mild cheeses are meant to be eaten young and fresh. Sometimes fresh goat's cheeses are rolled in ash, which gives them an attractive appearance but has little or no impact on taste. Soft goat's cheeses can also be matured and eaten semi-hard, or hard.

White, bloomy-rinded cheeses

Such as French Brie, Coulommiers and Camembert, English Wigmore, Tunworth and Flower Marie, and Irish Cooleeney. These are the trickiest cheeses to buy in good condition. They start out life with a snowy-white exterior and a firm, sometimes chalky interior. If you try to eat them in this state – and that is mainly how supermarkets sell them – they will have a mild smell, a bit like raw mushrooms, and taste of very little. To be appreciated as they ought to be, they have to be ripened. At this point they should look soft in the middle, the white rind should have a more wrinkled appearance with ridges of pale orange lines showing through the white, and they should have developed an attractive aroma. Cheeses of this type that are sunken, cracked, or smell of ammonia are past it. This type of cheese is best bought from a specialist cheese shop. If this isn't possible, then choose a whole small cheese that is still firm but has a little 'give' and leave it out to ripen in a cool, dark place. There is no possibility of properly ripening a wedge of cheese cut from an underripe whole cheese.

White, bloomy-rinded triple-cream cheeses

Such as French Vignottes and Brillat-Savarin, and English Finn. These are cheeses that are markedly rich with a buttery texture because extra cream is added.

Orange-coloured washed-rind cheeses

Such as Irish Gubbeen and Ardrahan, French Munster, Époisses and Reblochon, Livarot, English Stinking Bishop, Italian Tallegio, Welsh Celtic Promise and Scottish Criffel. These are pale orange in colour because their sticky exteriors have been bathed in liquids such as wine or mead to encourage the growth of bacteria that give the cheese a pungent savoury aroma. These cheeses usually smell more powerful than they taste and are best eaten fairly fresh, when the rind is still smooth and moist. When it becomes dryer and slightly cracked, the flavour and smell are too strong for most people.

Semi-hard cheeses

Such as Dutch Gouda, Swiss Gruyère and raclette, French Comté, English Cheddar, Caerphilly, Cheshire, Lancashire, Wensleydale, Berkswell, Spenwood and Cornish Yarg, Italian pecorino and Fontina, Spanish Manchego, Greek feta and halloumi, Welsh Hafod and Irish St Gall. This is the easiest, and most forgiving kind of cheese because it keeps well and isn't especially fragile.

With notable exceptions, such as feta and halloumi, which are aged in brine, semi-hard cheeses are best experienced when they have been traditionally matured by being stored in cool conditions and turned at regular intervals over a period of time so that they develop a hard rind. The longer they are matured the stronger, more complex and full their flavours become.

Hand-made Cheddar is always best cut from a large wheel, rather than as a small truckle of the type sold for the Christmas market. Small truckles will have a higher ratio of rind than a wedge cut from a large wheel, and don't usually have such a good flavour or consistency.

Rindless, semi-hard cheeses of the Cheddar type cut from long oblong blocks and sold in plastic vacuum packs, along with cheeses with wax coatings, do not taste as good as they are not matured in a natural way, which hampers the development of flavour. These rubbery, factory-made cheeses may look the part, but they are apologies for the patiently matured article. Block and waxed semi-hard cheeses are typically made in a highly automated, fast-track way and sometimes the acid level is manipulated to give a false impression of depth and maturity. Such cheeses often mug the tastebuds with an upfront, full-on acidic heat that can almost nip the mouth, hence the enduring popularity of milder block Cheddars. They may have very little taste, but at least whatever taste they do have isn't actively unpleasant.

Since block cheeses are so inherently boring, manufacturers have dreamt up additions to breathe an illusion of diversity into their otherwise tediously homogenous products. So you get a number of novelty cheeses, such as whisky- or curry-flavoured Cheddar, Wensleydale with cranberries and port and Stilton with apricots. These cheeses are best thought of as gimmicks and not to be confused with a genuinely diverse cheese selection. As a general rule, coloured cheeses are best avoided. There are certain cheeses, such as English Cheshire cheese, that were traditionally coloured with annatto, a natural red pigment from the achiote tree, but apart from these, coloured cheeses are fake.

Hard cheeses
Such as Italian Parmigiano Reggiano and well-aged French Mimolette, which have been matured for a long time, often years rather than months. These cheeses are wonderfully complex in flavour and immensely satisfying. Cheeses that are sold younger, such as French goat's cheese

'crottins', can be aged until they become very hard. Some people prefer them that way. Many semi-hard cheeses, such as Italian pecorino and Spanish Manchego can be aged further, which makes them become very hard indeed and more crumbly. The older the cheese, the more full-throated its flavours are likely to be.

Blue cheeses

Such as Italian Gorgonzola, French Roquefort and Fourme d'Ambert, English Beenleigh Blue, Stilton and Blue Vinney, Irish Cashel Blue and Scottish Strathdon. These can either be quite soft, or semi-hard. Often blue cheeses are saltier than other cheeses to balance the strong flavours of the blue veins, but they should never be over-the-top salty and the creamy white part of the cheese should have a rich flavour that balances the intensity of the blue veins. If a blue cheese is one-dimensionally salty and blue, or, alternatively, insipid, it isn't that great.

Smoked cheeses

Such as Italian scamorza affumicata and English Applewood. Smoked cheeses are never subtle and have a potentially bully-boy presence that can dominate other ingredients. Some are traditionally wood-smoked, others simply have artificial smoke flavouring added. Smoking has become a technique to add value to bland cheese. When cheese is smoked, it's impossible to tell whether or not it has any intrinsic flavour. Approach all smoked cheeses with slight suspicion.

Apart from the freshest, softest types, all cheese is best taken out of the fridge, unwrapped to let it breathe, and allowed to come to cool room temperature before eating. This is the way to appreciate it at its best.

Things to do with cheese

- Cheese on toast is never to be sniffed at, especially if you slip in an additional layer – ripe tomatoes, chopped chives, coriander, spring onion, tapenade, pesto, even last night's leftover broccoli – between the bread and the soon-to-be-melted cheese topping.

- Cheese soufflé is a happy exception to the general observation that recipes involving whipped eggs can be tricky. Even if yours doesn't stand to attention quite as much as you'd hoped, everyone will still love to eat it and think you're very clever.

- Salty, mature cheeses add meaty savouriness to a dish. Grated aged Parmesan – one of the foods richest in 'umami', the so-called fifth taste – enriches and adds depth to everything it touches.

....

- Crumbled mature goat's cheese or cubes of feta make vegetable dishes – think roasted aubergines, or a grain and vegetable salad – into a meal.

....

- A generous amount of cheese in a quiche recipe makes it rich and luxurious, rather than a wobbly invalid's custard imprisoned in a pastry shell.

....

- Strong blue cheese served with ripe pear, or Manchego or pecorino-type ewe's milk cheese served with fragrant quince paste, score highly for no-effort elegance.

....

- Macaroni cheese isn't a sophisticate's dish, but nearly everyone adores it; those who say they don't are probably fibbing.

....

- Cheese sauce, made with nippy Cheddar and some strong blue, forms a flattering duvet around the less popular brassicas, such as cauliflower and Brussels sprouts.

Is cheese good for me?
....

Cheese is essentially a concentrated form of milk (see MILK AND CREAM/ Are milk and cream good for me?). It consists mainly of fat and protein, which means that quite a small amount can satisfy the appetite. There is no need to eat large amounts of cheese, but in moderate quantities, cheese is very healthy food.

Supermarkets make great play of stocking low-, or reduced-fat cheeses, for which read reduced-taste cheeses. Such cheeses will always taste inferior to those made from full-fat, whole milk and won't be as nutritious because the fat-soluble vitamins which contribute to flavour have been skimmed off. The dietary gospel that saturated fat, of the type found in dairy products and cheese, is bad for you is now being challenged as there is no good evidence to support it (see BUTTER, GHEE AND BUTTERMILK/Are butter, ghee and buttermilk good for me?). If you do for some reason want to eat less fat, go for a rich, satisfying, full-flavoured, traditionally matured cheese and eat less of it. It is much easier to over-eat mild, bland cheese, simply because it is so unsatisfying.

From time to time there are food poisoning incidents involving cheese, and pregnant women are often advised to stop eating certain types. Cheese isn't a particularly risky food compared with other staples in our diet, such as chicken, and any risk that there is relates to soft cheeses. Very fresh cheeses, such as soft goat's cheese, ricotta or mozzarella are unlikely to present a problem because they will smell off long before they become dangerous. However, they should be eaten before the 'use-by' date and finished up quickly once they have been unwrapped. Harder cheeses, such as Cheddar, Gruyère or Parmesan are not risky because their dryness and acidity level create a hostile environment for food poisoning bugs. The potentially most risky category is soft cheeses with white bloomy rinds, such as Brie and Camembert. This type of cheese should be bought when ripe and ready to eat and consumed in one sitting, or used up in cooking, not left hanging around.

Cheeses made from raw (unpasteurized) milk are no more risky than those made from pasteurized. In fact, they may be safer because raw milk cheeses have more beneficial bacteria to keep the potentially dangerous ones in check. Pasteurized cheeses are sterile by comparison, which means that it is easier for them to be colonized by food poisoning bugs and for those bugs to multiply quickly to unsafe levels.

How is cheese produced?

The simplest types of cheese, such as fromage frais and cottage cheese, are made by warming milk and treating it with strains of lactic bacteria to help the cheese acidify, then allowing it to drain.

In the case of more complex cheeses, after lactic bacteria are added to the heated milk, the milk is curdled (coagulated) so that it sets and separates into curds (the solid part) and whey (the watery part). Traditionally, animal rennet, made from the lining of a calf's stomach, is used to achieve this. For vegetarian cheeses, extracts from plants such as cardoon and nettle are used. Yet another possible coagulant is chymosin, a genetically modified enzyme that mimics rennet. It is thought that most cheese made in industrial creameries in the UK and Ireland is made using this enzyme. Since chymosin is regarded by law as a processing aid, not an ingredient, it does not need to be listed on the label. If you prefer to avoid foods made using GM technology, avoid mass-produced cheese and vegetarian cheeses (unless the use of a plant-based coagulant is mentioned). Go instead for traditional and artisan cheeses, most of which are still made using animal rennet – both here and on the

Continent – or choose organic cheese. Organic rules outlaw the use of GM technology.

Once the coagulant is added, the cuts are made. Mozzarella-type cheeses are pulled and twisted in hot water to encourage the cheese to become stretchy and develop strings. For other cheeses, the curds are cut and slightly 'cooked' if the cheese is to be quite firm, then drained, salted and packed into moulds. Blue cheeses are pierced with thin needles to allow air and natural bacteria to penetrate that encourage the blue veins to develop.

The moulded cheeses are pressed for different periods of time according to the recipe, removed from the moulds and then stored in a cool, extremely damp cave-like atmosphere to mature. In smaller-scale, artisan cheesemaking, this maturing is slow and patient. For Cheddar, for instance, the cheeses are wrapped in cloth and left to mature for a minimum of nine months, and up to eighteen months, and turned regularly during this time. In this process the cheese dries out and the flavour develops. In the industrial creamery, the cheese is left to 'mature' in plastic so it doesn't lose weight, which makes it more profitable for its makers.

Although the key stages in any cheesemaking are much the same, there is a big difference between true 'farmhouse', or artisan cheesemaking, and large-scale factory production. In the former, cheesemakers have much more control over the source of their milk and many of the procedures are carried out by hand. Highly skilled and experienced cheesemakers are needed because they have to make key judgements about each stage in the process: how long to leave the curd with the whey, whether the acid level is right, and so on. Also, the maturing takes longer and is more labour-intensive, since, for instance, the cheeses are hand-wrapped and turned. In the latter method, the milk used is typically pooled from a number of different producers and each production stage is largely automated and computer-controlled.

Is cheese a green choice?

See MILK AND CREAM/Are milk and cream green choices?

Where and when should I buy cheese?

Cheese shops and delicatessens have the best selection of real, artisan cheese and the best ones also have the expertise and knowledge necessary to store and mature cheese. Both www.nealsyarddairy.co.uk/cheeses and www.mellischeese.co.uk/MellisHome.asp are great sites to look at for lists, pictures and descriptions of some of the artisan cheeses that are now available.

The cheese selection in most supermarkets is top-heavy with industrial cheeses sourced from vast creameries both here and abroad. More upmarket supermarkets do stock a small number of authentic, artisan cheeses, but these are best thought of as window dressing for the main business, which is selling great volumes of bland, mass-produced cheese.

OLD AND NEW TRADITIONS

The selection of cheese that's on offer in Britain or Ireland these days is more diverse and interesting than at any other point in our history. Small-scale, artisan cheesemaking is in an exciting, dynamic phase of its history. Old traditions are being honoured and new ones created.

Up until the Second World War, there were thousands of small producers making cheese in Britain, most of them with on-farm dairies, and British cheese was internationally renowned. The Somerset cheesemaking technique known as 'cheddaring', which involves repeatedly stacking up and turning over the curds so that as much whey as possible is drained off to make a smooth, close-textured cheese, had been taken up by cheesemakers around the world.

But in the drive for wartime economy, milk previously used to make a range of small-scale, distinctive cheeses was all sent to factories to make a standardized 'Government Cheddar'. The war ruptured our rich cheesemaking tradition and most of the on-farm dairies disappeared.

Small-scale cheese production in Britain and Ireland hit an all-time low in the 1970s. Many regional farm dairies and smaller creameries that were still making cheese using traditional methods were forced to close as cheese production became centred on larger, fewer, highly automated industrial creameries. These creameries churned out an homogenous product that made a mockery of terms such as 'traditional', 'farmhouse', 'mature' and 'vintage' and debased the

---

once-celebrated names of 'territorial' cheeses such as Cheshire, Wensleydale and Gloucester.

In the 1980s and 1990s, perhaps as a reaction to the woeful sameness of mass-market cheese, artisan cheesemaking underwent a revival. Belatedly, there was recognition of the need to protect producers who still make traditional cheese and help consumers distinguish them from inferior lookalikes. For instance, cheesemakers in Somerset, Devon, Dorset and Cornwall have been awarded Protected Designation of Origin (PDO) status by the European Union for their West Country Farmhouse Cheddar in recognition of the fact that their product has a unique authenticity. Cheese sold with this certification must be made and matured on a farm in one of the four counties, using only traditional methods and local milk.

This welcome reinforcement of traditional cheeses has been complemented by a new wave of cheeses from small-scale cheesemakers, who as well as looking to our cheesemaking heritage, have been influenced by European artisan cheesemaking techniques and traditions. While Britain's and Ireland's expertise was once in semi-hard cheeses, made mainly from cow's milk, cheesemakers are now also making many cheeses with sheep's and goat's milk. In the 1980s, when you walked into a delicatessen, any pungent, orange washed cheeses, goat's logs and bloomy-rinded white cheeses on offer were likely to have been trucked from France. Nowadays, they are just as likely to come from these isles. Our choice of cheese, both old and new, has never been better.

Will cheese break the bank?

The one thing to be said for the industrial cheeses that dominate supermarket aisles is that they aren't expensive. Real artisan cheese from small cheesemakers will always be much more costly, weight for weight, but the difference in quality is so apparent that unless you really are hard up, you may be prepared to pay it.

British and Irish artisan cheeses can often seem expensive in comparison to European imports. This is mainly because although many of our imported cheeses are packaged to look as though they come from small, traditional dairies, they are often made in large numbers in semi-industrial creameries that benefit from economies of scale. Like for like, real artisan cheese from the UK and Ireland is no more expensive than its true European equivalent.

If you feel that you need to justify the higher cost of real, artisan cheese, remember that because it has much more character, you don't need anything like as much to make an impact. A cheese sauce, for instance, made with a small amount of a properly made traditional Cheddar will have a more pronounced cheesy flavour and character than one made with twice the quantity of the mass-market equivalent. A modest amount of good cheese can also be used to add substance and interest to otherwise quite economical dishes. And if you routinely buy a standard lunchtime cheese sandwich, then by making your own at home using the pick of the country's finest artisan cheeses, you can actually save money.

Supermarket cheeses are sold with a 'use-by' date. While these do need to be observed with most soft cheese, they can be ignored with harder cheese. Any semi-hard cheese will keep well after the 'use-by' date and any mould can be pared off and the rest of the cheese eaten. Never throw out the hard rind from Parmesan. Think of it as a useful vegetarian bone and use it whole to flavour soups (minestrone) and tomato sauces.

Ice cream

(including sorbet and non-dairy ice cream)

Ice cream brings out the child in nearly everyone. Some of us have still not perfected the technique of licking a perilously topped cone or iced lolly without those rivulets of melting ice cream running through our fingers. There's a Doll's Tea Party appeal in small tubs of ice cream eaten with tiny spoons. Ice cream can fog – or should it be freeze? – the brain of the most issue-aware eater. Forget whether it's good or bad, we just want to eat it – and quickly too, like those chimpanzees with ice-cream headaches who cradle their heads in their hands.

Ice cream made at home is usually a delight. An ice-cream maker helps, but you can get more than passable results by stirring the mixture at intervals as it freezes, or settling for an easier parfait-style recipe that doesn't need to be churned. When it comes to fruity ice creams, the home-made sort is often streets ahead of anything you can buy, quite simply because it will have far more fruit in it. Rather than being a wishy-washy shell pink, or full of fake colours, as is the bought kind, your home-made raspberry ice cream can be a brilliant blushing pink, your blackcurrant a study in purple. At home, you can play around making ice creams that you will struggle to find in the shops – crème fraîche or yogurt sorbet tangy with lemon zest, peanut butter, rosewater, Indian pistachio kulfi maybe – and you can snap up some of summer and autumn's more fleeting fruits, such as gooseberry, damson or wild blackberries, to brighten up your winter eating.

Everyone has their favourites – nutty, fruity, with chocolate, marbled with caramel, and so on – but whatever sort you like, try to concentrate on the quality of the base ice cream rather than additions to it, which may skew your view of the overall product. The intrinsic quality of the main ingredients should shine through. A pretty ordinary, even inferior ice cream can seem quite delicious, only because it is studded with something sticky and sweet that you like: cookies, caramel or chocolate chips perhaps. If these add-ins are what really appeal, why not eat them in another, probably cheaper, form?

In terms of consistency, there are several styles of ice cream. The US-style 'premium' brands you can buy are heavy, solid and rich. European and Italian café-style ice cream is softer, lighter and more aerated. Middle Eastern ice cream and sorbet is often more icy. Industrial aerosol-type ice cream that spews out of a machine and stands in peaks is soft, smooth and full of air. Indian kulfi ice cream more resembles the home-made sort: it emerges hard and then melts to a runny creaminess. Unless you are vegan or have a dairy allergy, steer clear of non-dairy ice cream, which is usually the poorest quality around.

Many popular ice creams are complex concoctions, cloying, homogenous masses of hi-tech ingredients whose precise purpose would baffle all but a chemistry professor. These include ingredients worth avoiding, such as water, powdered egg, whey solids, emulsifiers and stabilizers – such as guar gum, carrageenan, locust or carob bean gum, hydrogenated vegetable fat and mono- and diglycerides of fatty acids – which give them a telltale synthetic texture and mouth feel.

Any really good ice cream, on the other hand, should contain only instantly recognizable ingredients that you would see in a recipe designed for home cooks. A true vanilla ice cream, for instance, will contain just whole liquid milk, cream, eggs, sugar and natural vanilla bean or extract. The only exception to this rule for commercial production is skimmed milk powder, which even high-quality ice-cream makers use in small quantities to give body and trap air.

The acid test of good ice cream is that a few seconds after eating it, the roof of your mouth should feel clean, with no greasy residue that would indicate the presence of highly industrial ingredients. Neither ice cream nor sorbet should leave a lingering taste in your mouth. It is arguable whether added flavourings – apart from classic ingredients like chocolate, vanilla or fruit – have any place in the best ice cream. Even when natural flavourings are used, they can produce a larger-than-life taste in the mouth and many commonly added synthetic flavourings are out-and-out mouth-muggers. Rather than offering full-on flavours, excellent ice cream woos you gently so that the last mouthful tastes every bit as good as the first. Flavourings are commonly used heavy-handedly in fruit ice creams and sorbets to give fruits that are underripe and characterless more 'oomph'. This is why so many of them taste more like fruit gums.

Appearance also provides a clue to quality. Good ice cream doesn't bark out at you with Day-Glo colours, so unless a naturally vibrant or dark ingredient, such as blackcurrants or chocolate, has been used, expect good ice cream to have a demure, pastel colour. A true pistachio ice cream, for instance, should have a colour similar to pale avocado flesh, not a green pea. Added colourings, whether natural (from carrots or beetroot perhaps) or chemical, are totally cosmetic and unnecessary. In ice-cream parlours, where the ingredients are rarely listed in any visible position, brightly coloured ice creams should be taken as a sign of synthetic production methods. Unless there is some reasonably detailed declaration on the premises that only natural ingredients are used, the opposite is likely to be the case.

Things to do with ice cream

- Pour a small, strong shot of hot espresso coffee over vanilla ice cream to make the classic Italian dessert, *affogato*.

- Match the richness and sweetness of ice cream with a tart fruit purée or compote.

- Drop a scoop of creamy ice cream into home-made lemonade or good-quality ginger beer to make an ice-cream float.

- Sandwich ice cream between chewy cookies to make an ice-cream sandwich. Serve instantly or freeze for later.

- If you haven't got an ice-cream maker, use a recipe that requires no churning. Indian kulfi – made from milk, cream, evaporated and condensed milk – is delicious. Flavour with cardamom, pistachio nuts, rose water or mango.

- Drizzle syrupy aged balsamic vinegar over milky dairy ice cream.

Is ice cream good for me?

It will come as no surprise to learn that ice cream is a fattening food. This is mainly a consequence of the large amounts of sugar and other sweeteners in it. These can destabilize blood sugar and insulin levels, encouraging fat production and storage in the body.

If lower-fat ice products appeal to you, ice cream made from sheep's milk is an interesting alternative to that made with cow's milk. It is much higher in solids than cow's or goat's milk with smaller fat globules that remain evenly distributed through the milk. This means that ice cream can be made out of whole, full-fat sheep's milk without the addition of further fats in the form of cream or eggs, so producing a naturally lower-fat ice cream.

Ice creams marketed as 'low fat' are often even sweeter than their higher fat equivalents and contain more additives to hold them together. So the best thing to do is to buy high-quality, whole milk and full-fat ice cream, but eat it only occasionally, and in modest amounts.

Cheaper brands of non-dairy ice cream often contain hydrogenated (chemically hardened) vegetable fats. These altered fats are now widely considered to be extremely bad for health.

There is some research to suggest that organic cow's milk is nutritionally superior to the conventional equivalent (see MILK AND CREAM/Are milk and cream good for me?), so organic ice cream may be a healthier choice.

How is ice cream made?

In its classic form, ice cream is based on a liquid custard with eggs, sugar, cow's milk and cream which is whipped and flavoured with anything from alcohol and fruits to nuts and chocolate, then frozen and churned. The eggs bind the creamy sweetened bulk to form a smooth, coherent texture. Ice cream made with sheep's milk is whiter in colour with a slightly richer, nuttier flavour. Variations on the traditional ice cream include the French parfait, and the Italian semifreddo (desserts with such rich ingredients that they require no churning), sorbets (fruit and sugar combinations that contain no dairy ingredients, but which may contain egg white) and the granita, an Italian type of sorbet that is not churned, but mixed with a fork so it forms larger, flakier crystals. Indian ice cream, or kulfi, is made in a different way, by evaporating milk with spices such as cardamom or other flavourings, such as saffron, then mixing in sugar and chopped nuts, such as pistachios, or fruit purée (such as Alfonso mango pulp) before freezing.

Although some smaller scale and upmarket 'premium' commercial ice creams are still made to a scaled-up version of the traditional method, for cheaper products made on an industrial scale, food technologists have devised ways of making ice cream more profitable, using specially formulated pre-mixes, in either powder or liquid form, containing milk solids, fats, vegetable oils, starches, chemical stabilizers, flavourings, colours and acidity regulators. These mixes are simply added to water and/or milk, then the whole thing is frozen and churned. Modern machinery also allows more air to be incorporated into cheaper, mass-market ice creams and sorbets.

Until richer, US-style ice creams came on to the market in the 1980s, the name of the game in UK ice-cream production was to reduce as much as possible the quantity of pricey ingredients needed and replace them with cheaper, more profitable industrial equivalents. To this day, by law, 'dairy' ice cream need only contain 5 per cent dairy fat and 2.5 per cent milk protein, so the bulk of an ice cream can be made up of all the other ingredients and air.

Is ice cream a green choice?

Many common brands of ice cream contain palm oil, either listed by name as an ingredient, or unannounced in ingredients such as vegetable oil or fat. Palm oil is a tropical oil with a venerable history that used to be grown in a traditional way to provide a source of food and income for small growers. Nowadays, it is cultivated on vast plantations owned by large companies and whole swathes of virgin forest in Malaysia and Indonesia have been cut or burnt down to make way for its production. This peaty forest is one of the most concentrated stores of carbon around and clearing the forest releases vast amounts of greenhouse gases into the atmosphere.

Expanding palm oil plantations have also had a drastic effect on wildlife. The only orang-utans now left in the world live in Borneo and Sumatra where the lowland forests that sustain them are being rapidly destroyed. Wildlife groups warn that without urgent intervention, the palm oil trade will make the species extinct within a decade. The Sumatran tiger is also threatened. Avoid ice-cream brands that use palm oil, along with brands that contain vegetable oil or fat from unspecified sources.

The refrigerants used in ice-cream freezers and chiller cabinets have been pinpointed as environmental hazards. The oldest sort – CFCs, or chlorofluorocarbons – were thought to cause ozone-layer depletion and were widely replaced by supposedly greener HFCs, or hydrofluorocarbons. Now these in turn have been linked with global warming, and large ice-cream makers are experimenting with alternative refrigerants.

One way to cut down the use of refrigerants is to buy ice cream made and sold as locally as possible. Many premium brands have their ice cream made in Europe and transported to the UK. The more environmentally progressive cafés and ice-cream parlours will keep ice-cream tubs covered with lids, inside refrigerators with doors, to save energy. Their display may not look such fun, but it will be greener.

Will ice cream break the bank?

When you buy cheap ice cream, you will be paying for air, water and additives, so it represents poor value for money. Middle-priced brands market themselves as though they were premium brands, but although they cost a bit less than those, a look at the ingredients label will reveal that they also contain many industrial ingredients, so they are not that much of a bargain. Most upmarket, more natural brands of ice cream and sorbet are quite expensive and best thought of as a treat. Organic ice creams cost little more, and are sometimes cheaper, than their non-organic 'premium' equivalent.

ICE CREAM WITH AN ENGLISH ACCENT

In the past, Britain's contribution to the world of ice cream was far from distinguished. Ice cream was made available to a mass market in the UK when Italian immigrants set up ice-cream parlours in the early twentieth century. Initially, the ice cream they sold was made in a traditional way using time-honoured ingredients, and very few flavours were offered.

From the 1960s onwards, UK ice-cream parlours started to use pre-mixes similar to those being used in industrial ice-cream production and to diversify into hi-tech synthetic flavours with implausible names, such as bubble gum, liquorice, peach melba and cola. Many ice-cream parlours, although they nurture a folksy image, continue to use pre-mixes, so temper nostalgia with realism when you queue up for your cone.

On the mass-production front, one uniquely British development was pioneered by a research team of chemists that included the young Margaret Thatcher. It worked out how to double the amount of air in ice cream, so allowing manufacturers to use less of each ingredient and reduce their costs. This innovation went down well in Britain because people liked the lighter texture. It spawned the 'Mr Whippy'-type machines that spewed out architectural towers of swirly ice cream from ice-cream vans.

When more upmarket US-style brands arrived in the 1980s, Britain was an easy market to conquer. Many people were disillusioned with the quality of ice creams which were increasingly criticized as low-grade, over-aerated, synthetic concoctions with little resemblance to the traditional product. The unique selling point of the premium US brands was that unlike most of the British opposition, they contained only natural ingredients. No chemical stabilizers were needed because of the naturally richer mix with thick cream and eggs – and they contained much less air. On the downside, people struggled to get a spoon in the tub because they were so solid.

Nowadays, although American-style ices further enriched with chunky additions such as cookie dough, chocolate fudge and cheesecake continue to be popular, Britain is rediscovering a new generation of artisan ice creams which are a little lighter than the US sort and which have more in common with traditional Italian ice cream, yet still made with first-rate ingredients: milk and cream from named farms, free-range eggs and whole ripe fruits rather than ready-to-use, bought-in fruit concentrates. Many of the emerging small-scale British ice-cream brands try to make use of more local ingredients, and unlike bigger brands that ape the heavyweight US style, their portfolio speaks with more of an English accent, offering flavours such as elderflower, honey, blackberry and apple crumble, strawberry, damson and Christmas pudding.

Fish

4

Cod and other white fish

(haddock, plaice, lemon and Dover sole, dab, witch, megrim, whiting, pollack, coley (saithe), hake, monkfish, gurnard, brill, turbot, halibut, huss (also known as dogfish and rock salmon), skate, John Dory, sea bass, sea bream, catfish (also known as sea wolf, sea cat or rockfish), stone bass (wreckfish), pouting, ling, mullet (red and grey), flounder, redfish (also known as Norway haddock, hoki, snapper), squid)

White fish are eternally useful, wonderfully versatile and speedy to cook. In the past, the prevailing wisdom was that simple, relatively unadorned, rather plain recipes were best, so as not to mask the natural flavour of the fish. Of course, old stalwarts – such as simply grilled or fried fish on the bone anointed with browned butter, capers and lemon, a comforting fish pie, and blisteringly hot fillets in crisp batter or breadcrumbs – are crowd-pleasers. But tradition needn't be a conservative straitjacket, rather a jumping-off point for more adventurous approaches. The truth of the matter is that white fish are suitable for all manner of treatments, from the demure to the decidedly bold, so never be afraid to throw lots of lively, robust flavourings their way.

The flavours of white fish vary only subtly from species to species. The main differences are less to do with taste than texture and consistency. At the more substantial end of the white fish spectrum there are firmer, almost meaty fish such as halibut and monkfish, which hold their shape well once cooked. At the opposite end of the spectrum come softer, more delicate, thinner fish such as witch, dab and plaice, which fall apart easily. Flaky species such as cod, haddock, gurnard, red mullet, hake and pollack come somewhere in the middle. Squid isn't strictly a white fish but a cephalopod, belonging to the same group as octopus and cuttlefish. It should have a springy, pleasantly bouncy texture but it should never be excessively chewy if properly cooked. There are two approaches to cooking it, either a high heat for a short time (say chargrilled or stir-fried), or gentle, slow cooking. Anything in the middle is disastrous.

White fish shine when they are truly fresh. Although they suffer less obviously from age than oily fish, they lose their lively, attractive marine flavours and become rather dull and uninteresting to eat.

You can use your nose and eyes to judge the freshness of fish. Any retail outlet, be it a traditional fishmonger, a fish van, a fish stall or a supermarket fish counter, should not smell strongly fishy. A bracing whiff of ozone and sea air is fine, a strong odour that resembles boiled fish or stinky cat food is not. It is easiest to judge the freshness of fish when it is whole and unfilleted. The fish should look sleek, toned and plump under its skin, which should be slippery, moist and sparkly. Its eyes should look full and bright, and its gills (the bits under its head at the top of its body) should be bright red. Any fish that appears apathetic and lacklustre, with sunken eyes and brown gills, is past it. Fillets that are matt and dry-looking without any sheen are probably old. Also avoid fillets that are sitting in a puddle of water, a possible sign that they may have been defrosted from frozen.

Fish freezes quite well, providing that it was really fresh when frozen; however it is best to buy fish that has been frozen when it is still in its frozen state, or buy truly fresh fish and then freeze it yourself. Fish sold as fresh, but labelled as 'previously frozen', is often waterlogged and the eating quality can be poor.

Things to do with white fish

- Thin fillets of plaice, dab, witch and lemon sole are lip-smacking when covered with equal amounts of lemon juice, double cream and grated Parmesan, all mixed together, then baked for minutes, or flashed under the grill, to produce a gratinated crust and a tangy sauce.

- In Latin American ceviche, slices of fillet are put raw into a lime juice marinade which firms them up and 'cooks' them – you know this has happened when the fish looks opaque – then served with chopped fresh chilli and leafy coriander.

- Steamed fish – either whole or filleted – bear no resemblance to pallid invalid food when you steam them with grated ginger, then finish them off in the Chinese fashion with a drizzle of soy sauce and a sizzling dressing of hot sesame oil with slivers of garlic fried in it.

- Caribbean cooks like to season their fish some hours before cooking in a vibrant liquidized marinade made from spring onions, turbo-charged Scotch Bonnet chillies, garlic, oil, lime, fresh thyme and parsley.

- White fish get along nicely with Indian spices, either rubbed with a moist paste that includes aromatics such as ginger, garlic and turmeric before baking or grilling, or in chunks, in a creamy, coconut milk-based curry.

- Potentially workaday fish cakes become positively exciting when you include some pungent smoked haddock or soaked salt cod in the mix.

- Saffron really infuses white fish with its earthy flavour and ochre colour. Toast, then lightly crush a pinch of saffron stamens and sprinkle them on fillets before steaming or baking, or incorporate the saffron into a tomato sauce.

- Salt cod, as its name suggests, has a quite pungent flavour. It is often used in Spanish and Portuguese recipes, either in small quantities to flavour bland ingredients such as potatoes, or in a tomato and red pepper sauce.

- Any white fish can be made special in minutes by slamming it into a high oven with a spoonful of potted shrimps on top, or under a cap of herby butter sprinkled with breadcrumbs.

- Dusted in flour, egg, then breadcrumbs, quickly fried white fish fillets go well with a cheat's tartare sauce. Just mix equal amounts of natural yogurt and mayonnaise, adding lots of very finely chopped rinsed capers, gherkins and green herbs, such as chives, dill or tarragon.

Is white fish good for me?

White fish has a lot going for it. Its main constituent is high-quality protein, which is essential for regeneration of the body. Since protein is filling, and the body takes some time to digest it, it keeps you going for hours at a time without feeling peckish. It is a rich source of selenium, which is thought to be protective against cancer, and contains significant amounts of vitamins B3, B6 and B12. White fish does contain some omega-3 oil (see SALMON AND OTHER OILY FISH/Is oily fish good for me?) which is really good for you, but at a much lower level than oily fish. Smoking does nothing to detract from the healthiness of fish.

How is white fish caught?

Most species of white fish are wild-caught. A few species – sea bass, sea bream, halibut, cod and turbot – can also be farmed in similar ways to salmon (see SALMON AND OTHER OILY FISH/How is oily fish caught?).

Methods for catching wild fish have changed radically. Traditionally, fishing fleets were localized and artisan. Small, low-tech boats fished relatively close to shore, returning to land either daily, or every two to three days, staying within their national limits. Since the 1950s, fishing has become progressively more industrialized. The invention of mechanized pulleys that could be attached to large nets revolutionized fishing because boats could scoop up and haul in unprecedented numbers of fish. Technological developments such as echo sounders and sonar allowed large fishing boats (trawlers) to detect the whereabouts of fish with great accuracy, so they can target whole populations and net huge catches.

Entire fleets of these ruthlessly efficient hi-tech trawlers now scour the globe, hoovering up massive catches as they go. Unlike smaller day boats that only store the fish on ice for a day, larger, more industrial trawlers are equipped with freezer tanks, allowing them to stay out on the high seas for weeks at a time.

Is white fish a green choice?

Modern fishing methods have triggered a grave ecological crisis: 70 per cent of global fish stocks are either fully fished, over-fished or depleted. In European waters it is thought that nearly 90 per cent of stocks are over-fished. Trawlers' ability to catch previously unthinkable numbers of fish has outstripped many species' ability to reproduce and this has significantly depleted fish stocks. As well as landing too many fish, many trawlers drag weighted nets along the seabed. This ploughs up and damages the marine ecosystem that sustains fish life. Unfortunately, only a tiny percentage of the world's seas are under any sort of legal protection, adequately policed or subject to any meaningful controls.

In the more regulated fisheries, remedial action is being taken to halt the collapse in stocks. This includes imposing strict quotas (limits) on the amount and the species of fish that can be landed, using more selective methods to allow young fish to escape so that they can reproduce, and using mesh panels in nets that allow non-target species to escape. However, restrictions on what fish can be landed have also led to a huge problem with discards, with a shockingly high number of high-quality, non-target species having to be dumped back into the sea because it was illegal to land them.

Environmental groups advocate the creation of marine reserves, expanses of water that are closed to fishing for a period, to allow fish stocks to regenerate. Encouraging data from New Zealand, where reserves have been introduced, suggest that stocks start recovering within two to three years, showing significant increases after five or six years. They also believe that fishermen in other fishing areas should have their days at sea restricted and use larger-sized mesh in their nets to allow juvenile fish that will breed and produce future stocks to escape. That done, they argue that fishermen should then be allowed to land absolutely everything they catch to stop the senseless waste of discards.

In recent years, guidance on identifying sustainable fish has been based on lists of 'good' species and 'bad' species. Although such lists do provide some guidance, they can be confusing. Because fish stocks are very localized, the same species often appear on both lists. So rather than saying that a certain species is off-limits altogether, as in 'Don't eat cod', the specific fishery it came from is more relevant. The term 'fishery' is used to mean one specific fish species from a specific marine location. For example, a scientific survey might suggest that stocks of sole in the Celtic Sea, Western Channel, Skagerrak and Kattegat are healthy, while those in the North Sea, Irish Sea and Bay of Biscay are not. Similarly, while North Sea cod is still considered by environmentalists as off the menu, cod fished around Iceland is widely seen as coming from a well-managed, sustainable fishery.

No one wants to think that they are eating the last few under-sized representatives of an endangered fish species, but identifying sustainable fish isn't easy. From a practical point of view, fish approved by the international Marine Stewardship Council (MSC) is currently the best bet. The MSC certifies specific, named fisheries as sustainable on a species-by-species basis. MSC-approved fish carry a blue label with a white tick on it. As yet there are relatively few MSC-approved fisheries, but many more are due to come on stream.

Fish that does not have MSC certification isn't necessarily unsustainable. It could come from a fishery assessed by international bodies as sustainable but just not be labelled as such. Be particularly vigilant, however, when buying monkfish, hake, cod, halibut, plaice, turbot or skate as there is a high chance that they come from endangered stocks. Only buy if MSC-certified, or when given some other persuasive assurances; for instance, a guarantee that the fish has been line-caught.

When trying to work out what fish to eat, there are three websites worth consulting: www.seafish.org/b2b/rss maintained by the Seafish Authority has responsible sourcing guides that will give you information on stock status and background on management for twenty-six species or groups of species. These are updated as regularly as possible. www.fishonline.org/advice/eat maintained by the Marine Conservation Society has lists of fish to eat and fish to avoid. And use the MSC Fish To Eat list at www.msc.org/cook-eat-enjoy/fish-to-eat.

RETHINKING OLD PREJUDICES

Cod has become symbolic of the deep crisis with our fish stocks. In living memory, it was in such abundant, affordable supply that it was a staple fish and chip shop choice. Now it is scarce and expensive. It was estimated that stocks of cod in the North Sea, our traditional source, had crashed by 86 per cent in the last century. Stocks were at such a low level for a while that many environmental organizations advocated that we should not eat it. Thanks to efforts to curb over-fishing, stocks of North Sea cod are now thought to have picked up encouragingly, but they are still low by historic standards. Seeing this improvement, the fishing industry is pushing for increased quotas, but environmental groups are maintaining their advice to avoid buying North Sea cod, on the grounds that stocks must bounce back further before we resume eating it, other-wise this promising recovery may be set back.

The shortage of traditional fish favourites, such as cod and plaice, and their escalating cost have forced us to find alternatives and pushed us into rethinking old prejudices. Species that were once thought of as the poor relatives, such as coley and pollack, are gaining new status. Once we were a bit sniffy about them, but now more people are warming to their charms and finding that they can taste surprisingly good.

Where and when should I buy white fish?

Unpredictable – fish stocks change all the time.

White fish has never been so expensive. The highly prized, very popular species such as cod, turbot and sole now cost the same as, or more than, prime red meat. But there are still bargains to be found if you look beyond the usual suspects like cod and haddock. If you want something more manageably priced, check out the less well-known species such as coley, gurnard, pollack, catfish, dab and megrim. They are cheaper just because they aren't so familiar and people aren't quite so sure what to do with them.

Whole fish are always cheaper than fillets because the fishmonger hasn't had to spend any time preparing them. Most people don't buy them because they aren't confident about cooking them, so if you do, you can net a bargain.

Salmon and other oily fish

(sea trout, mackerel, tuna, trout, herring, pilchards, sprats, eel, whitebait, sardines, swordfish, anchovies)

Salmon and tuna may be bestsellers, but, these species apart, oily fish are nowhere near as popular as white. Not everyone can get their head around the characteristic fishy whiff of the stronger-tasting, silvery-blue-skinned species, such as mackerel, herring, sardines, whitebait and sprats, or come to appreciate their more developed taste, or learn to ignore tiny bones. That's a pity, because these species can be magnificent in prime condition. They can make white fish seem lacking in personality by comparison, and their bones are not an insurmountable problem. Mackerel won't have any troublesome bones if it has been properly filleted. Smaller fish of this family, such as herring and sardines, have tiny, fine bones that can be eaten once cooked.

The pink-fleshed species such as salmon, trout and tuna are the least oily-tasting and will still be fine to eat quite a few days after catching, but others in this family group will not. They must be ultra-fresh because the oils that make them so tasty rapidly deteriorate and become unpleasantly pungent. An encounter with an ageing mackerel or tired sardines can put people off all oily fish for life. In truth, buying oily fish is much more of a lottery than buying white. So when buying silver-blue-skinned species, establishing that they are extremely fresh is an absolute must. For preference, buy the fish whole, as this allows you to assess its freshness more easily. For guidance about recognizing freshness in fish see COD AND OTHER WHITE FISH. Buying fillets of oily fish without first seeing the fish whole is rarely a good idea unless you can really trust your fishmonger.

If you find the whiff of fish like herring and mackerel off-putting, baking or roasting is the way to go, since frying or grilling is smellier. Fresh oily fish is best balanced with vivid, assertive flavours and partnered with refreshing ingredients that cut its richness and provide a contrast.

The most commonly eaten oily fish – salmon – offers very different eating quality, depending on whether it is wild-caught or farmed. Wild salmon can be from one of two different species. The finer, more delicate-fleshed Atlantic salmon is found in waters around Scotland, Ireland and Scandinavia. The meatier, slightly drier and deeper coloured Pacific salmon swims in North American waters. Chinook (King), Chum, Coho (Silver), Sockeye (Red) and Pink are all sub-groups of Pacific salmon. The colour of wild salmon flesh will vary from flamingo to orange, depending on what the fish has been eating in the wild. That flesh will be firm and athletic, as befits a powerful fish that swims thousands of miles in its lifetime. The natural oil in the wild salmon cannot be seen when looking at the flesh. During cooking, it gives off little or no oil and, if judged correctly, will remain pleasantly juicy in the mouth.

Farmed salmon comes a poor second best to wild. It is flabby compared to wild because it has had only a fraction of the exercise in the course of its life and so it lacks the muscle tone and all-round condition of its wild counterpart. Farmed salmon often has a visible herringbone mesh of creamy fatty veins running through its flesh. This occurs because farmed fish are given feed that contains high levels of fish oils to promote growth, and also because they are less active than the wild equivalent. When you cook farmed salmon, it will give off more oil than wild, and may taste watery and bland, with an ever so slightly tinny, bitter aftertaste.

Oily fish in tins make a handy stand-by. Those packed in oil taste better, and less salty, than those packed in brine. The more you pay, the better quality you get. For species such as mackerel, pilchards and sardines, cheaper types can be quite good, the main difference between these and more upmarket labels being that the fish tend to be larger in size and be more intact. More expensive tinned tuna will contain larger, more unbroken chunks of paler fleshed fish. If you intend to mash it up rather than use it in large flakes, then the outlay won't be worth it. Anchovies are one canned fish worth trading up on. You get what you pay for here because cheap anchovies can be absurdly salty, pungent and excessively bony, while more expensive brands are distinctly sweeter and fishy in a pleasant way and are packed in a better quality of oil. People who find salted anchovies packed in oil too powerful may prefer them pickled when they are sold as silver or marinated anchovies.

Smoked fish such as salmon, trout, mackerel and herring (kipper) will have been salted, often seasoned with spices and sugar or treacle, which firms up their flesh, before smoking. Styles of smoking vary from the light 'London smoke' which was developed by smokers in the East End of London, to the more assertive, woodier style associated with traditional Scottish smokehouses. Fish takes on a subtly different character depending on how it is smoked. Oak and beech are the most common woods used, and peat is another traditional smoking medium in Scotland and Ireland. Gravadlax is a Scandinavian way of curing salmon that doesn't involve smoking: the fish is salted until much of its moisture is lost, covered in fresh dill and sometimes spices, then weighted down until it firms up and loses moisture.

Things to do with oily fish

- Cover fillets for a few hours in a North African *chermoula* marinade – a mixture of onions, lemon or bitter orange juice, garlic, cumin and fistfuls of coriander and parsley all blended together – then bake them.

- Sandwich sardine fillets together with finely chopped pecans or pine kernels, sea salt, rosemary and parsley, leaving the skin-sides facing outwards. Sprinkle with breadcrumbs, drizzle with oil and briefly bake in a hot oven.

- Jars of cheap pickled herring take on a slinky Scandinavian quality when dressed in soured cream or crème fraîche and brightened up with peppery dill and chives. A spot of horseradish, either grated or in a ready-made sauce, adds a kick.

- Cans of sardines or pilchards in olive oil make a bargain-basement, stylish, near-instant supper, mashed up with red wine vinegar and black pepper, spread on toasted sourdough bread and topped with a tangle of fresh watercress. Add slivers of preserved lemon zest if you fancy it.

- In Malaysian and Indonesian cuisine, tiny whole fish (*ikan bilis*) are salted then dried until crunchy and eaten whole as a garnish for many savoury rice and noodle dishes, like the Asian equivalent of croutons, as in the popular Malaysian dish, *nasi lemak*.

- Whitebait or sprats, floured then deep-fried, work brilliantly tossed in smoked paprika and sea salt, then served with a crisp green salad featuring thin slices of celery, crunchy cucumber, lettuce and peppery greens such as rocket or mustard cress.

- Tuna makes an occasional treat when rolled in toasted seeds (sesame or nigella), seared for one to two minutes on each side, then chilled and served thinly sliced with soy sauce or an Asian-style dipping sauce.

- Salmon works well baked in parchment with salted butter and grated root ginger.

- Cheap herring roes taste great when quickly sautéed in butter, seasoned with sea salt, coarse black pepper and chopped flat leaf parsley, then served on toast.

Is oily fish good for me?

Oily fish is a supremely healthy food. Its main constituent is high-quality protein, which is necessary for regeneration of the body. Since protein is filling, and the body takes some time to digest it, it satisfies the appetite and keeps you going for hours at a time without the urge to snack.

Fresh oily fish is the best dietary source of the highly desirable long chain fatty acids EPA (eicosapentaenoic acid) and DHA (docosahexaenoic acid). A body of research now suggests that these omega-3 fats can have many beneficial effects, such as reducing blood pressure, stroke and heart disease, improving brain function and mental health, and reducing inflammatory conditions such as arthritis, psoriasis and colitis. The omega-3s in tinned tuna are reduced considerably because the fish are pressure-cooked beforehand, so tinned tuna fish is nowhere near as good a source as fresh, but tinned sardines, mackerel, salmon and pilchards are packed in such a way as to retain their omega-3s.

Oily fish is an excellent source of vitamin D, a vitamin that many people don't have enough of. The body makes vitamin D from sunlight, and many British and Irish people don't see enough of the sun to keep vitamin D at optimum levels. Vitamin D is currently the focus of much research and it is now thought that it plays a more important role in preventing a number of illnesses than was previously acknowledged. In addition to the role previously attributed to it as contributing to bone health, a shortage of vitamin D is increasingly being linked with cancer, heart disease, diabetes and multiple sclerosis. Fish is also a good source of vitamin A, important B vitamins and beneficial minerals and trace elements such as potassium, iron, zinc and selenium.

Marine contaminants from pollution, such as mercury and other toxic heavy metals and trace chemicals like PCBs (polychlorinated biphenyls) and dioxins, all of which are bad for health, can concentrate in the flesh of oily fish, particularly the bigger fish like tuna and swordfish. For this reason, it seems sensible not to eat excessive amounts. The UK Food Standards Agency advises pregnant or breast-feeding women, and girls who might want to have a baby some day – the groups most at risk from exposure – to eat no more than two portions of oily fish a week.

How is oily fish caught?

The most commonly encountered oily fish species on sale in the UK and Ireland are salmon, rainbow trout, herring, mackerel, sardines, pilchards, sprats, whitebait, anchovies and eel. These are all found in our traditional northern fishing grounds. Other oily fish, such as tuna and swordfish, are imported from Mediterranean or tropical countries.

Oily fish can either be wild-caught, farmed or ranched. The species farmed in Britain and Ireland are salmon and trout. The basis of fish farming is that juvenile fish, hatched from eggs, are put in tanks (in the case of trout), or wire cages suspended in water (in the case of salmon), either just off the coast, or at the mouths of rivers and sea lochs. The fish are fattened up on pelleted food and slaughtered when they reach their target weight. Tuna ranching, which is common in the Mediterranean, is a variation of fish farming in which wild tuna are first netted live at sea and then put in cages.

Fish farming can be seen as the marine equivalent of land-based intensive farming. Vast concentrations of closely packed fish are kept in a very small area of water, a huge restriction on their lives in the wild. Animal welfarists object to the whole concept of confining in a cage such free-ranging creatures as salmon that are genetically programmed to swim the oceans. They liken it to farming tigers. If salmon are farmed organically, then they are given more space.

Farmed fish are fed on pelleted food made from ground-up wild fish with added vitamins, minerals and binders such as wheatflour and soya, none of which figures in the diet of a wild fish. Salmon and trout usually also have chemical colourings added to their feed because they don't eat the varied diet of wild seafood that would naturally give their flesh an attractive pink hue. These colourings are not allowed in the feed of organic salmon and trout, which is why their flesh is paler.

Is oily fish a green choice?

Like all types of fish, wild stocks of some oily fish are at an all-time low, which means that identifying which species to eat or avoid isn't straightforward (see COD AND OTHER WHITE FISH/Is white fish a green choice? and How is white fish caught?). In the oily fish category, it's mainly the larger, highly popular species that give cause for concern. Only buy tuna if you have a solid, specific guarantee that it has been caught by the pole and line method, or it carries a blue label to show that it comes from Marine Stewardship Council (MSC)-certified fisheries. Otherwise your tuna may have been caught in purse seine nets using 'fish-aggregating devices' – man-made rafts that trap and kill other fragile, non-target species, such as turtles, dolphins, rays and shark. There are no known sustainable fisheries for swordfish. Only buy eel that comes from the UK and carries the Sustainable Eel logo.

When it comes to salmon, fish farmers present their industry as the saviour of wild fish. They claim that they are helping to take the pressure off endangered wild stocks by offering the farmed equivalent, but, globally, fish farming has been pinpointed as a net reducer of fish stocks. Farmed fish are fed on pelleted food made from stocks of smaller fish further down the marine food chain. Salmon, for instance, eat anything from three to five times their weight in wild fish, while tuna eat around ten times their weight in wild fish. So far from helping wild stocks, fish farming depletes them. (Organic farmed fish are the exception here because they are fed pellets made from the filleting waste – blood, guts, tails, heads – of fish harvested for human consumption that has been certified as sustainable, so they do not deplete wild fish stocks to the same extent.) Fish farmers are looking at the possibility of adding a proportion of food from plant sources to fish feed to cut down on the amount of wild fish used, but plant food stocks are also under pressure. It makes no sense to feed precious stocks to fish that could be used directly for human food.

In Scotland and Ireland, fish farming has been pinpointed as a significant contributing factor in the worrying reduction in numbers of wild salmon and sea trout. Large populations of farmed fish, just like land-based factory farms for livestock, are a magnet for disease. Sea lice infestations are endemic on fish farms and many farmed fish suffer sporadically from Infectious Salmon Anaemia, a disease specific to fish farming. It is thought that escapee fish from fish farms infect wild fish and interbreed with them, so reducing their ability to cope in the wild.

Another harmful impact of fish farming on wild fish is that a thick layer of uneaten feed and faeces often settles below the cages. Both conventional and organic salmon farmers use powerful, highly controversial chemical treatments in the water – some are thought to be carcinogens – to limit the numbers of sea lice. These also contribute to a reduction in overall water quality that is not helpful to wild fish. In recent years, the use of pesticides to control sea lice has been of extreme concern to wildlife groups who insist that it is damaging marine life.

Better alternatives to farmed salmon and trout are wild brown trout (which is rarely on sale commercially), wild sea trout, or wild Alaskan salmon, certified as coming from healthy, sustainable fisheries by the Marine Stewardship Council. This US salmon is frozen soon after catching and shipped to the UK and Ireland, and although it comes from thousands of miles away, for the time being it looks like the best all-round option. Because it comes from a sustainable fishery with a light carbon footprint, this offsets somewhat the fuel used in transport.

'Premium' brands of Scottish and Irish farmed salmon come from a number of independent salmon farms, some approved by the RSPCA's Freedom Foods scheme and others certified as organic. These brands are marginally preferable to the standard farmed salmon because such schemes require slightly higher environmental and fish welfare standards. For instance, the cages have to be situated further out to sea where there is a stronger flow of water, which makes for fitter fish, and fewer fish can be kept in one cage. However, these brands are just slightly more enlightened versions of intensive fish farming.

THE KING OF FISH AND BIG BUSINESS

Salmon should probably be a rare treat, but now it has become ubiquitous on the fishmonger's slab. This abundance is a relatively modern phenomenon. Until the 1970s, when you talked of salmon it was assumed that you were talking about wild Atlantic salmon, the 'King of Fish', a magnificent, romantic wild fish that swam thousands of miles before being caught by rod or netted in the mouth of rivers. It was a rare and special summertime treat, to be savoured with freshly dug new potatoes and freshly podded peas perhaps.

Then the first Scottish salmon farm opened in 1969 and a small-scale, cottage industry promptly sprang up in north-west Scotland along the coast and in sea lochs. Within a decade, Scottish salmon farming with its year-round consistent supply of fish boomed. Nowadays it is a huge international business, with over 80 per cent of 'Scottish' salmon farms operated by Norwegian-owned, trans-national corporations.

Massive amounts of public money have been channelled into salmon farming which has become a highly profitable industry, both on the home and overseas markets. Salmon farmers have argued that their industry has been a great boost to rural economies in remote spots, but anglers, hoteliers and shellfish farmers insist that the negative impact of fish farming on wild fish has blighted stocks and devastated their sport and their livelihoods. Interestingly, in Scotland stocks of wild salmon are healthiest along the east coast where there are hardly any fish farms, and lowest along the west coast, where nearly all salmon farms are situated.

Where and when should I buy oily fish?

The availability of silver-blue-skinned oily fish such as mackerel or herring is unpredictable, since fish stocks change all the time. Both farmed Scottish and Irish salmon and wild Alaskan salmon are available year round. Wild Scottish and Irish salmon is in season from May to September but is rarely on sale as most rivers now operate 'catch and release' schemes where anglers put back any fish they hook. If you are buying wild Scottish or Irish salmon – not highly recommended – then ask for assurances that it does not come from a river with depleted stocks. Wild sea trout is not, as yet, endangered, and is available from May until September.

Will oily fish break the bank?

The oily fish category always offers some bargains. As a general rule, the silvery-blue family of fish, from the largest (mackerel) down to the littlest (whitebait), are often quite cheap as many people are wary of their strong taste, having never tasted really fresh ones.

Farmed Scottish salmon and trout are ubiquitous and cheap. Imported Norwegian farmed salmon is even poorer quality and cheaper still. Wild Alaskan salmon is more expensive than the farmed Scottish, Irish or Norwegian equivalent, but because it is very meaty, a little is quite filling. You can pay a small fortune for wild Atlantic salmon because it is endangered. Wild sea trout is never cheap, but it is more affordable; it tends to be prohibitive at the start of the season, then the price drops somewhat.

When it comes to preserved fish, pickled herring makes a great budget buy and keeps well in the fridge. Very cheap tinned tuna is a false economy: it tends to be a mush and isn't great value for money because it is so full of brine or oil. Similarly, avoid cheap anchovies.

Prawns and other crustaceans

(scampi, shrimp, crab, lobster, langoustines)

Prawns can be one of the sweetest, most delicious, most succulent seafoods you are ever likely to encounter. Unfortunately, most just taste of salty water. There is no beating fresh wild prawns, straight from the sea, but they are hard to track down and usually extremely expensive, so frozen prawns are the obvious alternative. But while there is an argument to be made that fish doesn't suffer from freezing, there is no doubt that prawns do. This is not only due to the effects of freezing on this delicate protein, but also because of the way they are shelled and processed beforehand.

Fresh langoustines, also known as Dublin Bay prawns, are the pinnacle of prawndom, unbeatable for flavour. These sweet, fleshy wild prawns, which look like miniature lobsters, usually come from small-scale fisheries on the west coast of Scotland and Ireland. They are rarely frozen because they are a premium product. The same applies to lobster.

At the opposite end of the size spectrum, tiny, brown wild shrimp from Morecambe Bay and the North Sea, off Holland and Germany, have a deeper, more concentrated seafood flavour, more reminiscent of crab.

Those familiar pink curls – wild, cold-water prawns that come from northern waters in the North Atlantic – are ubiquitous. Who knows if they ever really taste of anything because they are almost always cooked and frozen before we get to eat them, making it impossible to tell if they once had more crustacean personality. Always sold frozen because they deteriorate quickly, pink cold-water prawns are best bought frozen, raw and unshelled. Most, however, are cooked at sea, cooled, then shelled and frozen in a factory when they are landed. Shelling is done using high-pressure water which leaves the prawns waterlogged and considerably dilutes their flavour.

Don't expect scampi to taste of anything much more than the batter or crumb that coats them. The term 'scampi' used to be taken as referring to the whole tail of a cold-water prawn or langoustine in a coating. Increasingly, it is a term used for broken bits of pink prawn tail and fish mince, bound together with additives and 're-formed' into a prawn shape before being battered or crumbed. Scampi may sound deluxe, but it rarely is. If you fancy a bit of battered or breaded seafood, go for fish, not prawns.

In recent years, wild-caught, cold-water prawns have had competition from the increasingly popular warm-water tiger prawns. These are chewier-fleshed and meatier than our traditional wild-caught prawn species and now turn up everywhere, on the fishmonger's slab, in supermarket ready meals, or floating in your Thai-style hot and sour soup. Tiger prawns usually have marginally more flavour than our pink prawns from northern waters when you buy them shelled and frozen, but considerably less than either fresh langoustine or brown shrimp.

If you are buying prawns from a wet fish counter or the fishmonger's slab, check that any apparently fresh prawns have not been previously frozen and then defrosted. The water that saturates them dilutes their flavour, as well as making it hard to sauté or fry them satisfactorily. If you have to use frozen, rather than fresh, prawns, buy them frozen and then defrost them yourself. That way, you will know that they are fresh, or at least, freshly defrosted, and that they have not been hanging around in a pool of salty water for some time.

Prawns sold both frozen, or cooked and chilled, usually have added salt. There is no good reason for this other than to compensate for their puny flavour. If you eat a lot of prawns and think that they are tasty, you might just be hooked on their saltiness. Try tasting them on their own before you use them or add any ingredients that might disguise their lack of taste, and see how you find them.

Unlike most prawns, crab usually delivers well in the taste department. It is best bought fresh and live, but if you can't handle dealing with the cooking and shelling, prepared white and brown crab meat, or dressed crab in the shell, are both very decent products.

Things to do with crustaceans

- Stir-fry raw prawns or langoustines, unshelled for preference, with black mustard seed, black pepper and fresh curry leaves, then deglaze with lime juice; or stir-fry with garlic and chilli, then deglaze with lemon juice.

- Pot brown shrimps or prawns in barely melted, unsalted butter, just enough to cover, with lots of chopped herbs – such as chervil, chives and dill – and serve with Melba or sourdough toast.

- Make a fennel-scented oil by gently warming olive oil, crushed fennel seeds and finely chopped fresh fennel, leaving the oil to infuse. Serve with spoonfuls of ready-prepared dressed crab (both white and dark meat) and wedges of lemon.

- Crack crab claws (see Will crustaceans break the bank?) and mash the meat lightly with half and half natural yogurt and mayonnaise, finely chopped capers, skinned, chopped tomato flesh, dill or fennel.

- Roast langoustines with garlic and herb butter, or briefly grill lobster with lime or lemon butter.

- Make a strong shellfish stock by sautéing leftover shells of crustaceans, sliced onion and fresh fennel in olive oil or butter, adding chopped fresh tomatoes and parsley stems and then only just enough water to cover. Simmer for twenty minutes, strain, add a splash of brandy or pastis, and then reduce to half the volume: Use as a base for Mediterranean-style fish soup, stew or in a seafood risotto.

- One sure-fire hit with uncooked prawns is the Chinese dim sum favourite, sesame prawn toast. All you need to do is make a food processor or blender paste with prawn, spring onion, egg, a little light soy sauce and sesame oil, press on to thin white bread, sprinkle with untoasted sesame seeds, then deep- or shallow-fry the toasts.

- Serve any lightly cooked crustacean with a Cambodian dipping sauce made from coarsely ground black pepper, sea salt and lime juice.

Are crustaceans good for me?

Prawns and other crustaceans may be small, but they are more filling than they might look because they are full of protein, a key nutrient that is essential if the body is to function properly. Protein helps satisfy hunger, so it is good for keeping hunger pangs at bay. Prawns and other crustaceans contain a significant amount of cholesterol but this does not mean that they should be avoided. It is now accepted that consumption of some cholesterol-rich foods is essential for good health. Without cholesterol, the body cannot make certain hormones – cortisol, oestrogen and testosterone. If cholesterol is too low, the body may not be able to use the sun to make sufficient amounts of vitamin D. Crab is a good source of the highly desirable long-chain fatty acids EPA (eicosapentaenoic acid) and DHA (docosahexaenoic acid). A body of research now suggests that these omega-3 fats can have many beneficial effects, such as reducing blood pressure, stroke and heart disease, improving brain function and mental health, and reducing inflammatory conditions like arthritis, psoriasis and colitis. Prawns also contain these desirable omega-3 fatty acids, but in lesser amounts than crab.

Eating prawns and other crustaceans is a good way to boost the level of certain nutrients in your diet that may be lacking. Beneficial minerals and trace elements in seafood include zinc, which boosts the immune system, iodine, which keeps the metabolism on an even keel and supports the thyroid gland, and selenium, which also aids metabolism and is thought to reduce the risk of certain cancers. British and Irish soils typically contain very low levels of selenium, so many people may be deficient in this trace element. Prawns also provide useful amounts of phosphorous, iron and potassium, along with vitamin B12.

In their raw form, prawns are an excellent food, but there are certain health issues to do with the way they are processed. Most frozen prawns have salt added, often in hefty amounts, as the prawns are frozen in a salty brine or 'glaze'. Prawns are likely to be one of the saltiest foods you can buy, which explains why that lunchtime prawn sandwich might leave you thirsty. Excessive amounts of salt are known to be associated with higher rates of stroke and heart disease. If you have been diagnosed with high blood pressure, then don't eat too many.

Some cooked, chilled prawns also have added sugar to make them sweet and added sodium metabisulfite, a preservative that can trigger breathing problems, gastric irritation and allergic skin reactions in some sensitive people.

Read the small print carefully on all prawns bought packaged and quiz the fishmonger about any bought loose to avoid those with added salt, sugar and preservatives.

How are crustaceans caught?

Prawns come to our tables via very different routes. Langoustines, lobsters and crabs are mainly caught using traditional fishing methods with creels or pots (mesh baskets) attached to lines that are left on the seabed, although langoustines can also be netted by trawlers.

Brown shrimp were once netted on the sand flats of Morecambe Bay in shallow waters using nets dragged by horses and carts, but now tractors do the same job. Brown shrimp from Holland and Germany are caught by smaller trawlers that stay near to the shore.

Pink cold-water prawns from the North Atlantic are caught by huge commercial trawlers that drag large nets through the sea.

Tiger prawns are either wild-caught by trawlers or cultivated in fish farms or 'ponds' in warm tropical waters. The ponds are 'seeded' with juvenile prawns then fed until they reach the desired weight.

Are crustaceans a green choice?

Creel- or pot-caught langoustines, lobster and crab raise no environmental concerns. They are caught using small-scale, sustainable fishing methods using static gear. This puts a natural limit on the size of the 'take' or catch. As a general rule, creel-caught langoustines are preferable to those caught by trawlers. Trawlers can catch many more langoustines at a time, so they can put more pressure on stocks, and are capable of doing considerable damage to the marine environment, depending on the methods used. However, some trawled langoustines, such as those from Stornoway, are thought to be sustainably fished.

Brown shrimp from Morecambe Bay used to be harvested in a very traditional, artisan way using horses and carts dragging nets to collect the catch. These have been replaced by tractors which have probably contributed to a decline in the stocks as they are capable of harvesting many more shrimp. The availability of brown shrimp from Morecambe Bay is not what it once was and many of the shrimps used for potted shrimp, or available from fishmongers, now come from Holland and Germany where stocks are healthier.

Pink, cold-water prawns from deep northern waters are trawled. Levels of stock vary from one fishing area to another, but they are usually considered to be within safe biological limits.

Tiger prawns raise many environmental concerns. Some of these tropical prawns are wild-caught by prawn trawlers that damage fragile coral reefs and produce a wasteful 'bycatch' of other wild fish that is then discarded, including endangered species such as sea turtles. Most of the tiger prawns we eat are farmed, but with no less environmental impact. In tropical countries, swathes of mangroves – fragile coastal forest that defends the coast against rising sea levels and tsunami – have been destroyed to create prawn farms. As a result, coastal rice paddies that locals rely on for food are often polluted by salt water from farms, and drinking water is contaminated.

Tiger prawn farming took off in the 1980s when, fuelled by loans from organizations such as the World Bank, prawn farming was hailed as 'the blue revolution'. This triggered a gold rush that has turned into an environmental disaster. On a typical tropical farm, the growing crustaceans are packed in and fed on pellets made from ground-up wild fish. This is extraordinarily wasteful because only about 17 per cent of it is converted into consumable meat.

These prawn ponds are a magnet for disease, so medication of feed becomes necessary. This has implications for prawn consumers, as, in the past, traces of drugs that are illegal in Europe have been found in tiger prawns. Even when the sites are 'rested', disease often restarts with production, so many are finally abandoned.

Prawn farms are notorious for not treating their waste, which consists of uneaten fish meal, prawn faeces, undigested drugs and chemical traces, simply pumping it into streams or waterways that flow to the sea, polluting the water and robbing it of the oxygen that sustains the wild fish on which many local people depend.

As prawn ponds are so disease-prone, organic production is especially difficult, although organically farmed prawns are thought to be more sustainably produced. Organic standards require that mangrove is replanted, stocking density is limited on farms and the use of pesticides and antibiotics is restricted, but there is no guarantee that workers or locals are treated any better.

Where and when should I buy crustaceans?

Look out for langoustines, crab and lobster from spring until the end of November. Their availability depends on the weather being fair enough to fish for them. Brown shrimp, pink prawns and tiger prawns are on sale all year round.

Will crustaceans break the bank?

Langoustines and lobster are fantastic, but very expensive. The bigger they are, the more you pay for them but it is best to go for plump ones as an occasional treat, rather than settling for slightly less pricey ones that have less eating on them.

If you are prepared to shell crab claws, then they can be a surprisingly good buy. Just put the crab in a strong plastic bag and bash it all over with a rolling pin or meat mallet. This stops the shells flying all over the kitchen. Then pick out the white meat from the shell. Prepared white crab meat costs much more if sold fresh, rather than frozen. Brown crab meat is often overlooked for white but it is a cheap way of getting a strong crustacean flavour into a dish and is great for spreading on toast. 'Dressed' or ready-prepared crab is an affordable and convenient way to buy crab. You can use a mixture of the white and dark meat to make crab cakes.

Brown shrimp, sold in packs by enterprising fishmongers, are manageably priced, as are tiger prawns and pink cold-water prawns.

Cheaper frozen prawns often contain up to half their weight in water so they work out more expensive in the end. Only buy prawns that state their weight 'exclusive of glaze'. The label should say either 'deglazed weight', 'after defrosting' or 'net of ice glaze'.

If you buy prawns with their shell on, keep the shells even if they have been frozen, as they will be loaded with flavour and you can use them to make a stock for a risotto, fish soup or stew.

IN THE POT

Potted brown shrimp is one of England's finest food traditions, most strongly associated with Morecambe Bay. The shrimps are warmed through in butter, seasoned with gentle spices – mace and nutmeg are preferred – then potted in small ramekins until the butter sets, then spread on brown toast with a squeeze of lemon. If you can find a source of brown shrimp, it is very easy to pot them at home but many supermarkets and fishmongers serve proper potted shrimp from small family businesses around Morecambe and the north-west of England.

Mussels and other shellfish

(scallops, oysters, cockles, razor, surf and Venus clams)

There isn't a member of the shellfish family that isn't packed with flavour. Meaty mussels deliver a punchy burst of seafood flavour, rivalled only in intensity by brown crab meat. It is best to buy cultivated rather than dredged mussels, because the former are cleaner and contain less sand. You can usually tell the difference because wild mussels have duller, thicker, more matt shells while the cultivated equivalent are smoother, shinier and sleeker with thinner shells. Most of the mussels on sale are cultivated.

King scallops, smaller queen scallops and razor clams are prized for their springy texture and gentle marine sweetness. When buying large king scallops, avoid those that have been soaked in water and polyphosphates to make them soak up water and plump up their weight. They might look good, but they will give off too much water when you cook them. Soaked scallops should be labelled as such but rarely are. You can ask the fishmonger, or have a good look at them yourself: soaked scallops will be shelled, look large and shiny, and will probably be sitting in a pool of water – never a promising sign with seafood. Also avoid frozen scallops, which tend to be waterlogged. Unsoaked 'dry' scallops should look firmer and smaller and will probably still be on the shell when you buy them.

Slippery oysters offer an exhilarating salty sea tang. Oysters vary subtly in flavour, depending on whether they are native wild or 'flat' oysters which are round in shape, or the cultivated, tear-shaped 'rock' (Giga) type that are cultivated from an imported species. Oysters also taste more or less salty and sweet, depending on where they have been cultivated, something you'll only really appreciate if you get a chance to taste oysters from different origins side by side. Venus and surf clams and cockles have a pleasantly deep fishy taste that can lend depth and aroma to other ingredients.

Things to do with shellfish

- Steaming scallops on the half shell for a couple of minutes with grated ginger and spring onion, then splashing with light soy sauce, shows off the delicate, sweet flesh of this beautiful, luxury bivalve.

- To cook the classic French *moules marinières*, simply sauté chopped shallots or onions in olive oil in a pot, add mussels and a little white wine, then steam with the lid on until the mussels open (discard any that remain shut). Stir in abundant amounts of finely chopped flat leaf parsley to finish.

- You can give moules marinières a Breton twist by using salted butter rather than oil, cider in place of wine, and stirring in thick cream at the end.

- A few shelled oysters added to a straightforward beef stew towards the end of cooking makes the flavour deeper and more savoury.

- Shelled mussels or oysters make an interesting fish stew or thick soup. Add to onions and potato that have been gently softened in butter, with fish stock or water, cream and fresh parsley, dill, chervil or chives.

- Mussels or oysters are brilliant grilled on the half shell with lemon and herb butter.

- Fry a Thai or similar Asian fresh curry paste in coconut oil, add mussels in the shell and coconut milk. Steam with the lid on until the mussels open (discard any that remain shut). Stir in chopped coriander to finish.

- Add surf or Venus clams to a basic tomato sauce, or cook as for moules marinières, then serve with spaghetti or linguine.

- Stir-fry mussels or razor clams fiercely with spring onions and garlic and finish off with black bean sauce.

Are shellfish good for me?

Shellfish score highly on the nutrition front. They provide high-quality protein in a very digestible form. Protein is essential for the regeneration of the body and is the best macronutrient for satisfying the appetite in a healthy way. In addition, shellfish are a rich store of beneficial micronutrients.

Of all shellfish, mussels have the most impressive nutritional profile. They contain more health-promoting omega-3 fatty acids than any other, and are an excellent source of the highly desirable long-chain fatty acids EPA (eicosapentaenoic acid) and DHA (docosahexaenoic acid), although oysters are also a good source. A body of research now suggests that these omega-3 fats can have many beneficial effects, such as reducing blood pressure, stroke and heart disease, improving brain function and mental health, and reducing inflammatory conditions like arthritis, psoriasis and colitis. Mussels also contain comparable amounts of iron and folic acid to red meats.

Shellfish are excellent sources of vitamins A and D and provide significant amounts of B vitamins. They also supply a number of important minerals that many people do not get enough of, such as magnesium, selenium, copper, iodine and zinc.

Green-lip mussels from New Zealand have attracted a particular following. They are rich in eicosatetraenoic acid which has anti-inflammatory effects and may be beneficial for people suffering from conditions such as arthritis. But the green-lipped mussels on sale in the UK have either been frozen, or chilled and air-freighted from the other side of the world, so they aren't as fresh as our own blue mussels. If you want to test out the supposed anti-inflammatory qualities of the green-lipped sort, the better option is mussel extract in supplement form.

Some research supports the belief that oysters have an aphrodisiac effect. They contain certain amino acids that may regulate mood and raise levels of the sex hormones, oestrogen and testosterone, along with dopamine, a neurotransmitter that may influence sexual desire.

All bivalve (two-shelled) shellfish are only as clean as the water they come from. If that water is polluted, say by sewage, heavy metals, food poisoning bacteria such as salmonella, or viruses such as gastroenteritis, then shellfish can be very dangerous. Even in usually clean waters, sudden algal blooms in warm weather can temporarily cause bivalves to produce natural toxins that can, very occasionally, prove deadly to humans. So never eat shellfish you have collected from the wild unless you are 100 per cent confident of the purity of your source.

Unlike fish, shellfish are sold live. Never buy them if they smell fishy – a sure sign that they are dead – they should just have a nice fresh smell of the seaside. Always inspect them carefully before you cook them. Rinse them in cold water to remove traces of sand – there should be very little, if any – and discard any with broken shells. In the case of mussels, pull off the little beards with your fingers. For all other shellfish, pick off any strands of seaweed, but don't worry about barnacles; they are fine. The shells should be tightly shut. You can check that any open mussels or clams are safe to eat by tapping them sharply against the side of the sink. Alternatively, slip the point of a sharp knife inside the shells. Either way, if they don't clam up, throw them away. Also ditch any that stay closed after cooking: they were dead before you got them.

How are shellfish caught?

Shellfish can be either wild or cultivated. Wild shellfish are harvested in different ways. Usually, they are brought up by fishing boats that dredge their favoured habitats of sandy estuaries and gravel-bottomed coastal inlets. A small number of large, prime king scallops and razor clams are harvested by divers. Shellfish such as cockles and razor clams can also be harvested at low tide from shallow water, foreshore and beaches, using a rake, or by suction. Scallops can sometimes be netted by small trawlers.

Most of the mussels and oysters on sale are cultivated. Scallops and clams can also be cultivated, but rarely are in the UK and Ireland. The basic procedure is to seed water with juvenile shells, and then grow them on until maturity. This procedure takes around two years for mussels, four years for oysters and up to five years for king scallops.

Mussels are grown on ropes suspended from floating rafts in inshore waters where they attach themselves by their hairy 'beards' and cling on until they reach harvestable size. Oysters are grown under water on mats, trays or trestles protected by nets or in net bags.

Shellfish pose a potentially high food poisoning risk because of the way they feed, so they must be free from contamination. If the mussels have been cultivated or fished in waters that are considered by marine authorities to be extremely pure, then they can go straight to market. In most areas, however, shellfish have to undergo forty-eight hours of 'depuration' to allow them to purge themselves of any harmful bacteria and toxins. This is done by moving them to suitably clean water, or by placing them in holding tanks of water purified with ultra-violet light.

Shellfish production in our waters is now concentrated mainly on the west coast of Scotland, Ireland, Wales and the English West Country around Devon and Cornwall.

Are shellfish a green choice?

While the farming of carnivorous (fish-eating) fish like salmon is mired in controversy, the cultivation of mussels and oysters is generally thought to co-exist harmoniously with the marine environment. Unlike farmed fish species such as salmon, cultivated mussels and oysters are not fed with fish feed because they fatten up naturally on plankton from the water, converting it very efficiently into nutritious flesh, so they do not deplete wild fish stocks. Unlike farmed salmon producers, the companies that cultivate mussels and oysters tend to be small-scale. Some research into mussel and oyster cultivation suggests that better than being 'carbon neutral' (all in all making no negative impact on the environment), they may actually be 'carbon positive' (having an overall positive effect) because mussels and oysters filter waste and phytoplankton and naturally purify the water.

Wild-caught shellfish are more problematic. They have traditionally been harvested by dredgers that can damage the seabed. These are boats with equipment, not unlike a giant rake, attached, which drags along the sediment that lies on the seabed. This type of fishing can damage the structure of the sea floor, and ruin the marine habitat for both the target shellfish and other species. One way to mitigate the damage caused by dredgers has been to close off fishing areas so stocks can regenerate. The industry has also put some effort into designing dredging equipment that is less destructive. But when faced with a choice between dredged wild shellfish or cultivated, the latter is generally the more ecological choice. Scallops that have been harvested by divers, or trawlers, are also preferable to their dredged equivalents. Native wild oysters are very special and relatively rare, so there are strict standards about how they can be harvested. Small fishing boats with dredging equipment are used, but the dredge is hand-hauled, not mechanically powered, so as not to damage the precious oyster beds.

Where and when should I buy shellfish?

Although shellfish can be bought all year round, there is still something to be said for the old wisdom that you shouldn't eat them unless there is an 'r' in the name of the month. In the warmer late spring and summer months there is a higher risk of shellfish being contaminated because of raised water temperature, and their meat may be of a lower quality because they are spawning. Native oysters are only available from September until April.

RAGS AND RICHES

Shellfish like cockles, oysters and mussels have been consumed for centuries around these shores, and in some bulk, quite commonly as a poor person's food. In Victorian times, dredging for oysters was such big business that our native (wild) oyster beds were over-fished and badly depleted. By the 1960s, a series of severe winters, over-fishing and disease had more or less put paid to them. In the 1980s the non-native rock (Giga) oyster was introduced and culti-vation made oysters reasonably plentiful once more. Consumption of oysters has since picked up, but is still only a fraction of what it once was and oysters are now considered as a luxury food, not the staple they once were. Careful environmental stewardship of our fragile wild oyster beds has seen native oysters become more numerous in coastal areas that were once famous for them, notably in Whitstable in Kent, Maldon and Colchester in Essex, Loch Ryan in Wigtownshire and in Cornwall around Truro and in the Fal estuary.

The cultivation of more affordable rope-grown mussels also took off in the 1980s, and their consistent quality and generally high standards of purity have helped break down the common prejudice that eating shellfish is risky.

Will shellfish break the bank?

Mussels are the most affordable of shellfish that don't require tricky cooking or need a lot of time and effort to prise them from their shells, and are a charitably cheap source of high-quality protein. Since they are extremely filling, you won't need huge quantities. A generous handful is enough for a substantial starter to serve most appetites and a large plate of mussels need never break the bank. They naturally produce a lot of flavoursome broth, so you won't need any stock or bouillon. Everything in the shell is edible. Most other types of shellfish are generally expensive and best looked on as a treat.

Fruit

5

Apples

A common verdict on apples is that they are just a dull staple of the fruit bowl and lunch box. You can see why many people arrive at this conclusion, presented with the typical selection of suspect varieties that have emerged from months in store and degenerated into balls of wool. But if you get to taste freshly picked, seasonal apples that haven't been through months of storage and its cosmetic pre-grooming processes, they can be glorious. You may be surprised at just how mouth-wateringly fragrant they are, and revel in their sweet, juicy crispness.

The style of apple you prefer is highly personal. There is a spiritual divide in the apple world between sweet and sharp, with modern tastes tending to favour the latter. Among the most ubiquitous apple varieties, the only truly acid type is Granny Smith, although otherwise it has very little personality. The others all tend to be sweet to a greater or lesser degree. The most reliable and characterful varieties among them in taste terms are Cox, Egremont Russet, Braeburn and the short-lived Discovery. Spartan, Gala, Jonagold, Fiesta and Golden Delicious are pretty uninspiring by comparison and probably owe their ubiquity to the fact that they store well, although if home-grown and left to ripen, they can taste like different apples entirely. Gleaming red Mac Red and Ida Red apples of the type that are popular in the US are tough-skinned, and rarely riveting to eat.

Bramley reigns supreme as a 'cooking' apple, although other countries prefer to use sweet apples in the kitchen, but if you can buy your apples from growers, there are other slightly acidic or 'dual purpose' apples with just as much going for them such as James Grieve, Peasgood's Nonesuch and Charles Ross.

Our traditional eating apple varieties tend to be quite sweet. They generally don't store as well as the more commercial varieties, although some late varieties will still eat well in spring, but most are best appreciated within a few weeks of picking. These 'heritage' varieties tend to be much more distinctive than the typical modern apple. A ripe Worcester Pearmain may develop an almost strawberry taste, Ellison's Orange has an aniseed character, Ribston Pippin is tangy, Irish Peach is aromatic and Ashmead's kernel is reminiscent of fruit pastels.

Slick, boutique 'club' varieties of apple, such as Pink Lady, Jazz, Kanzi and Cameo, discussed on page 236, are newer apple varieties with exceptionally good marketing behind them, but despite their premium price and polished packaging, they represent no obvious improvement in taste terms over less trumpeted varieties.

To get the very best from apples, eat them in summer and autumn when they are freshly picked and before they disappear into long, dark months of storage. Be led by the nose not the eyes. Forget what they look like and concentrate on their fragrance. If you have to buy apples from the supermarket, keep them in the fridge as the texture goes downhill rapidly if they are kept at room temperature. For cooking, unless you want an apple that breaks down into a fluffy purée, such as Bramley, experiment with sweeter varieties.

Things to do with apples

- Apple and onion slices, fried until golden, go well with black pudding.

- Gently braise chicken, rabbit or pheasant joints, or lean pork, with apples, onions and cider, then deglaze the pan with cider and/or a little Somerset brandy or Calvados, scraping to get all the bits into the sauce. Add thick cream and let it bubble up to thicken the gravy.

- Fry apple segments in unsalted butter and golden sugar until the apples caramelize. This is a simple, pleasing dessert to serve with a blob of natural yogurt or crème fraîche.

- Large Cox and Braeburn apples make a brilliant *tarte Tatin*.

- Make an unsweetened apple compote by adding a little water to peeled segments of eating apples and cooking gently in a covered pot until they collapse. Leave to cool, then mash the apples into a rough purée. Flavour with orange or lemon zest, cinnamon or cardamom and serve with toasted, flaked almonds.

- Hollow out the cores of large unpeeled cooking apples and score a line through the equator of each. Fill with a mixture of chopped raisins, nuts, coarse demerara, Barbados or muscovado sugar, a little unsalted butter and ground allspice or cinnamon. Bake under foil until the skin is golden and splitting to reveal oozing apple innards.

233

Are apples good for me?

A body of research suggests that eating apples is associated with a reduced risk of heart disease, cancer, asthma and type 2 diabetes. This may be because apples are particularly rich in many different types of phytochemicals such as the flavonols procyanidin, quercitin and catechin, and the phenol, chloragenic acid, which have been associated with a reduced risk of many chronic diseases. They are also a very good source of soluble fibre, which slows down the rate at which sugar is released into the bloodstream. In addition, apples have useful amounts of vitamin C, which boosts the immune system, and potassium, which helps moderate blood pressure. Most of the phytochemicals and much of the fibre in apples are in the skin, so to benefit from them most, they are better eaten unpeeled. Whole apples are better for you than apple juice, while cloudy apple juice, which retains more of its fibrous pulp, is better than the clear sort.

Apples are one of the very worst fruits for containing pesticide residues. Over the last few years, the problem has been so apparent that the European Commission has issued several EU-wide alerts. Tests have found that the vast majority of both eating and cooking apples are contaminated with multiple residues of up to eleven different pesticides. In addition, the use of illegal pesticides has been detected in some samples. Since pesticides are toxins it is best to avoid them as much as possible, and there is therefore an extremely strong argument for buying organic apples. Organic growers can use only two pesticides in apple production – conventional growers have an armoury at their disposal – and no residues have been detected in organic apples in recent years.

You need to accept that organic apples are more natural-looking, with the odd patch of russeting and blemish, and of varying size. Perfect, uniform apples owe their pristine appearance to pesticides.

How are apples grown?

Most of the British apples we eat come from orchards in Kent, Norfolk, Sussex, Herefordshire, Suffolk and Worcestershire. Imported apples tend to come from South Africa, New Zealand, Chile and the US.

Some apples, especially certain more traditional varieties that don't keep so well, such as Discovery, are simply put in cold, humid store and sold in the weeks following picking, but many commercially grown apples are given a post-harvest treatment. They are washed and lightly brushed, which removes the natural wax on their skin, leaving it looking dull, so the apples are then dipped in an edible wax. Various types of wax are used such as carnauba (from palm trees), shellac (from beetles), beeswax and petroleum wax. Waxing protects the fruits and makes them shiny but has no nutritional value, so you may prefer to avoid waxed apples. Duller-looking apples may not have been waxed.

After waxing, apples are put in large stores where the composition of the air has been modified so that most of the oxygen, which would cause the fruit to rot, has been replaced with carbon dioxide. Often a chemical growth regulator gas is also used. This manipulation of the air slows down the respiration rate of the apples and has the effect of delaying ripening which means that the apples can be stored for months and taken out when they are needed. In the past, most apples were stored for up to six months. Nowadays, increasingly sophisticated storage techniques mean that they can be kept for a year.

Are apples a green choice?

Apple trees absorb and store carbon from the atmosphere, which makes their fruits a sustainable, environment-friendly crop. Their roots also help stabilize the soil and prevent erosion. Apple orchards provide a wildlife-friendly environment, and contain several micro-habitats that support a multitude of wildlife: beetles, bats, birds, butterflies, moths and bees.

Unfortunately, our orchards have been in decline for decades. It is thought that over half of England's apple orchards have been grubbed up or fallen out of use since 1950. This situation has largely been created by the failure of supermarkets to give pride of space to home-grown apples. Even at the peak of the native apple season, the majority of fruits on sale are imported.

In the last few years, the growing interest in local food has seen the steady decline of apple orchards halted as more growers see a future in orchard fruits. Improved storage techniques now make it possible to eat English apples all year round. In terms of energy efficiency, the greener option is to store home-grown apples rather than shipping imports from the southern hemisphere. Now there really is no need to buy an imported apple, so check the country of origin of apples and choose those grown nearest to home.

Supermarkets' insistence on visual perfection has led growers to use more pesticides than is strictly necessary to ensure that their fruits are not rejected because of imperfections. Even a minor blemish or a tiny patch of russeting can lead to a consignment of apples being rejected. This is one reason for the extremely high levels of pesticide residues in apples as more chemicals need to be used to obtain the required supermarket appearance.

Supermarkets also encourage waste because they rarely stock anything other than evenly sized apples. This means that smaller and larger fruits, although perfectly good to eat, are commonly rejected as 'grade outs', often around 40 per cent of the crop. Growers have to try to find another buyer, or let them rot. Supermarkets insist that their cosmetic and size requirements are responding to consumer demand, but most people just buy from what they see on the shelves. If you only see apples in supermarkets rather than fresh from the orchard, then it can come as a surprise that they don't all grow to a uniform size and naturally fit into a moulded polystyrene pack of four. But growing awareness about the need to cut food waste is making more people open to the idea of more natural-looking fruits. Whether supermarkets will pay anything more than lip-service to this remains to be seen.

'Club' varieties of apples, such as Pink Lady, Jazz and Cameo, raise important questions about whether any company has the right to 'own' nature. To grow such varieties, growers must pay a fee to the patent-holder who has trademarked the variety. The issue here is that these club varieties were cross-bred from apple varieties that exist in nature and therefore belong to no one and are free for anyone to grow. If companies can take genetic material that was once part of our common genetic heritage and use it to make private profits, then this establishes a precedent whereby the genetic material of life is up for sale. If you object to this privatization of nature, then you may not want to buy club varieties.

Where and when should I buy apples?

British and Irish apples are picked from August until early November. Kept in cold store, some varieties will still eat very well until the following growing season. The early cropping varieties, such as Discovery and Katy, ripen in August through to early September, the midseason varieties such as Egremont Russet, Worcester Pearmain, Ellison's Orange and Spartan from September to October, the late-season varieties such as Kidd's Orange Red, Cox, Fiesta, Lord Lambourne, Bramley and Chiver's Delight in October. Make the most of Apple Day each October when there is a celebration of traditional varieties and lots of opportunities to sample them all around the country. Apples kept in modified atmosphere storage are on sale all year.

When home-grown apples are being picked, keep an eye out for fruit farms or market stalls that are selling the new season's crop. Throughout the year, traditional greengrocers are often a better source of English apples than supermarkets as they get supplies from regional wholesale markets that distribute produce from smaller, more local growers.

APPLES AND THE AMOROUS PLANT

The mistletoe we kiss under at Christmas is intimately intertwined with apple orchards. Mistletoe is a parasite on apple trees, forming large green balls of pretty leaves with pearly berries high up in the branches of the wintry trees. As orchards have declined, so has our mistletoe, to such an extent that there have been fears that in years to come we will have none for the festive season. Several mistletoe projects have been set up to conserve the much reduced apple orchards that still provide the creeper with its habitat. The UK capital of mistletoe is Tenbury Wells, the heart of mistletoe production in Worcestershire, Gloucestershire and Herefordshire, which currently struggles to provide enough of the plant to meet national demand. Other initiatives are under way further afield to restore apple orchards that have been neglected and plant new ones. Even five apple trees are enough to create an orchard that proves attractive to this amorous plant. At present, our mistletoe may travel hundreds of 'mistletoe miles' to get to us, a symbol of how close our once prolific apple orchards have come to collapse. Apples and mistletoe, like so many living things, are inextricably linked.

Will apples break the bank?

There is no point in shelling out more money for expensive club varieties as the eating quality doesn't merit the premium. Apples are cheaper when you buy them minimally packaged in a plastic bag, not in a tray of four. Cheaper apples, sometimes sold as Grade Two apples, usually taste every bit as good as more expensive ones. If you get stuck with some woolly-textured eating apples, chop and cook them in a little water and eat them as purée or apple sauce. Or if you have a machine for that purpose, juice them.

Avocados

The avocado's seductive charms are more to do with its velvety texture and its rich, rounded, mouth-filling creaminess than its mild, green flavour. The two main varieties sold here are the Hass, which has a darker, rougher skin, and the Fuerte, which is smoother and greener. Some US connoisseurs swear that the more fragile Fuerte is superior to Hass, but because its skin is not so robust, it is often picked so hard and underripe to prevent it from being damaged in transport that it never ripens up properly. So in practice, Hass avocados are often the better bet. As a rule of thumb, the larger the avocado, the better the eating quality.

Avocados need to be properly ripe to be experienced at their best. The best way to do this is to leave them at room temperature for anything from three days to a week and feel them gently from time to time. You can speed up the process by putting them next to bananas, or in a brown paper bag. Avocados shouldn't be refrigerated until they are ripe as the cold will stop them ripening, although ripe avocados will keep for some days in the fridge. A definite, all-round 'give' under the skin is an indication of ripeness, but you can never quite tell until you cut them open: avocados are a lottery.

Avocados shouldn't have a mesh of fibrous grey threads. This means that they have been affected by a rot that should never develop in good-quality fruits. These fibres won't do you any harm, but they are technically a fault rather than merely a consequence of overripeness. If you have the energy, take them back and ask for a replacement.

Never feel the need to be inventive with avocados. Recipes such as avocado soup, avocado mousse and baked avocado are a waste of both avocado and effort.

Things to do with avocados

- Use them in a salsa with over-ripe mango (preferably the very aromatic Indian or Pakistani fruits), finely chopped red onion and fresh coriander.

- Combine chunks of avocado with sliced chicory and thin slices of ripe pineapple. Dressed lightly with oil and vinegar, this is a good winter salad.

- Serve ripe avocados, mashed with lemon juice and a little skinned, deseeded and diced tomato, with crab meat.

- Fill bread rolls with avocado mashed with lemon, sea salt, black pepper, mustard cress and either potted shrimp or canned salmon.

- Combine leftover cooked, chopped chicken or turkey with chopped avocado and a little mayonnaise or soured cream. Serve with watercress and thin rashers of crisply grilled bacon or pancetta.

- Make a smoothie using a small amount of ripe avocado, pineapple or pineapple juice, natural yogurt or coconut milk and a little lime juice.

Are avocados good for me?

Avocados are largely composed of oil, mainly the monounsaturated sort which research suggests protects against heart disease and lowers blood pressure. The oils in avocados make them an excellent food for giving a feeling of fullness that can help quell the urge to over-eat. They are also a rich source of antioxidant vitamins, most notably vitamin E, which research suggests can help reduce the incidence of heart disease, certain cancers and strokes. Avocados have more soluble fibre than any other fruit, and this slows down the rate at which sugar is released into the bloodstream. They contain a number of useful minerals too, such as iron, copper and folate, and are a particularly good source of potassium, which helps to moderate blood pressure. This in turn may help protect against cardiovascular diseases such as heart disease and stroke. Several carotenes, such as zeaxantin and lutein, are found in avocados, which are thought to help keep the eyes healthy. Some research suggests that these carotenes also boost the absorption of micronutrients from other foods and combine with vitamin E to inhibit the development of certain cancers. In addition, avocados contain glutathione, consumption of which has been associated with reduced risk of some cancers.

How are avocados grown?

Avocados grow on trees in warm climates where the winter temperature is mild, and there isn't too much wind, because they are susceptible to frost. One crop each year is cultivated then harvested by hand. The avocados we buy tend to come from South Africa, the US, Spain, Peru, Chile and Brazil. They are harvested when they are mature, but still hard and underripe and these are generally sent by boat. Others are tree-ripened, or pre-ripened by being exposed to ethylene gas – like the gas given off by ripe bananas – then air-freighted.

THE CHOCOLATE OF FRUITS

The changing fortunes of the avocado speak volumes about how nutritional orthodoxy is first made and then unmade. When avocados appeared in our shops in the early 1960s, their foreignness made them highly desirable: to eat them was a way of demonstrating gastronomic sophistication. By the 1970s, avocados had been hybridized with that iconic 1960s dish, prawns Marie Rose, and a half avocado filled with prawns had became a restaurant and dinner party favourite.

But by the 1980s there was a question mark over the desirability of avocados. The public health dogma that dominated on both sides of the Atlantic, which then became enshrined in various popular diets, dictated that all fat was bad, and that calorie-heavy foods should be avoided. So oil-rich, calorific avocados – a large avocado can contain 400 calories – came into the line of fire. Avocados were seen as sinful and fattening, the wicked temptress of dieters everywhere, the chocolate of fruits.

Come the 1990s, this broad-brush, anti-fat guidance was weakening. It began to be acknowledged that far from being bad for the heart, monounsaturated fat might actually be good for it. So instead of being full of 'bad' fat, avocados became full of 'good' fat. But unable to make a total break from the low-fat/low-calorie prescription, the new nutritional gospel was subtly changed to say that avocado could be a healthy food, but only if eaten in moderation.

In the last decade, diligent slimmers and would-be healthy eaters up and down the land have continued to approach the avocado with caution and found themselves measuring out recommended servings of two tablespoonfuls of avocado, or composing salads that called for a sixth of an avocado, or using avocado as a 'healthier' alternative to butter or mayonnaise. Meanwhile, research that supports the all-round nutritional desirability of this fruit has stacked up. Some studies have found that eating avocados is associated not with weight gain, but weight loss. Increasingly, as more research explores its array of micronutrients, the avocado is now commended as a healthy, 'nutrient-dense' (nutritionally rich) food, although the habitual resistance to eating it in any quantity still lingers on.

Currently, the old simplistic dogma that all fat is bad is being unpicked. This was inevitable, given the absence of good evidence to support it and the growing body of evidence to challenge it. As we continue to struggle with the ever growing global problem of obesity, and low-fat/low-cal advice doesn't appear to be working, more research is focused on the question of satiety: the notion that eating more, not less, of foods that satisfy appetite may be the best long-term recipe for a healthy body weight. Bathed in this new nutritional light, the oily, filling avocado looks poised to secure its nascent 'superfood' status.

Who knows how avocados will, or won't, fit into nutritional orthodoxy in the future? And who cares? You may prefer just to take the view that avocados are a nutritious, whole food that people in warm countries have eaten for millennia without becoming obese or ill, and help yourself to a half, or even a whole, avocado when you feel like it.

Are avocados a green choice?

Avocado trees absorb and store carbon from the environment, which makes them a sustainable, environmentally friendly crop. These tall trees provide a wildlife-friendly habitat and a protective canopy that allows other crops to flourish below. Their roots also help stabilize the soil and prevent soil erosion after heavy rains and floods, extreme weather events that are becoming more frequent as a result of global warming.

However, all the avocados we eat are imported and travel very long distances, which is the opposite of environmentally friendly. That said, there is no substitute for avocados, so many people will feel that they will continue to eat them anyway. If you eat a lot of avocados, you might want to think about reducing your consumption. Choose hard avocados that have been shipped and then ripen them at home rather than pre-ripened avocados that have been air-freighted. Pre-ripened avocados also tend to come swathed in absurd amounts of unnecessary packaging when they have their own natural packaging: their skin. They cost more and are not always reliably ripe, despite the claim on the label.

Will avocados break the bank?

Unless they are discounted, avocados are rarely cheap, but as long as you don't eat too many of them, the cost is not that significant. You will pay a hefty premium for both the air-freighted 'ripe and ready to eat' sort, and gimmicky small avocados. You can get stunning avocado bargains from greengrocers and markets if you buy them when they are beginning to be overripe. Even ripe avocados with dark patches on the skin can be quite good, if you just cut away any bad bits.

Bananas and other tropical fruits

In the depths of winter, when boredom sets in with our stored apples and pears and small citrus fruits that are past their peak, the invigorating, zingy, larger-than-life flavours and perfumes of fruits such as pineapple and passion fruit are highly seductive. These two fruits, along with lychees and physalis (Cape gooseberry), travel reasonably well and when we get them in the UK they taste pretty similar to how they might on their home territory. Bananas, mangoes, guavas and papayas, on the other hand, rarely do, and other fruits, such as the pitahaya (dragon fruit), carambola (star fruit) and the kiwano (horned melon) are so spectacularly taste-free that they are best considered ornamental and left on the shelf. Plantain – the starchy, less sweet member of the banana family that is used for savoury cooking – transports reasonably well.

Almost all the tropical fruits we see on our shelves have come from a handful of commercial varieties that have been chosen, not for eating quality or taste, but because they can stand up to transport and look good, which means, among other things, that they must have a tougher skin than usual. Most mangoes on sale in Britain, for example, are from the visually attractive Tommy Atkin, Kent and Keitt varieties that were bred in the US, not in tropical countries. They look good with their shiny, smooth green and red skins, but lack perfume and are usually fibrous and turnip-like in the mouth. Indian Alfonso variety mangoes, or Pakistani Chaunsa and Langra mango varieties, on the other hand, are traditional varieties that look duller and their skins are often marked, but they are aromatic and full-flavoured with yielding flesh. These luscious mangoes are rarely found in supermarkets and are best sought out in Asian food shops.

Tropical fruits destined for supermarkets are usually picked underripe and immature – 'green and backward' as they are known in the fruit trade – so they can withstand transport either by air or sea. Not only do they never develop their full taste and scent potential, they can also remain unpleasantly acidic because they have been harvested before they would naturally sweeten. Pineapple and passion fruits often suffer from this problem. When they have ripened naturally, bananas, for instance, have lots of little brown specks on their skins, but our supermarkets would see these as flaws. When buying plantain, choose fruits with skins that are neither yellow nor too brown.

Although you can do a certain amount to ripen up tropical fruits at home, by leaving them for a few days at room temperature, say, or sticking them in a bowl with riper fruits to encourage them to ripen up also, their natural development has been disturbed much earlier in the supply chain, so there is only so much you can do with them.

Things to do with tropical fruits

- Bake bananas in orange juice along with a little lemon or lime juice and golden demerara or Barbados sugar to taste. Good warm with vanilla ice cream.

- Fry plantains sliced thinly on the diagonal until golden and crisp and serve with Caribbean dishes such as jerk chicken and rice and peas, or as an alternative to fried potatoes or chips.

- Use under-ripe green mango in a piquant Thai salad. Shred the fruit and mix with chopped shallots, basil and coriander leaves. Make a dressing by blending coriander stalks, lime juice, palm or caster sugar and a mild green chilli.

- Sprinkle sea salt, lime juice and chilli flakes on ripe mangoes and eat as a salad, or as a fresh pickle with Indian food.

- Serve strained, thick, Greek-style yogurt, flavoured with a little honey, a few crushed cardamom seeds and a pinch of toasted, crumbled saffron – in the style of Indian *shrikand* – then top with passion fruit pulp and seeds and a few chopped pistachios.

- Bring out the flavour of papaya by tossing slices with a squeeze of lime juice.

- Fry thin slices of ripe pineapple in golden caster sugar and unsalted butter. When golden, stir in some finely chopped ginger, either fresh or preserved in syrup. Slips down nicely with coconut ice cream.

Are tropical fruits good for me?

From a nutrition point of view, tropical fruits are full of beneficial vitamins, minerals and valuable micronutrients. Bananas, for instance, are loaded with potassium, which is thought to reduce blood pressure, pineapples and papaya are considered to be anti-inflammatory foods, while ripe mangoes are a good source of carotenes. Eating foods rich in carotenes is associated with a reduced risk of heart disease, stroke, certain cancers and cataracts. Tropical fruits do contain a fair amount of natural sugar, more than non-tropical, native fruits such as berries. This means that they aren't a great choice for anyone who is diabetic or trying to lose weight. That said, they make a much healthier alternative to sweet foods that you might otherwise eat, like cakes or biscuits.

From an overall health and safety perspective, the pesticide residues that commonly turn up in non-organic tropical fruits are a cause for concern. Government tests here show that the vast majority of bananas and pineapples, for instance, contain residues. Pesticide residues are toxins so it makes sense to limit your exposure, meaning it is probably a good idea not to eat tropical fruit in vast quantities. If you are a parent, you may want to restrict the amount of non-organic tropical fruits that you give to babies, toddlers and children who, because they are still growing, are more susceptible than adults to the effects of pesticide residues.

How are tropical fruits grown?

Our growing taste for tropical fruits has had fairly direct effects on the way that they are grown. If you visit many tropical countries, you will see different fruits growing alongside one another, mixed in with other food crops as just part of the natural vegetation. Since the 1980s however, with the spread of supermarkets, smaller-scale producers of bananas and other tropical fruits have been overtaken by the plantation-style production which is owned and operated by large transnational companies who use hired, often casual, often migrant, labour.

These plantations, be they in Costa Rica or Cameroon, are vast, stretching much further than the eye can see. Trade union groups and non-governmental organizations report that workers routinely earn less than a living wage while working in unhealthy and often hazardous conditions. In Latin America, for example, the banana has earned the nickname of 'the chemical fruit' because workers are so exposed to pesticides, often by aerial spraying. Costa Rican pineapple plantation workers frequently have deformed fingernails from planting pesticide-soaked plants with their bare hands. Many tropical fruits are also dipped in chemical fungicides before being dispatched to stop them from rotting en route. When you buy organic fruits, you know that workers haven't had to risk their health to grow them. Organic certification standards do not cover workers' conditions or pay, but mean that workers do not have to work with agrochemicals day in and day out and are likely to have a better working environment and conditions than the industry norm.

A string of reports has testified to how fruit workers are working for up to fifteen hours at a stretch, six days a week, and travelling (at their own expense and in their own time) another few hours to and from work. Once on the plantation, they are on 'piece' rates so have to work longer than their nominal hours just to make a living. It is estimated that banana plantation workers earn as little as 2–3 per cent, and no more than 5 per cent, of the final retail price consumers pay. This contrasts with small-scale producers who are Fairtrade, who get about 16 per cent of the final price.

On fruit plantations, tales of victimization and harassment of workers' organizations and representatives who try to improve working conditions are common. There have been several lawsuits (both successful and unsuccessful) where groups of plantation workers have sued for compensation for the adverse health effects they have suffered from unhealthy and dangerous working conditions. Most tropical fruits on sale in the UK, unless they are Fairtrade or organic, come from plantation-style production systems. Fairtrade bananas, which usually come from the Caribbean or the Dominican Republic, are grown on a much smaller scale and come from people who earn a living wage and who have reasonably equitable working conditions. Fairtrade producers are required to minimize their use of pesticides.

Are tropical fruits a green choice?

Plantation-style intensive fruit production is a disaster for the environment. It is standard practice to plant them in monocultures – kilometre after kilometre of the same fruit – since this makes it easier to cultivate and harvest mechanically and has lower production costs. Plantation production leads to a build-up of disease and pests because there is no rotation of crops and an absence of companion plants that would attract beneficial predators to outcompete with them.

Plantation production is also focused on a handful of highly commercial global crop varieties, which are selected mainly for their cosmetic appearance and also for their ability to stand up to long-haul transport. All bananas come from the ubiquitous Cavendish variety, while most pineapples are either of the Smooth Cayenne type or one of the new ultra-sweet golden sort. This narrow genetic base also makes them more susceptible to disease because they are not as well-suited or adapted to local growing conditions as more diverse native varieties, which have remained popular over time because of their disease resistance.

For all these reasons, any more natural production methods, such as organic, or even just a reduction in pesticide use, are out of the question, so plantation-produced tropical fruits are grown at all stages in their life cycle with regular treatments of agrochemicals. Environmental organizations in countries where intensive plantation-style fruit production is widespread have monitored how pesticide run-off from plantations has polluted rivers, killing off wildlife and aquatic species.

Tropical fruits are either sent by air, which generates substantial amounts of CO_2 and so fuels climate change, or they come by boat, which is generally thought to produce less carbon than air transport.

The only commercial source of organic bananas is the Dominican Republic because it has not been affected by the black sigatoka disease that has blighted production elsewhere, so natural production methods that do not rely on chemicals are viable there.

Where and when should I buy tropical fruits?

Tropical fruits are on offer all year round. Since the 1980s, supermarket distribution with its global reach has made tropical fruits seem as 'everyday' and reliably available as our native fruits. But on taste and environmental grounds it is better to think of them as fall-backs for times of the year when home-grown or European fruits are thin on the ground.

Given that so many of the tropical fruits on our shelves are disappointing to eat, it is very worthwhile considering tinned versions. Tinned Alfonso mango pulp is likely to taste much better than most of the 'fresh' mangoes you can lay your hands on. Lychees and rambutans also retain much of their aroma when canned. Drain off the syrup if you want to eat less sugar. Dried tropical fruits, such as mango and pineapple, often have an attractive, slightly concentrated flavour. They are often surprisingly good when rehydrated (soaked in liquid) and eaten as a breakfast compote, or used in baking (see DRIED FRUIT AND CANDIED FRUITS).

THE CARIBBEAN CONNECTION

The only perishable tropical fruit that figured in any quantity in the British diet before the 1980s was the banana. Nowadays it is the UK's most popular fruit. It was not until the beginning of the twentieth century that importers figured out a way to import bananas to Britain from our colonies without them arriving rotten. During the Second World War, bananas were unobtainable as banana ships with refrigerated holds were requisitioned for other cargoes. Shipments recommenced after the war.

Our main source of bananas until the 1990s was the Caribbean islands of Jamaica, St Vincent, Grenada, St Lucia and Dominica, where the fruit was grown on small, family-owned farms. Growers there earned a living wage and their conditions were negotiated by trade unions and enshrined in law. As supermarkets have largely taken over from the traditional greengrocer, and transnational companies have supplied them with cheaper, plantation-style bananas, Caribbean banana growers have been pushed out of the market. In 1992 there were 24,000 banana farms in the Caribbean; now there are fewer than 4,000. Caribbean banana growers got together and became Fairtrade to differentiate their fruits from the cheaper, more ubiquitous, plantation-style equivalent. If you think it is important to support more equitable banana production and support our traditional suppliers, seek out Caribbean bananas.

TROPICAL FRUITS

Tropical fruits are generally very expensive and often a bit of a let-down to eat, so they rarely justify the outlay. The one exception to this rule is bananas, which have reduced dramatically in price. For years, supermarkets have conducted regular 'banana wars' where they slash the cost of bananas. Bananas are what supermarkets call a 'known value item', a staple, everyday food, like sliced bread or milk, that consumers are known to use as benchmarks to gauge how cheap, or otherwise, a store is. If a chain can sell these price-sensitive essentials at a spectacularly low price, then this can be used to put a halo of good value around everything else in the store.

Trade unions and charities insist that the long-term effect of subsequent banana price wars has been to impoverish banana workers. They argue that the relentless downward pressure on price favours banana suppliers that do not pay their workforce a living wage or offer decent working conditions. Furthermore, they say that cheap plantation bananas are harming more ethically produced bananas by making them look extremely expensive in comparison.

Cherries

Botanically speaking, there are hundreds of different varieties of cherries. Britain alone has around 300, although commercial fruit production in the UK concentrates on a more restricted number of varieties. Sweet cherries vary in colour from the white, red-dappled Napoleon or Merton Glory, through red varieties such as Kordia and Penny to black cherries such as Waterloo and Hertford. Acid, sour cherries, such as Montmorency and Morello, are more translucent in appearance and are rarely grown commercially in the UK but do grow in domestic gardens. Duke cherries are a cross between sweet and acid, while cherries that grow in the wild are known as 'geans'.

Though imported cherries from sunny countries like Turkey and Spain are always sweet, cherry aficionados swear that our maritime climate produces crisper, better fruits with deeper, more intense flavours. Adding to the appeal of UK-grown cherries is their freshness. Chilean cherries, for instance, will have spent three weeks in cold storage being shipped to our shores and are likely to be a month old by the time we eat them. Many imported cherries are from firm-skinned modern varieties that have been bred to transport well, rather than selected for flavour.

Traditional English varieties famed for their flavour and worthwhile buying whenever you see them include:

Bradbourne Black, Merton Glory, Merpet,
Merton Premiere, Florence, Frogmore Early, White Heart,
Kentish Red, Early Rivers, Waterloo.

Newer, more commercial varieties with good eating qualities include:

Sunburst, Kordia, Penny, Summersun,
Lapins, Sasha, Stella, Van.

Things to do with cherries

- Make a French batter pudding or clafoutis.

- Use tart varieties of the fruit in a crumble or pie.

- A few fresh cherries make a big impression when stoned, halved and baked in muffins.

- Use cherries, in place of strawberries, to make a creamy Eton Mess. Stone cherries and mix with double cream, whipped to soft peaks, and crushed meringues. Drizzle on some Italian Amarena cherry syrup or Maraschino liqueur to serve.

Are cherries good for me?

Cherries give you useful amounts of vitamin C, which supports the immune system, and soluble fibre, which slows down the rate at which sugar is released into the bloodstream, and potassium, which helps moderate blood pressure. Some research suggests that the antioxidants in cherries may be protective against heart disease, cancer, diabetes and Alzheimer's. Other research supports the notion that they may have anti-inflammatory properties. This chimes in with the traditional use of cherries and cherry juice as a natural remedy for gout.

How are cherries grown?

In the past, British cherry trees were hard work. They were grown from rootstock that produced tall trees, as much as forty to sixty feet high, which had to be harvested rather precariously, while balancing on frighteningly tall ladders. They were also rather temperamental. All it took was a hard frost and the cherry blossom would not 'set' and the fruit would not form, meaning a poor or non-existent harvest. British growers have now started using newer varieties growing on dwarf rootstock. These smaller trees are easier to protect from birds and bad weather and can be harvested from the ground or with small, stable tripod ladders. Some English cherries are now grown under polytunnels.

Post-harvest, cherries can be washed and lightly brushed then dipped in an edible wax. Various types of wax are used such as carnauba (from palm trees), shellac (from beetles), beeswax and petroleum wax. Waxing makes them look shiny but has no nutritional properties, so you may prefer to avoid waxed fruit. Duller-looking cherries may not have been waxed.

Commercial cherries are grown in Kent, as well as in areas such as Buckinghamshire, Hampshire, Worcestershire and Essex.

Are cherries a green choice?

Cherry trees absorb and store carbon from the environment, which makes cherries a sustainable, environment-friendly crop. Cherry orchards provide a wildlife-friendly habitat, while the tree roots help stabilize the soil and prevent soil erosion after heavy rains and floods.

British cherry production declined to an all-time low in 2003 when the total area of our cherry orchards was reduced to a tenth of what it was in the 1950s. But since then, cherry orchards have been on the up as growers have started using this dwarf rootstock and cultivating newer cherry varieties that yield more consistently, and British fruit growers now see a future in cherries once again. New orchards are being planted and British cherry production is increasing significantly as these become fruitful.

Where and when should I buy cherries?

With our portfolio of heritage and new varieties, it is now feasible for growers to produce sweet English cherries commercially for a six-week season, from June to August. Our large food retailers have tended to rely on cheaper foreign imports that are more consistent in supply and appearance but often lack the flavour and character of the British crop. However, the proliferation of farm shops and farmers' markets has created an important new sales outlet for small- and medium-sized growers who lack the scale necessary to supply supermarkets. So come June, look out for vivid, scarlet, summer bursts of this juicy fruit enlivening market stalls, farm gate shops, pop-up roadside stalls and traditional greengrocers.

Outside the summer season, forget about eating cherries or use tinned or bottled ones. Sweet cherries lose a lot when frozen but sour varieties are still fine for pies and crumbles.

ORCHARD FRUITS SINCE ROMAN TIMES

Given the relative rarity of British cherries now, it is hard to believe that they were once common British fruits. The familiar cry of the cherry seller in the streets of seventeenth-century London was immortalized by the poet Robert Herrick, who wrote:

> Cherry ripe, ripe, ripe, I cry,
> Full and fair ones; come and buy...

In fact wild cherries are native to Britain and cherries have featured among our British orchard fruits since Roman times. The Tudor kings were especially keen on cherries and encouraged the planting of cherry orchards in Kent, which, to this day, is still the region that produces most of the British crop.

Will cherries break the bank?

Cherries, whether imported or British, will never be cheap and air-freighted cherries from countries such as the US and Chile are always scarily expensive. If you wait for the European and English season in June and July, you can expect prices to decrease as the season progresses. So it pays to keep an eye on the price of the early cherries then buy when availability is greatest and price lowest. Cherries, consumed in any quantity, are only ever going to be a once-a-year, seasonal treat.

Citrus fruits

(oranges and small citrus fruits (clementines, satsumas, minneolas, ortaniques), lemons, limes, grapefruit, kumquats)

They come in different shapes, sizes and colours, but members of the citrus family all have one thing in common: that refreshing, almost thirst-quenching quality. Oranges, and smaller citrus fruits such as clementines and satsumas with their likable sugar–acid balance, can almost double up as a drink. The slightly spicy, intense juice of the blood orange inhabits a magnificent category all of its own. The sourer, more bitter-tasting grapefruit and Seville orange wake up the senses in an invigorating way. A kumquat surprises with its sweet skin and sour centre while the zingy lime has an exhilarating perfume that enlivens everything it touches. The lemon, of course, is one of nature's key flavour enhancers, a fruit no kitchen should ever be without. A squeeze of lemon juice improves just about anything.

When choosing citrus fruits, appearance is a red herring. The shiny, plastic-looking identikit fruits that crowd our shelves look nothing like the ripe, naturally grown ones you'll find in producer countries. More natural citrus fruits are generally larger, less uniform in colour, often with green patches (in the case of oranges) and knobbly bits (in the case of lemons and limes). Smaller citrus fruits are picked for rapid eating, but larger citrus fruits are often picked not fully mature so that they are less fragile to transport and will store better. What that means in practice is that many of our oranges, lemons, limes and grapefruit are often underdeveloped; that is, they have too much peel and pith in relation to juicy fruity interior, their exteriors are ungiving and hard, and they have a surplus of pips. Go instead for softer, more yielding oranges, lemons, limes and grapefruit that feel heavy for their size. With a bit of luck, they will be sweet and juicy.

Things to do with citrus

- A last-minute dusting of fresh Italian gremolata – finely grated lemon zest, finely chopped parsley and garlic – enlivens and freshens up meaty stews.

- Lemon posset – just-warmed unwaxed lemon zest and juice with cream and sugar – is one of the very simplest, but most popular desserts. Add lime zest too, if you can get your hands on unwaxed limes.

- Make the classic Sicilian salad of peeled orange segments (preferably blood oranges) combined with thinly sliced fennel and red onion. Dress with olive oil. Good with roast pork belly and oily fish.

- Pour a little warmed maple syrup and Campari or vermouth over peeled segments of pink or white grapefruit.

- If oranges and chocolate is a marriage made in heaven, then steely grapefruit and cuddly avocado is a classic attraction of opposites.

- Make a quick sauce for duck by bubbling up and reducing mild honey (such as acacia) or maple syrup, orange juice and zest and stock. Bring the sauce together by swirling in a knob of cold unsalted butter.

- A few curls of orange zest provide an essential taste in the southern French beef daube or stew.

- Preserved, salted lime from Middle Eastern stores adds an agreeably sour taste to many Iranian dishes.

Are citrus fruits good for me?

Citrus fruits are a very good source of vitamin C, which helps protect cells against damage, supports the immune system and aids the absorption of iron. They contain pectin, a type of soluble fibre that aids digestion. This fibre is in the papery pith that encases each citrus segment, so eating whole fruits with it still intact is better for you than drinking only the juice. Citrus fruits also contain many beneficial phytochemicals. These include the flavonoid, hesperidin, which is thought to reinforce the antioxidant effect of vitamin C and have anti-inflammatory effects, and the terpene, limonene, which some research suggests may have an anti-cancer action. Blood oranges also contain a red pigment, or anthocyanin, which some research suggests may reduce the risk of heart disease, some cancers and cataracts.

Government tests show that almost all non-organic citrus fruits contain residues, typically multiple residues of anything up to seven different pesticides. Pesticide residues are toxins, so the less of them you eat, the better for your health. Since most of the residues on citrus fruits are on the skin, it is not a great idea to use your teeth to start unpeeling them. If you are going to eat the skin of the fruit, say in the form of zest, candied peel or marmalade, buy unwaxed or organic fruits which will not have surface pesticides. They feel softer and their skins look duller, but they are safer to eat. Seville oranges for making marmalade are routinely sold unwaxed.

How are citrus fruits grown?

Unless they are organic, citrus trees are heavily sprayed with pesticides in the field, then treated with further pesticides after picking. The fruits are either dipped in, or sprayed with wax from a plant, animal or petroleum source that has been mixed with fungicide. The purpose of this post-harvest treatment is to give the fruits an attractive cosmetic gloss and make them last longer in storage.

Most of the oranges, small citrus and lemons we eat come from Spain, Morocco, Israel and Italy. Outside winter, most imported ones come from South Africa and South America. Most of the grapefruit we eat come from the US, Israel or Cyprus. Limes are usually from Mexico or Brazil.

Are citrus fruits a green choice?

Citrus trees absorb and store carbon from the atmosphere, which makes their fruits a sustainable, environmentally friendly crop. These orchard trees provide a wildlife-friendly habitat. Their roots also help stabilise the soil and prevent soil erosion.

The UK and Ireland can't grow citrus fruits commercially, so unless you want to sign up for a citrus-free life, imports are a necessity. Since citrus fruits are reasonably robust, they are usually transported most of the way by road or shipped. Some small citrus fruits, such as limes and kumquats, are air-freighted. To lighten the load on the environment, buy citrus fruits grown in Europe or the Middle East and keep purchases of fruits from further afield to a minimum.

Where and when should I buy citrus fruits?

Winter is the best time to eat citrus fruits. They come into their own in the depths of winter when our native summer fruits seem like a distant memory, and autumnal apples and pears are beginning to show signs of having spent too long in store. January, February and March are the months for buying new season's European and Middle Eastern oranges, lemons and grapefruit. But these fruits last well in cold store and can be eaten for many more months.

FRUIT

Small European and Middle Eastern-grown citrus fruits, such as clementines and satsumas, are in season from November until February. If they still have fresh green leaves attached then they will have been freshly picked. They do not store well, so outside this time any small citrus fruits on sale will either be from the tail-end of the Europe and Middle East harvest, or have come from further afield. There is no especially good time to buy limes as they are imported from South American countries all year round.

When the Italian citrus crop is in full swing (from April until the autumn), it is worthwhile checking out enterprising delicatessens, specialist food shops and markets. They sometimes stock otherwise hard-to-find fruits such as perfumed lemons from Amalfi and Sicily and soft-skinned blood oranges (also known as Moro, Tarocco or Sanguinello) from southern Italy and Morocco.

AN EARLY INTERVENTION STUDY

We may not grow them, but citrus fruits are embedded in our history. Introduced to them by early spice merchants and sea explorers, we instantly saw their potential and promptly drafted them into service in cooking, medicine and perfume-making.

Long before scientists named it vitamin C or ascorbic acid, the beneficial effects of this vitamin that is so abundant in citrus fruit had been recognized. For centuries, citrus juice was used in traditional medicine as a cure for scurvy, the disabling disease that affected sailors and pirates on long sea voyages. In 1747 James Lind, a Scottish doctor and naval surgeon, observed that the cabbage-eating Dutch had fewer problems with scurvy than the British or the French. He carried out an experiment – one that would now be referred to as an intervention study – to see which substances were most effective in treating it. Some sailors were given a mixture of garlic, horseradish and mustard, some seawater and the others lemons and limes, which turned out to be the most effective remedy. Lind used this experiment to prove that something in these fruits effectively prevented the disease. His findings were not widely accepted at the time by the medical establishment, but they laid the foundations for the subsequent 'discovery' and naming of vitamin C in the 1930s.

CITRUS

The better looking citrus fruits are, the more they cost. The price difference between a large, shiny, cosmetic pink grapefruit, for example, and a smaller, duller yellow one that looks slightly bashed from being stored, can be substantial. One of the frustrating things about buying citrus fruits is that external appearance is a poor indicator of the eating quality, but what this does mean is that if you are prepared to try less prepossessing-looking specimens, you can find great-tasting fruits at a bargain price.

Think twice before you stump up for premium-priced small citrus fruits that still have their green leaves attached. They are certainly fresh, but may not actually taste any better than their cheaper, leaf-free equivalents.

In the depths of winter, if you are eating a lot of citrus fruit, it's a good idea to buy them from a greengrocer or market stall. These outlets are almost always cheaper than supermarkets, and if you can buy a whole box, say a case of blood oranges or a smaller, shoe-sized box of clementines, then you can drive an even harder bargain and make a massive saving on the supermarket price.

Currants

(blackcurrants, redcurrants, whitecurrants, gooseberries and jostaberries)

Although they are native to these shores, blackcurrants, gooseberries, white- and redcurrants have come perilously close to becoming 'forgotten fruits', losing out to the more instantly accessible delights of blueberries and strawberries, but, fortunately, they are undergoing something of a renaissance.

Traditional 'culinary' varieties of blackcurrants, gooseberries, red- and whitecurrants are generally considered tart and will usually need to be warmed and softened with a little sugar if they are to release their perfume and become palatable. But when they are left to ripen on the bush, they can be surprisingly sweet and you can eat them just as they come. Most modern 'dessert' varieties with their more honeyed flavours are designed to be eaten this way. Well-recommended, flavoursome currant varieties include:

> Ben Connan, Ben Lomond, Ben Sarek, Ben Hope,
> Ben Alder (blackcurrants)
> Whinham's Industry, Invicta, Careless (gooseberries)
> White Versailles (whitecurrants)
> Rovada, Jonkheer Van Tets (redcurrants)
> Jostaberry (a cross between a blackcurrant and a gooseberry)

Things to do with currants

- The presence of a generous amount of blackcurrants in its fruity interior lends a welcome acidic backbone to the classic summer pudding.

- One blackcurrant leaf will perfume a glass of chilled Pimm's.

- Sharp, clean redcurrant has an affinity with mint, and both work beautifully in a sauce with a summertime leg of lamb.

- Gooseberry crumble gives the popular rhubarb equivalent a good run for its money.

- By way of whipped cream puddings, it takes a lot to beat a gooseberry fool, perfumed with just a hint of elderflower cordial.

- If you can't be bothered topping and tailing blackcurrants, just simmer them with water and strain off the juice. Sweeten to taste with sugar and use as a cordial, or set with soaked gelatine to make a gorgeous, tart jelly.

Are currants good for me?

Blackcurrants' vibrant purple-blue colour signals the presence of health-promoting flavonoids, called anthocyanins, which are thought to be protective against myriad ills: heart disease, cancer, inflammatory conditions and urinary tract infections and more. They are also loaded with vitamin C – streets ahead of other fruits. Red- and whitecurrants, gooseberries and jostaberries are also an excellent source of vitamin C, which supports the immune system, potassium, which helps moderate blood pressure, and iron, which prevents anaemia.

Government tests show that about two-thirds of currants contain pesticide residues, typically multiple residues of anything up to six different pesticides. They have also found traces of illegal pesticides in blackcurrants. Pesticide residues are toxins, so it makes sense to limit your exposure by not eating large quantities of these fruits unless they are organic or home-grown.

How are currants grown?

Blackcurrants, red- and whitecurrants, gooseberries and jostaberries grow on bushes and thrive in the UK in berry-growing areas areas such as Perthshire and Angus because they like cool weather and tolerate shade, conditions that make for a certain acidity and allow the fruit to ripen slowly rather than being baked into maturity by a warmer sun. It is no coincidence that many currant varieties were bred in Scotland. Lower temperatures allow the fruit to go through a desirable period of dormancy.

Are currants a green choice?

Britain grows only 10 per cent of the fruit it eats so there is a pressing need for us to increase our fruit production. Bush fruits like currants are relatively easy to grow and the UK could easily increase its output if there was an increase in consumer demand. They are a category of fruit that Britain can grow exceptionally well. One mounting concern among growers is that global warming may encourage the plants to awaken too early, only to be killed off by frost, so reducing our future supply.

All year round, 'fresh' redcurrants, and sometimes whitecurrants, are air-freighted to the UK from far-flung countries generating unnecessary, environmentally ruinous food miles, just so they can be used to garnish desserts and cakes. These imported specimens cannot match the freshness or flavour of our native fruits in season and cost a bomb. Why bother?

Where and when should I buy currants?

Once stalwarts in the British summer fruit repertoire, British currants are in season in July and August but can be surprisingly hard to find in greengrocers and supermarkets, and when you do see them there, they can be quite expensive. It's much better to go to farm shops, farmers' market stalls or direct to growers. See www.pickyourown farms.org.uk for lists of farms where you can pick your own.

There is a very strong argument for getting your hands dirty and growing your own. Reasonably well-established bushes can be bought for around £5 from garden centres and mail-order specialist fruit nurseries and will give you fruits in the first year. This may sound like extreme lengths to go to just to taste these often overlooked summer fruits, but they require a minimum of cultivation, suit most soils and conditions and fruit for years and just one bush will reward you first with verdant green leaves, then pretty flowers, followed by buckets of jewel-like currants.

QUINTESSENTIALLY BRITISH SUMMER FRUITS

Traditionally, blackcurrants, gooseberries and redcurrants were staple summer fruits, the backbone of many quintessentially British dishes, such as summer pudding or Eton Mess, bringing some of the fragrance we often associate with sauvignon blanc wines. Of all the currants, blackcurrants are the most widely grown in Britain. Ninety-five per cent of home production provides the raw material for Ribena, while the remaining 5 per cent has been snapped up by enthusiastic jam-makers.

In recent years, blackcurrants and gooseberries have been eclipsed by berries that require no preparation, especially blueberries. The latter have found favour with modern consumers because they can just be popped in the breakfast bowl and eaten raw.

Received wisdom is that blackcurrants, gooseberries, red- and whitecurrants and jostaberries, on the other hand, need some preparation, either topping and tailing or removing from the stem. Unless you are obsessive about removing every little top and tail, this need not be too laborious. You may find that you can happily eat blackcurrants and gooseberries, without any topping and tailing whatsoever, in recipes like crumbles.

Will currants break the bank?

Apart from July and August, currants are all sold frozen, often in pricey summer berry selections. If you can get yourself organized to buy trays of currants when they crop direct from growers and then freeze them yourself, then they will be affordable. If you grow your own, better still.

Blackcurrants, redcurrants, whitecurrants, gooseberries and jostaberries all freeze well either raw (topped, tailed, destalked as appropriate) or picked over then softened with sugar to make a versatile compote or purée that can be packed compactly in the freezer then served at breakfast, or as a component in a dessert to add a dash of vibrant flavour during dark winter months. Compotes and purées use considerably less sugar than jam and so are much healthier.

Grapes

You usually have a very straightforward choice when you buy grapes: red or white, very occasionally black. The Thompson's seedless variety is ubiquitous, Flame and Crimson are well-represented and Autumn Royal and Midnight Beauty have walk-on parts. These varieties can be firm, juicy and not without charm, but they don't overwhelm with flavour or perfume. If they do have any smell, it's likely to be a dank one from their weeks in storage. 'Fresh' grapes may have been stored for months by the time you eat them, which is one reason why they often have a tinny aftertaste and leave a slightly unpleasant sensation in the mouth.

In supermarkets, the only grapes that really do have some personality are the large, white, seeded Muscat grapes with their appealing muscatel fragrance and taste. Greek grapes can also be better than average. In greengrocer's shops, you may be able to buy small, seeded Turkish sultana grapes that can often be exceptionally sweet. Taste-wise, any seeded varieties you can find are likely to be better than the seedless sorts. The pips may be irritating, but such varieties are usually more aromatic. When grapes have slightly twig-like brown stems attaching them to their clusters, rather than the usual green ones, this is an indication that they have been picked later and so ripened more on the vine. They should be sweeter, and have more flavour as a result.

Things to do with grapes

- Grape halves, chopped leftover chicken or turkey and chopped pecans, all coated in a mixture of soured cream, mayonnaise and fresh herbs – such as tarragon, parsley and chives – make a substantial, main course salad.

- Use small or halved seedless black grapes in place of raisins to make a fresher, less cloying bread and butter pudding.

....

- For an elegant but simple dessert, macerate halved, stoned Muscat or Italia grapes in Vin Santo or a similar dessert wine. Dust with golden icing sugar and add a squeeze of lemon juice. Good with sweetened mascarpone.

....

- Bake fillets of white fish in white wine, strain off the cooking juices and use these to make a thin white sauce. Add a little cream and halved, deseeded green grapes just before serving, in the style of the classic French sole Véronique.

....

- Clusters of small, sweet grapes really complement a strong, salty blue cheese, served at room temperature.

Are grapes good for me?

....

Grapes are a reasonably good source of B vitamins, which help give you energy and support brain function, and are one of the best sources of potassium, which helps moderate blood pressure. Otherwise their main health virtue is that they contain a number of beneficial phytochemicals. These include the stilbenoid, resveratrol, which some research suggests may have an anti-inflammatory and anti-cancer action, and the flavonol, quercitin, which may reduce the incidence of asthma and certain cancers.

Grapes are the very worst fruit for containing pesticide residues. Over the last few years, the problem has been so bad that the European Commission has regularly issued EU-wide Rapid Alerts. Tests have shown that almost all grapes are contaminated with residues, typically multiple residues of up to eleven different pesticides. In one case, German authorities found a sample containing residues of twenty-six. Grapes routinely contain residues over the maximum permitted limit. The problem has been most marked in grapes from Chile. There is therefore an extremely strong argument for buying organic grapes. Organic growers can use just two pesticides in grape production and only when there is no other option. Conventional growers have an armoury at their disposal and use them routinely. No residues have been detected in organic grapes in recent years.

Grapes can sometimes cause allergies because they have been fumigated with sulphur. This treatment is not permitted on organic grapes.

Grapes are cultivated on vines. They are imported to the UK and Ireland from Europe (Spain, Italy, Greece), the Middle East (Egypt, Turkey, Israel), and Morocco, the US, India, South Africa and Chile.

Unless grapes are organically grown, they are frequently sprayed with pesticides because they are very susceptible to insect and fungal attacks that damage the crop and reduce its value.

Once hand-picked, bunches of grapes are taken to a packhouse then put into cold stores. Since they are prone to fungal rot and infestation with insects such as spiders, the grapes are fumigated. A number of different chemical fumigants are used, the most common one being sulphur dioxide. Grapes are fumigated once a week during storage and can be kept for up to five months, depending on the variety.

THE INVALID'S FRUIT

Grapes are traditionally the invalid's fruit, the treat that sits on your hospital locker. But grapes have also landed a steady stream of people in hospital as patients, rather than visitors. Over the years, supermarket grapes have provided personal injuries lawyers with a regular source of income. The scenario for litigation is the unwary shopper who slips on a runaway grape then crashes down on the smooth, tiled, unforgivingly hard supermarket floor. To limit their liability, supermarkets strategically place mats around the grape gondolas, but some hefty out-of-court settlements with wounded parties have forced them to change their packaging. Nowadays, most supermarket grapes are sold in zip-up bags or sealed cartons to stop any escapees. This doesn't mean that grapes have lost their potential for litigation entirely. It still leaves that other occasional grape hazard: spiders. Black widow and false widow spiders love grapes and pickers do not always spot them on the clusters. If they make it to cold storage, they can curl up and go to sleep, then wake up again when they warm up to room temperature. A close en-counter with a comatose arachnid, however, is rarely dangerous, and tends to be dealt with by an offer of money back, not thousands of pounds in compensation.

Are grapes a green choice?

The heavy use of pesticides in grape production causes pollution, encourages soil erosion and has negative impacts on wildlife and the surrounding environment.

Imported grapes are generally transported by ship and lorry, but some grapes from further afield, such as Chile, are air-freighted, which uses up more fuel and produces more greenhouse gases. For us to eat grapes grown under the shadow of the Andes in Chile, or Table Mountain in South Africa, the environment has to pay a very high price.

When should I buy grapes?

Grapes are on offer all year round. The best time for buying European grapes that have not been fumigated and stored for weeks is August, September and October, when white Greek grapes, Italian Muscat grapes and Turkish sultana grapes come on to the market.

Will grapes break the bank?

Grapes are always a pricey buy. Prices tend to stay the same throughout the year, irrespective of seasonal availability. If you need to save money, consider other cheaper fruit alternatives first.

Nectarines, peaches and apricots

A really ripe nectarine, peach or apricot, fresh from the tree, and still with a little residual heat from the sun, is a wonderful thing: fragrant, sweet and dripping with juice. Unfortunately, the ones we see in our shops and supermarkets rarely live up to that promise. Most of them will have been picked immature to help them withstand transport, and they will have been refrigerated, which interferes with post-harvest ripening. It can be really challenging to find good ones and few people will be unfamiliar with the shortcomings of bad ones: the tendency to rot rather than ripen and those fudge-textured, juiceless interiors. It's not surprising that many people lose interest in buying these fruits and see them as a lost cause.

It is possible, though, to find nectarines, peaches and apricots that, although not outstanding, do offer very respectable eating quality. The key here is buying them at the height of the European summer season when they are at their best. Spring and autumn fruits are more of a mixed bag as the grower's emphasis is on selecting varieties for their ability to extend the season, rather than their eating quality. Imports from further afield, such as the US and South Africa, are almost invariably poor, doubtless a consequence of their lengthy transportation. They may look the part, but very rarely taste it.

Nectarines, which are just smooth-skinned peaches, are generally more reliable for eating quality than either peaches or apricots. White-fleshed varieties of nectarines and peaches are sweeter and more fragrant than the more commonly encountered yellow-fleshed sort, which, though sweet, are considerably more acidic. White-fleshed 'flat', 'doughnut' or Saturn peaches and nectarines (named after the planet's rings) are particularly perfumed. Happily, this fragrant type of peach is becoming more available.

Larger nectarines and peaches, sold individually from trays in greengrocers, usually taste better than the smaller sort. A slight 'give' under the skin is promising, but even hard fruits, given time, can ripen in a warm room. Small fruits in punnets should be bought hard, removed from the punnet, and left in a single layer to ripen. Nectarines seem to fare better than peaches when sold as small fruits in netted punnets. When buying loose or netted nectarines and peaches, fragrance is the best clue as to whether they will eventually ripen satisfactorily.

Peaches and nectarines sold in more expensive sealed plastic packs of four and labelled as 'ripe and ready to eat', are usually an expensive flop. It may sound as if they have ripened fully on the tree, but in fact they are likely simply to be larger fruits, grown to tighter cosmetic standards – often requiring the use of extra chemical treatments – that have been picked immature, refrigerated and then 'ripened' with ethylene gas. They may feel soft and not be obviously rotten, but because their development has been arrested by early picking and prolonged refrigeration, they hardly ever ripen properly.

Apricots, like nectarines and peaches, can announce their ripeness with a come-hither fragrance, but for the most part, colour is the best indicator of ripeness. The more orange-red the colour, the better they are likely to taste. They barely ripen once picked so there isn't much you can do with underripe ones, other than cook them. On the upside, even fairly poor apricots can be quite good cooked because the sharpness of the skins perks up the dull flesh and makes for quite an acceptable taste.

Things to do with nectarines, peaches and apricots

- Fill stoned fresh peach halves with a mixture of crumbled amaretti biscuits, golden sugar and enough egg yolk to make a paste. Bake in the oven in a buttered dish until the filling is crunchy and slightly set.

- Butter slices of brioche on both sides, top with sliced ripe peaches or apricots and a generous sprinkling of coarse demerara or Barbados sugar. Bake until the fruit softens and the brioche becomes golden.

- Cut ripe nectarines or skinned peaches into thick slices or chunks and macerate for an hour or so in Prosecco or other sparkling white wine.

- As summer desserts go, the classic peach Melba – poached or canned peaches with fresh raspberry coulis and vanilla ice cream – takes some beating.

- Unripe imported apricots make a great winter compote. Just stone and soften them with a little sugar and water in a lidded saucepan; they make a good, tart foil for sweet milky puddings such as baked rice, or potentially cloying meringue.

- Peaches and apricots are luscious baked into an almond or pistachio frangipane tart.

Are nectarines, peaches and apricots good for me?

Nectarines, peaches and apricots are all good sources of vitamin C, which, among other things, helps keep cells healthy, and beta carotene, which turns into vitamin A in the body and is thought to perform many useful functions including strengthening immunity to infections and helping vision. The deeper orange-coloured the fruit, the more beta-carotene it contains. Apricots are a particularly good source. Nectarines, peaches and apricots also have useful amounts of potassium, which controls fluid balance and helps moderate blood pressure.

Nectarines, peaches and apricots are a category of fruit that is particularly bad for containing pesticide residues, so you may want to consider buying organic. Government tests have shown that almost all samples, unless organic, contain residues of at least one, and up to six different pesticides. Pesticides are toxins and exposure to them is best kept to a minimum.

How are nectarines, peaches and apricots grown?

Nectarines, peaches and apricots are tree fruits and harvested by hand. Most of the European nectarines and peaches we eat come from France, Spain, Italy and, to a lesser extent, Greece. France is also the main summertime source of apricots, although a small number of English apricots, from Kent, are now coming on to the market. The breeding of new self-fertilizing varieties of apricot trees, combined with warmer English weather, has made apricot production in the UK commercially viable. Outside summer, most imported stone fruits come from South Africa, the US and Chile.

Are nectarines, peaches and apricots a green choice?

Nectarine, peach and apricot trees absorb and store carbon from the atmosphere, which makes their fruits a sustainable, environmentally friendly crop. These orchard trees provide a wildlife-friendly habitat. Their roots also help stabilize the soil and prevent soil erosion.

Eating nectarines, peaches and apricots that come from outside Europe is a bad idea, since this inevitably means thousands of environmentally destructive food miles which leaves a heavy carbon footprint. And for what? They are rarely worth eating. The fact of the matter is that if you live in northern Europe, these are fruits to be eaten only in summer.

When should I buy nectarines, peaches and apricots?

Spanish, Greek, Italian and French nectarines, peaches and apricots are in season from June until September. The first two are at their peak in July and August, the latter in June and July. Imports from outside Europe are on sale at other times.

Will nectarines, peaches and apricots break the bank?

Buying supposedly 'ripe and ready' nectarines, peaches and apricots is one sure way to burn money. If you are strapped for cash, netted punnets of smaller nectarines are the best buy.

Peaches survive the canning process beautifully. Tinned peaches may not seem so upmarket but they will often taste much better than their fresh equivalent, and they are considerably cheaper. Tinned apricots can be pretty good too. These stone fruits are the exception to the rule that fresh is best.

FRUITS FOR A SHELTERED SUNNY SPOT

We think of peaches, nectarines and apricots as fruits that must always be imported, yet we used to be obsessive about growing them. Apricots, known as the 'hasty peach' because it ripens earlier, were documented in English gardens in the early sixteenth century. From the mid-seventeenth century onwards, well-to-do, aristocratic gentlemen would devote prodigious amounts of energy to growing peaches and apricots, or, more accurately, having their gardeners grow them, as these trophy fruits were so highly prized for their exquisite perfume and delectable sweet flesh. They were cultivated in glasshouses and conservatories or along walls, or shaped into a zig-zag 'serpentine wall' to catch the heat. Perhaps it's time to revisit our early reverence for peach and apricot. They will produce fruit outdoors in the milder south of England, and even fruit further north in a warm conservatory, or in a sheltered sunny spot. Who knows, perhaps with global warming, there might be a future for growing more of them in these isles.

Pears

A ripe, mature pear is a wonderful thing. It offers sweet, juicy flesh with that distinctive 'pear drops' perfume that is reminiscent, in the nicest possible way, of acetone, or nail polish remover. Ripe specimens have soft, yielding flesh that collapses between the tongue and the roof of the mouth and which is highly digestible. That is one of the reasons why pears are often recommended as a first food for babies.

But pears are also one of the most exasperating fruits to get to grips with. It can seem that they are either as hard as a turnip, or rapidly deteriorating into a pile of mush. Many people have never had the pleasure of tasting a good pear and more or less given up buying them, which is a pity, because pears can be a delight to eat, and England is particularly good at growing them.

The eating qualities of a pear depend very much on its variety.

Comice, or Doyenne de Comice, is an old French variety that has long been grown in England. The Comice walks away with the prize for creamy, velvety flesh and fragrance.

Conference is an English variety that dates back to the 1890s and is the most commonly grown commercial variety. It is sometimes seen as a more humdrum variety, which is a bit unfair. When its thick skin is peeled off and it is properly ripened, it can taste wonderful. Chefs prefer Conference pears for poaching because they hold their shape better than other varieties.

Concorde, a variety mainly grown in England, is a modern cross of the Comice and the Conference that is sweet and firm-fleshed but not particularly perfumed.

William pears, which usually come from Italy or South Africa, are exceptionally aromatic but their soft flesh and thin, fragile skin mean that they are ripe one minute and past it the next.

Passe Crassane pears, usually imported from France or Italy, can have a good flavour but some people find them too big and the flesh too gritty.

Forelle pears, with their attractive orange-pink blush, usually from South Africa, Chile or Argentina, have some of the taste qualities of Williams pears but have slightly tougher skin. They can also be a bit 'mealy' in texture and low in juice. Supermarkets like them because they look pretty and are easier to ship and handle.

Packhams pears, generally imported from South Africa, New Zealand, Chile and Argentina, have flesh with some of the delicacy of a Comice without its beguiling taste.

Rocha pears, which come from Portugal, are juicy and soft-fleshed but easily turn to mush.

No variety of pear tastes good unless it is properly ripe. They ripen from the inside out and the only indication that they are ready to eat is a slight 'give' or softness around the stem and under the skin. Eat pears too soon and they will be dry and dull-tasting with hardly any juice. Leave them too long and they turn brown and mushy at the centre.

You can buy them rock-hard, either sold loose or in simple plastic bags, and put them in a bowl at room temperature in a heated house, then watch them like a hawk. The fridge is their enemy because it will inhibit their natural ripening process. It might take anything up to a week to ripen large ones and allow the starch to convert to sugar, so anticipate when you might want to eat them and buy them in advance. Squeezing them is out, but a very gentle palpation is fine. When the stem is beginning to feel a little pliable, they should be rewarding to eat. Large fruits are best for this type of ripening because they are more mature than smaller ones and will have more flavour and scent potential. Don't buy 'ripe and ready to eat' pears as the taste and texture usually disappoint. Whatever type of pear you are dealing with, remember that all pears are best appreciated peeled.

Things to do with pears

- Pears gently poached in syrup made from sugar, water or wine and a split vanilla pod are always a winner. Vary the syrup by adding just a few crushed cardamom seeds and/or a pinch of lightly toasted, crumbled saffron strands . Choose hard pears for this treatment; Conference are ideal.

- A winter salad of sliced ripe pears, watercress and chicory with blue cheese dressing is fresh and nice, but pretty effortless.

- Butter a slice of sticky gingerbread on both sides, top with ripe, peeled, sliced pears and golden sugar, then bake until the pear juices begin to run. Good with thick natural yogurt.

- Pears go brilliantly with sheep's milk cheeses, such as Berkswell, Ossau-Iraty and pecorino, or with grainy Parmesan or salty blue cheeses of all types.

- Ripe pears eaten with still-juicy new season's cobnuts, hazelnuts or walnuts make a memorable pairing.

- Use peeled, sliced, fresh pears dusted with ground cardamom seeds and golden sugar as a base for a crumble. Add some crushed hazelnuts to the topping.

- Even pear sceptics will like poached or canned pears swathed in a runny, dark chocolate sauce.

Are pears good for me?

On the nutrition front, the main claim to fame of the pear is as a good source of soluble fibre, which slows down the rate at which sugar is released into the bloodstream, and copper, a mineral that is often deficient in modern diets. Pears are frequently recommended as a weaning food for babies and people with food allergies because they are easy to digest and unlikely to provoke allergic reactions.

Pears have been one of the worst fruits for containing pesticide residues. Government tests have found that nearly all pears are contaminated with residues, usually multiple residues of up to ten pesticides. In addition, the use of illegal pesticides has been detected in some samples, although the problem may be historic. In the past, a growth regulator was used to produce fruits of a uniform size and appearance but it has since been banned on health grounds. This does underline, however, how many pesticides remain in the environment and contaminate our food many years, even decades, after they have been used. Since pesticides are toxins it is best to avoid them as much as possible. There is an extremely strong argument for buying organic pears, even if that means choosing less visually perfect specimens with russeting (natural brown patches) or superficial skin defects. Organic growers can use only two pesticides in pear production and only in extremely limited circumstances – conventional growers have an arsenal at their disposal – and no residues have been detected in organic pears in recent years.

How are pears grown?

Our native pear season is from September through to October, and this is when English pears are at their best. Pears, both English and imported, are picked in the orchard when mature but still hard. Thereafter they can be sold as the new season's crop after a brief period of chilling which helps develop their flavour, or put in cold stores or in 'controlled atmosphere' or 'modified air' storage where oxygen has been removed from the air and carbon dioxide and nitrogen added to aid preservation. Stored this way, pears can be kept for a year, but they don't have the same flavour as when they are at their seasonal peak because they lose their ripening capacity over time and are more likely to suffer from 'brown heart', when the core of the apple turns brown but the pear is still not ripe.

Pears sold as 'ripe and ready' have been ripened up by the importer. These often look shiny because they have been given a post-harvest wax treatment using an edible wax such as shellac or carnauba. This stops them wrinkling and keeps them looking good and attractively glossy. These waxes are approved as food additives but as their use is purely cosmetic and they offer no nutritional advantage, you may prefer to avoid them. Pears do not have to be labelled as waxed but any glossiness is a dead give-away. Unwaxed pears look matt by comparison.

A NATIONAL FRUIT COLLECTION RIPE FOR REPLANTING

We have been growing pears in Britain for hundreds of years, most notably in Herefordshire, Gloucestershire and Somerset. Our National Fruit Collection lists some 550 traditional varieties of pears such as the Arlingham Squash, the Barland and the Huffcap, some grown as table fruits, others as 'perry' pears to make English perry, the pear equivalent of apple cider. But unless you frequent farm shops or have a tree in the garden, you are unlikely to see them as only a handful of more commercial varieties dominate our shelves. According to Common Ground, which campaigns to encourage diversity in orchards, over half of our pear orchards have disappeared in the last thirty years. So by buying English pears, we can support the growers who are still in business and encourage them to plant more trees.

Are pears a green choice?

Some 80 per cent of the pears we eat in Britain are imported, clocking up unnecessary food miles. Although pears are not usually flown in from overseas, they do require shipping and road transport. Many of the pears we eat in autumn come from Holland, Belgium or southern Europe and compete directly with our English crop. At other times of the year, imported pears come all the way from the southern hemisphere. These do not represent an environmentally aware choice because they have travelled long distances by road and sea. On taste grounds, they might be preferable in spring to eating rather uninspiring home-grown pears that have been in storage for six months, but they rarely rival the taste of a home-grown autumnal pear.

'Ripe and ready to eat' pears come swathed in protective packaging with several layers of polystyrene and plastic that is almost impossible to recycle and have to be sold in chiller cabinets which use up more energy than open shelves, so they don't represent an ecological choice.

When should I buy pears?

Fresh pears are on sale all year round but the best ones are to be had when the new crop of English pears is on our shelves, from September until December.

Will pears break the bank?

Hard, fresh pears that you can ripen up at home are normally reasonably priced. 'Ripe and ready to eat' pears are usually super-expensive and rarely live up to the price tag. Some people are a bit sniffy about tinned fruit, but if you are looking for pears to use in desserts or baking rather than to eat from the fruit bowl, then tinned pears can be useful and cheap, allowing you to opt out of the pricey lottery of finding a fresh ripe pear.

Plums, greengages and damsons

A ripe, sweet plum is a glorious fruit to eat, offering that pleasing contrast of tart skin with sweet flesh. Finding plums that fit the bill requires some dedication, however, because our shelves are crowded with types of plums that regularly disappoint. A further complication is that the only real way to tell if a plum is sweet and ripe is by biting into it, although some of our native plums often hint at their ripeness with a light, enticing fragrance. But plums can be a bit hit-or-miss.

This may sound like blind patriotism, but when it comes to flavour and texture, English-grown plums take some beating. They have a short summer–autumn season, so eat them then until they are coming out of your ears. Characteristically, English plums are thin-skinned, oval in shape and the stone comes away cleanly from the flesh which is soft, juicy and slightly jelly-like. The most commonly encountered sorts grown in England are the red/gold Victoria and purple/green Marjorie Seedling, both traditional English varieties, but other excellent native plums still grow in less commercial production. The later they are picked, the juicier they are. When they have been picked reasonably ripe, English plums will soften, darken and sweeten up a little further in the fruit bowl. English damsons have the most astonishingly intense, purple-plum flavour and are eaten cooked, not raw. Non-native varieties that grow well in the UK and Ireland include Jubileum, Avalon, Opal and Czar. In the autumn, some fine plums come from France, notably greengages. Don't be put off by their powdery bloom. They are generally quite sweet, with a slightly grainy flesh that clings to the stone.

Outside the European plum season, the only plums that taste good, more often than not, are the red and yellow, rather fudgy-fleshed, thin-skinned sort that are imported from South Africa, such as Santa Rosa and Laetitia, which have a faint bubblegum flavour, and Songold, which is very sweet. Otherwise we are stuck with a year-round supply of imported plums that are dark red or blue, round and heavy with thick, tough skins and dry, almost taste-free granular flesh that sticks to the stone. These plums appeal to supermarket buyers because they have a long shelf life and stand up well to handling and transportation. They come from a different family from the plums and gages that are native to Europe, and are known as Japanese plums, the most common variety on sale being Angelino. This type of plum is the quintessential supermarket fruit. For eating fresh, the quality is lamentable, although they can be used to make a reasonable compote.

Things to do with plums, greengages and damsons

- Spice up simple plum compote with a couple of cloves and a stick of cinnamon. If made with restrained sweetness, this is a good foil for duck and venison.

- Bake sugared plums under a layer of fresh white breadcrumbs and coarse Barbados or demerara sugar, generously moistened with melted butter.

- Poach halved, stoned, firm, red plums in a syrup made with port, sugar and water, flavoured with star anise.

- Any greengages that are disappointing to eat will still make an excellent chutney.

- Stewed damsons make a superlative, magenta-coloured fruit fool.

- Sharpen up a rich crème brûlée by putting a layer of tart plum purée under the custard.

- Use hard, small, stony damsons to make damson gin.

Are plums good for me?

Plums are a good source of vitamin C, which supports the immune system and aids the absorption of iron from other foods, and beta carotene, which helps protect against infection and promotes eye health. Plums also have very high levels of certain polyphenols, such as chlorogenic acid. It is thought that these phenols have an antioxidant effect; that is, they help neutralize the damage done by harmful free radicals that can predispose the body to disease. Some research suggests that the phenols in plums are anti-inflammatory, beneficial for vision, and can inhibit the proliferation of certain cancer cells. These phenols are most concentrated in the skin of the plum, rather than the flesh, and dark-skinned plums contain more than lighter ones.

How are plums grown?

Plums are orchard fruits. In England, Worcestershire and Kent are the main centres for plum growing. The trees are picked over a two-week period. Pickers first take the ripest fruits and then return for a second time to gather those that have ripened later. Most imported plums come from France, Chile, the US and South Africa, and plums from outside Europe are usually picked slightly underripe so that they are less fragile to transport.

Are plums a green choice?

Wherever they are grown, plum trees absorb and store carbon from the environment, which makes them a sustainable, environmentally-friendly crop. These orchard trees provide a wildlife-friendly habitat. Their roots also help stabilize the soil and prevent soil erosion.

Eating plums that come from the other side of the world makes no sense. This involves thousands of pointless food miles and they don't even taste that good at the end of their long-haul journey. What's the point? A better approach is to look on plums as a seasonal fruit, one to be eaten in bulk when the native and European crop arrives in late summer and autumn, not a year-round fruit bowl staple.

THE DAMSON'S WINNING CHARMS

Never miss a chance to taste or buy damsons. These small, dark blue fruits with their vivid purple juices are as plummy as they come and one of the unmissable jewels in our food heritage. Damson trees, with their beautiful snowy-white blossom, were once a common sight in the countryside, where many orchards contained damson trees, and they were frequently grown in gardens too.

In the 1980s and 1990s, production of English plums of all types went into decline as the supermarkets put their retailing muscle behind imported fruit, and killed off many of the independent shops that had previously stocked them. Damsons particularly fell out of favour because, unlike sweet table plums, they are tart and need cooking. Until quite recently, damsons were prime candidates for the endangered fruits list. Supermarkets just weren't interested in them because they grow in small quantities, so they were hard to find, even in enterprising greengrocers.

Of late, damsons no longer seem to be in such acute distress. Once on the edge of commercial extinction, damson enthusiasts and the rump of commercial growers who still produce them have focused their efforts on protecting our existing damson trees and promoting their cultivation. These days, the hotspot for damson production is the Lyth and Winster valleys in the English Lake District, where growers have declared a national Damson Day to celebrate the fruit, but there are also damson growers in Herefordshire, Shropshire and Worcestershire who sell their fruits to independent shops via wholesale markets.

The best way to ensure that damsons never disappear from commercial fruit production is to eat as many of them as you can. Snap them up from greengrocers, markets and roadside stalls, so that beleaguered fruit growers see that they still have a future. This is no penance whatsoever, given the damson's winning charms.

When should I buy plums?

English and French plums are in season from mid-August until the end
of October. Dark, thick-skinned imported plums are available year round.
Thinner-skinned red and yellow plums from South Africa are in season
from January until March.

Will plums break the bank?

Plums are never very expensive and in the English season they can be
pleasantly cheap. With the exception of some of the thinner-skinned
varieties grown in South Africa, plums imported from outside Europe
are a total waste of money.

Plums are fruits that almost never need to be thrown out. Over-soft
plums, even slightly rotten ones, can be trimmed and used for crumbles,
Brown Betties or fruit fools. Many underwhelming plums can make a
surprisingly good compote as the heat releases the tart, sour flavour and
colour in their skins.

Pomegranates

The pomegranate remains a stubbornly archaic fruit. It looks as though
it has not changed significantly over the centuries, like a fruit that might
appear in ancient wall paintings. To date, plant breeders have not yet
remodelled it to meet supermarkets' body fascist cosmetic specifications.
Break into a pomegranate, however archaic and battered-looking, and the
interior sparkles with regal, jewel-like seeds, which readily disgorge their
juice – anything from blushing pink to vivid scarlet. There's nothing like
a scattering of lustrous pomegranate seeds to add a celebratory quality
to a dish, be it savoury or sweet. In the mouth, pomegranate is a most
three-dimensional fruit. The juicy sweetness of its seeds is tempered by
a bitter, slightly tannic note and slight astringency.

When choosing pomegranates for taste, don't head for the prettiest fruits
with perfectly smooth, thick, shiny pink skins. Beautifully round, orb-like
pomegranates are most likely underripe. For ripeness and sweet, dark
juice, go instead for those with deeper red, mottled, slightly matt, thin,

dry skin that is settling into an almost square shape, developing ever so slightly sunken sides or facets.

Things to do with pomegranates

- Juice pomegranates with oranges. The bitterness of the former balances the sweetness of the latter. Add sparkling white wine to make a gorgeous cocktail.

- The seeds from just half a pomegranate tart up a fruit salad made with less exciting fruits.

- Otherwise beige dishes involving grains, such as rice, couscous and bulgar wheat – either hot or in salads – look much more special when scattered at the last moment with pomegranate seeds.

- Pomegranate seeds look gorgeous scattered over crumbled white feta cheese, on top of a green salad.

- Oily, rich, toasted pine kernels make an inspired contrast to the bitter, juicy crunch of pomegranate seeds. Use together to bedeck grilled meats, Middle Eastern salads and grain dishes.

- Pomegranate molasses (a tart, syrupy condiment made by reducing pomegranate juice) provides a distinctive, sharp tang in many traditional Middle Eastern dishes, such as *Muhammara*, the Syrian pepper dip, and *Fesenjan*, chicken cooked in a walnut sauce.

Are pomegranates good for me?

The pomegranate's main claim to fame on the vitamin front is as a good source of vitamin C, which helps protect cells against damage, supports the immune system and aids the absorption of iron. Otherwise, the fruit's modern reputation for being something of a superfood rests on the phytochemicals it contains – tannins, polyphenols and anthocyanins. Some research suggests that these micronutrients have an antioxidant effect; that is, they neutralize disease-promoting free radicals in the body. As pomegranates have become quite fashionable, more research is being carried out to establish how beneficial they might be for health. Among all the current claims being made for them, so far, there is some evidence to indicate that they are good for the heart and may reduce the risk of heart disease. This chimes with the use of pomegranates in traditional Indian (Ayurvedic) medicine, where the fruit is used as a heart tonic.

Pomegranates do contain fibre, mainly of the insoluble sort. Nutritional opinion is divided on the relative merits of this type of fibre (see GRAINS/ Are grains good for me?).

How are pomegranates grown?

Most of the pomegranates in our shops are grown in Spain, India, Pakistan and the Middle East. You may find Iranian and Afghan fruits in independent greengrocers. Pomegranates are also cultivated in the southern hemisphere in countries such as Peru and South Africa. Pomegranates grow as orchard fruits. Once they are picked, they are usually washed and sometimes waxed and stored in a modified atmosphere in a similar way to apples (see APPLES/How are apples grown?).

Are pomegranates a green choice?

Pomegranate trees absorb and store carbon from the atmosphere, which makes their fruits a sustainable, environment-friendly crop. Their roots also help stabilize the soil and prevent erosion. Pomegranates are a drought-tolerant crop, which makes them particularly suitable for cultivation in hot, arid areas. Thanks to their tough skins, pomegranates are quite disease-resistant and need few, if any, pesticide or fertilizer treatments, enhancing their green credentials further.

As they are a reasonably resilient fruit, pomegranates are usually transported by ship and road, not air. As pomegranates store well, even out of their season, it makes sense to stick with northern hemisphere fruits over those that have been imported from the southern hemisphere, necessitating thousands of avoidable food miles.

Where and when should I buy pomegranates?

Pomegranates from Europe, the Middle East and the Indian subcontinent are in season from September until February. Outside this season, they are available from cold store. Southern hemisphere pomegranates crop from March until May.

Ready-prepared pomegranate seeds are now a fixture in supermarket chiller cabinets. Their popularity in this convenience form illustrates just how daunting most British and Irish people find the task of deseeding a whole fruit. How are you meant to liberate the seeds from their tough, tight red jackets? How can you avoid aerosol spraying of both the cook and the kitchen? What's the best way to part the seeds from that spongy yellow pith?

As pomegranates have become increasingly popular, even trendy, we have grappled with the best way to deseed them. Trade bodies promoting the fruit to the time- and effort-averse modern consumer suggest no-mess techniques that involve slashing the skins, excavating the seeds under water, then draining them in a sieve. This sanitized method guarantees that you lose most of the juice. If your supermarket 'ready to eat' pomegranates taste insipid and dilute, they were probably processed in a deseeding machine that used water. Other helpful suggestions involve halving the fruit with a knife and then hitting each half, cut side down, with a heavy spoon or rolling pin to encourage the seeds to jump out. Some people advocate gently pummelling the whole fruit first to loosen up the seeds, but this method risks escaping juice and smashed seeds.

Both botanically and culturally, the pomegranate belongs to Iran and the Himalayan region, so for guidance on the best way to get to grips with the fruit, we can learn from Iranian, Afghan, Indian and Pakistani communities. Here, the very idea of letting the seeds come into contact with water raises eyebrows.

A favoured technique is as follows: make a shallow incision in the pomegranate with a knife, just enough so that you can then pull it apart with your fingers. Better still, break the skin with your fingernails and then pull it apart. (A ripe pomegranate will have a little 'give' under parts of the skin – this is where to start.) Once you have forced the fruit apart, turn the rugged halves broken side down and then pull back the skin as though you were trying to turn the fruit inside out. The seeds, which should be exposed in uneven peaks and ridges, should then pop out with relative ease. Those that resist can be coaxed out with the fingertips.

Pomegranates give you a lot of bang for your bucks, so to speak, because although they are rarely that cheap, it doesn't take too many seeds to make a big impact in a dish. Even half a pomegranate's worth of seeds adds bling.

Pomegranates often represent some of the best bargains in the fruit department. They are commonly reduced when they become slightly sunken and their skin dries out a bit, but as long as they aren't excessively so, they often taste sweeter and juicier. Don't be put off by the appearance of battered, blemished pomegranates. As any good greengrocer will tell you, they usually taste good inside. If in doubt, buy one, split it open and check that the seeds are nice and red and not brown – an indicator of rot. If one passes the test, buy up as many more as you can afford and indulge in a pomegranate-fest.

Raspberries, blackberries and blueberries

It's an unusual person who doesn't love this colourful trio of berries. On the flavour front, raspberries earn the gold medal for that winning balance of sweetness and acidity and their alluring fragrance when they are at the peak of ripeness. The most perfumed raspberries tend to be those grown in summer, often varieties that have 'Glen' in their name, such as Glen Lyon. Later varieties, such as Autumn Bliss, don't have the same haunting scent, but they come into their own when cooked.

Cultivated varieties of blackberries, such as Loch Ness and Loch Tay, don't have the distinctive flavour you'll find in their wild-picked relatives, but, by way of compensation, they are larger, more luscious and have far fewer pips.

The fashionable North American blueberry is a relative newcomer, although its wild cousin, the bilberry, grows prolifically in upland parts of the UK and Ireland. Its desirability has less to do with its taste, which is rarely that exciting, than the way it pops so pleasingly in the mouth. Blueberries are more of a lottery than either raspberries or blackberries:

often they are soft and mushy. This is particularly true of those imported from the southern hemisphere.

Frozen berries are one of the key foods to keep in the freezer. Raspberries and blackberries freeze particularly well; blueberries, less so. Texture may suffer, but the flavour can be good, with the acid coming to the fore, so a little sugar may be needed.

Things to do with raspberries, blackberries and blueberries

- Raspberry and chocolate is a marriage made in heaven. A spoonful of fresh coulis or sauce of sweetened, sieved raspberries lightens up any heavy chocolate cake or pudding.

- Mix lightly whipped cream with a little toasted coarse oatmeal, golden caster sugar and a dash of whisky, then fold in fresh raspberries to make the traditional Scottish dessert, cranachan.

- Although you can vary the types and quantities of berries you use in the classic English summer pudding according to availability, the presence of raspberries is essential. It's the key berry that makes this recipe work. Blackberries add inky depth and vary the colour. Blueberries are wasted in a summer pudding. Go for red- and blackcurrants instead.

- Gently soften tart, firm blackberries with golden caster sugar and a couple of scented geranium leaves. Serve at breakfast or as a dessert.

- Freshly baked blueberry muffins put the bought sort to shame and are dead easy to make.

Are berries good for me?

Raspberries, blackberries and blueberries are excellent sources of vitamin C, which helps protect cells against damage and aids the absorption of iron, and manganese, which, among other attributes, helps regulate blood sugar levels. They also contain a useful amount of soluble fibre, which slows down the rate at which sugar is released into the bloodstream. These berries are extremely rich in phytochemicals, naturally occurring plant compounds, such as ellagic acid and kaempferol. The properties of these and other phytochemicals are still being researched but they are thought to have an antioxidant action that helps protect the body against a long list of diseases, and have an anti-cancer and anti-inflammatory action. Some research suggests that organic strawberries have higher levels of these phytochemicals than those grown with pesticides. Organic raspberries, blackberries and blueberries may offer similar benefits.

Berries are given repeated pesticide treatments in the course of a growing season. Raspberries and blackberries are particularly disease-prone and quite heavily sprayed. Government tests have found residues of pesticides in more than half the raspberries and blackberries tested and detected residues of between two and four pesticides in most of these. If you eat a lot of berries and want to limit your exposure to pesticide residues, then buy organic raspberries, blackberries and blueberries when you see them, and if you can afford them.

How are berries grown?

Raspberries and blackberries grow on canes. Traditionally, the canes were in open fields, but increasingly they are grown under polythene arcs to protect the crops from the effects of weather and disease and extend the growing season. Many of the home-grown raspberries and blackberries we eat are cultivated in Tayside. Those that are imported outside the UK growing season come from Spain, Morocco, Mexico and Argentina. Blueberries grow on shrubby bushes. The area of land given over to growing them in the UK is relatively small but rapidly expanding because of the blueberry's popularity. As UK-grown blueberries have a relatively short growing season, blueberries are commonly imported from Poland, Spain, Chile and Argentina.

Are berries a green choice?

Many people expect to be able to eat fresh raspberries, blackberries and blueberries all year, but doing so really doesn't make any environmental sense. In winter, they will have been flown from the other side of the world, refrigerated all the way, so they leave a very heavy carbon 'foodprint'. If you really must have berries on your January muesli, at least be aware of the environmental impact of that decision. A more aware option is to eat the frozen sort. When European berries come on to the market in early spring and you are desperate for something different, eat them in moderation. But otherwise, reserve your annual fresh berry-eating enthusiasm for a wall-to-wall berry fest in summer and autumn when home-grown berries are in season.

In the past, we managed to pick our own berries. The fruits were harvested by travelling people, casual workers who moved around the country looking for agricultural work, and children drafted in to help out with the harvest during the summer holidays. These days, our berries are unlikely to be picked by locals. Growers can't find local people to do the work and rely for harvesting on a limited number of young people, from specified eastern European countries, who are allowed into the UK under the Seasonal Agricultural Workers Scheme. Even so, growers regularly complain about how hard it is to find enough pickers and warn that this could lead to fruit rotting in the fields. A further worry is that seasonal workers from eastern Europe will choose to stay at home, or work in other countries in Europe where they are paid in euros, or take work in better paid industries, making the existing chronic shortage of pickers acute. The government is under pressure to look at ways of encouraging unemployed people to take up summer work picking fruit by re-jigging the benefit systems so that it is possible for them to do some temporary picking work without having their benefits stopped.

Where and when should I buy berries?

UK-grown raspberries and blackberries are in season from June to November. UK-grown blueberries are in season from June to September.

Pick-your-own farms consistently sell the best raspberries and blackberries. They are usually fresher, and picked riper, than those in the supermarket. More pick-your-own farms are now growing blueberries, but, as a general rule, they are currently best bought in supermarkets.

Will berries break the bank?

Berries are always pricey buys. They are time-consuming to pick by hand so growers have a high labour bill. They are fragile, so have to be carefully packed, which means high packaging costs. On the other hand, you don't need too many to brighten up a bowl of muesli or a plain sponge cake. If you can't afford to eat them in large quantities, even a mean scattering of berries will make more prosaic foods feel positively luxurious.

If you find yourself with a tasteless punnet of berries, don't lose interest and throw them out. They can be rescued by warming them up with a little sugar and lemon juice, or used up in a smoothie or hot pudding.

Supermarkets often charge over the odds for berries, so try to compare their prices with greengrocers and market stalls, which are often considerably lower. If you can get along to a pick-your-own farm and actually do your own picking, as opposed to settling for the lazy person's option of just buying those that have been already picked, then you can save a lot of money. A trip to a local pick-your-own enterprise is definitely a good investment if you want to freeze your own, make jam, or just indulge in a sea of berries.

In September, remember that wild blackberries are ripe and free for the picking, not just in the country, but also in urban green spaces. Any hedgerow or thicket is a promising place to look.

Rhubarb

Rhubarb offers a welcome flash of fruity pinkness at the bleak end of winter. It has an appealingly astringent, sharp taste and a rather unique texture when cooked, as it breaks down into silky strands. Although it is not aromatic, it marries well with stronger flavours such as orange, rosewater, strawberry and ginger.

Indoor- and outdoor-grown rhubarb are two different animals. Indoor rhubarb – known as forced rhubarb – is prized for its delicacy, the softness of its flesh and its pretty pink colour, but sometimes, especially when it is imported, the flavour can be muted. Outdoor rhubarb is more fibrous, and becomes more so as the growing season progresses. Outdoor rhubarb is at its best when it is deep red and will most likely have a more concentrated taste than the indoor kind. When outdoor rhubarb grows too fast or gets too mature, and has a mainly green stalk, sourness can dominate.

When buying rhubarb, always go for full-length stalks where only the leaves have been removed. Supermarkets usually cut the stalks to make them fit into plastic bags, which makes the cut edges brown, weakens the crispness of the stalk and encourages it to rot faster.

Call it prejudice if you like, but UK-grown forced rhubarb usually tastes better than the imported Dutch equivalent, which can often be puny and taste bland.

Things to do with rhubarb

- Gently soften chopped pink or red rhubarb and golden caster sugar over a low heat until the rhubarb collapses and becomes juicy. When cool, perfume with rosewater. Marvellous with a rosewater-scented pannacotta.

- Add freshly grated or chopped preserved stem ginger to the fruity base for a rhubarb crumble.

- Gently soften chopped pink or red rhubarb with golden caster sugar over a low heat. As it cools, stir in sliced strawberries. The slight heat brings out the scent and jammy fruitiness of the berries.

- Gently soften pink or red rhubarb with golden caster sugar and a little freshly squeezed orange juice over a low heat. When almost cool, stir in pith-free segments of orange; blood orange looks particularly pretty.

- Make individual rhubarb pies in a muffin tin in preference to one large pie that will lose its shape when you cut it.

Is rhubarb good for me?

Rhubarb contains some useful soluble fibre; robust outdoor rhubarb contains more than the indoor-grown sort. This fibre slows down the rate at which sugar is released into the bloodstream. Otherwise, it has only minor amounts of vitamins, notably vitamins C and K, and other beneficial micronutrients, so any potential health benefit from these is likely to be more than undone by the amount of sugar required to sweeten it. There are many reasons to buy rhubarb, but health isn't one of them. That said, rhubarb is a plant well used in traditional Chinese medicine, and is thought to have some laxative properties.

How is rhubarb grown?

Outdoor rhubarb grows well in Britain and Ireland, both in domestic gardens and commercially. Commercial growers usually dig up and divide the plants in winter, keeping a plant growing for three years. Forced rhubarb is grown by lifting outdoor roots once they have had a touch of frost, and then transferring them to warm, dark, indoor sheds. The lack of food and light triggers growth and 'forces' or makes the plant produce thin, tender, pale pink stalks with small, tightly curled yellow leaves. In Yorkshire, forced rhubarb is grown in purpose-built wooden sheds and the stalks are harvested by candlelight so that the younger stalks that are still growing are not exposed to light. In Holland, forced rhubarb is grown in glasshouses with blacked-out windows, harvested in electric light, and a plant hormone is used to stimulate growth in the plants for early production. The outdoor rhubarb we buy usually comes from the UK or Ireland.

Is rhubarb a green choice?

Once outdoor rhubarb plants are established in the UK and Ireland, they tend to be quite hardy and reasonably resistant to disease, so they don't get many, if any, pesticide treatments. Their expansive green leaves help shade out unwelcome weeds. They do need quite a lot of fertilizer, but most outdoor growers dig in old rhubarb plants, or use indoor spent plants that have been composted as a fertilizer. Forced rhubarb only has one season. Rhubarb is a crop that grows well organically in the UK and Ireland.

Heating the sheds for indoor rhubarb does require the use of fossil fuels and these are non-renewable resources that are depleting rapidly. However, the sheds are only heated from November until March, and the availability of home-grown rhubarb at this time of year does reduce our reliance on imported fruit transported from much further afield, frequently by air. Yorkshire growers are trying to find a more renewable type of energy.

Dutch forced rhubarb often comes on to the market a few weeks earlier than our home-grown crop, but it is worth waiting patiently for the latter. Dutch rhubarb rarely competes on taste with the Yorkshire sort and, because of its transportation, it leaves a heavier carbon 'foodprint'.

Rhubarb doesn't need to be refrigerated and requires only minimal packaging. In fact, full stalks of rhubarb almost defy packaging. A plastic band does the job.

Where and when should I buy rhubarb?

Forced Yorkshire rhubarb is available from the end of January until March. Outdoor-grown rhubarb crops in all areas from April until July.

As they sell the stalks whole, not cut, greengrocers, markets and farm shops are the best places to buy rhubarb.

THE JEWEL IN OUR FOOD HERITAGE CROWN

Rhubarb is a well-loved and familiar fruit. In Britain, it is most strongly associated with Yorkshire, home of the celebrated 'Rhubarb Triangle', a geographical production area that connects Leeds, Wakefield and Bradford, where production started in 1877. This area lies in the shadows of the Pennines, which act as a frost pocket, providing the perfect weather conditions essential to the plant. The then sooty, sulphurous atmosphere caused by heavy industry was actually good for rhubarb as it encouraged it to die back in autumn. Yorkshire was the first place in the world where special sheds were built for forcing the crop. Local sheep farms provided an ideal source of natural fertilizer in the form of 'shoddy', strands of wool, naturally rich in nitrogen.

Indoor-grown rhubarb from Yorkshire is one of the jewels in our food heritage crown and rightly inspires great loyalty. In recognition of its very special nature, Yorkshire forced rhubarb is now one of a handful of British crops that have been awarded Protected Designation of Origin (PDO) status by the European Commission, a scheme that recognizes foods that are unique within the European Union.

Will rhubarb break the bank?

At the back end of winter it's tempting to rush out and buy forced rhubarb whenever it first comes on to the market, as welcome relief from the limited winter fruit selection. But it tends to be Dutch, and is often very pricey. Get carried away stacking up those stalks for the first crumble of the year, and you can get a nasty shock at the till because of its high initial pricing.

Yorkshire forced rhubarb starts out expensive too, but rarely as expensive as the first Dutch stalks, and it does come down a little in peak season. Outdoor-grown rhubarb – often more reliable for flavour – has the additional bonus of always being democratically cheap.

Strawberries

There are few fruits more captivating than really good strawberries with their distinctive perfume and soft, sweet flesh. Botanically speaking, strawberries are classed as members of the rose family, *Fragraria*, from the Latin word for fragrant, which provides a clue to what they should be like. Good strawberries should announce their presence by their captivating perfume and be loaded with that often all too elusive strawberry flavour. Finding fruits that fit this bill can be a challenge. Many of those on our shelves have the texture of cucumber and about as little flavour.

Ripeness is the critical factor influencing their taste. When strawberries are red and mature, they are at their nutritional peak. At this point, all the naturally occurring chemicals that contribute to their alluring flavour and aroma – furanones, aldehydes, alcohols, sulphur compounds, phenols, flavonols, esters, terpenes – reach their fullest expression, and deliver that appealing strawberry bouquet. Strawberries taste best when they are allowed to ripen properly, by which point they are red all over, there is very little white 'core' at the base of the stem, the stem comes away easily from the berry and the flesh offers no resistance in the mouth. Those that are pallid pink, with white or green patches or 'shoulders' under the stem, are underripe.

Strawberries should really be picked when fully ripe and eaten as soon after harvesting as possible. But ripe berries are fragile and have a short shelf life, so in order to supply supermarkets and avoid potential rejections of consignments, growers have to pick them early, slightly underripe, so that they can stand up to several days in transport, storage and on shelves. This is particularly true of strawberries imported from Europe, which come by road and sea, and those from further afield that come by air. They will have been picked 'green and backward' to withstand the journey. One of the reasons strawberries from fruit farms usually taste better is that they are picked riper because they are sold direct to the consumer.

Of course, some strawberries are incapable of tasting of very much, no matter how ripe they are, or where they are grown, because they are of a variety that has been designed, not for flavour, but to meet other criteria such as firmness, shine and transportability. This is why it is important to look out for the name of the variety when buying strawberries.

The classic example of the modern, tasteless, fragrance-challenged strawberry is Elsanta, the modern Dutch variety that has dominated our shelves in recent years. Fortunately, although Elsanta is still the most commonly encountered strawberry, even large retailers are now acknowledging that it is somewhat lacking in the taste and perfume stakes and so they are introducing varieties with more intrinsic character. Fruit farms are also rediscovering traditional varieties and exploring alternatives to the dreaded Elsanta. Almost any other variety is preferable, but there are a few – you can tell them by their crunchy, firm, super-sized fruits – that are even worse and best avoided, such as Camarosa, Darselect and Selva.

Thankfully, consumer demand for more favourful, scented strawberries has seen Elsanta's grip on UK strawberry growing weaken as better tasting varieties have come to the fore. Prior to the era of Elsanta, growers cultivated a greater number of traditional varieties, selecting them for their taste, fragrance and suitability for local soil, growing a different sequence of varieties (early, mid-season, late) throughout a growing season. British heritage varieties renowned for their eating quality, such as Royal Sovereign, Hapil, Cambridge Favourite, Cambridge Vigour and Cambridge Late Pine are still popular with gardeners and highly rated by chefs and food enthusiasts, as are some of the celebrated French strawberry varieties, such as Garriguette.

Commercial growers rarely choose these traditional varieties, however, because when grown on a large scale they are prone to disease. So in preference to wall-to-wall Elsanta, they increasingly concentrate on newer varieties, such as Alice, Symphony, Florence, Sonata, Eros, Honeyoye, Jubilee, Evie, Ava, Sophie and Pegasus that have more essential taste than Elsanta, but better disease resistance than traditional varieties.

Strasberries are relatively new to the market but are actually an old variety. These look like a cross between a raspberry and a strawberry but taste like wild or Alpine strawberries. The pineberry is another speciality strawberry. White in colour with red seeds, it smells fragrant – like an Alpine strawberry – and is so named because it is meant to taste like a pineapple. Many people may find that its flavour is pretty much like any modern strawberry variety.

It may sound like a cliché, but UK-grown strawberries do taste better when cultivated in the traditional summer growing season when there is heat and sun. If you see strawberries as merely red and decorative and are not looking for taste, then those grown at other times of the year may have some appeal, but if you want strawberries that taste like strawberries, then it has to be a summer-grown fruit.

As a general rule, UK- and Ireland-grown strawberries taste better than imports. There are excellent strawberries grown abroad, but you will have to go there to experience them. The imported strawberries we see in supermarkets are grown mainly for export and come from varieties designed for long-distance travel, not delightful eating. Native strawberries will also be fresher: imports will be two to three days old before they even appear on the shelf.

To get the best from any type of strawberry, eat them soon after purchase, refrigerate as little as possible and serve them at room temperature so you can appreciate their perfume.

Things to do with strawberries

- A dusting of sugar and a sprinkling of lemon juice or pomegranate molasses enhances the flavour of strawberries. Some chefs recommend a grinding of black pepper.

- Give people their own plate of whole, unhusked strawberries along with little piles of crème fraîche and golden granulated sugar (vanilla sugar is perfect). Using their fingers, people can dip each strawberry first in the cream and then in the sugar, and from there right into their mouths.

- A spoonful of really ripe strawberries, mashed to a pulp with a little sugar, goes well with any buttery cake such as Victoria sponge, creamy cheesecake or pannacotta.

- Make the best of hard, unripe strawberries by combining them with rhubarb in a crumble base.

- Use over-ripe 'jam' strawberries to make a fool.

- Layer up thin shortbread biscuits with whipped cream and sliced strawberries.

- Mix smooth, sweetened strawberry pulp with sparkling white wine for a summer cocktail.

- Make a smoothie with strawberries, oatflakes, natural yogurt and a little honey or maple syrup.

Are strawberries good for me?

Strawberries are an excellent source of vitamin C, which may help to protect against cancer and heart disease, and also of the trace mineral, manganese, which helps bone health and supports the nerves and thyroid gland. Strawberries are also notable for their levels of phenols – anthocyanins and ellagitannins – that are thought to have an antioxidant effect (help protect cells against damage that may predispose the body to diseases such as cancer and inflammatory conditions). Other notable beneficial micronutrients found in strawberries include flavonoids, such as quercetin, which some research suggests are protective against heart disease and stroke. There is some research to suggest that organic strawberries may have significantly higher levels of antioxidants and vitamins than their non-organic equivalents.

Although in nutritional terms strawberries are brilliantly good for you, as a crop they are prone to disease and fungal attack and commonly have many pesticide treatments in the course of a growing season. According to the Pesticides Action Network UK, they are one of the ten worst foods when it comes to containing pesticide residues. Calculated over a five-year period, 69 per cent of strawberries we ate contained residues, while 42 per cent had multiple residues. They regularly crop up on international and national lists of the foods most likely to contain pesticide residues. Unless you feel reassured by the official line that traces of toxic chemicals in food pose no risk to human health, you may want to buy organic strawberries where possible, especially if you eat a lot of them.

How are strawberries grown?

Strawberries used to be grown mainly outside in open fields, often in the same place for several years at a time, which led to a build-up of disease in the soil. This was routinely controlled by using methyl bromide – a powerful soil sterilant – at the end of each season. Once this was identified by the United Nations as a 'Class One Ozone Depleter', its use was phased out in Europe. Growers can still use other soil sterilants, such as formaldeyhde and dazomet, which are considered to be less environmentally damaging. They are nevertheless toxic and tricky to apply as they are harmful to skin, eyes and also to the respiratory system if inhaled. Now, most strawberries are grown in polytunnels and a minority in glasshouses. Supermarkets insist on strawberries grown under protection because the fruits are cleaner and more attractive-looking as they are protected from the elements.

Cultivating strawberries under cover offers growers certain advantages. Workers have more protection when planting and picking and the sheltered environment makes for fewer pests and diseases and, because protected from rain, the berries are less prone to diseases like mildew and rot. In more enclosed types of polytunnels and glasshouses, the grower can introduce beneficial predators such as nematodes to discourage unwelcome insects. However, many growers still use the standard armoury of pesticide treatments since strawberries are a crop that is particularly susceptible to pests and disease.

Polytunnels and glasshouses have revolutionized strawberry growing, extending the growing season from the traditional end of May until end of July growing period to twenty-six weeks from May until autumn. Some growers with heated and lighted glasshouses are even producing strawberries as early as mid-March and continuing until the end of November. The best tasting fruits, however, are still produced in the summer months.

In polytunnels and glasshouses, as in open fields, strawberry plants can be planted directly in the ground or in raised beds. Usually they are planted through a polythene cover or 'mulch'. This keeps them warmer, so speeding up growth, raises them up above the muddy ground and also discourages weeds. Some growers still prefer to put straw around the growing plants to protect them.

Strawberries cultivated under polytunnels are sometimes grown not in soil, but in bags, and drip-fed nutrients. These bags can be raised off the ground to make planting and picking easier. The growing medium of choice used to be peat, but recognizing that this was not an environmental choice because the trade in peat was destroying natural peat habitats, growers have started using alternative mediums like those used to grow indoor tomatoes (see TOMATOES/How are tomatoes grown?).

Organic strawberries, whether grown in open fields or in polytunnels, tend to be few and far between, so worth snapping up if you see them. You'll find them only in the traditional British summertime strawberry season. Organic growers avoid the need for repeat treatments of pesticides and soil sterilization by selecting pest-resistant varieties, and using a mixture of crop rotation, fallowing (leaving the ground uncultivated) and natural pest control.

Are strawberries a green choice?

The dominance of the Elsanta strawberry has been an environmental, as well as a taste disaster because this ubiquitous variety is not at all disease-resistant. On the contrary, it is notorious for its susceptibility to crown rot and grey mould, so it requires extensive pesticide treatments. Indeed, after the UN agreed to phase out the use of methyl bromide, strawberry growers argued for some years for what is known as a 'critical use exemption', on the grounds that they simply could not control pests and diseases without it.

Large-scale strawberry growing can potentially damage soil through the heavy use of pesticides, soil sterilants and fertilizers. Strawberries are also a thirsty crop and when grown under protection are commonly 'trickle-irrigated'. This almost constant irrigation puts a heavy demand on water from rivers, streams and boreholes. Run-off from the excess water, and from rainfall that drips off the polytunnels, is thought to cause soil erosion and pollution of waterways. These impacts can be even more marked in hotter strawberry-growing countries where drought and water shortage is an ongoing concern. The World Wildlife Fund has urged consumers to stop buying strawberries grown in southern Spain in winter because it says that the irrigation required is depleting the region's water table and polluting it with pesticides and waste plastic from old polytunnel sheeting.

On environmental grounds, it makes sense to eat home-grown strawberries in summertime and ignore imports the rest of the year. European berries will have been transported by road and sea, while those from countries such as the US and Morocco will have been air-freighted.

STRAWBERRY VILLAGES

Strawberries used to be a short-lived summer fruit whose annual arrival caused much excitement. In the 1950s there was still a much awaited train, known affectionately in the fruit trade as 'the Strawberry Express', that delivered freshly picked berries from Kent to London where they were taken to Covent Garden market, and from there sent out to greengrocers and wholesale markets throughout Britain. Native strawberries served at Wimbledon were still seen as so special that they symbolized the start of English summer.

Nowadays, English strawberry production has been super-sized. Fruit-growing regions of the UK, such as Herefordshire, have witnessed an unsightly explosion of plastic as large areas are turned over to cultivation under protection. There have been numerous campaigns against extensive developments of visually intrusive polytunnels on the grounds that they spoil the beauty of the landscape. While some polytunnels are quite modest in scale, the 'Spanish' type of interlocking polytunnel can be up to 300 metres long, and is typically 6.7 metres wide and 3 metres high. The largest strawberry-growing enterprises are like villages in themselves. In addition to a sea of polytunnels, seasonal workers employed to harvest the fruit are accommodated in caravans, mobile homes or 'pods', with ancillary leisure (internet cafés, football pitches) and service buildings. In many cases, these complexes do not require planning permission because they are not considered to be permanent structures. The need for planning permission depends on the scale and type of the polytunnels in question. Transport used to carry pickers, and lorries taking strawberries to distant supermarket distribution centres, have been pinpointed as causing congestion and damage on narrow country roads.

Where and when should I buy strawberries?

Nowadays, strawberries are one of those 365-days-a-year fruits that are never absent from supermarket shelves, but that doesn't make them worth eating. Strawberries are still best enjoyed in the traditional UK season that runs from the end of May until the end of July. Some of the later home-grown varieties produced under polytunnels still taste reasonably sweet and perfumed in early September. Thereafter, although there are home-grown strawberries to be had from glasshouses, the eating quality is disappointing.

In June and July you can't beat strawberries direct from the garden or allotment, but berries sold ready-picked in farm shops are usually rather good too. It is worth making an expedition to farm shops just to buy strawberries. Apart from this being good fun, you will usually find more interesting varieties, and because the crop is being sold direct to the consumer, it will have been picked riper and so have a better flavour. If you can be bothered to pick your own, then you can personally select the ripest.

Will strawberries break the bank?

British-grown strawberries, like other berries, are never cheap, mainly because they take time to pick and so growers' labour costs are high. Strawberries could become more expensive still because of government restrictions on seasonal foreign migrant labour. Ironically, top-quality British summer strawberries are often more expensive than the imported ones that are on sale all year round, but they do taste a million times better.

It pays to keep an eye on the cost of strawberries, especially in supermarkets, where prices are commonly significantly higher than in local greengrocers and market stalls. Be especially wary of offers that say 'Now 50 per cent cheaper' or 'Larger, better value pack' or similar. Generally supermarkets set ludicrously high prices for strawberries at the start of the UK season so that they can then reduce them later and present a still high price as a bargain. Check the price and the weight to see exactly what you are being asked to pay for what amount.

The best value of all is to be had from farm shops which will often give you a keener price if you buy in quantity, as well as offering less perfect-looking 'jam' strawberries which are especially fragrant and particularly good for recipes like summer pudding, ice cream and fool or chopped up on breakfast cereal. Traditional market stalls and greengrocers tend to vary their strawberry prices throughout the season to reflect the market price, whereas pick-your-own outlets and fruit farms tend to set one price and maintain it throughout the season.

Larder

6

Eggs

(hen's, quail's, duck's and goose)

There is something pleasing about the smooth contours of an egg, and there is no food quite like it for instilling a sense of security in a cook. As long as there are eggs, there is the possibility of fast, healthy food whether they come boiled, poached, fried, scrambled or in an omelette. Centre stage, in recipes such as the classic French crème Anglaise – a custard sauce thickened only with yolk – and mayonnaise and soufflé, they show off their deluxe potential. Their simple goodness can upstage more complex dishes that require myriad ingredients.

If you have only ever eaten hen's eggs, then other types can look a little scary, especially goose eggs, which are so large you might imagine that they could hatch a small alien. Actually, eggs from different birds taste quite similar. That said, the yolks in goose and duck eggs are more velvety in texture and richer in the mouth. They also have slightly firmer whites when cooked. A goose egg is the equivalent of four hen's eggs, while most duck eggs are like extra-large hen's eggs. Quail's eggs are just like tiny, more delicate hen's eggs. Their main attraction is their size, which makes them a pretty addition to salads. If you are the sort of person who has the patience for fiddly canapés, then quail's eggs are prime candidates for this purpose.

Good eggs have strong thick shells, those of goose and duck being particularly thick. Whatever sort of egg you're eating, a deep ochre or orange-coloured yolk is an indication that the bird that laid them had a healthy diet feeding on grassy land with a variety of plants with natural pigments that colour the yolks. Eggs with pale yellow yolks and thin, fragile shells are poor quality and probably from grain- and soya-fed indoor birds. Some producers of intensive, indoor eggs use feed with synthetic colourings to make the yolks more yellow, however, so yolk colour is not a totally reliable indicator of a bird's diet. Free-range and organic eggs from birds that have been outdoors feeding on green pasture often taste noticeably better than those from their indoor, battery-farmed equivalent.

In the natural run of things, eggs are laid in different sizes, depending on the breed and age of the bird. Nowadays, when it comes to hen's eggs, farmers have a financial incentive to produce larger ones as they get paid more for these by retailers. Choosing certain breeds of bird, and feeding them on a high-protein diet – usually with extra soya – will result in larger eggs. Some producers argue that these larger eggs – perhaps because of the nature of their feed – have less flavour, and that the best size to buy for taste (and for a good, thick, healthy shell) is medium.

Some animal welfarists think medium-sized eggs are more humane because it is easier for the hen to lay them. For most cooking purposes, size of eggs makes precious little difference to the end result. Some chefs and food writers stipulate large eggs in baking, for recipes such as sponge cakes, probably as an extra insurance policy to make sure that they rise. If you only have medium-sized eggs, then you can use an extra egg but medium eggs should produce perfectly reasonable results. In recipes where egg yolks are used to thicken, such as custards, it's advisable to use the egg size stipulated or add an extra yolk to compensate for smaller eggs.

It's often a good idea to take eggs out the fridge to bring them up to room temperature before you use them, since the egg whites will stiffen quicker and the eggs will be less likely to crack when plunged into boiling water.

Hen's eggs with brown shells come from brown breeds of hen, such as Burford Browns, Marans and Columbian Blacktail. Cotswold Legbar hens produce eggs with pretty pastel-coloured shells, while eggs with white shells come from white breeds such as White Leghorn and Legbar. Speckled eggs come from speckled breeds such as the Hebdon Black and Speckledy, with smaller speckled eggs produced by quail. The breed of hen is less important than the bird's diet in terms of the taste of eggs.

Eggs are at their best when they are really fresh. The 'best-before' date is a guide but this relies on the trustworthiness of the supplier, the way they have been transported and stored, the weather and so on. A truly fresh egg should hold together well and the yolk should be sitting up to attention, supported by a thick, jelly-like white. If the white is watery and thin, and the yolk breaks on impact, then your egg may be less fresh than you think.

Things to do with eggs

- Breakfast or brunch on Indian masala scrambled eggs. Fry chopped red onions or shallots and green chilli in coconut oil or ghee until golden brown, add chopped ripe tomatoes, chopped coriander and sea salt and cook fast to a mush. Crack in your eggs and stir vigorously over a high heat until the eggs thicken the mixture.

- Eggs, a little sugar and a surplus of milk or cream are all you need to whisk up a simple, cheap but pleasing crème caramel.

- Almost anything tastes wonderful when it is napped with an eggy hollandaise sauce. A sauce thickened with egg yolk is so much more upmarket than one thickened with flour.

- As an accompaniment to steak, Béarnaise sauce, the little sister to the hollandaise, is hard to beat with its winning alliance of fragrant tarragon and shallots sharpened with vinegar.

- Half-fill ramekins with cooked spinach, crack in an egg and top with double cream seasoned with sea salt, black pepper and a grating of nutmeg. Bake until the egg white is only just set and the yolk is still soft.

- Make a delicious sauce that works well with asparagus, terrines, smoked meat or fish and most picnic foods by incorporating chopped hard-boiled egg yolks into a vinaigrette then adding chopped herbs (such as tarragon, parsley, chervil, chives), capers and cornichons (small gherkins), in the style of the French sauce Gribiche.

- Home-made chocolate mousse, using ultra-fresh eggs and really good chocolate, is hard to beat.

- Hand-made pasta really showcases the quality of your eggs. Organic and free-range eggs, with their bright orange-ochre yolks, will produce particularly rich, golden pasta.

- Finish off a kedgeree made with spiced brown rice and undyed smoked haddock with quarters of still-runny boiled egg (boiled for six minutes) and a handful of chopped parsley. Also good cold for a packed lunch.

Are eggs good for me?

For a time, eggs got a bad press because their yolks contain cholesterol, but now it is increasingly accepted that eating cholesterol in food such as eggs does not lead to clogged arteries and heart disease. Cholesterol is a vital component of cell membranes. Among other things, it helps the body heal and repair, supports brain function, and allows the body to make vitamin D and certain hormones.

Eggs offer high-quality protein. Protein is the macronutrient that best satisfies hunger, so it helps to keep you going for longer. Eggs are an exceptional source of vitamins, providing all the key vitamins apart from vitamin C. They contain vitamin A, which is needed for healthy skin and good vision; vitamin E, which research suggests can help reduce the incidence of heart disease, certain cancers and strokes; and vitamin D. It is thought that many British and Irish people may have insufficient levels of vitamin D, and deficiency is being linked to increased risk of heart disease, auto-immune diseases such as multiple sclerosis, and certain cancers.

Eggs also contain vitamin B2, which is needed for metabolizing food, and vitamin B12, which as well as helping brain function and providing energy, helps lower levels of undesirable homocysteine that can build up in the blood. High levels of this substance are associated with an increased risk of heart attack and stroke. Vitamin B12 deficiency is quite common, especially among older people and vegetarians. Eggs also have useful amounts of minerals such as phosphorous, which is needed for good bones and teeth, iodine, which is important for thyroid function, and selenium, which is thought to be protective against certain cancers.

All in all, eggs are highly nutritious, so they can be eaten freely. There is no need to impose any limit. As a breakfast food, they offer vastly superior nutrition to cereals. So if you feel like eating an egg every day, do so.

Some brands advertise that they contain higher levels than normal of the healthy omega-3 fatty acids that are present naturally in eggs. These higher levels are achieved by incorporating fish oil and/or flax seed into the bird's diet. People who want to eat more omega-3s may prefer to choose eggs from grass-fed, free-ranging birds as their eggs will have naturally higher levels of omega-3s than their grain- and soya-fed indoor counterparts because of their pasture-based diet.

In the 1990s it was revealed that most British eggs were contaminated with the food poisoning bug, salmonella enteriditis. Since then, many people have been wary about eating raw, or lightly cooked eggs for fear of food poisoning. Nowadays UK rates of salmonella contamination in eggs are low, as about 85 per cent of hens are now vaccinated against it. If eggs have a Lion stamp, this means that they were laid by vaccinated hens. Many small-scale producers of free-range and organic eggs do not vaccinate their hens, however, arguing that hens not kept in close confinement are less susceptible to salmonella and other diseases associated with intensive farming. Several scientific reports now support the view that caged hen farms are more likely to be infected with the salmonella food poisoning bug than those where hens are kept in free-range systems. There is also evidence that cage-produced eggs are more susceptible to absorbing salmonella.

If you intend to eat eggs raw, in a mousse perhaps, then make sure that they are very fresh as all food poisoning bugs multiply with age. The maximum legal 'best-before' date on eggs is twenty-eight days from lay and eggs must be sold to the consumer within twenty-one days of the eggs being laid; in other words, at least seven days before the 'best-before' date. When using raw eggs, aim to use eggs within the first week of that 'best-before' period. Older eggs are fine for recipes, like cakes or custards, where they will be very well cooked and any food poisoning bacteria present will be killed off by the heat. When making mayonnaise, the vinegar added will usually keep any potential food poisoning bugs in check, but for the best mayonnaise use really fresh eggs.

Unless you can be sure that your larder is always under 20 degrees C – the safe temperature for storing eggs – then refrigerate them. Store them pointed end downwards for maximum freshness and centred yolks.

How are eggs produced?

Eggs can come from either indoor or outdoor systems. The most inhumane system is the notorious battery cage. Hen's and quail's eggs are commonly produced this way. In this scenario, lines of wire cages filled with birds are stacked up upon one another in closed sheds that are artificially lit and ventilated. The largest battery units house nearly 100,000 hens. A cage for hens has four hens in it, leaving each bird a space smaller than an A4 page, and only just enough headroom to stand upright.

These barren cages provide no nest boxes, perches or litter so hens cannot express their natural behaviour. Hens are naturally gregarious creatures. If left to their own devices, they would live together as a flock with a distinct hierarchy or 'pecking order', spending their days outdoors foraging for food and only seeking the cover of trees for roosting or a safe hen house at night.

Intensive battery egg production is associated with a number of problems: birds often suffer fractures from brittle bones and lose feathers because they rub up against the wire of the cage and are pecked by other birds. Battery hens and quail usually have part of their beak removed to prevent this. The hens are confined in this way for the duration of their unnaturally short lives – sixteen months, as opposed to their natural lifespan of seven years – and pushed to their limits to produce about 300 eggs a year.

Thanks to campaigning from animal welfare groups, the battery cage as we know it will become illegal throughout Europe from 2012 to be replaced by so-called 'enriched cages'. These roomier cages have higher minimum space requirements for birds and nest boxes, litter, perch space and claw-shortening devices which help the birds express more of their natural behaviours. Animal welfare campaigners argue that the enriched cage is only a marginal improvement on its precursor because it still stops hens from fully expressing their natural instincts, like foraging, flapping their wings and dustbathing, so causing frustration, suffering and premature body degeneration. About half the hen's eggs eaten in Britain currently come from this intensive battery system, or 'enriched cages'. As quail eggs are thought of as a speciality, many people assume that they are free-range, whereas, in fact, most quail's eggs are from caged birds.

Hens and quails in battery cages are fed on a mixture of grain and soya. Some egg producers still use the synthetic colourant canthaxanthin, which is controversial on health grounds, to give their yolks a more wholesome-looking yellow colour so they look more like those from free-range, grass-fed hens. Other egg brands prohibit this colouring and use instead ingredients such as grass meal, maize, capsicum, marigold or citranaxanthin (from the peel of citrus fruits) to get the same effect. Battery eggs have to carry the label 'eggs from caged hens'.

Processed or pre-prepared foods are likely to be made using eggs from caged hens unless the ingredients listing specifically states otherwise. These eggs may come from intensive battery systems outside the EU. So if you look at an ingredients label on quiches, cakes, ready-to-eat custard and the like, and just see the word 'eggs', without any qualifying 'free-range' or 'organic', you can reasonably assume that they come from caged hens. The RSPCA says that 85 per cent of all eggs used in catering are from battery systems. So whether you're looking at school meals' sponge pudding, a lunchtime takeaway egg mayonnaise sandwich or that elegant lemon tart from an upmarket pastry shop or restaurant, there is a very strong probability that the eggs used came from caged hens.

For people who want to avoid eggs from caged birds, there are three alternatives: barn, free-range and organic. In barn or 'aviary' systems, the hens are kept inside in sheds for all their lives, but uncaged, using the floor space and tiers of perches. Barn birds can fly around a bit – although nothing like they can outdoors – and lay their eggs in a nest. Don't assume that eggs with a Freedom Food logo (the RSPCA's food labelling scheme) are free-range. Barn eggs can carry this logo. Barn-kept birds are fed a similar diet to those in cages and also have part of their beaks removed.

In free-range systems, hens, quail, ducks and geese are housed to a similar standard as barn hens but have more space and they must have constant daytime access to an outside range with grassy vegetation. There is no guarantee, but in practice, duck and goose eggs tend to come from free-range farms.

Some free-range systems are better than others. In smaller flocks, there is more chance of birds managing to get outside using available popholes. When flocks are large, there may not be sufficient popholes for most birds to get out, so all birds may not be able to access outdoor vegetation and exercise regularly.

Many free-range birds also have part of their beak removed to stop them pecking each other when they are indoors. Their diet is likely to be similar to their battery and barn counterparts but it does not always contain yolk colourings as the yolks will naturally be yellower if the birds can make it out on to grassy land.

Organic hens enjoy a superior sort of free-range with more space again (a minimum of ten square metres of outdoor range per bird) and they range over certified organic land that has not been treated with pesticides and synthetic fertilizers. Organic flock sizes are smaller to encourage better welfare. Organic hens are fed on organically produced feed and unlike conventional egg producers, organic farmers aren't allowed to use yolk colourants in their feed.

When buying eggs, don't rely on marketing terms like 'farm fresh' or 'farm assured', but look at the code stamped on the box and the eggs:

0 = organic   1 = free range   2 = barn   3 = cage

Farmers' market and farm shop eggs don't have to be stamped, so check directly with the producer.

Eggs from all types of birds have been a staple in our diet for centuries. In the first half of the last century they were seen as a super-healthy, nutritious food to be enjoyed on a daily basis. This perception was encapsulated in the classic 1957 advert 'Go to work on an egg', featuring the popular comedian Tony Hancock. As late as the 1960s, our average egg consumption was five eggs per person a week.

As eggs fell foul of the anti-cholesterol lobby, consumption dropped to its current level of two eggs per person per week as people were exhorted to restrict their consumption. In the US, the low-cholesterol 'omelette' made only with egg whites became fashionable. As this negative perception of eggs has been debunked, eggs are back on the menu.

Heightened awareness of the cruelty of the battery cage has radically changed the type of eggs we eat. In the mid-1990s, eggs from caged hens accounted for more than 85 per cent of the eggs consumed. Sales of eggs from caged hens have declined markedly and they now account for about 50 per cent. It looks likely that sooner rather than later sales of eggs from caged hens in the UK will be overtaken by those from higher welfare systems. Some progressive retailers have already stopped selling battery eggs altogether and some have also removed them from their processed food.

Are eggs a green choice?

The familiar cardboard egg box is one of the greenest and most minimal forms of packaging around. Unlike polystyrene egg boxes, which cannot be recycled, and rigid plastic egg boxes that are harder to recycle, most councils have collections for recycling cardboard. Cardboard egg boxes are biodegradable and compostable. If you want to compost them or use them in a wormery – they are good for this, as they soak up excess moisture – dip them in water first and break them up a bit. For gardeners, egg boxes are also useful for chitting (sprouting) potatoes and as mini-pots for seedlings.

Many farmers' markets and farm shops will gladly take back already used cardboard egg boxes and refill them, so if you shop there, you may not even need to recycle egg boxes yourself.

Many hens are fed in part on soya, which raises a number of issues for the environment (see SOYA FOODS/Is soya a green choice?).

Where and when should I buy eggs?

Hen's, duck's and quail's eggs are available year round. Goose eggs are usually only available in spring and summer. Free-range and organic quail's eggs aren't easy to find, but they do exist. Try farmers' markets, farm shops and specialist food shops.

Will eggs break the bank?

Free-range and organic hens that are fed primarily on a grass-based diet, and those from older, traditional breeds, produce fewer eggs and their eggs cost 25–30 per cent more to produce, so they are pricier to buy than the caged alternative. But even if you buy organic, or top-end free-range, which cost more than eggs from caged hens, eggs are still a relatively cheap source of high-quality protein.

Don't assume that supermarkets are cheaper for eggs. They do sell the cheapest eggs from caged birds, but organic and free-range eggs are often cheaper in farm shops and farmers' markets.

Good eggs have gone up in price and are not to be wasted, but many recipes call just for yolks, so whites are often left over. Meringues used to be recommended by baking experts as a way of using up surplus whites, but these days many people are put off by the large amounts of sugar required, not to mention the technique and experience necessary to produce the perfect meringue – all that whisking to a peak, the lining of the baking tray and the long slow baking. The French financier, less fussy cousin to the madeleine, is a more forgiving recipe for putting whites to good use. Financiers use considerably less sugar than meringues and the inclusion of ground almonds, although upping the cost, considerably improves the overall nutritional profile.

Grains

(rice, wheat, bulgar, cracked wheat, couscous, polenta, spelt,
quinoa, buckwheat, millet, barley, rye, spelt, teff)

There is something empowering about having a selection of grains in your storecupboard. With grains to hand you can really ring the changes and guide the same ingredient down very different routes. Take rice, for instance. Fragrant basmati rice is the staple of the Indian repertoire, but if you're cooking Thai food, then sticky rice is the natural partner. Chinese people like to start the day with a glutinous, savoury rice porridge (congee), Iranians adore rice when it's cooked to form a crunchy mat, while Italians look at short-grain arborio, carnaroli or vialone nano rice and think risotto. Serve brown, as opposed to white rice, and you instantly give a dish nuttiness and substance. While a salad made with white rice seems dated, like a rather sad throwback to the 1960s, one made with brown rice, slightly mineral-tasting wild rice (actually a grass not a grain), or red Camargue rice feels altogether more modern. As for rice pudding, here's one recipe that comes in hundreds of incarnations. A Scandinavian approach flags up the addition of sweet green cardamom and lemon peel, or a spoonful of cheery red lingonberry purée cuts the creaminess. Turkish rice pudding is more of a perfumed jelly than a filling bowl of stodge, aromatized with a dash of rosewater and a dusting of cinnamon. This same obliging versatility applies to other grains: one ingredient, a world of recipes. Each grain has a subtly different taste and texture that suits different uses.

Grains that cause some confusion because the names are often used interchangeably are couscous, cracked wheat and bulgar. What are they, exactly? Couscous is made from rolled semolina made from durum wheat, the sort used to make pasta (see PASTA/How is pasta made?) and wheat flour, salt and water. Correctly cooked couscous – a minimum of water is the key – provides a dry, free-flowing medium for soaking up gravy. Mograhbieh and maftoul are larger types of couscous. Bulgar is made from wheat that is soaked and steamed before drying and crushing, while cracked wheat is made while the grain is raw. Both bulgar and cracked wheat have more body than couscous. They are easier to cook because the amount of water used is less critical, so they are less likely than couscous to turn mushy.

Quinoa makes an interesting alternative to couscous. There are two sorts: creamy white and red. Both are ever so slightly bitter and when cooked, the grains form little white curls around them, like Saturn's moons.

The slippery-smooth contours of pearled (husk removed) barley or spelt come into their own in a peasanty vegetable broth with root vegetables and dark greens like cavolo nero or kale. Rye and buckwheat have a deeper, almost smoky quality that makes most other grains seem bland by comparison. In its whole form, not everyone instantly takes to the smoky strength of buckwheat, but milled, fermented and transformed into blini daubed with crème fraîche mixed with horseradish and chopped dill, then topped with a curl of smoked salmon, few will turn up their noses.

Milled maize, or cornmeal, is one of the most distinctive grains, announcing its presence with its sunny yellow colour. A tortilla made with cornmeal, for example, has a much bigger personality than one made from wheat. If porridge (see BREAKFAST CEREALS) is a dish to split opinions, polenta (another form of cornmeal) is just as controversial.

Relative newcomers to these isles, ever so slightly malty amaranth, kamut – an unhybridized type of wheat (see BREAD/The rise of the British loaf) – and millet can be used in pilaf or porridge, or substituted in recipes for better-known grains. They are increasingly used as flours in artisan bread, and turn up in whole foodie alternatives to popular breakfast cereals. Without teff, a relative of millet, there's no *injera* – Ethiopia's staple pancake with its distinctively sour edge that comes from fermentation.

Things to do with grains

- An earthy-tasting, golden risotto Milanese using arborio, carnaroli or vialone nano rice, onion, meat stock and Parmesan is the best recipe for making a big impression with a parsimonious pinch of expensive saffron.

- Make an easy but unusual Asian rice pudding using sticky black rice, palm sugar and coconut milk.

- For a colourful, interesting risotto, sweat rice with onion and smoked bacon or cured ham, add chopped radicchio, then follow the standard risotto recipe using red rather than white wine.

- Use pearled spelt or barley instead of rice in a risotto.

- Couscous and cracked wheat make mild-mannered companions to piquant grilled merguez sausages and spicy harissa paste. They also obligingly soak up the juices from soupy meat and vegetable stews.

- Add toasted pine kernels, chopped flat leaf parsley, slivers of preserved lemon or olives, pomegranate seeds and cubes of salty white cheese or cold roast chicken to quinoa, rice, couscous, bulgar wheat or brown rice to make a main-course salad, perfect for the lunchbox.

- Some like polenta soft and sloppy, perhaps topped with wintry greens cooked with chilli under a cap of molten blue cheese. Others go for it when it has been cooked firm, allowed to set, then crisped up by frying or char-grilling, served in fingers to dip into fiery pepper or tomato salsa.

- To experience the palate-filling potential of corn, the simple add-wet-to-dry recipes for US-style Deep South corn bread (buttermilk, eggs and oil to cornmeal, flour, baking powder and salt), with additions, perhaps, of crisp bacon, cheese and Jalapeño chillies, are there to explore.

- Combine equal amounts of warm cooked brown or green lentils and brown rice. Anoint with olive oil and season with sea salt and pepper. Serve warm or cold with natural yogurt, dark-fried onions, toasted pine kernels and chopped parsley on top.

Are grains good for me?

Grains have a very healthy image, yet their benefits may have been over-hyped. Grains vary in their precise nutritional make-up, but, taken as a category, the main attributes of these carbohydrate-rich foods are that in their whole (unprocessed) forms they supply a number of B vitamins, which help give you energy and support brain function, some vitamin E, which is thought to promote heart health, and useful minerals, such as manganese, magnesium and selenium. But all the vitamins and minerals found in grains are found in greater quantities in other foods, such as eggs, meat and fish.

Whole grains contain fibre. There are two sorts of fibre: soluble and insoluble. Soluble fibre is found in fruits, vegetables and beans. Insoluble fibre is the sort usually found in grains, such as wheat bran, although an exception here is oats, which contain soluble fibre. Soluble fibre is generally considered to be very useful in the diet. It can help to keep waste matter moving through the body, so encouraging regular bowel movements. It can also slow down the rate at which food leaves the stomach, delaying the absorption of sugar into the bloodstream after a meal. Nutritional opinion is divided on the relative merits of the insoluble sort. That said, some nutritionists believe that grains are inherently pro-inflammatory and will worsen any condition that has chronic inflammation at its root, such as coeliac disease. Some studies suggest that insoluble fibre can worsen digestive problems such as irritable bowel syndrome, while soluble fibre is generally well tolerated.

There is also a school of nutritional thought that argues that whole grains should not be eaten uncooked or unsoaked. The concern is that whole grains contain natural toxins, or anti-nutrients – enzyme blockers, lectins and glycoalkaloids – that impair the body's ability to digest protein and starch and which could play a role in digestive disorders. Cooking is thought to remove some, but not all of these anti-nutrients, as is fermentation (see BREAD/Is bread good for me?).

While the overall merits of whole grains are debatable, they are more nutritious than refined grains, such as white rice, couscous and wheat. Refining destroys most of the vitamins and minerals, leaving refined carbohydrate that is rapidly converted by the body into sugar. Rapid surges and dips in blood sugar levels like this can cause cravings, lead to over-eating and encourage a surge in the fat storage hormone, insulin, which encourages the body to lay down fat. High levels of insulin in the blood are increasingly being pinpointed as a cause of weight gain and one of the factors at play in conditions such as diabetes and obesity. It is also easier to eat, or over-eat, large quantities of refined grains than it is to eat them in their whole form. A small portion of brown rice, for instance, takes longer to chew, and is more filling, than a large helping of white rice. In short, if you eat refined grains and cereals made from them, you are more likely to put on weight than if you eat whole grains.

Grains do contain protein, although at a much lower level than animal foods such as eggs and meat, but they can be a useful protein source for vegetarians. Higher protein grains include amaranth, oats, quinoa, teff, kamut, wild rice, buckwheat, rye and spelt.

Grains are typically grown with frequent pesticide treatments. Refining reduces these substantially, but if you usually eat wholegrain bread and whole grains, rather than the refined sort, and want to minimize your exposure to any pesticide residues they may contain, buy organic ones.

Stone-ground grains are preferable to grains milled on a more industrial scale between steel rollers, when the friction and heat generated reduce their micronutrients.

How are grains produced?

Whole grains are harvested from field-grown crops. They can then be milled to remove their exterior husk, polished or pearled to make them softer to eat and quicker to cook. Alternatively, they can be made into flours that have a wide range of food manufacturing uses.

Are grains a green choice?

Staple grains, such as wheat and corn, are commonly grown in large-scale monocultures (only one crop) and their cultivation relies heavily on artificial fertilizers, derived from potash. Potash is a non-renewable natural resource; in other words, the earth cannot make it at a rate that keeps up with its usage, and so stocks are rapidly depleting. Grains are widely grown using multiple pesticide treatments. These are mainly derived from oil, another depleting, non-renewable resource. Synthetic fertilizers and pesticides are major contributors to pollution worldwide. Grain production leaves a very heavy carbon footprint and is rarely wildlife- or environment-friendly. By choosing organic grains, you can substantially reduce the environmental impact of those crops. Organic growers are not allowed to use synthetic chemical fertilizers and have to use crop rotations, natural nitrogen-fixing crops, like clovers, and animal manures to build soil fertility naturally. Only six pesticides are permitted in organic growing, and they may only be used as a last resort, while over 300 are routinely in use in conventional agriculture.

Where should I buy grains?

Check out wholefood shops for grains. They stock an eclectic selection of grains and cereals that is usually much wider than the supermarket offers and usually have a bigger choice of organic grains.

Will grains break the bank?

Even if you eat the highest quality and rarest types of grains, these are never expensive foods in the context of total food expenditure. Apart from anything else, they swell up massively in cooking. Even expensive wild rice becomes quite cheap when you think of it in this way.

Leftover grains need never be binned. Last night's risotto can be dipped in flour, egg and breadcrumbs then fried to make *arancini*, or rice balls. Uneaten cooked grain of all sorts can provide bulk and interesting texture for a vegetable rissole or stuffing for poultry.

HERO OR VILLAIN?

Traditionally, grains were seen as fattening foods for both humans and animals. Grain-fed farm animals, for instance, will put on more weight, faster, than their pasture-fed counterparts, and the meat of grain-fed animals usually has a higher fat content than that of grass-fed livestock.

Until the 1970s, it was taken for granted that eating too many starchy foods, such as grain, would lead to weight gain. There are various reasons why this might be the case. A high-carbohydrate diet may cause your body to store away more energy in fat tissue and prevent it from being released and burnt. Carbohydrate is also less inherently satisfying than either protein or fat. A large pile of couscous, for example, may leave you feeling full-up one minute, then hungry an hour or so later, looking for something further to eat, so encouraging you to eat more in the long term.

This long-standing perception of carbohydrate, grain-based foods was turned on its head as public health advice on both sides of the Atlantic embraced the notion that the main cause of obesity is over-consumption of saturated fat. This gospel is beginning to unravel, not least because there is an absence of good evidence to support it. Apart from anything else, statistics show that saturated fat consumption has reduced, but obesity continues to be an ever-expanding problem. Increasingly, the finger of blame points to an overabundance in the diet of carbohydrate-rich, grain-based foods – particularly of the refined 'white' sort – and sugar.

When evidence of how refined carbohydrate could cause surges in the fat storage hormone, insulin, emerged, fibre became the new dietary saviour. There were 'good' carbs (the wholegrain sort) and 'bad' carbs (the refined sort). But once again, the benefits of the insoluble type found in whole grains may have been exaggerated. You will often hear, for instance, that fibre can help prevent colon cancer, but there is no good evidence to support this.

Currently, the first tip in the UK Food Standards Agency's eight-tip healthy eating advice is to 'base your meals on starchy food'. It advocates that a third of all the food we eat should be starchy. The 'logic' here is that weight-for-weight, starchy foods have less than half the calories of fat. But increasingly, research suggests that there is much more to weight gain than eating too many calories for our body weight and activity level. Healthy eating paradigms, once established, are not easily shifted, but in the fullness of time, nutritional orthodoxy may yet turn full circle and carbohydrate-rich grain foods will no longer be seen in quite such a flattering light.

Breakfast cereals

Breakfast cereals take us back to childhood: the soothing familiarity of the cartoon-covered box, the rustle and shake of its contents, the snap, crackle and pop as you pour over cold milk, that dependable crispness. Day or night, a bowl of cereal is a stalwart, instant standby. Nostalgia apart, the childish appeal of the popular breakfast cereals, however tarted up with supposedly wholesome bran and fruits for an adult market, is mostly about crunch. It's no exaggeration to say that minus their added ingredients – notably sugar and salt and often artificial flavourings – they would taste about as thrilling as a mouthful of sawdust. Chuck in a sliced banana or a fistful of blueberries, by all means, but you can't turn a pig's ear into a silk purse.

Muesli is marketed as the grown-up's breakfast. And if you eat a lot of it, then it's worth considering making, or rather assembling, your own, if only so you can combine your favourite ingredients in the proportions that you enjoy and ditch those you don't like. Muesli is like a box of chocolates. Just as there is always someone who avoids the marzipan and the Turkish Delight, there's always someone who picks out the banana chips and the super-sized raisins.

Granola is European muesli's sweet and oily US cousin, once again offering the sweetness and crunch of our ubiquitous breakfast cereals, but in a more plausibly healthy form.

Porridge appeals to traditionalists and trumps the opposition in winter because it is served hot. Purists insist on oatmeal – fine, medium or pinhead – that has been pre-soaked overnight. For them it must be made with water, salt and served with cold milk. But for the spontaneous eater, porridge oats are a more convenient option. Many people find the water-only porridge concept too frugal and prefer it made with milk, or at least half and half milk and water.

Things to do with breakfast cereals

- Porridge offers a wonderfully blank canvas for the open-minded eater, the warm, cuddly foil for a compote of dried fruit, or sharp plum or apple purée. A spoonful of frozen red berries stirred into hot porridge will turn it a fruity purple-pink. Ripe pear or banana, along with a grating of fresh root ginger, adds sweetness and aromatic warmth to porridge.

- For those who like to take porridge down the sweet route, maple syrup and honey come into their own, while a grating of nutmeg, a blade of mace and a cinnamon stick can add sweet, spicy undertones.

- Try adding some millet or quinoa flakes (see Things to do with grains) to porridge made with porridge oats and stir in some sunflower or sesame seeds to add interest and vary the texture.

- Bircher muesli, with its natural yogurt-soaked oats, toasted nuts and grated apple combines the homespun charm associated with rice pudding with the wholesomeness of the health spa. Add red berries to make it even more irresistible.

- Make your own muesli and you can customize it to suit your taste, often upping the quality of the ingredients in the process, and making it more interesting, perhaps by incorporating barley, spelt and rye flakes into the basic mix, as well as the more usual oats and wheat. By lightly baking grains and nuts for muesli in a low oven before combining them with fruits and seeds, you can enhance their nuttiness.

- Beef up the nutritional value and the eating quality of the standard, processed breakfast cereals by adding protein in the form of nuts (cashews, almonds, pecans, hazelnuts) and fresh or defrosted berries.

Are breakfast cereals good for me?

Breakfast cereals tend to have a healthy image because they are grain-based, but the nutritional benefits of grain may have been overstated (see GRAINS/Are grains good for me?). All the vitamins and minerals found in breakfast cereals are found in greater quantities in other foods, such as eggs, fish and meat.

Breakfast cereals and cereal bars are highly processed foods but promoted as healthy because the nutritional benefits of the whole grain are used to give them an aura of health. Many breakfast cereals, for instance, trumpet that they contain fibre. Manufacturers also advertise that their breakfast cereals 'supply energy' and are 'part of a balanced diet'. That sounds good, but it is just another way of saying that the product, like any food, contains calories. This type of marketing has been successful, so much so that a bowl of refined breakfast cereal is widely seen as a healthier option than an egg, or the traditional cooked breakfast, when the opposite may be the case.

The older generation of refined breakfast cereals – cornflakes, rice crispies and puffed wheat – have large quantities of salt and sugar added. High intakes of salt in processed food are associated with an increased incidence of high blood pressure and stroke. Sugar may contribute to weight gain, a factor in many chronic diseases.

Cereals such as Shredded Wheat and wheat biscuits claim to be more nutritious because they are made from whole wheat, but most people find that those that do not already contain added salt and sugars are boring to eat, so they sprinkle them liberally with sugar to make them palatable, which defeats their supposed purpose.

Newer generation breakfast cereals, especially those targeted at children, are typically made from refined grain flours and meals. They are mixed with a number of obvious, and less obvious, sweeteners, such as added honey, malt, rice, milk powder, whey and high-fructose corn syrup, flavourings, both natural and artificial, and often colourings, even chocolate, then re-formed into appealing shapes. Cereals of this type often have levels of sugar to rival confectionery and are best thought of as sweets.

CEREALS

Most breakfast cereals aimed at children are fortified with synthetic vitamins and minerals. These are there to make up for the natural vitamins and minerals that have been removed in processing, but it is likely that their 'bio-availability', or the body's ability to absorb them, is more limited. But long lists of vitamins and minerals down the side of packs give parents the idea that these cereals supply all the micronutrients children need, when in fact they fall very short of being an all-round healthy food.

Another ruse to make breakfast cereals seem healthy, usually those aimed at adults, is to label them as low fat. Since cereals are naturally low in fat anyway, this is only what you might expect, but it is a red herring that helps distract attention from all the fattening sugars and sweeteners in the product. Besides, there is nothing intrinsically good about a product being low in fat. Contrary to what we have been led to believe, there is an absence of evidence to support the nutritional mantra that fat is bad for health, or even to back the assumption that the naturally occurring fat that you find in whole foods is intrinsically fattening.

Breakfast cereals of the muesli type are marketed to adults. Muesli may be quite healthy, although there is a school of nutritional thought that argues that whole grains should not be eaten uncooked or unsoaked. The concern is that whole grains contain natural toxins, or anti-nutrients – enzyme blockers, lectins and glycoalkaloids – that impair the body's ability to digest protein and starch and which could play a role in digestive disorders. Cooking is thought to remove some, but not all of these anti-nutrients, as is fermentation (see BREAD/Is bread good for me?).

Many of the most popular brands of muesli contain sugar and/or other sweeteners. On closer examination of the contents, they often owe much of their bulk, not to minimally processed cereals, but to composite flakes where grain flours have been mixed with sugar of some type. 'No added sugar' mueslis frequently have sugar levels to match the sweetened sort because the manufacturers have bumped up the quantities of sweet fruits like raisins, dates and banana chips and other miscellaneous sweeteners found in modern refined cereals. Both unsweetened or minimally sweetened porridge and Swiss-style Bircher muesli – a home-made blend of oats soaked in yogurt and milk with grated apple, fresh berries, nuts and seeds – are healthier options.

Granola-style mueslis, in the North American style, are stuck together with large quantities of oil and sugar, or other sweetener such as maple or golden syrup or honey. That they can be delicious to eat is undeniable, but they are by no stretch of the imagination a health food. Granola-style breakfast cereal bars commonly contain a full complement of all the undesirable additives and ingredients found in breakfast cereals targeted at children. The vegetable oils used in granola products are almost invariably highly refined and raise health issues (see OILS/Is oil good for me?).

Some research suggests that breakfast cereals packed in recycled cardboard boxes can become contaminated with toxic mineral oils. These come from the printing ink on newspapers used to make the recycled cardboard. These oils have been linked with adverse health effects – inflammation of organs and cancer – and have been shown to migrate from the cardboard box into the foods, even passing through thin internal plastic bags. The longer cereals stay in the box, the more these toxins accumulate in them. If this concerns you, go for cereals packaged in bags, virgin unrecycled cardboard, or unpack cereals and store in jars or containers when you get them home.

How are breakfast cereals produced?

See GRAINS/How are grains produced?

Are breakfast cereals a green choice?

See GRAINS/Are grains a green choice?

Where should I buy breakfast cereals?

Wholefood shops often stock a more eclectic range of breakfast cereals, mueslis and muesli bases and granolas, often organic. These typically contain more intrinsically nutritious grains, such as spelt, amaranth and millet, and substitute sweeteners that may have some marginal nutritional advantages over white sugar, such as honey.

Will breakfast cereals break the bank?

Popular, familiar breakfast cereals such as cornflakes and rice crispies may not seem like expensive purchases, but given the minimal cost of the ingredients and the fact that they are mass-produced, they represent rotten value for money. Most of what you are paying for is not the ingredients, but packaging, marketing and advertising.

If your regular breakfast is ready-made muesli or granola, then this will cost you quite a bit. By assembling your own you can reduce the cost a little. By swopping to a porridge, yogurt or egg-based breakfast, you may be able to save a significant amount of money.

THE GREAT NATIONAL SWITCH

Breakfast cereals have largely displaced the traditional British or Irish cooked breakfast and long since relegated it to an occasional weekend treat. Nowadays, in those whirlwind minutes when we rush out of the house, it's the breakfast cereal, even a cereal bar, (usually laden with sugar or sweeteners and a generous sprinkling of chemical additives) that we reach for, not the eggs and bacon.

This national switch to grains might seem like a healthy trend. The classic fry-up has had a bad press, making us worried about fat in bacon and sausages and cholesterol in eggs, and feeling that we lacked the time to cook. So the lure of a ready-to-eat cereal, in a box plastered with lithe bodies and scientific information that appears to vouch for the healthiness of the contents, has proved irresistible to many. But when you take a harder look at many of our most popular cereals, this confidence is misplaced. In the fullness of time, this change in our eating habits may look like nutritional folly. The net effect has been that we have deserted tried-and-tested whole foods, and started eating many more new, and relatively untested, highly processed foods. The results of this eating experiment are yet to emerge.

Bread

There are few smells quite so enticing as that of baking bread. Like a cosy hot-water bottle, the aroma of bread fresh from the oven has a reassuring homeliness about it. And if there's a sound guaranteed to soothe the soul, it's the cracking of crusty hot bread or the crunch of crisp toast. Dame Nellie Melba simply took this quality to its logical extreme with her eponymous, audaciously thin toast, at the same time unleashing its luxury potential.

On the face of it, we are in a 'never had it so good' phase of our bread history. We can now buy an unprecedented array of breads from almost every culinary tradition on the planet. Artisan bakeries, making bread to time-honoured principles, are a growing feature of our food landscape. Our bread possibilities are undoubtedly on the up. Yet in many places, you will still be presented with a 'choice' of bread that really doesn't deserve to be eaten. Whether it's the cheap and un-cheerful sliced and wrapped loaves that are rolled off the assembly line by a handful of industrial plant bakeries, or the supposedly just-made 'speciality' sort that appear miraculously from supermarket in-store bakeries, the taste and texture is frequently lamentable, unless, that is, you have a taste for the pappy, cotton-wool-meets-loft-insulation variety.

Few of us hold out high hopes for the standard sliced loaves, but many breads initially look more promising. It isn't always glaringly obvious whether they have better eating qualities. Supermarkets' more artisan-looking breads, for instance, often look as if they came straight from the hearth, with slashes in the crust and dustings of flour. It's only when you start eating them that it becomes clear that you have a lookalike impostor on your hands. When you're buying bread, that old maxim, 'appearances can be deceptive', is spot-on.

To get the measure of any bread, taste it when it is cold. Hot, fresh bread can cast spells on you, as almost any bread tastes reasonable when it is hot. But, like weighing up the virtues of a new lover the morning after the night before, only when it cools down can you really judge it objectively. Also base your judgement on the simplest, most straightforward loaf on offer. This allows you to concentrate on the intrinsic quality of the basic dough and your perception won't be skewed by the distracting presence of added ingredients – such as nuts, onions, raisins, sun-dried tomatoes, added whole grains and seeds.

There is a diverse and fascinating world of different styles and types of bread, each with its own taste characteristics, but good breads share certain common features. As far as white breads are concerned, look for those with a crumb that is off-white and slightly grey in colour. This suggests that they have been made with stoneground, unbleached flour. Breads with snowy, spongy white innards will be made from porous, roller-milled flour that has been chemically bleached. Crusty white breads, such as baguette, should make an enticing cracking noise when you squeeze them. If they break up in bits, seem powdery or extremely light and fragile, then they will have been made from dough that has risen too quickly, probably thanks to a combination of large amounts of yeast, poor-quality absorbent flour, and the use of industrial additives.

Any bread that calls itself brown, granary or wholemeal should feel relatively solid and dense. When you bite into it, it should not be tough, but the crumb should have a satisfying, reasonably substantial texture, and it should have a true crust and a good chewy 'sole' (base), so you have to use your teeth and jaws to eat it. In the mouth, well-made brown bread should offer an underlying nutty flavour, while bread made with sourdough leaven will have a slightly tangy taste. Different temperatures and levels of moisture promote different kinds of fermentation. Long, cool ferments produce more of an acetic acid, slightly vinegary flavour, while wetter doughs and warmer ferments have more of a lactic acid character, like the sharpness of yogurt.

If you get the chance, ask the baker how long the bread took to make from start to finish. It takes a minimum of five hours to produce a decent light white loaf in a traditional way, and a truly hand-crafted, slowly risen loaf made from wholemeal flour may take more than a day, depending on the type of flour used.

Whether they are white, brown or wholemeal, be suspicious of breads that become biscuity when toasted. This may be an indication of too much yeast, too rapid a rise and the presence of too much air and retained water. Well-made bread should still retain its moisture after a few days. Even baguette should still be good toasted on the second day. A telltale sign that bread from supermarket in-store bakeries has been baked from frozen, pre-formed, sometimes part-baked dough is that it hardens and dries out within a day. Sourdough bread, although often more substantial and less springy in style, keeps better than other types of bread and should toast nicely for days. Some legendary sourdough breads last for weeks.

It is hard not to be familiar with the woeful standard of the factory-made industrial sliced and wrapped loaves that dominate our shelves. Very few people eat it because they actively love it; it's just what happens to be around. These wrapped and sliced breads have no crust in the true sense of the word, more of a spongy skin and a pappy centre that is soft and squidgy and tastes of curiously little other than a vague sweetness. This ubiquitous sort of bread doesn't leave the mouth clean as good bread does, instead it forms a sticky mass on the roof and sides of your mouth and on your teeth. It appears to stay fresh for days, but this fake freshness is achieved by the use of crumb-softening enzymes. In a few days, the retained water in the loaf will suddenly turn to mould. When you find yourself stuck only with a selection of mass-produced bread, look at the ingredients label. Choose bread made with the four essential ingredients: flour, water, yeast, salt. Any other ingredients should be readily recognizable ones – sunflower seeds, olive oil, buttermilk and nuts, for example – that you would find in a well-stocked domestic larder. Avoid those that list flour treatment agent, emulsifier, improver, flavouring and preservative. Even then, the bread may have been made using controversial enzymes that do not appear on the label.

Things to do with bread

- Buttered crumbs, gently fried in foaming butter, turn any plainly cooked fish or vegetable into a feast.

- Make a salad of bitter chicory or frisée endive, chopped hard-boiled egg and fried breadcrumbs and serve with a sharp vinaigrette.

- Use soft white bread, brioche or panettone to make a bread and butter pudding.

- Serve any type of smoked fish on thin slices of pumpernickel rye bread spread with horseradish and soured cream.

- Light, soft rye breads piled with pastrami or corned beef, sauerkraut or shredded gherkins and mayonnaise spiked with hot English mustard make excellent sandwiches.

- Yesterday's croissants, halved horizontally and flattened with a rolling pin, make deluxe French toast when soaked in eggs, cream, icing sugar (and a little orange liqueur if you fancy it), then fried in butter. Serve as a dessert with fruit compote and extra cream.

- Fried croutons of good sourdough bread add interest to any green salad.

- Melba toast is made by toasting slices of white bread, cutting off the crust, slicing them horizontally through the middle and toasting once more the two thinner slices until they go brown in parts and curl up.

- Toast slices of white sourdough bread, rub with a cut clove of garlic and drizzle on extra virgin olive oil. Top with any of the following: tomato salsa, black olive paste, or warm fried mushrooms.

- Make up a white bread sandwich with thinly sliced melting cheese and cooked ham, then dip it in egg and milk and fry to make a French croque monsieur.

- Dry, rustic, country-style white bread is ideal for making an Italian panzanella bread salad. Just tear up the bread (crusts removed), add twice as much chopped fresh tomatoes, some chopped red onion and sea salt, then anoint generously with olive oil and wine vinegar. Allow to sit until the juices from the tomatoes have been soaked up by the bread, add torn basil and black pepper and serve.

- Make a grated cheese and chopped spring onion sandwich, butter it on the outside as well as inside, then grill it on a ridged cast-iron grill until it becomes crunchy and has nicely charred lines.

Is bread good for me?

Some wholemeal breads, and all white breads, have high glycaemic indexes which means that they can cause surges of blood sugar and the fat storage hormone, insulin. In other words, consuming large quantities of many types of bread can be fattening, even though they contain little or no fat. Foods with high glycaemic indexes tend to encourage inflammation and thrombosis in the body, which in turn has been linked with increased risk of heart disease. Sourdough and pumperknickel breads tend to have a lower glycaemic index, as a result of their long fermentation.

Another way in which bread might promote weight gain is that, unlike protein-rich and fatty foods, it is not that effective at satisfying the appetite. So it may leave you hungry after an hour or two and craving something else to eat, thus encouraging over-eating in the longer term.

Wholemeal bread made from properly fermented wheat, rye or any other grain does have some nutritional good points. It naturally contains B vitamins, most notably vitamin B1, which is needed for healing and maintaining the nervous system; vitamin B3, which is also necessary for the nervous system; vitamin E, which research suggests can help reduce the incidence of heart disease, certain cancers and strokes; and several useful minerals. It also contains a lot of insoluble fibre, which speeds up the transit of food through the body, and slows down somewhat the speed at which sugar, broken down from carbohydrate, is released into the bloodstream. Good wholemeal bread is typically quite substantial, which makes it more effective than lighter, whiter breads in satisfying the appetite and giving you a sensation of fullness.

White bread has much less going for it. The bran and germ of the whole grain, which contain the lion's share of the vitamins and minerals, are milled away. White flour usually has anything from 25 to 30 per cent of the whole grain removed, while brown flour has 10–15 per cent removed. By law, breads made using white and also brown flours that are not wholemeal must have synthetic vitamins B1 and B3, calcium and iron added to replace some of those lost, but this does not restore the full complement of micronutrients found in bread made from 100 per cent wholemeal flour. Extraction also removes the useful fibre. Some breads are marketed as super-healthy because they have a proportion of whole grains or fibre added back in. These are best thought of as breads that have been stripped of most of their nutritional integrity, then put back together in more profitable form.

As bread made from lighter, whiter flours is more insubstantial and less filling than the wholemeal sort, it is easier to eat more of it. The refined carbohydrate in white bread is rapidly converted by the body into sugar. Rapid surges and dips in blood sugar levels can cause cravings and lead to over-eating and encourage a surge in insulin. High levels of insulin in the blood are increasingly being pinpointed as a cause of weight gain and one of the factors at play in conditions such as diabetes and obesity and also many other diseases.

A growing body of research supports the idea that sourdough breads are better for you than breads made only from commercial baker's yeast because the natural bacteria in the dough produce lactic and acetic acids which go to work on the proteins in the gluten, making them easier to digest. These bacteria have also been shown to help the body absorb better the beneficial vitamins and minerals in the flour. This may be because they help neutralize the anti-nutrients that are naturally found in grains (see GRAINS/Are grains good for me?). Sourdough bread may also be preferable to yeasted breads because, the acids slow down the rate at which sugar is released into the bloodstream.

Whether flour is wholemeal, brown or white, stoneground flour is preferable to milled. When grains are milled between steel rollers, the friction and heat generated reduce the micronutrients. Stoneground flours, even the lighter ones, still retain very fine traces of the bran and germ of the whole grain, so they are slightly more nutritious.

Since modern breadmaking techniques have only been with us since the 1960s, we can't yet know what, if any, impact they are having on human health. However, the ingredients and methods used in industrial breadmaking have been pinpointed by some bakers and nutrition experts, as a likely contributory factor to the rise in the numbers of people now suffering from intolerance to wheat or gluten, coeliac disease, irritable bowel syndrome and other conditions that affect the gut. The thinking here is that because many modern breads are made to rise rapidly, they do not undergo the slow, natural fermentation that would make the gluten in them more digestible. Certain grains also have lower levels of anti-nutrients than others, which make them easier to digest (see BREAKFAST CEREALS/Are breakfast cereals good for me?). Spelt, for instance, is lower in phytic acid, an anti-nutrient that can make it harder to absorb certain minerals. Also the gluten in spelt is more brittle and soluble than in other wheats, which is why it is often recommended as an easier-to-tolerate alternative for people who experience problems digesting standard wheat baked by fast-track industrial methods. Rye bread, too, is generally better tolerated by people with food sensitivities. Other medical authorities, however, simply attribute the apparent increased incidence of these conditions to better detection methods.

Modern breads are made using considerably larger quantities of yeast, and faster acting sorts of yeasts, than were ever used in the past to speed up the whole breadmaking process. As a result we are eating more yeast than we ever used to, which may trigger or exacerbate problems in some people who suffer from fungal infections such as thrush and candida.

Other ingredients in industrial bread raise health issues. Chemically hardened oils are added to the dough to extend shelf life and keep the bread soft. In the recent past these have included partially hydrogenated vegetable fat which produced trans-fats that cause heart disease. Now the big bakeries are replacing this type of fat with fractionated, or interesterified, fats which are said to be less harmful, but they are, as yet, relatively untested (see MARGARINES AND SPREADS/Are margarines and spreads good for me?).

A number of enzymes are used to facilitate various aspects of the industrial baking process and to give the bread its profitable shelf life, bulk and feel. As these are classed as 'processing aids' rather than additives or ingredients, they do not appear on the label. Some of them are known allergens.

Pesticide traces are commonly found in bread samples. These are more often found in brown and wholemeal bread because residues tend to collect on the outside of the whole grain. Fewer residues are found in white bread because the bran is removed during the milling process. If you eat a lot of bread – more than a loaf or equivalent every week– and want to minimize your exposure to pesticides, there is good reason to buy bread made with organic flour, especially if you eat brown or wholemeal bread.

How is bread made?

Most of the sliced and wrapped bread on sale is produced by a fast-track method, known as the Chorleywood Bread Process, which was designed for industrial breadmaking plants. It does away with the long, slow, first rise or bulk fermentation stage which, until the mid-twentieth century, was seen as a necessary stage in breadmaking, instead using high-energy, high-speed mixing. The process is entirely automated and computer-controlled. It makes it possible to produce those oh-so-familiar rectangular pan or tin-baked loaves, all cooled, sliced and wrapped in three and a half hours from start to finish.

The process starts with finely milled absorbent flour that has been whitened using chlorine gas to toughen the protein in it. This allows the dough to soak up more water than it otherwise would. More generous amounts of yeast are added to the dough than are used in traditional breadmaking to speed up the time it takes to rise. A number of other items go into the mix, some of which are referred to in the bread industry as 'improvers'. Their main functions are to produce bigger, airier, more voluminous loaves, speed up the production process and keep the crumb soft and squidgy to give the bread a longer shelf life. Such additions to bread include soya flour (to whiten the flour and make it hold more water), emulsifiers such as soy lecithin and diacetyl tartaric (acid) ester of monoglyceride (to give it volume and softness), caramel, sugar, malt and milk powder (to impart a sweet taste), fat or oil (to make the crumb stay soft for longer), preservatives, notably vinegar and calcium propionate (to make it last longer), reducing agents, such as L-cysteine hydrochloride (to make the dough more workable and elastic), ascorbic acid (which strengthens the gluten and helps the dough rise) and enzymes.

Enzymes are naturally present in flour, yeast and sourdough starters and are needed for fermentation. But many of those used in industrial baking are controversial, either because they have been made using genetic modification, or developed from animals, using sources such as feathers and pig's pancreas. Vegetarians, people from certain religions and those who do not want to eat food made using GM techniques may want to avoid this sort of bread. Organic bread can be made using enzymes, but not the GM sort.

Smaller-scale bakeries make bread using different methods. Most of the longer-established 'craft' bakeries still use slower, smaller mixing machines and produce breads other than the standard, pan-baked sliced loaf. But many of them make full use of the same bleached, roller-milled flours and improvers along with large quantities of fast-acting yeast. These breads generally look more promising, more rustic and more homespun, but in taste and quality terms there is often little to choose between these and the standard factory-made sliced loaf.

A similar range of crusty, more exciting-looking breads is offered by supermarket in-store bakeries. Most of them do not bake from scratch on the premises, but the minority that do simply weigh out flour, add water and a 'pre-mix' of flour improvers.

As a reaction to the joyless, uniform hi-tech bread that dominates production, a new wave of small, artisan bakeries is sprouting up making bread more slowly, doing much more of the work by hand and allowing the dough to rise at its natural pace without the addition of large quantities of yeast. Typically, they use less industrial flour and avoid all the unnecessary additives used in the industrial process. They tend to be more experimental and bake with grains other than just wheat, such as rye, spelt, barley, oats, kamut, millet and quinoa. Some of them make bread that has been raised using only a 'leaven' or sourdough starter. This can either be made by mixing flour and water, then allowing it to be colonized by wild yeasts that are naturally present in the flour and the environment, or by keeping back a little dough from a previous batch of bread made with commercial yeast, mixing in flour and water, then leaving it to ferment naturally as lactic acid bacteria develop in the dough. Many bakers also make breads using a combination of sourdough leaven and yeast for a slightly lighter result.

The varieties of wheat that are native to Britain and Ireland are not considered by industrial bakers to be the easiest for breadmaking. Although the soft flours produced from these wheats work well for other sorts of baking, and have a very good flavour, they are quite low in protein, which can make it a bit tricky to make well-risen loaves.

In the past, British bakers got round this by combining these with flours from harder, higher-protein wheats, imported from North America. Modern wheat strains have been bred with shorter straw to make them easier to harvest and to have bigger yields that depend on heavy applications of chemical fertilizers. These strains have been selected, not for flavour, but for their higher protein content and ability to ripen earlier.

These hybrid strains have upped our production of home-grown wheat and considerably reduced our reliance on imported flour. This has strengthened the country's self-sufficiency in food and reduced food miles, but it has also had negative effects. Bread bought in Britain and Ireland more often than not contains residues of pesticides, and the new hybrid wheats are also less nutritious; that is, they produce flour with significantly lower levels of vitamins and minerals than did the old 'unimproved' strains, such as spelt.

As well as eating flour from a reduced number of varieties of wheat, we are also buying bread from a drastically reduced number of bakeries. Over the last few decades, the majority of smaller independent bakeries that were trying to compete with the big industrial bakeries have closed. They have been unable to match the bargain-basement price of the pappy bread churned out by the industrial plant bakeries that are owned by a handful of big companies, or to compete with their marketing strength.

Is bread a green choice?

Both the soya flour and the vegetable fat used in baking are problematic. Soya is increasingly grown on rainforest or savannah that has been cleared for this purpose and the vegetable fat often includes palm oil, produced from trees planted on cleared tropical coastal forest. The clearance of land for these crops releases carbon dioxide that has been locked in the soil, adding to global warming, and destroys wildlife habitat.

The concentration of breadmaking in industrial plant bakeries leaves a heavy carbon 'foodprint'. These out-of-town factories require a whole rapid distribution network of depots and haulage that is necessarily more carbon-intensive than a local bakery supplying its local area.

Where should I buy bread?

Unlike the traditional small bakeries of the past that tried unsuccessfully to compete head-to-head with the large industrial bakeries by turning out a similar range of products, the new artisan bakeries are making breads that are distinctively different and appeal to people who will pay more for bread, provided that they consider them to be of better quality. Some of these new-wave bakers do not have shops, but they have stalls at farmers' markets and/or sell their bread through wholefood shops, delicatessens and bread clubs.

The Real Bread Campaign has a website that allows you to find your nearest supplier using your postcode: www.sustainweb.org/realbread/bakery_finder

Will bread break the bank?

The trouble with buying properly made, high-quality bread is that it can seem unaffordably expensive because we are so accustomed to bread being the cheapest of cheap commodities. Ever since the 1960s, supermarkets have been using the low price of sliced and wrapped, mass-produced, plant-baked loaves to attract people to their stores.

Sliced bread is known in supermarket-speak as a 'known value item'; in other words, it is one of those foods that consumers use to compare the value offered by rival chains. So the supermarkets have bought the bread cheaply and sold it at unrealistically low prices, using this as a device to put a halo of good value around everything else that they sell. Not only has this forced smaller bakeries out of business by leaving them unable to compete on price, but it has also devalued bread and encouraged consumers' unrealistic expectation that all bread should be cheap. By comparison, the cost of good bread can seem exorbitant.

The fact of the matter is that if you want to buy nutritious, patiently crafted, hand-made bread, made with wholesome flour, and free from industrial additives, then you have to think in terms of pounds rather than pence. The upside is that it represents much better value for money than the mass-market, industrial sort, tastes a million times better, is more filling, and is likely to be more nutritious. If you think of it in the context of an overall food budget, better bread is still a relatively modest expenditure.

One of the bonuses of proper bread is that although it costs more, it should keep well. Don't expect it to be soft and squidgy like the factory equivalent that owes its apparent perpetual freshness to additives, but it should retain moisture and last for a week, or even more, especially if you toast it. Some sourdough rye breads, wrapped in foil, will keep for weeks. Many artisan bakeries sell bread with good keeping qualities left over from the day before at half-price. Buying bread this way is an easy way to afford better bread.

If you like the idea of eating better bread, but worry that you won't get through it fast enough and so will end up wasting it, slice the bread when fresh, freeze it, and take out a slice at a time, as and when you need it.

If you can't find a source of good, affordable bread, consider making your own at home, using unbleached, stoneground, preferably organic flour. You can make great bread at home by hand, without having to invest in a kitchen mixer with a dough hook, or a breadmaking machine.

If you buy or make decent bread, you won't want to waste it. Slightly stale bread has multiple uses. Any bread that looks as if it might not get eaten can be made into breadcrumbs and frozen for later use. For instance, you can make meatballs much more economically by adding breadcrumbs and cutting down on the quantity of minced meat you use. Breadcrumbs can also be dried out in a low oven and blitzed in a food processor. These can then be kept in a jar at room temperature and used for coating fried foods such as fish or vegetable patties.

Pasta

Few of us are immune to the charms of pasta. Cheap, versatile, quick, easy to cook and indisputably comforting to eat, this Italian import has become a mainstay of our national diet, putting the more traditional potato on the back foot. The popularity of pasta owes much to its chameleon personality. Depending on how you choose to anoint it – with a tomato sauce perhaps, or with richer cream, ham and cheese, a simple pesto, or a full-blooded red meat ragù – it can seem like a different meal entirely.

Freshly hand-made, silken pasta, golden yellow with egg yolks, plunged briefly in boiling water then finished with butter and freshly grated Parmesan, is one of the simplest but most special of foods. Pasta like this can be made at home if you invest in a small, relatively inexpensive, domestic pasta machine. A food processor will speed up the initial kneading. Otherwise, all you need is good flour and fresh eggs.

Home-made pasta is not to be confused with the 'fresh' egg pasta that is sold chilled in supermarkets. It is made on a commercial scale, often using pasteurized (heat-treated) liquid egg, rather than freshly shelled eggs. Some brands of filled 'fresh' pasta contain ingredients that you would never use for the home-made equivalent, unless, that is, your kitchen also serves as a science lab. These include cheap bulking agents such as potato starch and whey powder, emulsifiers such as mono- and diglycerides of fatty acids, acidity regulators such as lactic acid and both natural and synthetic flavourings.

In order to give it an unnaturally long shelf life, this pasta is packed in a modified atmosphere (a mixture of carbon dioxide and nitrogen) to prevent it from spoiling and to keep it looking fresh. Such pasta tends to be a bit characterless and stodgy, lacking the truly fresh, eggy quality and delicate, springy texture of pasta eaten soon after it is made. To be brutal, good-quality dried egg pasta will often have a less glutinous texture and a better flavour.

Plain dried pasta is cheap and ubiquitous, but that doesn't mean that it's inferior to the egg equivalent, it just has a different place in cooking. Basic dried pasta, made with flour and water, has little intrinsic taste. Rather than being something to be appreciated in itself, it provides a medium for showing off the sauce. While popular brands of dried pasta made on an industrial scale are fine for most purposes, some smaller, artisan brands of dried pasta that are made in a more traditional way are worth trying, once in a while, if you want to make a dish extra special. They have a slightly different, more interesting texture as a result of their production method (see How is pasta made?).

LARDER

Whatever type of pasta you are eating, the trick is not to overcook it, so that it is still slightly bouncy in the mouth and firm to the bite (al dente).

THE POTATO CHALLENGER

We have been fascinated by pasta ever since we first tasted the contents of those long, blue paper-wrapped rolls of spaghetti sold in food shops run by families of Italian immigrants. Pasta became a mainstream foodstuff in Britain after the Second World War and a challenger to our staple potatoes, a trend immortalized in the lyrics of the 1960s song 'Bangers and Mash' sung by Peter Sellers and Sophia Loren:

Her: Eat your tagliatelle, Joe.
Him: That's all I've heard for years.
Her: Eat your vermicelli, Joe.
Him: It's coming out me ears!
Her: You've got to fill your belly, Joe, Joe for heaven's sake!
Him: Well then, give us a bash at the bangers and mash me
    mother used to make.

Quick and easy to cook, pasta has suited a nation that has been increasingly reluctant to spend time in the kitchen, and where cooking skills have been on the decline. Spaghetti Bolognese – our variant on Bologna's speciality, *tagliatelle al ragù* – remains enduringly popular as one of our favourite 'national' dishes, while the more or less instant bowl of pasta, anointed with pesto or ready-made sauce, has become a popular stand-by option.

Britain has embraced all types of pasta with open arms, but since pasta has not been part of our indigenous food, we don't always know how it would be used in Italy. As a rule of thumb, fresh egg pasta is traditionally a northern Italian speciality, so it is part of a richer cuisine that makes more use of ingredients such as cheese, ham, cream, butter and mushrooms. Dried pasta, on the other hand, is the preferred type of pasta in southern Italy where it is used for fresher, lighter sauces that major on sunnier ingredients such as tomatoes, olives, anchovies, aubergines, chilli, garlic, fish roe and olive oil.

Things to do with pasta

- Toss cooked spaghetti or bucatini with anchovy and garlic softened in olive oil, fried breadcrumbs and chopped parsley.

- Combine a chilli-spiked tomato sauce with soft roast or fried aubergines, mix with cooked penne or rigatoni and garnish with a crumbly salted white cheese such as Cheshire, salted ricotta or feta.

- For a heartening gratin, par-boil penne or macaroni and bake in a thin béchamel sauce with plain or smoked mozzarella and leftover cooked smoked ham, topped with Parmesan and breadcrumbs.

- Add room-temperature chopped tomatoes, red onions, garlic, chilli, capers and/or olives, olive oil and basil leaves to hot cooked pasta to make a fresh summer supper.

- Cook garganelli, or any other small egg pasta shape, and sauce with cream, lemon juice and zest and ample grated Parmesan.

- Sauté chopped broccoli stems, anchovies and chopped chilli in a mixture of olive oil and butter. Mix together with boiled broccoli florets and orecchiette (little ears) or conchiglie (small shells) and lots of grated Parmesan.

- Toss cooked spaghetti, spaghettini, tagliatelle or linguine with a mixture of tomato sauce and ricotta.

- Serve thick ribbons of pappardelle with any rich meat stew.

Is pasta good for me?

Regular pasta consumption fits in snugly with government nutrition advice that encourages us to base our meals on starchy foods because they are low in fat. However, many doctors and nutritionists see pasta, along with other refined carbohydrate foods, as a food that can cause weight gain and which offers little in the way of beneficial nutrients. The main objection to the typical pasta, made from refined wheat flour, is that it disrupts blood sugar and insulin levels, which in turn encourages fat production and storage in the body. In other words, consuming large amounts of pasta may be fattening, even though it contains little or no fat.

Another way in which pasta might promote weight gain is that unlike protein-rich and fatty foods, it is not that effective at satisfying the appetite long-term. So although a plate of pasta instantly makes you feel full, it may leave you hungry after an hour or two and craving something else to eat, so encouraging over-eating in the longer term.

Italians, of course, eat masses of pasta and still remain slim – or at least reasonably so – but this may be to do with how they integrate pasta into their diets. In Italy, pasta in itself does not usually form the basis of a whole meal. Traditionally, it is served in a relatively small portion as just one of the savoury elements in a meal, the sequence being first antipasti (a selection of cured meats, fish and vegetable dishes), then the *primi* (a starter-sized amount of pasta, risotto or polenta), then the *secondi* (the main event, usually fish or meat) accompanied by *contorni* (vegetables).

So the British idea of making a meal of a bowl of pasta, perhaps with nothing much more than a tomato sauce, or pesto, is a departure from the customary Italian consumption pattern. By the time Italians get round to eating their pasta course, they are likely to have consumed a good amount of vegetables and protein in the form of antipasti and are leaving room for the protein-based *secondi*. They do not expect to fill up solely on pasta.

The other objection to basic pasta, made from refined white wheat flour and water, is that it offers empty calories. That is to say, it gives you energy, but provides little else in the way of nutritional value in the form of beneficial vitamins, minerals and micronutrients. Wholefood shops now stock some interesting new pastas made using inherently more nutritious wholemeal flours such as spelt and hemp. They do have more to commend them on nutritional grounds because they have the advantages associated with whole, unrefined grains, but most people find them rather heavy. These tend to be products that you eat because you think they are better for you, rather than because you actively prefer them. Egg pasta, whether fresh or dried, has a preferable nutritional profile to pasta made with just flour and water, thanks to the inclusion of eggs, which are a good source of high-quality protein, vitamins and minerals.

How is pasta made?

Dried pasta is made from wheat flour and water. The flour is milled from the heart, or endosperm, of durum wheat semolina, a hard wheat that is grown specifically for making pasta because of its colour and firmness.

The flour and water are mixed together and any eggs, or natural flavourings and colourings, in the form of dehydrated extracts of spinach, beetroot, saffron, truffle or squid ink, are added. The dough is kneaded, rolled into sheets, pasteurized to kill off any harmful bacteria, then either cut into noodle shapes (such as tagliatelle or fettucine) or squeezed ('extruded') through metal discs with holes in them known as dies, to produce characteristic shapes such as fusilli or penne, and, finally, dried.

Dried pasta with a more yellow appearance and a higher price tag will have been made by a more artisan method. Extruded pasta shapes will have been formed using traditional copper dies (moulds) rather than the modern, smoother, Teflon-coated steel dies that are used for mass-market pasta production. These copper dies produce a rougher texture which is said to hold the sauce better. In smaller-scale pasta production the pasta is slowly dried at a lower temperature for as much as two days, whereas in large-scale production it is dried for a matter of hours at a high temperature. This gives it a longer shelf life, but traditional pasta-makers insist that slowly dried pasta tastes better, retains more of its proteins, and its more open-pored texture makes the starches more digestible.

Is pasta a green choice?

Almost all the dried pasta, and much of the fresh pasta we eat in Britain, is made in Italy and imported by road and sea to the UK, so for all that it weighs little, pasta leaves a surprisingly heavy carbon 'foodprint' and does nothing to support the local food economy. Realistically, no one is going to renounce pasta-eating entirely, but before giving in to that knee-jerk 'Let's have pasta again tonight' reflex, it might be good to consider using other home-grown alternatives instead, such as barley, spelt or potatoes, where the recipe allows.

Will pasta break the bank?

Dried pasta is one of the cheapest foods you can buy, whereas 'fresh' chilled pasta is one of the most expensive, especially when you consider the gulf between the cost of the raw ingredients and the price tag. The cost of a portion of dried pasta, even the more artisan brands, can be measured in pence, while the cost of the 'fresh' equivalent is measured in pounds. And while other categories of convenience food save you time, the difference between cooking dried and 'fresh' pasta is minutes. Up to you to decide if the significantly heavier outlay is worth it.

Nuts and seeds

(almonds, hazelnuts, walnuts, Brazils, macadamias, pecans, pistachios, pine kernels, coconut, chestnuts, peanuts and sunflower, sesame, flax, pumpkin and hemp seeds)

Nuts have multiple, fascinating personalities that almost defy description. Brazil nuts, pine kernels and macadamias are distinguished by their creamy nuttiness, while pistachios and cashews share a similar texture, but have their own unique characters. Pecans, peanuts – technically legumes, not nuts – and almonds are chewier, but there the resemblance stops. Walnuts and hazelnuts are bigger presences, the former more robust and bitter, the latter sweeter and more mellow. Chestnuts have a sweet, almost smoky flavour. For a small nut, pistachios pack a big punch and milky coconut transports you to tropical shores.

Nuts are hugely versatile but have a special affinity with cheese, fruit and chocolate. They are one of the plant foods that come close to having the body and substance of meat. No wonder nut roasts figure so prominently in the vegetarian repertoire. Chestnut purée often features in desserts involving chocolate where it has the effect of lightening up chocolate pudding recipes that might otherwise be rather rich. Chunks of fresh coconut also make a great snack to nibble away on. True, shelling coconuts is a pain – think in terms of a hammer and a fit of temper, and try not to grate your knuckles – but the effort is well worth it.

The spectrum of seed tastes goes from the neutral (flax), through the mildly nutty (sunflower and sesame) to the bossier flavours of pumpkin and hemp.

Baking, dry-roasting and toasting nuts and seeds bring out and substantially develop their flavours and make their textures crunchier. Toasted hazelnuts, for instance, are the basis of the Piedmontese Gianduja chocolate and French praline. A dusting of toasted pine kernels gives a finishing touch to many Middle Eastern dishes, while roasted, salted peanuts are the global bar snack. Toasted sesame oil is one of the bedrock flavours in Chinese cooking and there is no Greek halva without sesame seeds. When baked, pecans transform themselves from their soft, pliable state to take on an engaging, sweet crunchiness. And you'll appreciate the point of the seemingly mild and inconsequential macadamia when you bite into one in the centre of a crisp, freshly baked cookie.

The best way to bake or dry-roast nuts or seeds is in a low oven, tossing them as often as you remember and giving them as long as it takes to turn an even golden colour. Tossing them around in a hot skillet or grilling them is trickier because they tend to 'catch' and become over-browned in parts while still pale in others. Burning nuts and seeds degrades their oils (along with their nutritional content) and masks their flavour.

Some recipes using ground almonds tell you to buy whole almonds and grind them yourself, the idea being that they will be fresher than the sort you buy pre-ground. For most purposes, this is unnecessary. You probably won't be able to tell the difference and grinding nuts is time-consuming. But if you are making a fresh marzipan, where you will really taste the fresh creaminess of the nuts, then the extra effort may be worth it.

The oil in nuts is relatively stable, but it does go rancid over time and this process is accelerated if they aren't stored properly or are broken. The more intact nuts are, the less likely they are to be rancid. Walnuts and Brazil nuts are particularly prone to rancidity, so much so that they may already be stale by the time you buy them. If you buy unshelled nuts and shell them yourself, you will often find that they taste remarkably different from the shelled equivalent, particularly if you are lucky enough to get unshelled nuts that have not first been kiln-dried.

If nuts have a bitter or stale taste, this is not normal and means that they are rancid; they should smell fresh and nutty. Buy nuts from a shop with a good turnover to ensure freshness. Ignore the 'best-before' date on nuts and treat them as a fresh food, albeit one that doesn't have to be kept in the fridge. Aim to eat them within weeks, for preference, and no later than six months after you bought them. Store them in a cool, dark place and in an airtight jar or packet to keep them as fresh as possible.

Things to do with nuts and seeds

- Ground almonds enrich and thicken a creamy lamb pasanda.

- Cashew nuts are a reasonable meat substitute in a vegetarian stir-fry or curry.

- If your crumble topping is beginning to bore you, a handful of finely chopped walnuts, pecans, hazelnuts or flaked almonds in the mix will ring the changes.

- Make a more or less instant dessert by combining sweetened chestnut purée with whipped cream, grated chocolate and broken meringue in the style of the Milanese Monte Bianco.

- Nuts work well in salads. Combine toasted hazelnuts with little chunks of goat's cheese and lamb's lettuce, then dress with nut oil and a little white wine vinegar or Seville orange juice. Or team walnuts with slices of apple or pear, crumbled strong blue cheese and radicchio, or other bitter leaf, and anoint with nut oil and cider or apple balsamic vinegar.

- Coconut deserves a much better fate than being dried and desiccated for sprinkling on jam sponges. Fresh coconut is an indispensable ingredient in the aromatic Indonesian rendang spice paste and appears in many Asian spice blends in toasted form.

- Crush toasted sesame seeds, hazelnuts or almonds along with a little cumin seed, coriander seed and sea salt, then use this as a dry dip for warm bread dunked in olive oil.

- Make a Middle Eastern sauce for falafel or vegetable crudités by combining tahini (sesame) paste with lemon juice, a little crushed garlic, sea salt and water.

Are nuts and seeds good for me?

For decades, nuts were exiled to the nutritional wilderness. High in fat and calories, they didn't fit in with low-fat, low-cal orthodoxy. Currently, the anti-fat dogma is being called into question because there is no good evidence to support it (see BUTTER, GHEE AND BUTTERMILK/Are butter, ghee and buttermilk good for me?). Equally, the simplistic calorie theory that weight gain is simply a matter of too many calories in, and not enough energy out, is being challenged. Nowadays, nuts, along with seeds, are increasingly seen as foods that offer excellent nutrition in a compact and highly portable form, making them a handy snack.

With the exception of the chestnut, which is best thought of as a starchy food, nuts and seeds are largely composed of oil, but they do also contain a significant amount of protein, essential for the regeneration of the body, and soluble fibre, which helps digestion. Most of the oil in nuts and seeds comes in the form of monounsaturated fats (omega-9s), which research suggests protect against heart disease, lower blood pressure and reduce levels of bad fats in the blood. This combination of fat, protein and fibre means that nuts and seeds are digested relatively slowly, providing the desirable long, slow release of energy that helps keep blood sugar levels stable. Research is piling up to suggest that eating nuts is good for the heart. Some research links eating nuts with weight loss, since when people eat nuts, they tend to feel satisfied and eat less of other foods. It is also thought that nut eating may stimulate the metabolism.

Nuts and seeds vary in their nutritional composition but, taken as a group, they share certain characteristics. They contain vitamin E, which is thought to be good for the heart and useful for countering antioxidant damage, and B vitamins, which help give you energy and support brain function.

Nuts and seeds are also very rich in beneficial minerals and trace elements, particularly manganese, which helps make enzymes; copper, which plays an important role in energy production and keeping arteries in good condition; and magnesium, which is vital for strong bones. Brazil nuts are an especially good source of selenium, which is thought to protect against cancer. British and Irish soils are usually very low in this trace element so it is likely that many people are deficient in it. Nuts and seeds are typically rich in amino acids, which build and repair muscle and are vital for many other body processes.

Many phytochemicals – naturally occurring plant compounds that are thought to promote good health – are being identified in nuts and seeds. Peanuts, for instance – strictly speaking, legumes rather than nuts – contain resveratrol, which research suggests may have several health benefits, such as aiding the flow of blood to the brain. Walnuts have ellagic acid, which may strengthen the immune system and have an anti-cancer action.

All these attributes make eating nuts and seeds a particularly healthy proposition, a good way of picking up traces of lots of beneficial micronutrients.

Nuts of all kinds are common allergens.

How are nuts and seeds grown?

Nuts are tree fruits. The tree flowers and produces a pod (fruit), which develops a hard shell. The seed, or inner part of this fruit, is the edible nut. An exception here is the peanut, a legume that grows as a plant above ground then buries itself in the soil and matures there. Seeds are grown as open field crops.

Almost all the nuts and seeds we buy are imported. China is the biggest source of most seeds, walnuts and chestnuts. Iran and Turkey supply almonds, hazelnuts, pistachios and pine kernels. As well as supplying pecans and peanuts, the US is also an important source of almonds. Most cashews come from India, Brazil nuts from Latin America and macadamias from Australia.

If you are buying nuts grown in less affluent countries, choose Fairtrade nuts whenever you get the chance. In many countries, the shelling and processing of nuts is typically carried out by women, who are paid a pittance and endure bad working conditions. In India, for instance, women workers shell cashews by hand, while kneeling on the ground. The interior of the shell contains a caustic resin and many women have permanent scars on their hands and deformed nails as a result. Fairtrade nuts come from growers' co-operatives where pay and working conditions are well above the industry norm and the benefits of the trade are shared more equitably with the communities who do the work.

Are nuts and seeds green choices?

Nut trees absorb and store carbon from the environment, so nuts are a very sustainable, environmentally friendly crop. Nut trees also provide a protective canopy, which allows other crops to flourish below. Nut trees, like all trees, provide a wildlife-friendly habitat. The roots of nut trees stabilize the soil and help prevent soil erosion after rains and floods. This is a growing global problem because of global warming. Nut trees usually require very little or no pesticide treatments.

Nuts and seeds are imported but, like pulses, they do still fit in with environmentally aware eating (see PULSES/Are pulses a green choice?).

Where and when should I buy nuts and seeds?

The English cobnut season runs from late August until October. The early crop are sold green and resemble fresh coconut in taste. By the middle to end of September they will turn a brown-gold and taste sweeter and juicier as their starch turns to sugar. For a supply of cobnuts see www.cobnuts.co.uk/info.htm.

Undried 'wet' walnuts from France are sometimes available in specialist shops in the early autumn. The run-up to Christmas is the best season for kiln-dried, unshelled nuts.

Wholefood shops often have a better selection of shelled nuts and seeds than supermarkets and tend to stock Fairtrade nuts. Unfortunately some smaller wholefood stores have a rather sluggish turnover, which means that their nuts can be less fresh than is desirable, especially those that they buy loose and pack themselves. Asian and Middle Eastern grocers also stock a wide range of pre-packed nuts and seeds.

I HAD A LITTLE NUT TREE …

All the nuts we buy are imported, except for the cobnut or filbert, a type of hazelnut, which is grown in Kent and, to a lesser extent, in Devon, Sussex and Worcestershire. Never miss a chance to buy and taste this sweet juicy nut.

Cultivation of nuts in the UK and Ireland wasn't always so rare. Up until the early twentieth century, cobnuts were commonly eaten, but, as with our fruit orchards, they were labour-intensive to harvest and so their cultivation took a nosedive in the face of cheaper imports.

It may come as a surprise to learn that our climate is not entirely hostile to nuts. Hazelnuts and walnuts that were once used as a food source now grow in the wild, and some enthusiastic gardeners have had success with almonds. The problem for would-be amateur nut growers lies in the words of that old nursery rhyme: 'I had a little nut tree … Nothing would it bear'. It's one thing to grow a nut tree, another to produce a harvest of edible nuts.

While we are maintaining the small number of cobnut trees we do still have, and some enthusiastic growers are planting more to meet the demand, no serious research and development effort has gone into assessing the potential for growing more nuts commercially in these shores. An early casualty of food globalization, our native nut trees are overdue for a revival. After all, no one ever thought England would successfully grow grapes for wine.

Will nuts and seeds break the bank?

Apart from peanuts, nuts are always quite costly. Weight for weight, they can work out as expensive or even dearer than meat or fish. On the upside, nuts are so satisfying that it's hard to eat them in the sort of quantities that you might eat meat or fish. If you panic when you look at the price of nuts, remind yourself of how good they are for you. Plus, a few nuts go a long way. A handful of crushed nuts can make an otherwise lightweight, pedestrian salad seem substantial and interesting, or elevate a humdrum compote made from the tired remains of the fruit bowl.

If you buy nuts then find that they that are rancid even though they are still within the 'best-before' date, take them back to the shop or supermarket and ask for a refund. Nuts should never be rancid – this is a fault – and they are too expensive to write off a bad batch as just the luck of the draw.

Dried and candied fruits

(raisins, sultanas, currants, dates, figs, apricots, prunes, peaches cherries, blueberries, pears, apples, papaya, mango, banana, candied fruits and glacé cherries)

Dried fruits are one of nature's handiest, most portable preserved foods. Dates, figs and unsulphured apricots tend to have a slightly fudge-like taste. The small, pitted-looking Pakistani Hunza apricots are particularly fragrant, slightly reminiscent of peaches and with caramel undertones. It isn't instantly obvious to many people that a prune is a dried plum, because prunes have that unique black, tarry personality redolent of liquorice and treacle. Currants (also known as Corinth raisins or Zante currants), raisins and sultanas have a more neutral sweetness that comes into its own when teamed up with sweet spices: cinnamon, nutmeg, allspice, mace, cardamom and cloves. If you're lucky enough to find unseeded Muscatel or Malaga raisins, the aristocrats of the raisin world, then these retain some of the alluring perfume and taste of the fresh grape and it doesn't make sense to mask that. When dried, apples and pears lose much of the perfume that makes them so attractive when fresh, and given that you can now buy our fresh native apples and pears throughout the year, why bother? Conversely, the flavour of peaches, and some tropical fruits – notably mangoes and bananas – can be intensified by drying. Others, like papaya, usually taste of nothing much other than sugar. Dried banana chips, that staple ingredient in the cheap muesli mix, are a love-it or loathe-it item. They resemble the larger-than-life artificial flavours found in children's sweets and bubblegum.

Commercial candied fruits, citrus peel and glacé cherries add more sugariness than freshness to a recipe and lack the zesty, zingy excitement of the fresh equivalent. Add glacé cherries to a recipe – these are sweet varieties of cherries that have been candied – and you might as well be adding straight sugar. In many cake and pudding recipes, glacé cherries can be omitted and dried sour ones substituted, or some more imaginative ingredient used. But if you feel that your recipe needs the colour and brightness of glacé cherries soak them in boiling water for a few moments to rinse off some of the sugar. Candied peel will benefit from the same treatment. Some delicatessens and upmarket shops sell more expensive candied fruits from smaller producers. These will have been candied in smaller batches than their mass-produced equivalent and may contain fewer or no additives. The taste may be superior, but if you are after a strong fruit flavour, go for citrus fruits: orange, clementine, kumquat and lemon. Even high-quality candied fruits can taste of very little.

Things to do with dried fruits

- Use dates and apricots in Moroccan tagines, but do so with restraint as too many can change this savoury dish into a dessert.

- Dried, sour Morello cherries and cranberries can bring a welcome acidity and fruitiness to traditional recipes such as mincemeat and Christmas pudding that can seem extraordinarily cloying to a modern palate.

- The trinity of prunes, figs and apricots is the bedrock of a breakfast-time dried fruit compote. Just pour over boiling water, or, for a more fragrant compote, Earl Grey or Lapsang Souchong tea, cover, and let the fruits rehydrate. Cutting the fruits into quarters or thin slices speeds up the process and makes the compote daintier and more enticing. A dash of rosewater or orange flower water turns it into something more exotic. Include some sliced mango and peach for a fruitier, less caramel effect.

- Soaked prunes can be tarted up for dessert with the addition of brandy, Marsala or Armagnac and orange zest.

- Raisins soaked in Sicilian Marsala or Spanish Pedro Ximenez sherry, spooned over a plain dairy or vanilla ice cream, make a patrician but effortless dessert.

- Pre-soak unstoned Pakistani Hunza apricots in a mixture of fresh orange juice and water, then simmer them in their soaking liquid until soft. Marvellous with thick Greek yogurt.

Are dried and candied fruits good for me?

Dried fruit is not as good for you as fresh. When fruit is dried, 80–90 per cent of the water is removed, some of the vitamins (mainly vitamin C) are destroyed and the natural sugar in the fruit is concentrated. This intense sweetness does not make them the dieter's friend, but eaten in small amounts they do have some health benefits. On the plus side, dried fruits such as prunes and dates are a good source of soluble fibre (see GRAINS/ Are grains good for me?) and beneficial minerals/micronutrients such as iron, potassium and selenium. If your digestion is sluggish, then prunes are helpful because they have a laxative effect.

Dried fruits such as apricots can be treated with sulphur dioxide to preserve their colour. This chemical can trigger adverse reactions, such as asthma, in sensitive people, so this type is best avoided. Switch to organic dried fruits, which will be sulphur-free. Some dried fruits are still oiled with hydrogenated (chemically hardened) oils that can contain artery-clogging, unhealthy trans-fats. Check the label to see what type of oil, if any, has been used.

FOREIGN FRUITS, BRITISH RECIPES

Given that all the dried fruits we eat are imported, it may seem surprising that they are so prominent in our culinary tradition, an essential item in festive recipes like Christmas pudding and Easter-time hot cross buns. But ever since the Crusaders returned home in the eleventh century from their travels through the Mediterranean and Middle East loaded up with dried fruits, we have had a taste for them. By the middle of the fourteenth century, currants and raisins were an important part of our cuisine, and, in an echo of the North African tagine – where meat is sweetened with dates or apricots – it was commonplace to combine meat with imported spices and dried fruit. The earliest mince pies we ate consisted of meat mixed with raisins or currants. Somewhere in the mists of time, the meat got left out and the all-fruit mincemeat pie we now know was born.

All the dried fruits available in the UK are imported. The traditional sources of raisins, currants and sultanas (all just different sorts of dried grapes), apricots and figs were Turkey, Greece, Iran, Syria and Spain, but nowadays they also come from Chile, California, South Africa and Australia. Our candied citrus peel, glacé cherries, prunes and peaches tend to come from France or the US. Sour cherries, blueberries and cranberries are usually imported from the US or Canada. Dried bananas, mango, papaya and pineapple are generally sourced from Africa or India. Most of the dates we buy originate from either the Middle East or North Africa. Be aware that dates labelled 'West Bank' are not Palestinian but come from Israeli settlements in the Israeli-occupied West Bank.

The time-honoured way to dry fresh fruits is to seed or stone them, as necessary, then leave them to shrivel in the sun, either on the vine or spread out for several days in the sun. Nowadays it is more common for them to be dried on a wooden rack in a heated chamber or in a kiln with hot air. Either way, they are ready when only 10–20 per cent of their original moisture remains. Sometimes they are 'nitrified' before drying; that is, given a pre-treatment to speed up the drying process either by dipping them into, or spraying them with, an alkaline solution, usually prepared using caustic soda or potash. This treatment is considered harmless and does not need to be listed on the label, but if you prefer more rustic, natural fruits, look out for those described as 'naturals' and choose fruits with a darker appearance.

Allowed to dry naturally, dried fruits are dark and dull-looking and may develop a harmless, whiteish bloom over time, so if you buy fruits that are brightly coloured, these have probably been fumigated with sulphur dioxide. A sulphur dioxide-treated dried apricot, for example, looks orange, while an unsulphured one looks brown. 'Golden' sultanas and 'green' raisins also owe their colour to this chemical. Glacé cherries are first 'brined' in sulphur dioxide solution before being processed further. Potassium sorbate is also used on dried fruit to extend its shelf life. Neither of these preservatives plays anything other than a cosmetic role so you may prefer to buy fruits without either. Both these preservatives are banned under organic rules.

The list of additives and added ingredients in dried fruits doesn't stop with preservatives. Colourings (synthetic or natural) are added to glacé cherries to make them red, green or yellow as required. Almond flavouring may also be added in a doomed attempt to reintroduce the natural cherry taste that the sugar has overwhelmed. Many dried fruits owe their attractive sheen to added glucose or corn syrup, which makes them sweeter still, while others are oiled. This type of oil is also prohibited under organic rules.

Since dried fruits are not produced in this country we know very little about the working conditions of the people who pick and process them. So if you are buying dried fruits from poorer countries, Fairtrade labels are attractive because they mean that workers get a better price and have reasonable working conditions.

Are dried and candied fruits a green choice?

As there are no 'local' alternatives to dried fruit, unless we want to give up eating favourites such as Christmas cake entirely, then we have to import them. Dried fruits do travel long distances to get to us, but because they are transported in a compact form, by road or boat rather than plane, and do not require any refrigeration, their carbon 'foodprint' is lighter than fresh imported fruits from the same sources.

Check labels to make sure that your dried fruits do not have added palm oil. This is the most common oil used to process dried fruits, yet palm oil plantations are the major cause of the destruction of virgin forests in tropical countries (see MARGARINES AND SPREADS/Are margarines and spreads a green choice?).

Where should I buy dried fruits?

The widest range of dried fruits is to be found in wholefood shops, which commonly stock several different types of raisin and Pakistani Hunza apricots as well as the standard sort. Church and charity shops sometimes sell less commonplace dried fruits such as sun-dried mango, papaya, banana and Palestinian dates.

Will dried fruits break the bank?

For commercial purposes, 'quality' in dried fruit means larger (jumbo) fruits that look good; taste is more or less irrelevant. So unless you feel that every raisin or currant you use must be beauty-pageant-perfect, it is worthwhile trying out cheaper grades of dried fruit, as long as you have checked the label and know that they do not also contain unwelcome added ingredients. When it comes to larger dried fruits, such as apricots, figs and prunes, soaking your own will save you some money. If you buy the 'ready-to-eat' or 'no-soak' sort, you will be paying a premium for the privilege of having just a few per cent more moisture left in your fruit. Some upmarket shops sell more naturally and slowly dried fruits. This treatment is usually reserved for the rarest, most special fruits, such as Muscatel and Malaga raisins, to retain more of their scent and taste. These sell at a premium and are best considered as a treat, not as a standard buy.

For people who want to avoid sulphur, there is a persuasive argument for buying organic dried fruits even though they are more expensive.

Many of us have half-used, half-forgotten dried fruits languishing at the back of the kitchen cupboard that have gone past their 'best-before' date. But don't chuck them out. Dried fruits never go off, they just become harder and all but the most fossilized specimens can be revived by immersion in hot water with a little lemon juice in it.

Consider candying the skins of organic or untreated citrus once you have eaten the fruit inside or used the juice. This is surprisingly easy to do, means that you get more from any citrus you buy, and the taste is light years ahead of the sort on sale.

Pulses

(chickpeas, kidney beans, butter beans (gigantes), borlotti beans, aduki beans, cannellini beans, black-eyed beans, haricot beans, fava beans (broad beans, ful), black beans, mung beans, flageolets, marrowfat peas, pinto beans, split peas and lentils)

Pulses are easy-going, obliging storecupboard items with stunning versatility. Their mild flesh makes them an ideal vehicle for showcasing other bolder flavours, while their mealy centres and more fibrous skins bring texture and body to dips, hearty soups, curries and stews. The bulk and sturdiness of pulses can make for a stick-to-the-ribs combination when used along with meat, but they rub along nicely with vegetables, adding a welcome solidity, hence their perennial popularity in beanburgers, the vegetarian riposte to the beefburger. Pulses beef up salads and, properly seasoned, make a cold, wintry, salad-centric lunchbox feel much more satisfying. Of the larger pulses, chickpeas have the most distinctive character.

Beans tend to get typecast in recipes that involve tomatoes and spices. You can see why, because this formula works well. But pulses do respond to more subtle treatments and sit happily in many different culinary traditions.

Pulses can seem to be much of a muchness, but there are distinctions to be drawn on quality. The key characteristic of the pricier gourmet pulses, such as Puy or Castelluccio lentils, is that they hold their shape much better when cooked. Lower-grade pulses have a habit of going mushy the minute you take your eye off them.

For certain purposes, such as making falafel, cooking your own pulses is preferable. Some recipes will tell you that tinned pulses will perform just as well, but that is debatable. Lentils are best avoided in canned forms, unless you like paying for slurry. Besides, they are quick to cook at home. For many purposes, however, cooked tinned beans have their uses. They do save time – a rapid chilli con carne for instance – but their flavour and texture are rarely as good as those you might soak and cook yourself. And, perhaps due to the extreme heat of the canning process, tinned beans often don't absorb other flavours quite as effectively, and are more likely to be rather soft and prone to falling apart than those that have been cooked from scratch.

Things to do with pulses

- What easier soup can there be than a can each of chickpeas and tomatoes, blitzed with cumin and sweated onions, slackened with water, sharpened with lemon, then served with a blob of yogurt?

- Warm green lentils dressed with good extra virgin olive oil, a drop of lemon juice and generous amounts of flaky sea salt and coarse ground pepper make a less predictable accompaniment to a weekday supper of sausages than a quotidian mash.

- A slowly simmered bowl of plainly cooked *ful médames* – Egypt's national dish which dates back to the time of the Pharoahs – allows dried broad beans to shine when spiked with garlic, lemon and onions and livened up on serving with fresh parsley and mint.

- In the staple Caribbean rice and 'peas' dish, black beans peep out from fluffy white rice cooked in coconut milk along with those favourite West Indian aromatics: Scotch Bonnet chillies, spring onion, thyme and allspice.

- There's something rather miraculous about how a pot of pretty dull boiled lentils is transformed by the addition of an Indian 'tarka', a seasoned oil or ghee in which garlic and onions have been browned along with whole and ground spices.

- Boiled sweet potato or squash, mashed up with the same quantity of cooked chickpeas, some tomatoes, spinach and spices, or fresh green herbs, makes a substantial, filling dish.

Are pulses good for me?

Their individual nutritional make-up does vary, but as a food category pulses provide lots of useful soluble fibre (see GRAINS/Are grains good for me?). Pulses are carbohydrate-rich foods, but they also contain a significant amount of protein. This combination of protein and soluble fibre makes them very filling, so they are great for satisfying the appetite for hours at a time. They provide small amounts of B vitamins, primarily vitamin B1 which is useful for energy and the nervous system, but they are also useful sources of minerals, notably molybdenum and manganese, which helps produce key enzymes, and folate, which is crucial for the production of red blood cells and the prevention of certain birth defects.

Pulses naturally contain certain toxins or anti-nutrients that can trigger allergic reactions and food intolerance and impair digestion. Along with the substances that cause flatulence, these are largely neutralized by lengthy soaking, sprouting and cooking. However, it may be a good idea not to overdo the amount of pulses that you eat. It is also important to start with fresh pulses. It is easy to forget how long they have been languishing at the back of the kitchen cupboard because they don't go off like other foods. Try to buy unsoaked pulses from a shop with a healthy turnover as they are likely to be fresher and take much less time to cook. The older they are, and the harder and drier they get, the less likely it is that a normal length of soaking/sprouting/cooking will make them digestible.

It is advisable to soak pulses for at least eight hours and change the water at least once, preferably more, then to boil them rapidly for ten minutes before reducing the heat to help neutralize their anti-nutrients and make them more digestible. Some types of lentils don't need soaking to soften, but, nevertheless, it may be a good idea to soak them for an hour or two and boil them rapidly for a few minutes. In traditional Indian cooking, lentils are almost always soaked before cooking and spices such as asafoetida, turmeric and ajwain seeds are usually added to assist digestion further.

Our staple tinned baked beans have a healthy image because of the fibre they contain. Unfortunately, they usually also contain large amounts of sugar, which somewhat spoils their otherwise good nutritional profile.

Never assume that a ready-made beanburger is good for you just because it contains beans. Many such products aimed at the vegetarian market are chock-a-block with ubiquitous processed food ingredients that you might do better to avoid, such as maltodextrin, soya protein isolate (see SOYA FOODS/Is soya good for me?), and chemical colourings and flavourings. If you buy pre-prepared beanburgers, read the ingredients label so that you are aware of exactly what you are eating. Better still, mash some beans with onions and spices and make your own.

How are pulses grown?

Pulses for human consumption are a category of food not commonly grown in the UK or Ireland. Most of the dried pulses we eat are grown in the Middle East, China, the Indian subcontinent, and a few – mainly lentils – in Europe. Pulses are grown as open-field crops. Once harvested each year, usually by machine, but in peasant production, by hand, some pulses simply need to be podded. Others need to be processed to make them edible: they have their husks removed mechanically or can be soaked or steamed to soften the husk as a prelude to removing and splitting the pulse.

Are pulses a green choice?

As a general rule it makes sense to eat local, or at least UK- and Ireland-grown foods as much as possible, but strictly applied this would mean no pulses, apart from dried marrowfat peas. But despite this, pulses do seem to fit in with an environmentally aware diet. Pulses usually come by boat and/or road, which is less of a concern than air freight. They can be stored at ambient temperature, so no energy-intensive refrigeration is required. The compact nature of pulses means that they take up relatively little storage space when being transported, and because of their sturdiness require only minimal packaging. Being the opposite of perishable, pulses generate very little in the way of food waste. Once cooked or sprouted, tiny amounts of pulses produce generous quantities of edible food. Although pulses do not contain as much protein as meat, they do contain much more than most plant foods, so they are a progressive option for those who want to reduce or avoid consumption of grain- and soya-fed, factory-farmed meat.

'MARXIST LENTILLISTS'

Eating dried beans and lentils came into vogue in the 1960s along with flower power and hippies. Until then, the range of pulses eaten was restricted to marrowfat peas, red lentils and yellow split peas, most of which were sold as minor ingredients in broth mixes for traditional broths, not cherished in their own right.

The wholefood gospel of this period preached a preference for plant foods with a strong critique of meat-eating. This agenda was passionately advanced in Frances Moore Lappé's bestselling 1971 book, *Diet for a Small Planet*. Lappé introduced vegetarians to the idea of combining high-protein vegetable foods, such as pulses, with other plant foods, such as brown rice, so that their combined amino acids would provide vegetarians with 'complete proteins' like those found in meat.

This philosophy spawned a wave of vegetarian dishes that mimicked popular meat classics by substituting pulses for meat, such as lentil lasagne, beanburgers and red dragon pie, the vegetarian answer to shepherd's or cottage pie, which is made with aduki beans instead of beef or lamb mince. These western vegetarian 'analogue' recipes bore no resemblance to the traditional usage of pulses in many foreign cooking traditions, where they are valued in their own right, not as a meat substitute, and the gastronomic image of pulses suffered as a consequence. Quips about 'Marxist Lentillists' and 'sprouting your own sandals' followed.

In more recent years, western vegetarian cooking has moved further away from the concept of meat substitutes and borrowed more from culinary traditions that make many inspired uses of pulses. From French cassoulet through to Mexican re-fried beans, pulses are no longer seen as the sole preserve of meat avoiders.

Where should I buy pulses?

Wholefood shops, Middle Eastern, Indian and Pakistani grocers usually have a much more comprehensive range of pulses than supermarkets. Wholefood shops are best for organic pulses. Indian and Pakistani grocers commonly stock an impressively wide range of various types of lentils.

Will pulses break the bank?

Pulses are a gift to people who need to produce a lot of food for very little money. Some of the world's most sustaining, cheap foods revolve round pulses, dishes such as Indian dhal, Italian *pasta e fagioli*, or British lentil soup. It's no coincidence that pulses figure prominently in poor person's cooking the world over.

By swapping, or partially substituting pulses for meat products, you can substantially reduce your food costs. Instead of having a pile of cheap, factory-farmed sausages with some sweet tinned baked beans on the side, you can produce a bean or chickpea stew, flavoured with a small amount of higher welfare, better quality sausage/chorizo/black pudding, and still be quids in.

Sugar and other sweeteners

(honey, treacle, palm sugar, maple syrup, high-fructose corn syrup, artificial sweeteners)

A little sprinkling of sugar brings out the flavour of summer strawberries, and without any sugar at all, we probably wouldn't eat chocolate, rhubarb, Bramley apples, blackcurrants, chutney and many other unpalatably bitter or acidic foods, but white sugar is a poor choice. It is 99.9 per cent pure sucrose and brings no flavour to a recipe other than sweetness. Less processed raw cane sugars – golden or muscovado sugars – are preferable because they still retain a very small amount of their molasses. These contain a collection of esters that gives the sugar its aromas of fudge, butterscotch, caramel and treacle and which produce a more interesting flavour in cooking and baking.

Sugars from date and coconut palms and other trees such as maple offer a more intense version of these same flavour characteristics. Honeys can be quite neutral, such as acacia honey, or exceptionally fragrant, such as pine or heather honey. Treacle has that faintly bitter, black, almost metallic taste that makes it a full-bodied partner for pungent, warming ginger.

High-fructose corn syrup and artificial chemical sweeteners have no secondary flavours or aromas. They are just extremely sweet.

Things to do with sugar

- For a cheat's crème brûlée, put a layer of halved grapes, whole berries or orange segments in ramekins, top with a thick layer of half-and-half natural yogurt and whipped cream, sprinkle over a thin, but covering, layer of coarse Barbados or demerara sugar and refrigerate for several hours or overnight. The sugar forms an even caramel surface.

- Just before baking, sprinkle coarse demerara sugar on top of uncooked cakes to produce a golden, crunchy surface.

- Use golden syrup mixed with fresh breadcrumbs to make a 'treacle' tart.

- Show off the deep, dark character of treacle by making a traditional Scottish gingerbread.

- For an instant pudding, drizzle a teaspoon of treacle over natural yogurt.

- Stir honey and lemon into boiling water to make a soothing hot drink. Add a generous splash of whisky for a knock-out invalid's hot toddy.

- Palm sugar dissolved in a little water makes an instant 'caramel' that can be used as a sauce with any milky pudding such as sago or semolina.

Is sugar good for me?

It is well known that sugar rots the teeth, but its role in causing ill-health goes way beyond that. The main problem is that it destabilizes blood sugar and insulin levels, encouraging fat production and storage in the body and triggering processes that can lead to type 2 diabetes and high blood pressure. Forsaking sugar entirely isn't realistic for most people, so even if you want to eat healthily, chances are that there will be some sugar or sweeteners in your larder.

When it comes to table sugar, the less refined raw cane type – derived from sugar cane that grows above the ground rather than sugar beet which grows below it – has a very slight nutritional advantage. While white sugars are more or less 100 per cent pure chemical sucrose, the molasses, or treacle, that is left in unrefined raw cane sugars contains a tiny amount of beneficial micronutrients such as manganese, copper, calcium, vitamin B6, potassium, zinc, magnesium and iron. Raw cane sugar is typically 87–96 per cent pure sucrose, depending on the type, the rest being made up of molasses. Muscovado sugar will contain the highest proportion of molasses. If, however, you are only interested in using highly refined white sugar, then it makes no difference whether you go for sugar from sugar cane or sugar beet because, refined to this degree, they are identical.

Sugars and syrups that are made from trees (palm, maple, nutmeg) tend to be less refined than table sugars and are a better choice nutritionally.

Treacle has some good points. It is surprisingly rich in certain beneficial minerals – iron, calcium, copper, manganese and potassium – and contains useful B vitamins which help give you energy and support brain function. Treacle has been used in traditional medicine as a tonic, and figures prominently as a laxative in folk medicine.

Honey, along with its by-products, propolis and pollen, is another sweetener that has a respected place in many traditional medicine systems as a treatment for coughs, colds, hay fever and stomach problems. Research is beginning to confirm that it does indeed have some medicinal properties, seeming to have an anti-bacterial, antibiotic, antiseptic and anti-microbial action. Raw Manuka honey has been shown to be remarkably effective in healing wounds and is thought to be effective against certain infections, such as MRSA, that show resistance to commonly used antibiotics. To benefit from the healing potential of this natural sweetener, buy cold-pressed honey that hasn't been heat-treated.

High-fructose corn syrup, also called corn sugar and fructose-glucose syrup, is a relatively new sweetener derived, as the name suggests, from corn. It is 20 per cent sweeter than ordinary table sugar and is now commonly used in processed foods such as breakfast cereals, fromage frais, ice cream and biscuits, and is found in abundance in soft drinks and colas. It is heavily implicated in the obesity epidemic that is sweeping through the US. There is a body of research to suggest that it can damage the metabolism and cause a number of health problems, including raising blood pressure and increasing the incidence of heart disease, diabetes and gout.

Some artificial chemical sweeteners are based on amino acids, the building blocks of protein in food, but they use them in new configurations and in quantities that do not occur in natural food. Other types are made by binding chlorine with sucrose. Such products claim to be a solution to the health issues presented by sugars. Their marketing pitch is that they provide the body with a sweet taste, minus the calories that normally accompany it, so their use in diet and low-calorie food and drinks is now widespread. But a body of research is now stacking up to suggest that although sweeteners can convince the taste buds that they are sugar, the brain cannot be tricked.

Some studies have shown that consuming artificial sweeteners is more likely to make people pile on weight, rather than reduce it. There are several lines of enquiry open as to why this might be the case. One theory is that our bodies, which are programmed to deal with natural foods, expect a very sweet taste to be accompanied by calories, and when it isn't, they go on a calorie hunt. In other words, you drink the diet cola but still feel like eating something sweet. Another possibility is that artificial chemical sweeteners don't satisfy the reward areas of the brain as sugar does, so they cause a craving for more sweet food and create a dependency on it. Rather than consuming less sugar overall, artificial sweeteners may encourage us to eat more. Yet another explanation is that a sweet taste in itself increases hunger. So the sweeter the sensation – bear in mind that artificial sweeteners are anything from 30 to 300 times sweeter than ordinary sugar – the greater your appetite may be. There is not one single properly conducted study that shows that artificial sweeteners are superior to sugar in terms of controlling weight.

Some scientific studies used to establish the safety of artificial sweeteners were sponsored by the companies that make them. Since then, several independent studies on laboratory animals have suggested that these modern sweeteners can pose some serious problems for health. These include neurological problems, such as memory impairment and learning difficulties, decreased liver function and weight gain.

One way to take more control of your sugar intake and your appetite is by eliminating, or severely restricting, key categories of processed food and drinks that commonly contain high levels of sugar, high-fructose corn syrup or artificial chemical sweeteners. The most glaring offenders here are not solids but liquids: diluting and fizzy drinks. It is fairly obvious that sweets, jams and ice creams are going to be sugary, but most people don't realize how much sugar is in everyday processed foods, such as refined breakfast cereals and apparently healthy foods such as fruit yogurt. Sugar and high-fructose corn syrup appear by stealth in savoury foods too, everything from mayonnaise and ketchup to ready meals and pre-cooked barbecued poultry.

You can also experiment with cutting down the amounts of sugar you use in home cooking. Many older recipes (such as jams, cakes) often use excessive amounts and can be adjusted downwards with no negative effect on the end results.

How is sugar made?

The most long-standing source of sugar in the world is sugar cane, a tall plant with bamboo-like stems and wavy green leaves that flourishes in tropical climates. It is produced in local sugar mills by squeezing the sugar cane stems to produce juice, clarifying and removing impurities by adding lime, then evaporating it until it forms crystals. Cane sugars can be sold as 'raw' (less processed) retaining a little of its molasses or it can be refined further. Some sugar is also made from sugar beet, a root crop that looks a bit like a bulbous parsnip and which grows under the ground in temperate climates. Unlike cane sugar, beet sugar has to be totally refined and have all its impurities removed because they are inedible to humans.

Sugar refining, whether cane or beet, takes place in an industrial refinery where the sugar is clarified using phosphoric acid and calcium hydroxide and the purified syrup is bleached using activated carbon.

In Asian food stores, speciality and wholefood shops you may come across palm sugars (jaggery, gur, raspadura, gula melaka) or sugars from other trees. They are made by tapping the tree sap then evaporating it until it crystallizes. These sugars can be used in place of white or raw cane sugar in some recipes, although, because they have a stronger taste, the end product may turn out a little differently.

Both beet and cane sugar are sold in grades from powdered (icing sugar), through caster sugar (fine) to granulated (coarser) to demerara (coarser still). Demerara sugar takes its name from the eponymous area in Guyana where it was first produced. True demerara is a natural golden-coloured sugar with large crystals and should be labelled as cane sugar. Very occasionally, some brown-looking sugars are just 99 per cent refined white beet sugar that has been coloured brown with the addition of caramel or molasses. So if you like your sugar more naturally refined without all the nutrients stripped from it, check that the bag says 'unrefined raw cane sugar' or similar. Beet sugar is sometimes coloured with molasses after refining to make it look like the real thing. It is known as 'London demerara'. Muscovado sugar, which is made in lighter and darker versions, is a darker, moister type of raw cane sugar with a distinctive treacle smell that is made in the time-honoured way by letting the molasses slowly drain away rather than removing them by centrifuge. The word comes from the Spanish *mascabado*, meaning 'more finished'.

Is sugar a green choice?

Using the logic that it is good to support home production, it might seem preferable to buy beet sugar since we grow it in the UK. But due to its susceptibility to weeds, sugar beet is a pesticide-intensive crop, so much so that it is well nigh impossible to grow organically. So home-grown sugar beet is not exactly a 'green' or particularly sustainable crop.

Globally, plantation-grown sugar cane has also been linked with a number of environmental problems such as habitat destruction, soil erosion from over-use of agrochemicals and the depletion of scarce water resources. That said, sugar cane, grown less intensively, can be a sustainable crop in the right circumstances and, unlike sugar beet, it can even be grown organically on a commercial scale.

High-fructose corn syrup is made in the US using mostly genetically modified corn. It doesn't have to be labelled as a GM sweetener because even though it comes from GM corn, no GM material remains in the finished syrup. GM foods are to be avoided (see SOYA FOODS/Is soya a green choice?). If you want to avoid GM completely and discourage the planting of GM crops, don't buy high-fructose corn syrup.

Where should I buy sugar?

Most of the sugar on sale in supermarkets is imported from the large sugar refining companies that dominate the European market. A much more interesting and varied range of raw cane sugars from small-scale producers and co-ops, some of it Fairtrade and/or organic, is to be found in wholefood shops, Oxfam and church shops, and specialist food shops. Asian supermarkets and shops are good places to look for unrefined palm sugars.

THE SWEET TASTE WITH A BITTER HISTORY

Until the eighteenth century, when the German scientist Andreas Marggraf figured out how to extract sucrose from sugar beet, all our sugars were made from sugar cane imported from tropical countries. Sugar was the lifeblood of the infamous 'triangular trade', or slave trade, grown, harvested and milled forcibly by enslaved Africans in the colonial plantations of rich nations like Britain, then profitably traded in Europe. So for all its sweetness, cane sugar has an unpalatable history. To this day, although sugar is no longer harvested by enslaved people, the day-to-day reality for sugar workers in many countries is still low wages and hard labour, so this makes Fairtrade sugars – where producers are reliably paid above the market price and earn a premium that is invested in local community projects – a particularly attractive, more ethical option.

In recognition of centuries of exploitation, Britain, along with other European former colonial powers, has traditionally had very strong links with sugar producers in former colonies. Previously, small-scale farmers and co-ops in the Caribbean, African and Indian Ocean countries such as Barbados, Guyana, Malawi, Zambia and Mauritius had preferential trading relationships with Europe but this protection has been removed. Now they have to compete on the world market, not only with heavily subsidized EU-grown beet, but a flood of cheaper cane sugar grown intensively on plantations from countries such as Brazil and Australia. As a result, they could be forced out of the market with disastrous results for their economies. So there is a strong argument for buying sugars from these traditional suppliers, just to keep them in business.

Will sugar break the bank?

Raw cane sugars cost more than the standard white but are still very affordable. Choose the best ones and use as little as possible, then the price differential is insignificant. Palm sugar bought in Asian shops is cheap.

SUGAR

Oils

Whether it's for frying, or for dressing food, it's hard to imagine a kitchen free from oil. Cheap 'cooking' oils are the bulk cooking oil of choice, but whatever type of seed, nut, fruit or bean is used, these oils are industrially refined, producing anonymous oils with no discernible flavour or smell. They are to be avoided, whether as single oils, such as sunflower or corn, or in blended vegetable oil. For flavour, you have to use cold-pressed oils as this method of extraction retains the healthy micronutrients in the oil that also give it its taste and aroma. They need to be stored in a cool, dark place to keep them fresh.

Our ongoing love affair with olive oil shows no signs of cooling. When buying olive oil, always go for extra virgin – the purest sort. The taste and smell will vary. Extra virgin olive oils vary widely in character, everything from light, buttery and grassy to strong and intense, with a peppery kick that catches the back of the throat. Whatever type you choose, it should always have a fresh and appetizing aroma and never smell rancid (like an old, stale nut).

Cold-pressed nut oils, such as walnut and hazelnut can be quite powerful, so some people prefer to use them along with olive oil in a fifty-fifty ratio. Brazil nut, pine kernel, cashew and macadamia oils are milder, and are expensive rarities.

Cold-pressed oils derived from seeds, such as rapeseed, sunflower and hemp, don't have such an appealing smell or taste as those from olives or nuts. They have a flatter flavour profile and a dryer, sometimes bitter taste. They can be very dominant in a salad dressing because they taste really strongly of the seed. This can come as a shock if you are used to refined oils that taste of nothing. Roasted seed oils, such as burgundy-green pumpkin seed and brown sesame seed, have an even more pronounced flavour, although their toasty character also makes them more palatable than when they are unroasted. Use sparingly. A teaspoon of roasted sesame oil, for instance, goes a long way

Coconut oil looks like white butter. The refined sort is as flavour-free as other refined oils, but the cold-pressed, virgin sort has a gentle aroma and taste reminiscent of freshly grated coconut. It is excellent for cooking in dishes like stir-fries, curries and soups when you want to introduce a slightly tropical taste. But its use doesn't need to be limited to Asian dishes. Although it has a definite coconut smell in the jar, it seems to blend seamlessly with many ingredients. A little coconut oil added at the end of cooking will give many savoury dishes added flavour and smoothness without bringing an obvious coconut taste to the table.

Things to do with oils

- A last-minute splash of extra virgin olive oil vastly improves vegetable and bean broths and soups that haven't been liquidized, such as the north Italian *ribollita*.

- To improve the appearance of Middle Eastern dips, such as hummus and aubergine *baba ganoush*, make circular hollows on top with a teaspoon then anoint with green-gold olive oil and a dusting of ground sumac or chopped parsley.

- Nut oils are especially good with chicory or other bitter winter salads, green beans, celeriac, cauliflower and broccoli.

- The natural sweetness of coconut oil really suits carrot, squash and sweet potato soups and flatters the entire family of brassicas: cauliflower, Brussels sprouts, cabbage and so on. It also gets along well with chicken, beef and white fish.

- Nut oils and roasted pumpkin seed oil work well balanced by stronger vinegars, such as sherry or apple balsamic.

Are oils good for me?

For half a century, vegetable oils have been promoted as healthy by the nutrition establishment because they contain mainly polyunsaturated fats. These fats were said to be better for us than the saturated and mono-unsaturated fats in foods such as meat and dairy, avocados and nuts. This dietary gospel is now beginning to crumble as there is no good evidence to support it (see BUTTER, GHEE AND BUTTERMILK/Are butter, ghee and buttermilk good for me?). Nevertheless, many people still try to choose products containing fats with unsaturated oils, such as vegetable oils, in preference to those containing saturated and monounsaturated fats.

There is no argument that polyunsaturated fats, in their natural forms, such as fish, grains and green vegetables, are healthy, but the same is not true of polyunsaturated fats or oils that have been processed or refined – the kind you get in cooking oil. Unlike saturated fats, the polyunsaturated fats in vegetable oils are unstable and easily become rancid and degrade when exposed to the heat, oxygen and humidity involved in cooking or refining. At this point, they lose their nutritional integrity and become rather dangerous. The rancid oils produce compounds known as free radicals that cause damage in the body. There is some evidence to suggest that high consumption of polyunsaturated oils can increase the risk of obesity, cancer, heart disease, strokes, diabetes and depression. So the problem may not be that we don't get enough polyunsaturates in our diets, but that we get too many, and in a degraded form.

As well as adversely altering the nature of the polyunsaturated fats in nuts, fruits, seeds and beans, high-temperature oil refining destroys the vitamin E that protects the body from free radicals and acts as a natural preservative. Two preservatives, butylated hydroxyanisole (BHA) and butylated hydroxytoluene (BHT), are sometimes added to the oil as a preservative, and some research links these to cancer. The solvents used in oil extraction are known toxins and traces may remain in the oil.

Unrefined olive oil (preferably extra virgin) is the best all-round oil. Its history of safe (and pleasurable) human consumption goes back to ancient times. It is mainly made up of monounsaturated fat (omega-9), which research suggests protects against heart disease, lowers blood pressure and reduces levels of bad fats in the blood. It is a relatively stable oil and doesn't go rancid quickly as polyunsaturated oils do. As well as being useful for dressings, olive oil can be cooked at a moderate temperature – although not allowed to burn – without losing all its nutritional integrity.

Research suggests that extra virgin olive oil has very many health benefits: it is rich in vitamin E and other antioxidants, including chlorophyll, carotenoids and phenols, and there is evidence to suggest these may be protective against heart disease, breast and colon cancer, and inflammatory conditions.

Cold-pressed nut oils, such as walnut and hazelnut, are also monounsaturated. Like olive oil, they are best bought in a dark glass bottle, or in a tin and kept in a cool place. They contain a number of beneficial antioxidants and phytonutrients (see NUTS AND SEEDS/Are nuts and seeds good for me?). These are not oils to be used for cooking but as dressings.

Cold-pressed flax seed oil is an extremely good source of omega-3s, but it goes rancid quickly. It is not suitable for cooking and should be kept in the fridge.

Cold-pressed, extra virgin coconut oil (which is actually quite solid) consists mainly of saturated fat. This means that it can be kept at room temperature for many months without becoming rancid. The fatty acids in coconut oil have many health benefits (see NUTS AND SEEDS/Are nuts and seeds good for me?).

Rapeseed oil is becoming more common in our diet, usually as a component of blended vegetable oil and spreads. In its unrefined form, it is promoted as the gastronomic answer to imported olive oil. Using rapeseed for human food is a very recent development. In the past, rapeseed oil was known to be toxic to humans because of its erucic acid content. A new hybrid strain of rapeseed with a low erucic acid content (called canola in the US) was developed and is now cultivated to provide oil for human consumption. Its big selling point is that it is high in omega-3 fatty acids, which are thought to be beneficial for the heart.

This new rapeseed oil is regarded as safe by regulatory bodies but there is no long-term research on its effects on human health. Some research carried out on animals suggests that it may cause heart problems. There are also many anecdotal accounts from people who think they have an allergic reaction to rapeseed when it is flowering in the field, either caused by the pollen, the volatile organic compounds released by the plants, or a cross-reaction with grass pollen.

Depending on what else you eat, it may make sense to limit your consumption of sunflower, corn, groundnut, safflower, soy, cottonseed (common components of blended vegetable oil) along with sesame, grapeseed and hemp oil, even if cold-pressed. They are high in omega-6 fatty acids and it is increasingly thought that a preponderance of omega-6s in the diet may be bad for health. Consumption of omega-6s is thought to have increased substantially as more processed food has found its way into our diet and people have followed advice to eat more polyunsaturated fats. The ratio of omega-6s to omega-3s in western diets has been estimated to be anything from 10:1 to 20:1. There is no consensus on the ideal ratio, but it is thought to be more like 2:1, or even 1:1.

Cold-pressed oils need protection from light, so it is best to buy them either in a dark glass bottle, or in a tin and keep in a dark, cool place, although there is no need to refrigerate. Shops and supermarkets often sell oils in clear glass bottles because they look good, but this is a bad way to store them.

How are oils produced?

The traditional way to extract oils is to crush the fruit, nut, seed or bean between slow-moving stone presses. These days, it is more common for steel rollers to be used, but, either way, when no heat is used to extract the oil, it is referred to as 'cold pressed'. Another modern way to obtain cold-pressed oil is vacuum extraction. The fruits, nuts or seeds are crushed and ground, then mixed with water and churned in a vacuum and the oil is drawn off. The friction caused by grinding in cold pressing does generate some natural heat, but for an oil to be sold as cold pressed, the temperature must stay very low.

Most oils, however, are processed in industrial plants or refineries and are referred to as refined oils. The fruits, nuts, seeds or beans are crushed and then squeezed out under intense pressure at an extremely high temperature and mixed with a toxic chemical solvent, usually hexane, to extract the maximum amount of oil. These procedures destroy all the natural flavour, colour and aroma of the fruit, nut, seed or bean. The solvent is then evaporated, but traces may remain in the oil. The oil, which is by this point rather dark and unattractive-looking, is then bleached, so that it looks an appealing golden colour, and deodorized, to remove the taste left by the refining process. Two preservatives may be added to prevent the oil going rancid: BHA and BHT. The goal of refining is to produce an almost tasteless oil with a long shelf life. Organic standards do not allow oils to be extracted using this industrial refining process. Organic oils are not extracted using high heat and are mostly cold pressed. They cannot be bleached and any deodorization is done with steam. No chemical solvents or preservatives are permitted.

Are oils a green choice?

Rapeseed, whether grown for oil for humans or biofuel, is an extremely fertilizer-hungry crop. The nitrates from nitrogen-based fertilizers can leach into local water and pollute it. This is a problem caused by many different types of non-organic cultivation but particularly associated with rapeseed. Rapeseed is also a very pesticide-dependent crop, which is why it is almost impossible to grow it organically. It is extremely prone to attack from a range of insects and diseases and has to be given repeated sprayings of fungicides and insecticides. Two of the pesticides routinely used on rapeseed are suspected hormone disruptors or 'gender bending' chemicals.

OLD FATS AND NEW FATS

The use of oil for cooking and dressing food is relatively recent. In the past we relied on fats from animal sources such as beef dripping, lard from pork, butter and chicken fat. Chip shops, for instance, used beef dripping for frying their chips, and lard was the fat of preference for a raised pork, chicken or game pie. Olive and almond oils were only used medicinally.

As the dominant nutrition view of the last fifty years has been that saturated fats from animals are unhealthy, many people have followed advice to replace them with more liquid polyunsaturated oils from vegetable sources that have been promoted as being healthier. Liquid vegetable oils are good, solid animal fats are bad, was the message. Chip shops ditched dripping and advertised their switch to supposedly more healthy vegetable oils. Animal fats in products such as margarines and biscuits were replaced with hardened (partially hydrogenated) vegetable oils, now known to form deadly trans-fats.

To date, the introduction of olive oil and nut oils with a venerable pedigree represents a healthy, welcome addition to our culinary repertoire. By contrast, our major switch to other highly refined liquid cooking oils may well end up looking like a nutritional disaster.

Will oils break the bank?

Cold-pressed, unrefined oils are always much more expensive than the cheap, industrially refined sort, but even if you find it hard to justify the outlay on taste grounds, think of the benefits for your long-term health.

For other cooking uses such as frying, it is not always necessary to use relatively expensive cold-pressed oil. Fats such as beef dripping, duck and goose fat, lard, butter, ghee and coconut oil often make cheaper, but still wholesome, alternatives.

If extra virgin olive oil is your oil of preference, settle on one brand that you particularly like and consider buying it in five-litre tins. Mail-order companies or food co-ops often offer the keenest bulk prices. This is a much cheaper way to buy extra virgin olive oil so you can make a big saving, just as long as you can manage the initial outlay.

Margarines and spreads

The best one can say for margarines and spreads is that they are neutral-tasting, although most chefs and food lovers find them pretty repellent. If in doubt, compare a Victoria sponge made with butter and one made with margarine. Not only do margarines and spreads lack the rich flavour of butter, their consistency is less agreeable too. While butter is undoubtedly fatty, it leaves the palate clean after swallowing. Margarine-type fats, on the other hand, leave a residual greasiness on the roof of the mouth. This is one pleasure-free processed food you can easily live without.

Things to do with margarines and spreads

- Leave them on the shelf.

Are margarines and spreads good for me?

It is now widely accepted that margarines and spreads made with hydrogenated fats are extremely bad for our health as the hydrogenation process creates artery-clogging trans-fats that are now thought to be a likely cause of heart disease. When the damage wreaked by trans-fats became widely known and consumers grew concerned, manufacturers began to reformulate their margarines and spreads, using different methods to harden them. There are still margarines with hydrogenated fats on our shelves, and they are commonplace in processed foods, but most manufacturers of margarines and spreads now say that their products contain only minimal traces of trans-fats.

These newer margarines and spreads are made with oils that have been hardened by the alternative, supposedly safer method of interesterification, described on page 366. These interesterified fats have been radically altered from their liquid form and have only been in our diet for a relatively short time, so their long-term effects on human health are as yet unknown. Given that margarines and spreads have a poor health record in the recent past, it seems a sensible precaution to avoid them and stick with tried and tested fats like butter. Some epidemiological evidence suggests that margarines and spreads may be worse for health than butter. What's more, a major plank in the sales pitch for margarines and spreads is that they are low in saturates, but as there is no good evidence that saturated fat causes heart disease, this claim is irrelevant.

Some spreads can be considered as 'functional' foods or 'nutraceuticals' as they have been designed to have a health-promoting or disease-preventing property. The idea is to isolate a useful health property or characteristic from some natural source and introduce it into a new or 'novel' product that can be said to have a particularly healthy profile.

Functional foods are best thought of as marketing gimmicks. All unprocessed foods have health-promoting qualities anyway, but in a naturally occurring, time-honoured form. Some spreads now include plant sterols or stanols because some research demonstrates that these lower cholesterol in the blood. However, the simplistic theory that cholesterol is always bad for us is being unpicked and it is now debatable whether lowering cholesterol improves health outcomes, or whether it has an overall beneficial effect on health. The evidence suggests that taking dietary steps to reduce cholesterol does not have broad benefits for health. A food can reduce cholesterol levels, but this doesn't mean that it's good for you.

Furthermore, isolated health benefits that have been engineered into a functional food may come at a price. It is known, for instance, that plant sterols may reduce the body's absorption of certain vitamins. And since functional foods of this type are highly processed, any possible benefit from the introduction of one added health property needs to be weighed up against the possible risks of other unhealthy ingredients in such processed products.

Margarine-type fats, made from partially hydrogenated oils, are ubiquitous in many processed foods, particularly in cakes, biscuits and confectionery and fried food. You can avoid them by not buying products that list 'vegetable fat', 'partially hydrogenated vegetable fat/oil' or 'shortening' as an ingredient, opting instead for products made with pure butter, liquid oils or, in the case of chocolate, natural cocoa butter.

How are margarines and spreads made?

Spreads and margarines are technically complex, highly processed products, about as unnatural as they come, and made in a thoroughly industrial way. They can be manufactured using fish oils and animal fats, but most are now made with cheap commodity oils from vegetable sources such as rape (canola), sunflower, corn, soya, palm and cottonseed.

Some health-conscious brands, mainly sold in wholefood shops, use cold-pressed oils, but the oil used in most margarines and spreads is extracted under pressure using solvents. This crude oil is steam-cleaned at a high temperature, bleached and deodorized with more chemicals until it is colourless, odourless and light brown in colour, then chemically hardened.

The most common way to harden the oils for margarines and spreads used to be to hydrogenate them by bombarding them with hydrogen gas. As the health risks associated with hydrogenated fats emerged, manufacturers of margarines and spreads have moved away from hydrogenation. Increasingly they take the 'fractions' of the liquid oils which are most solid at room temperature, then harden them using a technique called interesterification. This treatment rearranges the fat molecules under high temperature and pressure, using enzymes or acids as catalysts.

This hardened oil is then blended with a mix of salty water to form an emulsion, with the help of emulsifiers, such as lecithin, ascorbyl palmitate, mono- and diglycerides of fatty acids, modified starch and milk powder. Antioxidants, such as butylated hydroxyanisole, and preservatives, such as potassium sorbate and tert-Butylhydroquinone, are added to stop it going rancid. Synthetic vitamins are also added to mimic those in butter and to compensate for the natural ones destroyed by processing. Since the refined hardened oil has a rather unappealing colour, colourings (usually natural ones or ingredients that have a strong colour such as carrot juice) are incorporated to make it a more appetizing-looking golden yellow. Flavourings, both natural and synthetic, are included in the mix to make it taste better. Sometimes a proportion of butter or olive oil is blended in to improve the flavour.

Are margarines and spreads a green choice?

Palm oil is a very common ingredient in margarine and spreads. Palm oil does not need to be labelled as such if it is in a blended 'vegetable' oil.

Despite efforts to establish a reliable source of ethical palm oil, environmental groups say that 99 per cent of the palm oil used in food production has not been produced sustainably.

Unless the label explicitly states otherwise, palm oil is very likely to come from tropical countries where rainforest has been cut down to make way for palm oil plantations. The global demand for palm oil has seen whole swathes of virgin forest in Malaysia and Indonesia cut or burnt down to make way for palm oil production. This peaty forest is one of the most concentrated stores of carbon around. Clearing the forest on top, draining the peat and burning it, releases vast amounts of greenhouse gases into the atmosphere. In Borneo this clearance leads to the destruction of orang-utan habitat and wildlife groups warn that without urgent intervention the palm oil trade will make the species extinct within a decade. The Sumatran tiger is also threatened. Land clearance for palm oil plantations has also seen indigenous people and small growers displaced from their land and, according to environmental groups, they have suffered human rights abuses as a result.

If these issues are of concern to you, you can stop buying margarines and spreads that list vegetable oil of unspecified origin as an ingredient. Opt instead for butter, or a spread that uses named oils such as olive, sunflower, corn or peanut.

Soya oil is a common ingredient in margarine and spreads. Soya cultivation, along with cattle ranching, is now one of the two main causes of deforestation in South America, where vast expanses of rainforest and grassland are being cut down to make way for huge soya plantations. These plantations are managed in a very intensive way using high levels of synthetic fertilizers and pesticides. The destruction of these precious habitats has a catastrophic effect on biodiversity and wildlife and is a major contributor to climate change because the carbon that was fixed in the soil is released into the atmosphere.

Will margarines and spreads break the bank?

Margarine and spreads are usually cheaper than butter, but some spreads that make particular health claims can cost more than butter. You can make a small saving by using margarines and spreads, but given the question mark over the overall healthiness of such products, you may not wish to do so.

Margarine always used to be seen as an inferior substitute for butter, and indeed this was the purpose for which it was designed. The idea was to take cheap fats, usually of animal or fish origin, such as beef and whale fat, and process them, then colour and flavour them to look like butter.

From the 1980s onwards, the public perception of margarine improved as food processors saw the potential to reinvent it as a health food. They cashed in on the scientific orthodoxy that foods containing some saturated fat from animal sources, such as butter, were bad for you and best avoided, while polyunsaturated fats from vegetable sources were healthy.

When it emerged that the trans-fats in margarines and spreads were little short of deadly, manufacturers changed the way they hardened liquid oils and began re-emphasizing the supposed health benefits of their products. Time will tell whether margarines and spreads made with interesterified fats merit this profile, but given manufacturers' track record to date, there are grounds for extreme caution. For traditionalists who have always had a hunch that chemically altered fats would turn out to be bad news, the history of margarine and spread production simply reinforces the prejudice that it is better to stick with tried and tested foods that contain saturated fat.

Soya foods

(soy sauce, soya milk, soya protein shakes, edamame beans, tofu, miso, tempeh, vegetarian substitutes for meat and dairy, such as veggie burgers, non-dairy ice cream and vegan cheese, and textured vegetable protein)

Unless you are vegetarian, the only soya-based food in your larder may be soy sauce. But for vegans and meat- and dairy-avoiders, there is now a plethora of soya-based products on the shelves, everything from milk and vegetarian 'mince' to protein shakes.

In their fresh form, soya beans taste pretty much like other pulses. The only fresh form of soya beans on sale is edamame beans, which are underripe, immature soya beans with a bland, slightly nutty taste. Tofu, or soya bean curd, is more or less tasteless, with a blancmange-like consistency. It is best thought of as a vehicle for other flavours and often appears in Chinese vegetarian recipes. Soy sauce has a deep, rich, meaty flavour, the cheaper, more chemically made types tasting sweeter than the more traditional ones. Miso is a thick, fermented soya paste with a rich, meaty, savoury flavour, and is a staple soup base in Japanese cuisine. Sometimes rice or barley is fermented with the paste to add an extra flavour dimension.

Natto is a paste made from fermented, cooked whole soya beans. It is sticky to the touch and pungent, a bit like cheese, and is used as a spread or in soups. Tempeh is a fermented soya bean cake which is firm, chewy and nutty-tasting, commonly used in Indonesian cooking.

In various forms, industrially produced soya protein is a key ingredient in many vegetarian processed foods and ready-meals. It is best thought of as a firmish texture rather than a taste, as in its unflavoured form it has very little taste.

Things to do with soya foods

- Dry-roast unsalted peanuts or cashews and, when still hot from the oven, sprinkle them with soy sauce, stirring all the time, then allow to cool. These salty, crunchy nuts make a good nibble with drinks.

- Use miso to make a nutritious, savoury broth base. Tart it up with strips of seaweed or cubes of tofu.

- Give fatty meats (knuckle, ribs or belly of pork, duck or goose legs) the Chinese treatment by braising them gently in soy sauce/shoyu and sherry or rice wine, along with lots of fresh ginger, a cinnamon stick, a few spring onions and some palm or dark raw cane sugar. Remove any excess fat and serve with Chinese greens, such as kailan, or any other leafy brassica, and a little boiled rice.

- Barbecued meat is more exciting if you lightly marinate it first in a mixture of soy sauce/shoyu, honey and vinegar, with added chopped fresh chilli, garlic and ginger.

- As an easy, cheap supper, reinvent leftover long-grain rice by stir-frying it with spring onions, frozen peas, strips of omelette, and fresh chopped coriander, and finish it off with enough soy sauce to turn the rice an appetizing golden brown. Make it more substantial by adding prawns or squid.

Is soya good for me?

Soya has been heavily promoted as a health food in recent years. The soya industry, which is controlled by powerful transnational corporations, has sponsored a number of studies that suggest that modern processed soya products are a healthy alternative to traditional foods such as cow's milk, cheese, meat and butter. A number of benefits have been attributed to eating soya, such as reducing the incidence of certain cancers, improving bone density and alleviating menopausal symptoms. Vegetarians and vegans like soya because it comes from a plant, not an animal source, and it is the only plant food that comes close to providing the complete protein and amino acids found in meat or dairy products. It is also attractive to people with allergies to cow's milk, because it doesn't contain lactose.

The long-term safety of the soya products we now consume is not known, but there is good reason to show extreme caution. Soya beans contain naturally occurring toxins or anti-nutrients. For instance, soya has high levels of phytic acid, which can reduce the body's ability to assimilate essential minerals – calcium, magnesium, copper, iron and zinc. This acid is not neutralized by soaking or normal cooking. Soya also contains trypsin inhibitors which impair the body's ability to digest protein and have been linked by some research to pancreatic disorders and stunted growth. The industrial processing of soya is designed to remove these toxins but traces may remain.

The isoflavone oestrogens in soya have been linked with thyroid problems, since they mimic the female hormone oestrogen and have the ability to disrupt endocrine function. Some research suggests that soya oestrogens could affect reproductive development, have a negative effect on fertility, and encourage the development of breast cancer.

Several aspects of soya processing raise concerns. The acid washing of the soya protein is often carried out in aluminium tanks and this heavy metal, which is bad for the brain and the nervous system, can leach into the product. Processing of soya protein results in the formation of an amino acid, lysinoalanine, that can be toxic. The hexane that is used as a solvent is a known neurotoxin. Processing also creates free glutamic acid that can trigger allergic reactions and food intolerance symptoms in some people. Soya is one of the most common food allergens. Nitrosamines, which can be carcinogenic, can be formed during processing. The rapid hydrolysis process used to make non-brewed soy sauce can produce small quantities of 3-MCPD, a known carcinogen.

Traditional forms of soya, such as soy sauce, tempeh, miso and natto are likely to be much healthier than modern types of soya because they undergo a long fermentation process that neutralizes their toxins. Tofu is not fermented, so it may be a good idea to eat it, as is done in the traditional Asian diet, only in relatively small quantities. Edamame beans are not fermented either, so they also should be eaten only in small quantities.

The use of genetically modified soya in food manufacturing raises a potential health issue for humans. GM foods are simply assumed to be safe because the big, transnational biotech companies that promote them managed to persuade regulators at the outset that they would be 'substantially equivalent' to natural foods, so they have not had to go through rigorous safety testing.

The only countries where GM ingredients are common in food are the US and Canada. GM advocates argue that trillions of meals have been eaten there with no obvious casualties, and say that this shows that GM food is safe for humans. GM ingredients are used there in highly processed forms, in products such as vegetable oil and corn syrup that don't contain GM protein and DNA, which are theoretically more likely to cause health problems. Crucially, GM ingredients do not have to be labelled in these countries (despite huge public support for labelling), making it impossible to trace who has eaten what, and when – an essential prerequisite for studies looking at possible human health effects. So scientific research into the safety, or otherwise, of GM foods relies on results extrapolated from laboratory animals. In this context, 'safe' is interpreted as meaning an acceptable degree of risk.

Gradually, independent scientists are doing animal research on these new genetically engineered foods that have only been grown since the 1990s, and are beginning to find evidence that GM crops can have negative effects on animal health, including damage to the immune system, kidneys and liver, and negative impacts on fertility. The long-term effects on humans of eating GM food are as yet unclear, but you may feel that if GM foods aren't that great for your pet mouse, then you would rather not eat them yourself.

A DEBATABLE HISTORY

The health claims made for soya are often based on the observation that foods made from soya have long featured in traditional Asian diets without causing any problem. Some advocates of soya argue that soya is a miracle food that explains Japanese women's low levels of breast cancer and reported menopausal problems.

This version of soya history is debatable. Soya foods have been consumed in Asia for centuries, but mainly in their fermented forms, usually as a condiment, where the toxins are neutralized. Asian people have never eaten unfermented soya foods in large amounts and soya has never been the main source of dietary protein in Asia. When Asian people do eat unfermented soya foods, they eat them along with, not as a substitute for, meat and fish. Needless to say, modern, highly processed forms of soya, such as soya protein isolate and textured soya protein, did not figure in traditional Asian diets.

Some western people, often vegan or vegetarian, now consume unprecedented quantities of soya, in products such as milk, yogurt, spreads and soya substitutes for animal products, and as an ingredient in processed foods. This western soya-based diet bears little resemblance to traditional patterns of soya consumption in Asia.

How are soya foods made?

If soya beans are to be made into milk, they are cooked in hot water, mixed with more water, and crushed. The milk is strained off, then flavourings, sugar and, usually, synthetic vitamins are often added. Nearly all soya milk is pasteurized or sterilized at a very high temperature so that it has a long shelf life and can be sold without refrigeration. Tofu is made by adding a coagulant, generally calcium sulfate, to soy milk. This forms curds that are then shaped and pressed into cakes.

For most other purposes, the soya beans are processed using a highly industrial process. The beans are immersed in a high-temperature liquid bath that contains the petroleum-based solvent, hexane. The oil is extracted for margarines and spreads and the remaining soya protein slurry is bathed in alcohols such as methanol or ethanol, then the beans are treated with acid and alkaline solutions to adjust the pH. The idea is to remove the toxins in the raw beans.

The remaining protein can then be spray-dried under heat to produce a high-protein meal. Most of this is sold for animal feed. Alternatively, it can be used for human food, and in the form of a powder, soya protein isolate, it provides an ingredient for many processed foods. It can also be used to produce textured soy protein (also known as textured vegetable protein). This process involves cooking the soya meal in water at a high temperature, which converts the water to steam, then passing it through an extruding machine, which produces fibrous chunks of soya in various shapes and sizes.

Foods based on soya protein isolate and textured soya protein usually contain salt, sugar or other sweetener, thickeners, firming agents, fillers and synthetic flavourings since, after all this processing, they do not have a very appetizing taste. These additions also help them resemble traditional foods. Vegetarian 'bacon', for instance, will usually contain synthetic smoke and bacon flavourings. Vegan cheese is likely to contain artificial cheese flavouring.

The traditional way to make soy sauce involves cooking the beans, sometimes with roasted wheat, inoculating the mixture with a natural mould, mixing it with water and salt, then leaving the sauce to ferment and mature at ambient temperature in wooden barrels for a year or more. This process makes the beans digestible by neutralizing their toxins. Hardly any soy sauce is now made this way; instead, two modern methods are used.

If the soy sauce is to be sold as 'naturally brewed', the traditional production process is speeded up by using de-fatted soya protein meal, extracted using hexane. The sauce is matured more rapidly in steel tanks using heat so that it is ready in three to six months.

If the sauce is to be sold as 'non-brewed', it is made using a process known as rapid hydrolysis, which takes around two days. De-fatted soya flour is mixed with hydrochloric acid at high temperature, and under pressure, to create hydrolyzed vegetable protein. Salt, sugar or other sweeteners like high-fructose corn syrup, caramel colouring, chemical preservatives and synthetic flavourings are then added.

Is soya a green choice?

Soya is rarely an environmentally benign crop. Very little soya production is either small-scale or organic. Soya cultivation, along with cattle ranching, is now one of the two main causes of deforestation in South America, where vast expanses of rainforest and grassland are being cut down to make way for huge soya plantations. These plantations are managed in a very intensive way using high levels of synthetic fertilizers and pesticides. The destruction of these precious habitats has a catastrophic effect on biodiversity and wildlife and is a major contributor to climate change because the carbon that was fixed in the soil is released into the atmosphere.

You are unlikely to come across foods containing GM soya, because of vociferous opposition in Europe. Supermarkets have declined to stock them because consumers don't want to buy them and some leading food manufacturers have also developed GM-free sourcing policies, so it pays to ask about these before buying.

Unlike in the US, where key crops such as soya, oilseed rape (canola) and maize have been extensively planted, currently only two GM crops can be grown in Europe: a type of maize (mainly used for animal feed) and a type of potato (for use in industrial starch production and then animal feed). A type of US GM soya and many GM maize varieties that can be used for human consumption have import licences for the European Union, but any product including them would, by law, need to be labelled as such.

But although foods containing GM ingredients have been largely kept off our shelves, GM soya is being fed to farm animals in the UK and Europe – mainly poultry and pigs – and meat, eggs and milk from livestock fed on them can still be sold without any GM label. The most progressive UK food retailers, and some food manufacturers, now say that any own-label animal products they sell come from livestock fed on GM-free rations. But there is a question mark over the robustness of these guarantees, so ask for clarification. If you want to be absolutely sure of avoiding food from GM-fed animals, choose organic. All organic food is GM-free: genetic modification isn't permitted under organic rules.

There are sound reasons for boycotting GM food. The basic idea underpinning this technology is that by taking out or adding genes, geneticists can alter crops and animals in a beneficial way. This sounds good. The sales pitch for GM was that it would feed the world and reduce the use of pesticides without doing any harm to humans, animals or the environment, but it has not delivered on its promises.

As a credible answer to world hunger, GM is unconvincing. The largest study in the world to review research, the IAASTD report (International Assessment of Agricultural Knowledge, Science and Technology for Development), carried out under the auspices of the United Nations and the World Bank, consulted over 400 eminent scientists from different countries. They found little evidence to support a conclusion that genetic engineering can meet the needs of small-scale and subsistence farmers, especially in the Third World. Indeed in India, buying GM seed has forced poor farmers into a spiral of debt and crop failure. Some estimates suggest that thousands of farmers there have committed suicide as a result.

While GM crops have not lived up to the claims made for them, scientists have showed impressive results improving crops using natural breeding methods. Crop breeders in Wales, for instance, have bred new varieties of organic potatoes with much better resistance to blight – the disease that caused the Irish potato famine – than any existing conventional varieties. So far GM scientists have not produced a commercial strain with good blight resistance. Scientists in Italy have developed a tomato variety with 50 per cent more of the health-promoting phytonutrient, lycopene, once again using non-GM, natural plant breeding techniques. Increasingly, people are challenging the very need for GM, when natural methods can produce better results without the risks, and more quickly.

In terms of environmental impact, GM crops such as soya have increased, not reduced, pesticide use, and encouraged the emergence of worrying new super-weeds and super-pests. The planting of GM crops has not increased yields, and genes from them have been shown to escape, crossbreed and survive in the wild. The worry here is that these rogue genes could recombine with those in other plants so that they pass on these very undesirable rogue traits with each generation. Many GM crops, for instance, have been altered to include an antibiotic-resistant marker gene, which can potentially hop or transfer into the guts of animals and humans. Thus a new strain of pathogenic bacterium could be created, further reducing the effectiveness of these invaluable drugs in both animal and human medicine.

Where should I buy soya foods?

Soya foods are on sale everywhere. Wholefood stores are generally the best place to look if you want traditionally made, long-fermented soy sauce. Japanese brands of soy sauce (shoyu, tamari) contain few, if any, of the additives found in mass-market soy sauce.

Will soya foods break the bank?

Soya products are usually affordable though more traditional, craft-made soy sauces will cost quite a bit more than the chemical non-brewed type. Soya alternatives to meat usually work out cheaper than meat, while soya 'dairy' products are more expensive than their animal-derived equivalents.

Chocolate

Might this be our most popular food? Put it this way, it's rare to come across anyone who doesn't appreciate its charms. The essential character of chocolate comes from cacao, the cocoa bean that is used to make chocolate, which is bitter and slightly fruity. There are three main types. The most common, but most one-dimensional is the Forastero, a high-yielding bean with a good, strong chocolate taste, but little in the way of secondary flavours. Most mass-market chocolates are made from this bean. Chocolate enthusiasts and chocolatiers are much more keenly focused on the less abundant Criollo bean, which has a higher acidity and much more complexity of flavour, and the Trinitario, a hybrid of Forastero and Criollo. It is easier to cultivate than the relatively rare Criollo, but is more fruity and aromatic than the Forastero.

Grown in different climates, the cocoa bean takes on different characteristics. As in the case of wine, the soil affects the taste. Beans grown in the Caribbean are often described as having earthy, tobacco, slightly spicy flavours, those in Central America and Indonesia are thought to have an acidity reminiscent of red fruits, while those grown in South America are said to have a more floral character. If you want to explore the flavour nuances of the Criollo and Trinitario bean, then this leads you to specialist chocolate shops and top brands, since few of these beans find their way into commonly encountered brands.

Beans apart, there are three different types of chocolate. Milk chocolate is the forces' sweetheart, a familiar taste which many people fondly associate with childhood and home. The most basic sort contains only 20 per cent cocoa solids and has added vegetable fat as well as natural cocoa butter. Any cocoa taste is drowned out by sugar. Upmarket milk chocolate contains more cocoa solids – anything from 30 to 40 per cent – so the cocoa flavour stands more of a chance against the dominant sugar.

If you want to experience high-quality milk chocolate, avoid brands that contain vegetable fat. It is used to reduce the ingredient cost and give the product a longer shelf life, but it leaves a greasy film on the roof of the mouth. Vegetable fat also lacks the unique crystalline structure of cocoa butter, so chocolate made from it doesn't snap cleanly as true chocolate does.

Dark chocolate contains no milk or vegetable fat. By law, anything labelled simply as chocolate, as opposed to milk chocolate, must contain at least 35 per cent cocoa solids but nowadays, good, dark, cocoa-rich chocolate starts at not less than 55 per cent cocoa solids, while most are around 70 per cent. Specialist chocolatiers make chocolate with 85 per cent cocoa solids and upwards, but it is too bitter and intense for most palates, at least until you become accustomed to it.

Strictly speaking, white chocolate isn't really chocolate because it contains no cocoa solids, just cocoa butter, so it doesn't have that essential bitter chocolate character. Its appeal lies in its milky-rich butteriness, its texture rather than its flavour. Some cheaper brands also contain less desirable vegetable fat.

Whether it's milk, dark or white, a hallmark of good chocolate is that only natural flavours are used, everything from vanilla extract, orange and peppermint oils to candied ginger, citrus zest, alcohols, salt and coffee. Packaging can be deceiving: even some luxurious-looking brands use artificial flavourings, most notably the synthetic chemical vanillin, in place of natural vanilla. It pays to read the ingredients label.

Things to do with chocolate

- Dip strawberries in melted chocolate.

- A square of dark chocolate stirred into a rich game or red meat stew will make the gravy more glossy and homogenous and lend depth.

- Make your own truffles. Melt equal weights of dark chocolate and double cream or crème fraîche and add a dash of spirit of your choice, such as brandy, whisky, or Grand Marnier. Refrigerate until the mixture is firm enough to form into balls with your fingers, then roll in unsweetened cocoa powder and allow to set.

- Grate dark chocolate over a thinly sliced ripe pear, or canned pear, and serve with a dollop of whipped cream or thick yogurt.

- Bake cookies with chunks of chocolate in them.

Is chocolate good for me?

The capacity of chocolate to lift the spirits isn't just wishful thinking. Chocolate contains natural 'happy' chemicals such as theobromine, tryptophan and phenethylamine, which are known to have a mood-elevating effect. Chocolate also contains certain flavonols, which some research suggests can be protective against high blood pressure, heart disease and stroke. To benefit from these flavonols, however, it is thought you have to eat very dark chocolate. The higher the percentage of cocoa solids, the higher the amounts of flavonols and the less sugar you will be eating.

Most of the chocolate we eat cannot by any stretch of the imagination be thought of as a health food. The natural cocoa butter isn't a worry, as it is generally thought to be healthy and it is exceptionally stable at room temperature, so not prone to rancidity. But the hardened vegetable fats added to some milk chocolate, which are similar to those used in margarines and spreads, are a cause for concern (see MARGARINES AND SPREADS/Are margarines and spreads good for me?).

All chocolate contains sugar. Without it, chocolate would taste too bitter. The more cocoa solids it contains, the less sugar and vice versa. So, a 75 per cent chocolate bar will contain 25 per cent of sugar, a 65 per cent bar will contain 35 per cent, and so on.

If your preference is for milk or white chocolate, then you will be eating rather a lot of sugar. A typical milk or white chocolate will be over 50 per cent sugar. And if you are partial to sweet liquid fillings, such as caramel or fondant, then these will be primarily sugar, often in multiple forms, such as lactose, corn syrup, polydextrose and malted barley. To be sure of getting a product that is more cocoa than sugar, avoid products where the first ingredient listed is sugar. If you do buy products that list sugar before either cocoa solids, sometimes listed as cocoa mass, or cocoa butter, then be aware that however much you like it, it isn't good for you. A little dark chocolate could be beneficial for you. A load of milk or white chocolate is not.

People who call themselves chocaholics may like to consider whether they are hooked on the sugar in chocolate, rather than the healthy cocoa component. If this applies to you, then it might be an idea to try buying chocolate with a higher percentage of cocoa. For instance, if you have been used to eating milk chocolate with 20 per cent cocoa solids, try one with around 30, then another that contains nearer 40 per cent. If you become accustomed to this, and the chocolate you used to eat now tastes too sweet by comparison, you can start working your way up the dark chocolate ladder, trying out darker sorts from 55 to 70 per cent cocoa. Dark chocolate is better for you, and you will also get more of that intrinsic cocoa taste. Since the flavour is more intense and three-dimensional, it is extremely satisfying, so you are unlikely to eat too much of it.

How is chocolate produced?

The raw material for chocolate is the beans that grow inside the heavy pod-like fruits of the tropical cacao tree. Most of the chocolate we eat is made from Forastero cocoa beans grown in West Africa, mainly in Ghana. Rarer Criollos and Trinitarios usually come from South and Central America, Madagascar, the Caribbean and Indonesia. Wherever they grow, the ripe pods are harvested by hand, split open, and the beans are scooped out. The beans are then fermented by spreading them out in shallow wooden boxes covered with leaves over a period of days, which develops that distinctive chocolate taste. They are then dried, usually in the sun. All this work is done in the country of origin.

Numerous reports by international agencies and charities have drawn attention to the use of child labour on cocoa farms in West Africa where many families are so trapped in poverty that they need their children to help them earn money. In cocoa growing, children do a lot of the hard manual work, such as cutting down pods with machetes and applying pesticides. Workers spraying cocoa trees frequently do so without safety training and without protective clothing, so the pesticides often drip on to their skin or are inhaled.

These are very strong reasons for buying chocolate that is both Fairtrade and organic. Fairtrade rules outlaw child labour. They also guarantee that producers get a more equitable set price for their beans and have working conditions that are better than the norm. When you buy organic chocolate, you know that the growers didn't have to risk their health to produce it as pesticides are not used in organic cocoa bean growing.

Some chocolate you come across in specialist chocolate shops may not come with a Fairtrade label, but this doesn't necessarily mean that it has not been equitably produced. Chocolate companies often use more expensive Criollo and Trinitario beans from other parts of the world where living standards and working conditions are too high to qualify for growers to be eligible for Fairtrade status. They say that the premium price they pay for such beans means that cocoa producers can afford to pay their workers above the Fairtrade rate.

Once they leave the farm, the dried, fermented beans are shipped to factories all over the world to be made into chocolate. The beans are roasted, their outer husks are removed, then they are ground to produce a chocolate liquor which is a mixture of cocoa solids, and cocoa butter. This can either be separated into cocoa butter and solids (cocoa powder), or it can be made into chocolate. This involves mixing into the chocolate liquor sugar and vanilla extract or flavouring. In the case of milk chocolate, milk powder or condensed milk is also added. The chocolate mixture is then pressed and more cocoa butter is added, along with soy lecithin, an emulsifier. In the case of British-style milk chocolate, 5 per cent hardened vegetable fat from non-cocoa sources can be added. The resulting paste is then 'conched' or worked back and forth with rollers. After that it is 'tempered' – heated, cooled and reheated – so that it remains glossy. Then it just needs to be moulded into the desired shape.

Is chocolate a green choice?

The heavy use of pesticides in West African cocoa production is well-documented, in particular, the use of lindane, a neurotoxin and possible carcinogen, that has exceptionally long persistence, which means that traces remain in the soil for decades after spraying. Lindane is to be banned globally after 2014, but many other pesticides used in cocoa production worldwide are still a cause for concern. Cocoa producers are looking at greener ways of growing cocoa. These include planting more disease-resistant trees, cultivating the cocoa trees under the shade of other trees rather than in plantations in full sun, using beneficial insects to control the unwelcome ones and boosting soil fertility using natural methods. When you buy organic chocolate, you help demonstrate that there is a market for cocoa grown in a more environmentally benign way.

Some of the vegetable fat added to milk chocolate is likely to come from tropical countries where rainforest has been cut down to make way for palm oil plantations. The global demand for palm oil has seen whole swathes of virgin forest in Malaysia and Indonesia cut or burnt down to make way for palm oil production. This peaty forest is one of the most concentrated stores of carbon around. Clearing the forest on top, draining the peat, and burning it, releases vast amounts of greenhouse gases into the atmosphere. This clearance leads to the destruction of orang-utan habitat in Borneo. Wildlife groups warn that without urgent intervention, the palm oil trade will make the species extinct within a decade. The Sumatran tiger is also threatened. Land clearance for palm oil plantations has also seen indigenous people and small growers displaced from their land and, according to environmental groups, they have suffered human rights abuses as a result.

Where should I buy chocolate?

Ubiquitous brands of chocolate with a low cocoa solid content are everywhere. Supermarkets, wholefood shops and delicatessens usually stock a choice of mid-market brands that are still affordable, but which represent a huge leap in quality. Independent chocolate shops are springing up all over. Check them out from time to time to keep up with trends and experience new tastes, but establish first whether they actually make their own chocolates – the more interesting option – or just buy them in.

Will chocolate break the bank?

Cheap chocolate is likely to be bad chocolate. No one needs to eat a lot of chocolate, particularly not the poor stuff. Buy better chocolate and eat less of it.

The UK fought a long hard battle in Europe to defend the very particular sort of chocolate many British people adore. The problem was that most other European countries had difficulty recognizing it as chocolate. Milk chocolate in countries such as France and Switzerland generally contain between 30 and 40 per cent cocoa solids, and no vegetable fat. They took the view that mass-market British milk chocolate, which contains just 20 per cent cocoa solids and 5 per cent added vegetable fat, did not merit the chocolate label and wanted to have it re-named as 'vegelate'.

After twenty-seven years of wrangling, in 2000 a compromise emerged. Those familiar bars could continue to be sold as 'milk chocolate' in Britain but had to be labelled as 'family milk chocolate' when sold abroad. In both cases, the further phrase 'contains vegetable fats in addition to cocoa butter' had to appear on the packaging.

Since then, chocolate appreciation and expertise has soared in the UK. The country that came late to the world of fine chocolate has produced some first-class chocolatiers whose products can command respect anywhere. But however much our chocolate palates are extended, that deep-seated fondness for the least chocolaty chocolate in Europe still endures.

Salt

Salt is our oldest food additive, a cornerstone of taste in savoury foods. Societies all around the world have used this white crystalline mineral since time immemorial, not only to preserve food, but also as a natural flavour enhancer. Saltiness, along with sweetness, acidity and bitterness, is one of the fundamental characteristics we use to describe the taste of food.

Sea salt is the runaway favourite with chefs and food lovers who believe that it has a more complex and interesting marine flavour than common-or-garden table salt, which is a highly refined form of rock salt. Fans of the world-famous Guérande sea salt from the west coast of France, for instance, swear that the first bloom of salt crystals that forms on the sea water has a distinctive perfume akin to violets. Since salt of any kind has such a concentrated flavour, it is well nigh impossible to set up a comparative testing to work out whether the foodie preference for sea salt is objective, or merely a romantic prejudice. One clear difference, however, is that because it is flakier and coarser, sea salt can be used to create pockets of saltiness in otherwise quite unsalty foods, whereas the standard table sort adds a blanket, all-pervasive saltiness.

Some rock salt, such as Himalayan pink salt, is sold in a hard, coarse form, designed for milling in a salt grinder. This looks more like sea salt but lacks the flaky texture.

Both sea salt and table salt taste better than low-sodium salt, which tends to taste bitter.

Things to do with salt

- Adding sea salt to caramel when making millionaire's shortbread makes the flavour more interesting and the sweetness less cloying.

- Bake a whole, gutted fish in a crust made from rock or sea salt mixed with a little water or egg white. When this is removed, the flesh remains strangely unsalty and moist, and becomes particularly flavoursome.

- Just before putting a classic Italian focaccia in the oven to bake, sprinkle the surface with sea salt flakes, rosemary and olive oil. Tart up a ready-made focaccia the same way and give it five minutes in a hot oven.

- A dusting of crunchy roughly crushed or ground sea or rock salt adds a sparkling, lively finish to roast or fried potatoes and chips.

- Serve a slice of rich meat or game terrine with melba toast, cornichons (small gherkins) and a little pile of sea salt.

Is salt good for me?

In recent years, salt has been identified as a substance that can raise blood pressure, which in turn can increase the risk of heart disease and stroke. The potential problem here is that people who eat a lot of processed food have little control over their salt intake. As much as 90 per cent of the salt we eat comes in familiar processed foods. Relatively little of it comes from the salt cellar on the table, or the tub that sits beside the cooker.

Refined salt vies with sugar for number one position in the food industry's armoury of additives. Without it, everyday foods such as cornflakes and crackers would taste of precious little. It disguises the dullness of commodity ingredients such as white flour and seeks to replace the intrinsic flavours in fresh foods that are destroyed by industrial food-processing methods. The heavy-handed presence of salt in such foods sets up an expectation that every mouthful of savoury food must deliver a mouth-mugging dose of sodium.

As our diets have become more reliant on ready-made convenience food, our salt consumption has become cause for concern. Largely because processed foods have supplanted natural, unprocessed foods in the modern diet, most British and Irish adults eat between eight and ten grams of salt a day when the World Health Organization recommends only five grams as the upper limit.

But the widespread recommendation needs to be approached with common sense. If your diet isn't based on processed food, then it is hard to eat unhealthy amounts of salt. And some people, those with adrenal fatigue for example, can benefit from more salt in their diet. While we are advised to avoid salty foods, certain high-salt foods in the natural food category, such as olives, anchovies and capers, have such an intense and concentrated flavour that it is hard to eat any great quantity of them. Cured fish such as smoked salmon, and cured meats, such as salami, ham and bacon are fairly obviously salty, as are crisps. The tricky foods are those that we often consume in substantial quantities, but which do not taste so noticeably salty. Surreptitiously salty foods to look out for include bread, frozen and chilled prawns, breakfast cereals, sandwiches, ready-made soups, sauces and prepared meals, stock cubes and bouillon powder.

If you eat a lot of processed food, check the nutrition label on the product, and at least you will know how much salt it contains: high salt is more than 1.5g salt (or 0.6g sodium) per 100g; low salt is less than 0.3g salt (or 0.1g sodium) per 100g.

If you eat mainly unprocessed food that you cook yourself, you can control what type and amount of salt goes into your food and don't have to worry too much about overdoing it. If you suspect that you have an overly salty palate, then you can experiment with using less salt than the recipe specifies and reduce or even eliminate salt in some old recipes that have too much. Many traditional sweet baking recipes, for instance, include salt when it is not necessary. Another option for people with high blood pressure is using low-sodium salts. These are just standard table salts that substitute healthier potassium chloride for a proportion of the sodium, but some people find they taste bitter and irritate the stomach.

Iodized salt is refined table salt with added iodine. This type of salt originated in the US in the 1950s when its use was encouraged to reduce the incidence of goitre (thyroid enlargement) in the population. Unless you suffer from this condition, there is no reason to use iodized salt.

Sea salt has a superior health profile to other types of salt because it contains minute traces, some would say negligible amounts, of a number of desirable trace elements and minerals naturally present in sea water, such as iron, manganese, zinc, calcium, magnesium, cadmium and sulphur, that are sometimes at a lower level than is ideal in our diets. This doesn't make sea salts 'health foods', but it does give them a very marginal health advantage over standard table salts which have had all potentially beneficial trace elements and minerals removed.

How is salt produced?

Salt or sodium chloride, to give it its chemical name, is produced in different ways. Rock salt is, as the name suggests, extracted from underground sources. Hard deposits of salt in rocks are mined from underground deposits – salt mines – by blasting or drilling, then crushed. Most rock salt is used for non-food purposes like road gritting, but some rock salts are sold as hard crystals to be used in a salt grinder.

Refined table salt is usually 'solution mined'; that is, the underground salt chamber has been flooded with water to make a brine from which the salt is then evaporated and refined in an industrial process, the end result being a chemically pure salt that looks snowy white. This type of table salt is fine and free-flowing because anti-caking agents, either magnesium carbonate or sodium hexacyanoferrate, are added. The addition of these chemicals bestows no health advantage. They are simply there to make sure that the fine salt doesn't clog up.

The other main type of salt, sea salt, is obtained from shallow sea water using the time-honoured techniques of filtration and evaporation. Some French and Italian sea salts are still sun- and wind-dried in natural salt ponds or lagoons that have formed along the coastline. English and Welsh sea salts are produced by feeding the salty water into open tanks and warming it to encourage the water to evaporate and form flaky salt crystals which are then dried.

Sea salt production in the UK can be traced back to the Iron Age. Small-scale sea salt production is still thriving on Cornwall's Lizard Peninsula, on the Blackwater Estuary in Essex and in the Menai Straits between mainland Wales and Anglesey. Most table salt from the UK comes from rock salt mines in Cheshire, Yorkshire and Northern Ireland.

Is salt a green choice?

Most sea salt is still produced using quite low-tech methods, variations on techniques that have been used since time immemorial. The main issue is what is done with the water left over when the salt crystals have been formed. Care has to be taken not to extract so much salt from the water that it affects marine life, and the water has to be returned at a low temperature. Done carefully, sea salt production can have no negative impact on its local environment. Rock salt is produced by mining and then refined in a factory on an industrial scale with everything that those technologies imply. The production of rock salt is likely to leave a heavier carbon 'foodprint' than relatively artisan sea salt production.

Where should I buy salt?

Wholefood shops usually have the best range of more interesting, more natural sea salts.

Will salt break the bank?

Sea salt is significantly more expensive than standard table salt but if you use it only in restrained quantities, the cost is pretty inconsequential among other items in the typical household budget.

Spices and aromatics

Spices and aromatics are magic. They allow you to take common ingredients on a world tour, nudging them down very different culinary highways and byways. They endow you with the alchemist's ability to reinvent ingredients that are often mundane and familiar in myriad forms. A whiff of floral rosewater or orange flower water steers a dish towards the Levant; pungent fish sauce to South-East Asia; nutmeg and allspice to the Windward Islands. Smoked paprika and saffron speak of the Iberian peninsula, turmeric and coriander of India and Pakistan, vanilla of Madagascar and Mexico. Whatever culinary route you choose, spices and aromatics are the tools you need to produce three-dimensional flavours that make dishes taste distinctive and genuine.

The flavours and aromas of spices are thrillingly different and absolutely unique; this is what makes them so exciting. And teamed up in spice blends, such as the Indian garam masala, the Chinese five spice, Middle Eastern z'aatar and Ethiopian berbere, they create a further tier of fascinating flavour possibilities. Combinations of roasted, ground seeds, such as the Indian panchphoran, add yet another toolkit of flavourings. Even the variation within one spice category can be remarkable. They are all chillies, but the rocket-strength Scotch Bonnet and Habanero are poles apart from the mild, relatively fruity Ancho and the sour Guajillo. But in their simple forms, spices do broadly hang together in six main groups:

Fruity
Coriander, Nutmeg, Mace, Cloves, Allspice

Sour
Sumac, Amchoor (green mango powder), Lime powder

Sweet and fragrant
Vanilla, Green cardamom, Fennel seed, Dill seed

Pungent
Cumin, Chilli, Ginger, Black peppercorns, Ajwain

Earthy
Saffron, Fenugreek, Black cardamom, Nigella,
Black mustard seeds, Paprika, Turmeric, Asafetida

Potentially overbearing (use in moderation)
Star anise, Cinnamon, Sichuan peppercorns, Juniper berries
Caraway, Pink peppercorns, Dried bay leaves

Although they don't go bad, spices deteriorate dramatically in flavour with time. Old spices smell, look and taste like shadows of their fresher selves and will have a correspondingly duller, more muted effect in cooking, so it's important to buy spices from a source with a fast turnover, and use them up quickly. Although it's tough, you really have to be ruthless and chuck out those that are past their prime.

Aromatics also provide a defining X factor in many dishes. Horseradish root injects heat that makes its presence felt at the back of the nose. Fresh ginger adds heat and liveliness. Galangal has a similar effect but is slightly more medicinal. Krachai root, most commonly used in Thai cooking, is also engagingly medicinal but punchier and fruitier than galangal. Fresh turmeric is peppery, earthy and slightly bitter. Fresh curry leaves add haunting aroma without heat and find their perfect partner when used in south Indian dishes with black mustard seed. In South-East Asian cooking, sticky black-brown tamarind pods add mouth-puckering sourness, while lime leaves and lemongrass add zingy, almost lemonade-like perfume. The sweet, sultry aroma of vanilla is a knock-out. Whole pods, slashed down their length so their seeds can escape and stipple a dish, are best, but high-quality vanilla essence is a more than respectable second best – the stickier and thicker, the better. The heady, floral notes of rose- and orange flower water add an intoxicating perfume as well as flavour.

Whether you're talking Indian, Malaysian, Thai, Indonesian, Iranian or any other cuisine that uses a rich array of spices, if you want to cook food that tastes like a reasonable approximation of that served in its mother country, it's a good idea to make a small, one-off investment in a spice grinder. This means that instead of using ready-ground spices that are more prone to fade and lose their aromas, you can grind your own. The difference is dramatic: freshly ground spices are much brighter and more vivacious than the ready-ground sort. Many of the more authentic spice blends stipulate that you first roast spices before grinding them, and if you skip this stage, the dish just won't taste as good. Freshly ground spices can even make all the difference to your Christmas cake. A simple coffee grinder will do the job, but the ideal piece of equipment is a cheap 'wet/dry' spice grinder that allows you to make a paste of wet aromatics, such as galangal, ginger, lemongrass, lime leaf and garlic, as well as grind dry spices.

Things to do with spices and aromatics

- Get the best from saffron threads by toasting or baking them very lightly for a minute or two, crumbling them, then infusing them in a little liquid (water, stock, wine, fruit juice) before adding to a dish. This helps release the intrinsic aroma and colour.

- Infuse a teaspoonful each of fennel and fenugreek seeds and a piece of root ginger the size of a 50 pence coin in boiling water to make a pleasant, warming tea that will stimulate your digestion.

- A sprinkling of sour-tasting, red sumac powder is the customary Middle Eastern finishing touch that makes dips such as hummus and *baba ganoush* look more exciting.

- Nutmeg and vanilla transform potentially plain rice pudding and custard into positively refined and aristocratic dishes.

- Bruise the bulbous lower stem of lemongrass and pour on boiling water to make a fragrant infusion with more subtlety than any heavy-handed, commercial fruit tea.

- Traditional Scottish gingerbread made with treacle showcases the heat of ginger and the fruitiness of allspice.

- Roughly cracked coriander seeds add texture and fragrance to minced lamb kebabs.

- Get to grips with the addictive heat of Scotch Bonnet chillies by making West African Jollof rice: long-grain rice cooked with fried onions, tomatoes, root ginger, stock and as many Scotch Bonnets as you can handle. Often served with chicken and okra.

Are spices and aromatics good for me?

Culinary spices figure prominently in traditional medicine systems worldwide for their disease-preventing and curative properties. Caraway, for instance, is often cooked with cabbage and other brassicas to prevent wind, while asafoetida and ajwain do the same job for pulses. Chilli, peppercorns and ginger are all thought to stimulate the digestion; dill, fennel and bay often figure in popular folk remedies for colic and stomach pains; juniper is said to have antiseptic and antibacterial properties; turmeric has an anti-inflammatory effect; and clove oil soothes toothache.

Even though we consume spices in small quantities, they may have a significant, positive effect on health when eaten regularly over time. The

389

National Institute on Aging, part of the US government's National Institutes of Health, has developed a unit of measurement – ORAC (Oxygen Radical Absorbance Capacity) – to measure the antioxidant capacity of foods; that is, how effectively they neutralize disease-promoting free radicals in the body. When measured on the ORAC scale, spices show some of the highest antioxidant values. Cloves, sumac, cinnamon, turmeric and cumin earn particularly impressive scores.

Those who rubbish herbal medicine, or who see it as an ineffective second best to modern pharmaceutical medicine with precious few demonstrable results, won't rush to include spices in their cooking for any reason other than taste. But if you have a different philosophical mindset, then Hippocrates' famous saying, 'Your food shall be your medicine and your medicine shall be your food,' was never more apt than in the case of spices. You may want to eat them as much as possible.

SPICE ADDICTS

When chicken tikka masala regularly tops polls for the nation's favourite food, trumping fish and chips and roast beef, what more proof is needed of how spices and other aromatic plants have seduced their way into the heart of our national diet? But in fact long before Indian and Thai restaurants were a feature of every high street, we were spice addicts. The Normans introduced them to Britain and Ireland, beginning a national love affair with spices that flourished in medieval times. Our taste for the exotic was boosted by our colonial adventures in the tropics, consolidating a national taste for spice that shows absolutely no sign of waning.

In the past, British food has been depicted as being rather plain and unseasoned, yet many traditional recipes that are deemed quint-essentially British, such as chutney, gingerbread and mincemeat tarts, rely on spice. Perhaps we took to them as a contrast to the flatter, duller flavour profile that then characterized our cuisine. The contemporary British or Irish cook is now one of the most open-minded in the world, seeing a reasonably ambitious array of spices as essential kit. We rely on spices and aromatics much more heavily than other Europeans and are much bolder in our use of them. Our food is all the better for it.

How are spices and aromatics produced?

Some spices and aromatics grow in Europe and the Middle East. Spain, for instance, produces saffron, Germany grows dill seed, but the bulk of spices, and most aromatics, come from tropical countries such as India, Cambodia, Tanzania and Madagascar.

In traditional farming, spices are grown in among fruit, nut and cacao trees by small farmers, then sold on to middlemen. They have typically travelled through a long supply chain before they get to us, which has two consequences. First, we know little about the working conditions of the people doing the growing, who, even if they aren't exploited by middlemen, are usually excluded from the more profitable 'value-added' parts of the supply chain such as packaging, and unlikely to earn anything more than a tiny proportion of the end price paid by consumers. So if you get the chance to buy Fairtrade spices, or those that come from companies with explicitly ethical sourcing methods, then these deserve support. Second, the lack of transparency in the spice chain offers lots of scope for frauds and scams. Big scandals have surrounded Spanish saffron: product sold as the top grade La Mancha type has turned out to be inferior-quality saffron from other countries. In 2003 Sudan 1, a toxic dye used for petrol, solvents and floor polish, turned up illegally in chilli powder. This contaminant had been used as a colouring, and triggered one of the biggest product recalls in food retailing history. It's impossible to take individual action to protect yourself from such scams, other than buying your spices from reputable companies. But if you end up with spices that don't meet your expectations, such as duff saffron without any real taste, colour or aroma, take it back and ask for a refund.

Are spices and aromatics green choices?

Spices and aromatics are the opposite of local food. Enterprising growers in these isles have shown that chillies, for example, can thrive here, but as a general rule spices have to be imported. Fresh aromatics, such as lemongrass and lime leaf, are either air-freighted or shipped, which isn't brilliant for the environment. But as we only use them in relatively small quantities, and as they can't usually be cultivated here, they don't compete with any home-grown equivalent. Spices are shipped, weigh light, and need no cold storage, so their carbon 'foodprint' is slight compared to other imported foods. Spices and aromatics may be foreign, but they are invaluable ingredients that allow us to ring the changes with the home-produced foods that can make up the bulk of our diets.

Where should I buy spices and aromatics?

The best places to buy spices and aromatics are Asian and Middle Eastern grocers and Chinese supermarkets, which stock a wide range. In good ones you'll find things like krachai and turmeric root, along with curry, fenugreek and lime leaves in their fresh forms. For speed of turnover – the best guarantee of freshness – they are better than regular shops and supermarkets too as they have many more customers, often trade as well as retail, for this type of produce.

Will spices and aromatics break the bank?

Spices and aromatics allow you to cook something cheap and delicious with almost anything. The initial investment in them pays off over and over again, but watch where you shop.

Spices and aromatics sold in mainstream supermarkets routinely carry unjustifiably high mark-ups. Spices sold in glass jars are the most extreme examples. The price might not seem that high, but in terms of value for money they constitute a rotten deal. You can buy them at a fraction of the price in packets or tubs in Asian and Middle Eastern grocers, and Chinese supermarkets. Investing in some spice jars for spices you regularly use, then refilling them from packets, will also save you a lot of money.

Mainstream supermarkets treat items such as lemongrass and ginger as specialities or 'queer gear' – always a licence to print money. By contrast, in Asian and Middle Eastern grocers and Chinese supermarkets, they are just seen as part of their core range and competitively priced.

Lists

p = Pesticide residue concerns
h = Health concerns
e = Environmental concerns
a = Animal welfare concerns
u = Unfair trade/workers' conditions concerns
o = Over-processed/too many additives concerns
£= Pricey
c = Attractively cheap

....

Green List

....

These are foods that you can be quite relaxed about eating.
They don't raise any overwhelming issues. Only low vigilance required
when buying them.

Free-range eggs
Organic eggs (£)
Grass-fed beef
Lamb
Rabbit (c)
Goose (£)
Venison (£)
UK-reared veal (£)
Organic/free-range chicken, duck,
    turkey and other poultry (£)
Organic/free-range pork (£)
Organic cow's milk, cream,
    butter, natural yogurt,
    ice cream, cheese
Sheep's, goat's and buffalo's milk
    and dairy products
Mussels (c)
Oysters (£)

Mackerel (c)
Herring (c)
Scallops (£)
Sprats (c)
Sardines (c)
MSC-certified fish, such as
    Alaskan wild salmon
Cold-water prawns
Crab
Lobster (£)
Venus and razor clams (c)
Less well-known white fish
    species (coley, rockfish,
    megrim, pouting) (E)
Wild sea trout
Nuts (£)
Nut butters
Seeds

393

Pulses (lentils, beans, etc) (C)
Extra virgin olive oils
Cold-pressed nut oils (£)
Cold-pressed seed oils (£)
Unrefined coconut oil
Duck and goose fat
Sea salt
Spices
Asparagus (UK-grown)
Aubergine
Broccoli
Cabbage (C)
Cauliflower
Brussels sprouts
Kale (C)
Cavalo nero (C)
Bok/pak choy (C)
Romanesco
Kohlrabi (C)
Radishes (C)
Chinese leaves (C)
Spring greens (C)
Carrots (C)
Turnips (C)
Parsnips
Jerusalem artichokes (C)
Celery (C)

Courgettes (UK-grown)
Marrow (C)
Onions (C)
Mushrooms (C)
Garlic
Leeks (C)
Potatoes (H) (C)
Shallots
Swiss chard
Tomatoes
Tomato paste (C)
Broad beans
UK- or EU-grown squash
    and pumpkin
UK-grown herbs
Organic fruits (£)
Oats (C)
Wholegrain rice
Quinoa
Millet
Rye
Spelt
Buckwheat
Kamut
Teff
Sourdough bread
Cocoa and dark chocolate (U)

....

Amber List

....

These foods raise some concerns that you might want to know about.
Some vigilance required when buying them.

Non-grass-fed beef (E)
Non-organic cow's milk, cream,
    butter, ghee, natural yogurt, ice
    cream, cheese (A)
Imported spring onions (E)
Imported green and runner
    beans (H) (E)
Non UK-grown herbs (E)

Non-organic lettuce and other
    salad leaves (P)
Imported peas, sugarsnaps, green
    and runner beans (E) (£)
Peppers (P)
Grapes (P)
Imported courgettes (P)
Spinach (P)

Cod, monkfish, hake, halibut, plaice, turbot, haddock and other prime white fish (E)
Imported tropical prawns (E) (U)
Apples (P)
Avocados (E)
Bananas and other tropical fruits (P) (E) (U)
UK- and EU-grown cherries (P)
Imported cherries (non EU) (P) (E)
Citrus fruits (P)
UK- and EU-grown black-/red- and white- currants (P) (E)
UK- grown black-/red- and white- currants (P)
Nectarines, peaches and apricots (P)
UK- and EU-grown pears (P)
UK- and EU-grown plums (P)
Pomegranates (P) (E)
UK-grown raspberries, strawberries, blackberries and blueberries (P)

Imported raspberries, strawberries, blackberries and blueberries (P) (E)
Rhubarb (H)
Breakfast cereals (commercial blends), granolas and mueslis (O) (H)
Commercial bread (H) (O)
Pasta (H)
Dried fruits (H)
Milk and white chocolate (H) (U) (O)
White rice (H)
Couscous, bulgar and other wheats (H)
Barley (H)
Polenta/maize/cornmeal (H)
Honey (H)
Treacle (H)
Maple syrup (H)
Palm sugar (H)
Rapeseed oil (H) (E)

....

Red List
....

These foods raise major issues that are hard to ignore.

Non-free-range chicken, duck, turkey and other poultry (A) (E)
Non-free-range pork (A) (E)
Imported veal (A)
Farmed salmon (E) (A)
Wild Atlantic salmon (E)
Eggs from caged hens (A)
Tuna (unless canned, and with a solid guarantee of sustainable fishing method) (E)
Swordfish (E)

Skate (E)
Sugar (H)
Golden syrup (H)
Artificial sweeteners (H)
High-fructose corn syrup (H)
Non-organic blended vegetable and seed oils (H) (O)
Margarines and spreads (H) (O)
Unfermented soya products (soya vegan foods, protein shakes) (H) (O) (E)

Acknowledgements

This book would never have seen the light of day had it not been for the substantial help I received on the health front from Dr John Briffa, who read the manuscript and gave me his comments. John is Britain's most thoughtful, informed and truly independent commentator on nutrition matters. His book, *Waist Disposal*, is essential reading and his blog (http://www.drbriffa.com) provides invaluable insight into contemporary health debates.

At many points while writing this book, I relied on the unstinting support and advice of my dear friend and colleague, the food writer and author Lynda Brown. She is a mine of food information, insight and experience, and as always, exceptionally generous with it.

Once again, I count my lucky stars that I have an editor who is as patient, loyal and determined as Louise Haines at Fourth Estate. Her calmness, composure and dogged confidence make her a tower of strength.

A number of other busy and impressive people have made time to help me with this book, by reading sections and commenting on them, or by providing information: Chef Roy Brett who runs the brilliant fish restaurant in Edinburgh, Ondine; environmental journalist, Rob Edwards; venison authority, Nicola Fletcher, Sascha Grierson of Hugh Grierson Organic, Philip Lymbery and Peter Stevenson of Compassion in World Farming; Iain Mellis, pioneer of British and Irish artisan cheese; Pete Riley, of the tireless and much-needed GM Freeze campaign, local food pioneer, Mike Small; Matthew Roberts, of the inspiring Steamie Bakehouse, and Richard Young, of Kite's Nest Farm, whose knowledge on all aspects of livestock production is breathtaking.

To all these people, I extend the very warmest thanks.